The New Black Renaissance

The New Black Renaissance

The *Souls* Anthology of
Critical African-American Studies

Edited by

MANNING MARABLE

Professor of Public Affairs, History, and African-American Studies
Director, Center for Contemporary Black History
Columbia University

Associate Editors
KHARY JONES
PATRICIA G. LESPINASSE
ADINA POPESCU

Paradigm Publishers
Boulder • London

Published in the United States by Paradigm Publishers, 3360 Mitchell Lane, Suite E, Boulder, CO 80305 USA.

Paradigm Publishers is the trade name of Birkenkamp & Company, LLC, Dean Birkenkamp, President and Publisher.

Library of Congress Cataloging-in-Publication Data

The new Black renaissance : the *Souls* anthology of critical African-American studies / edited by Manning Marable ; associate editors Khary Jones, Patricia G. Lespinasse, Adina Popescu.
      p. cm.
  Includes bibliographical references and index.
  ISBN 1-59451-141-1 (hc) — ISBN 1-59451-142-X (pb)
1. African Americans—Study and teaching. 2. African Americans—Intellectual life. 3. African Americans—Politics and government. 4. African Americans—Social conditions—1975- 5. Afrocentrism. 6. Transnationalism. 7. Ethnicity—United States. 8. Multiculturalism—United States. 9. United States—Race relations. 10. United States—Social policy—1993- I. Marable, Manning, 1950-
  E184.7.N48 2005
  308.896'073—dc22

                              2005012208

Printed and bound in the United States of America on acid-free paper that meets the standards of the American National Standard for Permanence of Paper for Printed Library Materials.

Designed and Typeset by Cheryl Hoffman

09 08 07 06 05   1 2 3 4 5

Contents

Introduction

Because of the reality back of it, we continue the use of the older concept of the word "race," referring to the greater groups of humankind, which by outer pressure and inner cohesiveness, still form and have long formed a stronger or weaker unit of thought and action. Among these groups appear both biological and psychological likenesses, although we believe that these aspects have in the past been overemphasized in the face of many contradictory facts. While, therefore, we continue to study and measure all human differences, we seem to see the basis of real and practical racial units in culture. We use then the old word in new containers. A culture consists of the ideas, habits, and values, the technical processes and goods, which any group becomes possessed of either by inheritance or adoption.

Looking over the world today we see as incentive to economic gain, as cause of war, and as infinite source of cultural inspiration nothing so important as race and group contact. Here if anywhere the leadership of science is demanded not to obliterate all race and group distinctions, but to know and study them, to see and appreciate them at their true values, to emphasize the use and place of human differences as tool and method of progress; to make straight the path to a common world humanity through the development of cultural gifts to their highest possibilities. . . . A new view of the social sciences is necessary, as comprehending the actions of men and reducing them to systematic study and understanding. In this way we foresee a reinterpretation of history, education, and sociology; a rewriting of history from the ideological and economic point of view.[1]

—W. E. B. Du Bois, 1940

In 1906 at Columbia University in New York, South African student Pixley KaIsaka Seme gave a stirring lecture, "The Regeneration of Africa," upon which the university bestowed its most prestigious prize for oratory. In the talk, Seme declared that the people of Africa were prepared for a new realization of their capacity for redefining their destinies: "the ancestral greatness, the unimpaired genius, and the recuperative power of the race, its irrepressibility, which assures its permanence, constitute the African's greatest source of inspiration. . . . The regeneration of Africa means a new and unique civilization is soon to be added to the world."[2] After completing his law degree at Columbia, Seme was admitted to the bar at London's Middle Temple, returned to South Africa in 1910, and in 1912 became cofounder of the protest organization that would later become the African National Congress (ANC). For

Seme, an African "regeneration" or "renaissance" had embedded within it the concepts of black consciousness, a challenge to European hegemony, and the popular reawakening of the African people.

For Seme, John Langalibalele Dube, and other African intellectuals who founded the ANC, the concept of an African or black renaissance was an attempt at renegotiating the relationship between the black world and European domination, political as well as cultural and ideological. Embedded in this concept as well was the recognition that people of African descent now lived in new contexts as a result of the consolidation of European direct rule throughout most of the African continent in the late nineteenth century. Black intellectual and cultural production aimed at subverting European power over blacks' lives soon dovetailed with the concept of black renaissance.

In the century since Seme's oration, the concept of a black or African renaissance has been popularized throughout the African diaspora and on the African continent as well. In 1937, Nigerian nationalist Nnamdi Azikiwe had predicted this emergence in his book *Renascent Africa*. About a decade later, Senegalese intellectual Cheikh Anta Diop produced an influential essay, "When Can We Talk of an African Renaissance?" Since the dismantling of the apartheid regime in South Africa, the public discourse and growing debate about the meaning of an African renaissance has escalated sharply. In 1994, President Nelson Mandela called for an "African renaissance" at the 1994 meeting of the Organization of African Unity. Major conferences around the concept of an African renaissance were held in Johannesburg in 1998 and at the Africa Centre in London the following year. Mandela's successor, President Thabo Mbeki, has become particularly identified as the "primary articulator" of the African renaissance concept.[3]

In the context of the United States, the concept of "black renaissance" is most closely linked with the Harlem Renaissance, the explosion of literary, artistic, and political activity concentrated in black Manhattan immediately following World War I. Again, as in Africa, the call for a black renaissance was precipitated by fundamental changes within the political economy of African-American life. Beginning in 1915, hundreds of thousands of blacks had migrated from the rural South into the rapidly expanding ghettoes of the U.S. northeastern and midwestern states. Black folk culture and blues traditions gave way to jazz and urban life. Philosopher Alain Locke attempted to capture the intellectual vibrancy of this new generation of urban-based black artists and scholars in his famous March, 1925, edited issue of the *Survey Graphic*, on the "Harlem Renaissance."[4]

African-American studies as an interdisciplinary field of scholarship builds upon the legacies of Seme, Locke, and a host of other brilliant scholars, writers, and artists. In the wake of the black freedom struggle and civil rights movements of the 1960s and 1970s, black studies became institutionally consolidated at hundreds of U.S. colleges and universities. By 2004, there were at least forty formal departments of African-American or Africana studies including those at Brown University, Cornell University, Harvard University, Michigan State University, Ohio State University, The Pennsylvania State University, Rutgers University, the University of

California at Berkeley, the University of Illinois at Chicago and Urbana-Champaign, the University of Maryland, the University of North Carolina, the University of Wisconsin, and Yale University. More than two dozen master's degree programs in black studies had been established, and doctoral programs had been formed at nearly a dozen institutions, including Emory University, Harvard University, the University of Massachusetts, Michigan State University, Temple University, and Yale University.

Paradoxically, the widespread popularity and institutionalization of African-American studies occurred at the same historical moment that programs of affirmative action and race-based scholarships in higher education were being dismantled at hundreds of colleges. The growth of black studies unfortunately did little to transform the traditional racial hierarchy of the most prestigious research universities. For example, Columbia University did not hire its first tenured African-American faculty member, anthropologist Elliot Skinner, until 1959. Yale University's first black faculty appointee, Michael G. Cooke, was hired in 1962, and Cooke did not receive tenure until 1971, the first black professor there to do so. Princeton University appointed its first black tenured faculty member, economist W. Arthur Lewis, in 1963. The University of Pennsylvania's first tenured black faculty member, James W. Lash, was hired in 1969. African-American literary scholar J. Saunders Redding received tenure at Cornell University only in 1970. After three decades of struggle at these elite institutions, blacks have barely made a dent in their racial hierarchies. As of academic year 1999–2000, for example, Brown University had only seventeen full-time African-American faculty members, a modest 3.1 percent of that institution's total faculty. Most of the other Ivy League institutions have lower percentages of black faculty: Cornell, 2.7 percent; Yale, 2.7 percent; University of Pennsylvania, 2.6 percent; Harvard University, 2.1 percent; and Princeton University, 2.0 percent. When I was hired at Columbia in 1993, the entire College of Arts and Sciences had a grand total of five tenured African-American faculty members. As of fall 2003, there were only 12 tenured black faculty members in the College of Arts and Sciences, out of about 450 tenured professors. Those figures reveal a deep pattern of apartheid in U.S. higher education, and with the elimination of affirmative action programs and minority scholarships, this pattern will probably become even more pronounced.[5]

African-American studies increasingly became a lightning rod for attacks by political and ideological conservatives, who denigrated its substance and content. Prominent black studies intellectuals such as Cornel West were widely criticized for not producing "serious academic work."[6] Critics claimed that an African-American studies undergraduate major led to a career dead end, because students were inadequately prepared for advanced research in major disciplines. Indeed, there appeared to be some evidence that early in the new millennium, black students in large numbers were being discouraged from engaging in critical intellectual explanations of their own heritage and culture. According to the U.S. Department of Education, in the year 2000, only 782 African Americans graduated with B.A. degrees in black studies nationally. By contrast, 22,478 blacks earned B.A. degrees in business management, almost 29 times as many. Such comparisons were unfair because the vast majority of U.S. colleges had never established formal departments of African-American, Africana, and/or ethnic studies that permitted the granting of B.A. degrees. According to the *Journal of Blacks in Higher Education*, as of 2002 about 83 percent of the approximately 2,300 four-year colleges and universities in the United States had no African-American studies programs. At most elite research universities, about one-half to as many as three-fourths of all black undergraduates enrolled in at least one or more black studies courses.[7]

The effect of such criticism, combined with the more conservative political and ideological environment, contributed to a quiet "depoliticization" of many African-American studies programs and departments. Greater emphasis was given within many curricula to issues of identity, cultural representation, and social lifestyles, largely divorced from any concrete discussions of political economy and social class stratification. Many colleges redefined black studies as part of their overall commitment to "diversity," which eschewed any serious interrogation of the structural roots of racism and poverty. African-American studies increasingly presented itself as completely outside of the realm of politics for purposes of social change. In an April 4, 1998, debate with Harvard University Director of African-American Studies Henry Louis Gates, Jr., published in the *New York Times*, I challenged the field to reground itself in the activist traditions of scholars such as W.E.B. Du Bois, who did not separate intellectual engagement from the struggles of the real world beyond the academy.[8]

It became clear to me that African-American studies had to transform itself as an intellectual project, to address the vast transformation underway within the world of how the black experience was now evolving in the context of neoliberal, globalized capitalism. "Race" in the United States, which until 1965 was defined primarily as a black-white paradigm, was rapidly being reconfigured. Historic urban neighborhoods identified as "black" such as Harlem, Chicago's South Side, and South Central Los Angeles were becoming increasingly Latino. By the year 2000, about 7 million Americans defined themselves as "biracial" or "multiracial"—illustrating the acceleration of new racialized identities and cultural norms. In 2003, "Hispanics" surpassed African Americans, according to the U.S. Census, as the nation's largest minority group. Yet despite these demographic changes, the old pattern of anti-black oppression endured within the U.S. economic system and society. Blacks still experienced unfairly higher rates of unemployment and substandard health care, education, and housing; racist stereotypes of African-Americans continued to influence unfair sentencing patterns in the courts, contributing to more than 1 million blacks who were incarcerated nationwide as of the year 2000. Black studies has to effectively address the continuing stigmatization and exploitation of people of African descent both in the United States and transnationally, while at the same time, incorporating new information about the substantial ethnic and cultural shifts in how race is being "lived" in contemporary societies.

What was most disturbing to me was the almost complete silence of African-American studies as a field of scholarship to engage critically or discuss the prison-industrial complex and the devastating effects it was producing in the lives of black people. In early 2002, the Open Society Institute (the George Soros Foundation) provided a grant to me for the establishment of what we called the "Africana Criminal Justice Project" (ACJP). Our aim was to create a new interdisciplinary subfield in black studies to examine the links between structural racism, crime, and justice. Toward that objective, ACJP compiled research on the patterns of racialization within U.S. criminal system personnel, including judges and corrections officers; the racial disparities in sentencing patterns, especially those experienced by African-American youth; the political consequences of ex-felon disfranchisement and the subsequent deterioration of black electoral influence in both national and state politics; and the ideas about the "meaning of justice" that African-American intellectuals and human rights activists from Frederick Douglass to George Jackson had theorized over the past two centuries. In 2004 ACJP initiated a class inside New York City's Riker's Island Correctional Facility, working with black and Latino teenage men to encourage them to use "spoken word" poetry to examine their own personal stories and experiences during incarceration. That same year, ACJP also conducted a national survey of African-American studies programs to determine whether similar interdisciplinary courses were offered or were under development on race, crime, and justice. With fewer than five exceptions, black studies did not teach these topics that had become so vital to the welfare and advancement of black people both in the United States and transnationally.

When I began my academic career three decades ago, African-American studies experienced marginalization and exclusion on many campuses through the deliberate isolation of its course offerings by traditional departments. Its faculty were often deemed unqualified and unsuitable for integration into the academy; programs were "ghettoized" and denied resources by central administrations. By early in the new millennium, many of those barriers had been overcome. The new challenge, however, was failure of black studies departments overall to come to terms with how the "new racial domain" of color-blind racism was remaking America's contemporary racial and ethnic realities. The entire field required a new intellectual architecture, a "refoundation" based upon the evolving political economies of race, gender, class, and power that presently exist. African-American studies standard texts rarely incorporated discussions about globalization or the unprecedented mass migrations by people of African descent from the "global South" into Europe and North America. Despite the recent emergence of black feminist thought and a body of brilliant and provocative scholarship about gender and black women, too few of these writings had been included in standard African-American studies curricula. New theoretical approaches addressing these problems required the creation of new texts that could serve the needs of both higher education and the larger black community.

It was these concerns that led to the founding of *Souls: A Critical Journal of Black Politics, Culture, and Society* in January 1999. I invited the participation of a number of progressive scholars of the black experience who had prestigious histories of both academic rigor and political engagement. But I also endeavored to reach a new generation of intellectuals who had come to maturity in the 1980s and 1990s, whose work incorporated a theoretical orientation of "intersectionality"— bringing together an analysis of race, gender, sexuality, and class—in all of their scholarship. *Souls* solicited research papers examining the changing contours of racialization and the relationship between race and power inside Cuba, Jamaica, South Africa, and other countries outside the United States. The journal critiqued the growing scholarship on "whiteness studies" and tackled the question of how corporate capitalization distorted African-American popular culture through commercialization.

The New Black Renaissance is organized in three broad sections: "Remapping the Black Experience," "Old Constructs, New Contexts," and "Beyond Traditional Boundaries." "Remapping the Black Experience" includes essays employing the methodologies of history, cultural anthropology, and political sociology to examine the recent African-American past. Because "Harlem" has become so symbolic for the modern black urban experience, *Souls* has frequently published scholarly articles about this community, and this theme is represented here. Also in this opening section are articles that explore the recent history of African-American protest activism and political culture. "Remapping the Black Experience" suggests that the African-American experience has been uniquely distinct from that of the American mainstream; for blacks, "freedom" was not something bestowed from above by the state but achieved only through collective struggle. As a consequence, the texture of black political thought and practice is distinctly to the left of that of most white Americans. Instead of marginalizing or excluding the rich heritage of black radicalism, revolutionary nationalism, and Marxism, which is the standard approach taken in the academy, *Souls* has attempted to unearth and critique these elements of black political culture. Some of the very best articles that we have published on these themes are collected here.

The section "Old Constructs, New Contexts" examines how issues such as gender, youth culture, and racism within the criminal justice system have changed for African Americans in recent decades. The old structures of racialized power and domination that were previously embodied in Jim Crow segregation and South African apartheid have morphed into a new regime of "color-blind" structural racism that perpetuates the burden of inequality. How these processes of racial, gender, and class inequality are now being lived and experienced, and the ways black people resist them, are taken up in this section. A major theme addressed by *Souls* from its founding was the richly complex body of scholarship in the field of black feminist thought. Here I have selected several important articles reflecting that literature.

The section "Beyond Traditional Boundaries" presents the thesis that black studies needs to break its conceptual and thematic limitations, exploring "blackness" in new ways and in different geographic sites. Unlike the racial essentialism of many Afrocentrists, a critical black studies perspective argues that "race" is situational, always contested, and reflects the unequal relationships between different groups. "Whiteness" and "blackness" are both being restructured and redefined in the United States and *The New Black Renaissance* explains how this change is taking place. The contributors to this section are among the country's preeminent theorists and interpreters of the shifting dynamics of "racialization"—how "race" is being remade today. This section also argues that African-American studies scholarship must help shape and redirect public policies that affect black communities, working with government, foundations, and other private institutions on such issues as housing, health care, and criminal justice. It suggests that a critical black studies perspective must translate artistic and aesthetic creativity into a political commitment to challenge structural inequality and social unfairness in all its forms. The section's contributors outline creative ways for intellectuals to make a critical difference in policy debates.

The New Black Renaissance represents much of the best scholarly work appearing in *Souls* over the past seven years. Taken as a whole, it may assist in the construction of a "renaissance" or "refoundation" of the black intellectual tradition in the neoliberal age of empire and globalization. It breaks with the simplistic black-white template for race relations without sacrificing a moral and political commitment to the project of black liberation. It incorporates the new ethnic and racial diversity within U.S. urbanism with examination of what these developments mean for black Americans. *The New Black Renaissance*, like Seme's and Locke's earlier interventions, points toward the future emergence of a new praxis of black liberation that is just now on the horizon. In the radical tradition of W. E. B. Du Bois, this volume proposes "a new view of the social sciences . . . a reinterpretation of history, education, and sociology; a rewriting of history from the ideological and economic point of view."[9]

—*Manning Marable*

NOTES

1. W. E. B. Du Bois, "Apology." *Phylon: The Atlanta University Review of Race and Culture* 1 (First Quarter 1940), pp. 3–5.

2. See Chris Dunton, "Pixley KaIsaka Seme and the African Renaissance Debate," *African Affairs* 109, no. 409 (October 1, 2003), pp. 555–573. The most comprehensive work available on Seme is Richard Rive and Tim Couzens' study, *Seme: The Founder of the ANC* (Johannesburg: Skotsville Press, 1991).

3. Ibid., pp. 556–559. Certain South African leftists have also become extremely critical of the African renaissance concept espoused by Mbeki. See, for example, Sean Jacobs and Richard Colland, *Thabo Mbeki's World: The Politics and Ideology of the South African President* (Pietermaritzburg: University of Natal Press, 2002). George Clement Bond provides a more balanced analysis of the African renaissance construct in "Anthropology and the 'African Renaissance': Social Crises and the Potential for Complex Emergencies in Northeastern Zambia," in Debie LeBeau and Robert J. Gordon, *Challenges for Anthropology in the 'African Renaissance': A Southern African Contribution* (Windhoek: University of Namibia Press, 2002), pp. 2–9.

4. See Alain Locke, "Enter the New Negro," *Survey Graphic* 6, no. 6 (March 1925), pp. 631–634.

5. See Manning Marable, "Introduction: Reflections on Rituals of Passage," *Souls* 6, no. 3–4 (Summer/Fall 2004), pp. 1–4.

6. See for example, John McWhorter, "Cornell West Gives Black Scholars a Bad Rap," *Wall Street Journal,* April 15, 2002, p. A.20.

7. "News and Views: Black Studies Is an Unpopular Major," *Journal of Blacks in Higher Education* 36 (July 31, 2002), p. 14.

8. See Henry Louis Gates, Jr., "A Call to Protect Academic Integrity from Politics," and Manning Marable, "A Plea that Scholars Act Upon, Not Just Interpret Events," *New York Times,* April 4, 1998.

9. Du Bois, "Apology."

Part I. Remapping the Black Experience

1. *Rethinking Black Studies*

Manning Marable

Living Black History: Resurrecting the African-American Intellectual Tradition

I

We all "live history" every day. But history is more than the construction of collective experiences, or the knowledge drawn from catalogued and stored artifacts from the past. History is also the architecture of a people's memory, framed by our shared rituals, traditions, and notions of common sense. It can be a ragged bundle of hopes, especially for those who have been relegated beyond society's brutal boundaries.

I believe that historically oppressed people in the United States generally think about "living history" very differently from those closer to centers of power. The oppressed tend to privilege myth over accuracy, romantic resistance over silent subordination. To my knowledge, very few black poets have written lyrics in praise of Booker T. Washington, Condoleezza Rice, or Clarence Thomas. By contrast, there are literally hundreds and hundreds of powerful poems, plays, jazz symphonies, and even an opera inspired by Malcolm X. Blacks even make critical distinctions about "authenticity" among their most celebrated and popular public figures. Several years ago, for example, I inquired about the critical differences between Dr. Martin Luther King, Jr., and Malcolm X to the students in my Malcolm X seminar at Columbia. One black student quickly responded that the distinction was easy to make: "Dr. Martin Luther King, Jr., belongs to the world, but Malcolm X belongs to us."

At Malcolm X's Harlem funeral in 1965, Ossie Davis's eulogy and memorable description of Malcolm X as a "black shining prince" captured both the tragedy and triumph of the moment. Several months ago, interviewing my friend

3

Ossie for Columbia University's Malcolm X Project, I asked why he had used that particular word—"prince." Ossie replied that Malcolm X had inspired awe and admiration among black people worldwide, and deep love among the residents of Harlem in particular, because he consistently spoke truth to power. "He was the person that we wished we all could be." But blended throughout the fabric of myth and legend was also tremendous pain and sadness. "A prince," Ossie explained, "is not a king." Malcolm's greatness is found in his personal determination to become more than he was. His life's journey had been brutally cut short, his full potential unfulfilled.

C.L.R. James, the Trinidadian radical intellectual, made a similar observation in a 1967 London lecture. James described Malcolm X as "that great fighter whose potentialities were growing so fast that his opponents had to get rid of him."[1] James did not share Malcolm's black nationalist political philosophy, but it is not difficult to imagine "Nello" (as he was generally and widely known among friends) interrogating the militant black Muslim in an intense but casually intimate, lengthy conversion. Nello had an enormous curiosity about peoples and cultures of all kinds. He particularly wanted to identify and to comprehend the historical and social forces that constructed and produced a personality such as Malcolm X.

My theoretical approach to black studies, and my understanding of what "living history" means for the African American community, is best represented by James's remarkable 1970 essay, "Black People in the Urban Areas of the United States." "The [black] people who dominate the inner cities numerically cannot possibly work out a plan or have any programme by which they can improve their own situation which does not take into consideration the city as a whole," James observed. "A new situation has arisen for the urban black, for thinking in terms of the whole city means that you are automatically thinking in terms of the state and from the state you find yourself facing the whole nation."[2] Social historians have said for decades that the resis-tance movements of the African-American community throughout its history, but especially dating from the Great Migration of the early twentieth century, have been the basic template for other American social protest movements. This is undeniably true, but not only in the United States but throughout much of the modern world. The "Civil Rights Movement" (historian Clayborne Carson and I, among others, strongly prefer the term "Black Freedom Movement") spawned the modern women's rights movement, the gay and lesbian rights movement, the Chicano liberation struggle, as well as many others. The Black Panthers directly inspired the Puerto Rican Young Lords Party, AIM (American Indian Movement), and even struggles among white American senior citizens calling themselves the "Gray Panthers." Few Americans, regardless of race, can recall the most memorable words or ideas expressed in a George W. Bush presidential address. Few will ever forget "I Have a Dream," uttered by Martin on the steps of the Lincoln Memorial that hot August afternoon in 1963. Stamped deeply on public memory, it is now central to our understanding of what American democracy should be.

Martin's language still resonates for us today, not simply because he was a moving and powerful orator, but because what he was talking about actually had real depth and social meaning to every American. Even the white segregationists who hated him and rejected his politics understood the significance of what was being said. This explains to a considerable extent why most white Americans refuse to interrogate the meaning of "whiteness," or how white racial identity was historically constructed from the social processes that directly involved the trans-Atlantic slave trade, chattel slavery, and massive American Indian removal to reservations. White Americans are reinforced to handle the common history they share with African Americans very differently than we do. They have, in short, not a clue that virtually every major advance in expanding and reforming this nation's democratic institutions was directly caused, or profoundly influenced by, the black American struggle for freedom.

Most white Americans, for example, do have a somewhat vague awareness of what the American Civil War was, but possess no detailed, personal understanding about slavery, abolitionism, and why the conflict came about. Because my great-grandfather, Morris Marable, was sold on an auction block in West Point, Georgia, at the age of nine in 1854, I have acquired consequently a very different relationship to those distant events 150 years ago. When we feel personally connected with events from the past, they help to shape our actions today, thus bending the construction and trajectory of future history. Knowledgeable civic actors can draw important lessons from history, which does incrementally increase civic capacity. Historical amnesia blocks the construction of potentially successful social movements. As the distance between the past, present, and future becomes shorter and closer, individuals can acquire a greater sense of becoming the "makers" of their own history.

C.L.R. James understood all of this, and much more:

> The black people in the United States are the most socially united group in the country; they all have one unifying characteristic—they suffer from that historical development which has placed them in the role of second class citizens. There is no other national group which automatically constitutes one social force with a unified outlook and the capacity to make unified moves in politics and to respond to economic problems. . . . It is from America's urban blacks that many people all over the world have historically gained a consciousness of the problems that black people suffer and their attempts to overcome them.[3]

"Race" has always been the fundamental contradiction within the American state, and its politics. That is because, as King and Malcolm X both completely understood, U.S. democracy was constructed on a distinctively *racial* foundation. The nation's first law, the 1790 Emigration Act, limited citizenship solely to "free white persons." That helps to explain why most Asians born in continental Asia could not legally become U.S. citizens until 1952. That is why the majority of black voters could not cast ballots in a U.S. presidential election until 1968. Racism *matters* in the United States.

II

"Leadership" is the creative capacity of individuals of any group to realize that group's specific objective interests. Black leaders from abolitionist Frederick Douglass to former presidential candidate Jesse Jackson have therefore interpreted black leadership primarily as capacity-building-from-below: building structures of group advocacy and resistance, which were genuinely and organically linked throughout black civil society and its varied institutions. Intellectuals who assumed leadership roles in the black community have in very general terms endeavored to make vital contributions to that struggle through their own work and research. Any scholar who, like W.E.B. Du Bois or myself when I was a boy, was forced to sit in the Jim Crow section at the back of a public bus usually feels much more like a black person and much less like a Ph.D.

Malcolm X did not think of himself as an "intellectual," in the traditional sense of the term. Much of the historical literature and political commentary highlights Malcolm X's oratorical ability, his great skill as a debater, and overwhelming charisma as an individual. In certain respects, perhaps Malcolm's widely recognized mastery as a public speaker detracts attention from his impressive analytical contributions as a leading public intellectual.

What, after all, is an "intellectual," and what comprises intellectual leadership? Marxist theorist Antonio Gramsci suggested that "all men are intellectuals," although "not all men have in society the function of intellectuals. . . . Each man . . . carries on some form of intellectual activity, that is, he is a 'philosopher,' an artist, a man of taste, he participates in a particular conception of the world, has a conscious line of moral conduct, and therefore contributes to sustain a conception of the world or to modify it, that is, to bring into being new modes of thought."[4] Gramsci's model of the intellectual is also linked to the practical tasks of transforming theoretical concepts into real social forces, which in turn have the potential for influencing the events of daily life. In other words, the intellectual is not removed from the society, but instead conceives the spectrum of possibilities for a new social world, and through articulation seeks to persuade others to accept that vision. "The new intellectual," Gramsci observed, "can no longer consist in eloquence, which is an exterior and momentary mover of feelings and passions, but in active participation in practical life, as constructor, organiser, 'permanent persuader' and not just a simple orator."[5] This captures the essence of what Malcolm X attempted to accomplish, for himself and his people: to break the devastating mental shackles of dependency and self-hatred imposed by centuries of slavery and segregation, to imagine a world without white supremacy and black inferiority, and to construct strong social institutions to perpetuate and protect the cultures and communities created by people of African descent. Central to this effort are the contestation of the "master narrative" and the construction of an alternative history.

Gramsci considered the public intellectual to be both critic and catalyst, the source of new insights about society, while possessing the ability and dedication to turn ideas into new realities. These criteria for intellectual engagement have, interestingly enough, been the standards which have been integral to the intellectual traditions of black America. African-American intellectual work, since the middle of the nineteenth century, has been largely anchored to three great principles and practices. As I have suggested in other works, the black American intellectual tradition has been first "descriptive, that is, presenting the reality of black life and experience from the point of view of black people themselves." Second, it has been "corrective," a concerted attempt to challenge and to critique the racism and stereotypes that have been ever present in the main discourse of white academic institutions. And third, this tradition has been "prescriptive," an intellectual orientation which consistently connected scholarship with collective struggle, social analysis with social transformation.

Most of the classic texts which comprise the canon of African-American studies are firmly anchored within this tradition. W.E.B. Du Bois's entire intellectual life and magnificent body of scholarship are obviously the standard by which the entire field can be judged. And to a surprising degree, this model of intellectual praxis, of theoretical interrogation and practical political activity, appears and reappears generation after generation. James Weldon Johnson (1871–1938) is today perhaps best known as a literary scholar, novelist, and lyricist; he co-authored with his brother J. Rosamond Johnson the black national anthem, "Lift Ev'ry Voice and Sing," and wrote *The Autobiography of an Ex-Colored Man* (1912), *God's Trombones* (1927), *Black Manhattan* (1930), *Along This Way* (1933), and other works. But Johnson saw himself, and was largely viewed by his contemporaries, as a public intellectual engaged in practical political struggles for the empowerment of black people. Johnson served as United States counsel to Venezuela and Nicaragua, worked as an attorney and political journalist, and was from 1920 to 1930 the Executive Secretary of the National Association for the Advancement of Colored People (NAACP). Richard Wright (1908–1960) was an outstanding novelist and social critic, the author of *Native Son* (1940), *Black Boy* (1945), and *Pagan Spain* (1957). But Wright was also an activist in the U.S. Communist Party during the Great Depression, and in the 1950s was a leading figure in the pan-Africanist movement. He attended the historic 29-nation gathering of African and Asian countries at the 1955 Bandung Conference in Indonesia, and authored a blistering attack against racial prejudice, *White Man Listen* (1957), which anticipated many of Malcolm X's key ideas.

Malcolm X was born in an extraordinary generation of black intellectuals whose lives and careers were all profoundly defined by the chaotic events of the Great Depression, the Second World War, the global struggle between Communism and capitalism represented by the Cold War, and the eruption of anti-colonial political movements and social revolutions throughout the Third World. Within Malcolm X's cohort, some of the most prominent black activist intellectuals were novelist/social critic James Baldwin, Julius Nyerere of Tanzania, Eduardo Mondlane of Mozambique, Agostinho Neto of Angola, Amilcar Cabral of Portuguese Guiné, Harold Cruse, Ella Baker, Vincent Harding, Septima Clark, Bayard Rustin, and of course, Dr. Martin Luther King, Jr. Malcolm X's closest counterpart in the post–World War II black diaspora was Frantz Fanon (1925–1961), born in Martinique, who became the leading theorist of the anti-colonial revolution against

French rule in Algeria, and author of *The Wretched of the Earth* (1963). Like Malcolm X, Fanon was a relentless critic of "whiteness," and rejected the philosophy of nonviolence. Fanon not only believed that the oppressed had the right to use violence to defend themselves against the colonizer, but that such violence was essential in purging the self-hatred and cultural dependency which characterized the minds of non-whites within racialized societies.

Any close reading of both *The Autobiography of Malcolm X* and *The Wretched of the Earth* illustrates some striking similarities in a theoretical outlook. Malcolm X, reflecting back to his first experience of straightening or "conking" his hair, admits, "how ridiculous I was . . . stupid enough to stand there simply lost in admiration of my hair looking 'white,'"[6] The psychological makeup of the colonized black mind leads to self-mutilation, and the assimilation of white standards of beauty. Similarly, Fanon sharply condemns the desire among non-Europeans to achieve "whiteness at any price." The black colonized mind desired "all manner of possession: to sit at the settler's table, to sleep in the settler's bed, with his wife if possible." Both Malcolm and Fanon attempted to create new racialized subjects, black people who actively rejected the materialistic values and cultural traditions of the white world. Fanon believed that blacks "must leave our dreams and abandon our old dreams. . . . Let us waste no time in sterile litanies and nauseating mimicry . . . if we want humanity to advance a step further, if we want to bring it up to a different level than that which Europe or America has shown it, then we must invent and we must make discoveries. . . . We must turn over a new leaf, we must work out new concepts, and try to set afoot a new man."[7]

Both Malcolm X and Fanon also vigorously condemned the black bourgeoisie, the "House Negroes" who loyally supported the white power structure at the expense of the interests of the black masses. In his famous "Message to the Grassroots" address delivered in Detroit on November 10, 1963, Malcolm charged that black middle-class leaders committed to racial integration were ideologically descended from the plantation "Uncle Toms" of a century before:

> The slavemaster took Tom and dressed him well and even gave him a little education—a *little* education; gave him a long coat and a top hat and made all the other slaves look up to him. Then he used Tom to control them. The same strategy that was used in those days is used today, by the same white man. He takes a Negro, a socalled Negro, and makes him prominent, builds him up, publicizes him, makes him a celebrity. And then he becomes a spokesman for Negroes—and a Negro leader.[8]

Similarly, Fanon described the black middle class in colonial societies as a buffer elite used to dominate the masses. Both men were presenting alternative histories of enslavement and colonialism from the vantage point of society's marginalized groups.

Black public intellectuals in the age of racial revolution saw their scholarship as contributing to a building of a necessary intellectual rationale for the destruction of legal structural racism. Ironically, during the past quarter century, as legal barriers and restrictions on racial advancement have in many respects come down, the overall character of black studies scholarship is largely disengaged with the problems of the urban poor. Today's elitist discourse of liberal multiculturalism speaks the safe language of symbolic representation, but rarely of resistance. Our scholarship indeed must be rigorous and objective, but if it lacks vision or is not informed in its substructure by passionate collective memory, how meaningful can it be to the one million African Americans who currently are incarcerated in this nation's correctional facilities? Glittering public intellectuals may appear to offer a depth of social commentary in the media, but too frequently their politics and comprehension of history have shallow roots.

III

Perry Anderson once observed that historians work in the realm of the dead, a place where all of life's struggles have already been won or lost. This unfortunately gives history as a field a kind of grim, deterministic character. However, borrowing from the rich insights of cultural anthropology, a more useful ethnographic framework is that of the "living dead." African philosophy and cosmology suggests that the social weight of the ancestors frequently transcends the physical boundaries of life and death, as narrowly defined in the West. The black public intellectual must *actively* engage the past in such a way that tends to obliterate the boundaries that appear to divide the past from the present, and from the future.

In 2003, the Center for Contemporary Black History at Columbia University, which I direct, attempted to develop a unique public policy project in partnership with Myrlie Evers Williams, former national chair of the NAACP and widow of the martyred civil rights leader, Medgar Evers, that sought to use reconstructed history as a vehicle for racial reconciliation and social fairness in Mississippi. Our project, "Freedom Summer 2004," hoped to mobilize 250 college-aged students across the state of Mississippi next year to organize "freedom schools" and register voters. The project was timed to coincide with the fortieth anniversary of the historic "Freedom Summer" of 1964 when 1,000 Northern, mostly white students traveled to Mississippi to organize voters in poor, black, rural communities. That summer, in Mississippi, 1,000 civil rights organizers were arrested, 80 seriously beaten, 39 black churches and 30 black schools firebombed. Five civil rights activists were murdered—including Michael Schwerner, Andrew Goodman, and James Earl Chaney. This is the terrible history white Mississippians desperately want to forget.

The next year, in 1965, Congress passed the Voting Rights Act. The percentage of registered black voters soared from 6.7 percent in 1964 to over 61 percent in 1967. Jim Crow laws were overturned. But today, second-class citizenship has reemerged across the South, because of the adoption of repressive voters laws. In Mississippi, a citizen convicted of a felony loses the right to vote for life. Thirty percent of black male adults in Mississippi today cannot vote. The purpose of the Freedom Summer 2004 field organizing campaign was to focus public awareness on the social unfairness of these restrictions. In concert with members of the Mississippi Legislative Black Caucus, we planned to push for the adoption of liberalized voter laws. Part of that effort must involve reconciling Mississippi with its own turbulent racial history. New media resources, archival research, and oral history methodologies would have incorporated old films, newspaper accounts, photos, and recent interviews with the veterans of the original Freedom Summer, with multimedia materials generated by next summer's planned activities. We also proposed the organizing of a "Families of the Disenfranchised" group, documenting how losing the right to vote affects everyday people, white and black. Myrlie Evers Williams attended and spoke briefly at Columbia's tenth anniversary black studies conference, and we used the opportunity of her visit to New York to work on a comprehensive grant proposal, which was subsequently submitted to several foundations. However, with the growing climate of political conservatism in the wake of the "War on Terrorism" and the suppression of black voting rights in Florida and other southern states during the presidential election of 2004, foundations were reluctant to fund our progressive proposal. Without financial backing, the plan had to be shelved. Laurent Alfred, the coordinator of the Center's "Africana Criminal Justice Project," and I nevertheless travelled and spoke in Mississippi in April 2004, laying the ground for future activities there.

The purposes of the Center's Malcolm X Project are therefore similar to those of the Freedom Summer Project. It starts with the concept that a dialectical interpretation of events, whether they happened 100 years ago or tomorrow, requires a 360-degree, comprehensive approach. There is a "Rashamon story" to be told in all major historical events, like Malcolm's assassination at the Audubon Ballroom on February 21, 1965. Oral history and new media should critically explore all the divergent points of view of the assassins, the Shabazz family members, political friends and associates of Malcolm's, the New York City police, as well as the FBI, who certainly must have had its paid informants in the ballroom that terrible afternoon. If the educational project can help answer the question of what those in law enforcement and government know, and when did they know it, we may bridge the distance between our divided racial past and the present. The knowledge we produce can be incorporated into the curricula of public schools, and serve as an educational resource for the Audubon Ballroom Memorial and Cultural Center, when it opens sometime in 2005. Students trained in the Malcolm X seminar at Columbia will probably be employed as staff members and guides at the Audubon, as well as working with public schools.

Behind the idea of "living history" is the core belief that *powerful narratives we construct about the past have the potential capacity to reshape contemporary civic outcomes*. One excellent example of this was C. Vann Woodward's 1955 book, *The Strange Career of Jim Crow*, which was instrumental in destroying the myth that racial segregation had always existed in the South. Woodward's work convincingly laid the historical rationale for King's argument that biracial peace and cooperation were indeed possible in the South. Another element of living history that I find especially attractive is its ethnographic dimension of participant observation. The "living historian" is obligated to become a civic actor, as innovative knowledge collected and drawn from the past shapes important legislative initiatives and enriches public school curricula. The goal is not just to educate and inform, but to transform the objective material and cultural conditions and subordinate status of marginalized groups, through informed civic engagement, and by strengthening civil society. In effect, we attempt to reconstruct America's memory about itself, and our collective past.

The larger objective of the Malcolm X Project is not only to build a rich multimedia version of *The Autobiography of Malcolm X*, but to create a model for producing "living black history"—a critical intellectual project which utilizes the interdisciplinary methodologies and tools of new media, oral history, field research, and traditional archival research to construct a truly "thick description" of significant personalities, events, and social movements that were central to the construction of both black American and urban society. New media allow an unprecedented, rich interrogation of the past. In the context of recent U.S. history (post-1945), we can also employ oral history interviews to lift up and reconstruct fractured public memory. Throughout 2003 and 2004, for example, the MXP staff interviewed a series of eyewitnesses to Malcolm's assassination at the Audubon Ballroom.

Most of our students have acquired a depth of familiarity with the intimate details of Malcolm X's life that would truly rival or surpass most of the scholars who have written and published about him. We constantly look for inconsistencies in oral responses, and can easily inquire about very specific points. James Shabazz, Malcolm X's personal secretary, later confessed to me after a four-hour grilling that it was the most thoughtful but intense emotional interview he had ever experienced since Malcolm's death. Our research has revealed new questions about the actual number of individuals directly involved in the 1965 assassination. The real question to be exhaustively explored is how much federal, state, and local law enforcement authorities knew in advance, or perhaps if they participated in Malcolm X's killing.

The MXP is reconstructing the past, providing a more balanced and richer interpretation of a remarkable black leader. But its broader purpose transcends nostalgic walks down black history's memory lane. A fuller portrait of Malcolm X as a complicated and often internally conflicted human being does much more to empower urban youth than the frozen portrait of an icon. It helps us toward a realistic understanding of Malcolm X when we learn that back in the summer of 1944 Malcolm performed briefly as a drummer and dancer at Abe Goldstein's Lobster Pond in midtown Manhattan; that when he was arrested on burglary and gun possession charges in Boston, in January 1946, and detectives promised him that they would go lightly if he betrayed his accomplices, he immediately did; that his first extensive tour of the Middle East and Africa was in 1959, not in 1964 following his break from Elijah Muhammad and the Nation of Islam; and that Alex Haley and

Malcolm X collaborated to construct, for very different purposes, a partially fictive Malcolm X. That's a shame, because the actual man is far more attractive and powerful than that skillful literary representation of him in the Malcolm/Haley text called *The Autobiography*.

Virtually all of Malcolm X's opponents *and* defenders, both those who hated him and those who adored him, constructed him as a static figure. While he was alive, the mainstream civil rights leadership and media critics dismissed him as a black nationalist extremist and zealot. After the publication of *The Autobiography*, Haley's liberal integrationist interpretation convinced them that Malcolm had converted over to their gradualist, pragmatic philosophy. To his nationalist defenders, Malcolm would be fixed for all time as a "black shining prince," virtually incapable of making political mistakes or errors of judgment. By the late 1960s, Malcolm had been tragically reborn as "St. Malcolm," placed on a lofty pedestal far above the black masses. Witnessing this sad process of iconization, black cultural critic Harold Cruse wrote, in 1967: "The last outstanding leader was Malcolm X, but did his followers really understand the man's positive side, or why he acted as he did? Did they see any Afro-American historical trends repeating themselves in Malcolm X's career? Unfortunately, they did not."[9] They did not understand that while Malcolm indeed "made history," he could not freely make it in any way that he chose.

Malcolm and Nello as human beings were very different individuals. What links them together in my mind is neither race nor ideology *per se*, but their passionate belief in the power and integrity of ideas in action. They were unafraid to pursue the "truth," regardless of the costs and consequences. Perhaps this is the radical meaning of Rosa Luxemburg's quotation: "Freedom is always and exclusively freedom for the one who thinks differently."[10] Myths, even well-meaning ones, simply make oppressed people feel good about themselves. But it is only the truth that will set them free.

This "long view of black history" may help to explain why James, one of black studies' greatest intellectuals, rejected the concept of black studies. In 1969, before an audience of militant Black Powerites at Washington D.C.'s Federal City College, James announced that "I do not recognize any distinctive nature of black studies. . . . I do not know, as a Marxist, black studies as such. I only know the struggle of people against tyranny and oppression in a certain social and political setting . . . it is impossible for me to separate black studies from white studies in any theoretical point of view."[11] What James means is that writing solely from American history's racial mountain can give us a remarkably long, yet incomplete, view of the complex human condition. Malcolm's story is simultaneously authentically black and deeply and profoundly American and human. Identities are multiple and situational. A mature, wiser Malcolm X, weeks before his death, commented that the fundamental division of humanity was found in the deep structural inequalities separating the global "haves and the have nots." This explains why the late Malcolm rejected the call for "civil rights" and embraced the struggle for "human rights."

To enrich the black intellectual tradition, we must push the boundaries of what has become black studies well beyond black studies. The historical construction of racialization in the United States was largely, *but not exclusively*, framed by the black experience. Can anyone doubt that Asian Americans also encountered structural processes of racialization in California in the late nineteenth and early twentieth centuries? If not, why the massive construction of internment camps for Japanese Americans during World War II? Today, over 40 percent of the people in the combined neighborhoods of Harlem (West, Central, and East) are Spanish-speakers. Harlem's Dominican immigrants mostly dream at first of scaling the hierarchy of American whiteness, and when most fail, they turn angrily against the dream deferred. Puerto Ricans consistently nationwide have a lower household income than the average black household. History never exactly repeats itself. The next Malcolm X will probably speak Spanish as *her* native language. The once apparently fixed and immutable barriers of race are rapidly being reconstructed through the forces of globalization and mass migration of the global South's poor to the North's wealthy metropoles.

"Living history" must incorporate a dialectical method and appreciation of what history has in store for us in America's and the world's ghettoes and barrios. As the numbers in our prisons swell, as the millions of new politically disenfranchised grow, new social protest movements will undoubtedly emerge. Many of the new leaders may speak different languages, have different demands and grievances, and have different agendas for action. But I believe that they will all also quote and honor Malcolm X as one of their own.

NOTES

1. C.L.R. James, "Black Power Lecture," London, 1967, in Anna Grimshaw, ed., *The C.L.R. James Reader* (Oxford: Blackwell Publishers, 1992), pp. 362–374.

2. C.L.R. James, "Black People in the Urban Areas of the United States," in ibid., pp. 375–378.

3. Ibid., pp. 375–378.

4. Antonio Gramsci's analysis of the formation and social function of intellectuals is found in Quintin Hoare and Geoffrey Nowell Smith, eds., *Selections from the Prison Notebooks of Antonio Gramsci* (New York: International Publishers, 1973), pp. 3–23.

5. Ibid.

6. Malcolm X, as told to Alex Haley, *The Autobiography of Malcolm X* (New York: Grove Press, 1965), p. 56.

7. Frantz Fanon, *The Wretched of the Earth* (New York: Grove Press, 1963), pp. 315–316.

8. Malcolm X, *Malcolm X Speaks* (New York: Grove Weidenfeld, 1965), p. 13.

9. Harold Cruse, *The Crisis of the Negro Intellectual* (New York: William Morrow, 1967), p. 563.

10. From a prison cell, Luxemburg wrote: "Freedom is always and exclusively freedom for the one who thinks differently. Not because of any fanatical concept of 'justice,' but because all that is instructive, wholesome and purifying in political freedom depends on this

essential characteristic; and its effectiveness vanishes when 'freedom' becomes a special privilege." Rosa Luxemburg in Bertram D. Wolfe, ed., *The Russian Revolution* (Ann Arbor: University of Michigan Press, 1961), p. 69.

    11. C.L.R. James, "Black Studies and the Contemporary Student," in Grimshaw, ed., *The C.L.R. James Reader*, pp. 390–404.

~

HOWARD WINANT

Teaching Race and Racism in the Twenty-First Century: Thematic Considerations

This is a crucial moment for those of us who teach about race and racism. People, there's a crisis of racial meaning going on out there. In the classic definition, a crisis is a situation in which "the old is dying and the new cannot be born." Well, that's the situation in which racial pedagogy finds itself at the start of the twenty-first century.

There is a lot more at stake than just what we teach. What we teach is what people learn, and what they learn is what they know. Of course, there are many forms of knowledge, especially about race, but higher education curricula, taken as a whole, still embody what is known in a given society at a given time.[1] What I'm talking about here is courses and programs that deal with the complex subject of race: its history, theoretical and philosophical status, multiple manifestations in socioeconomic, political, and cultural relationships, embodiment in artistic production and in the toils of the human psyche, etc. Race is a big topic. Sociopolitical confusion, uncertainty, and anxiety about such a complex theme will be reflected in curricula focused upon it, and will be fostered in the hearts and minds of those students who seek knowledge about it. Such is the present situation in the academic treatment of race.

    It's no secret that much of what is taught about race is outmoded, that ethnic studies departments are often riven by fierce controversies and antagonisms, and that in mainstream disciplinary settings too there is confusion: the post–civil rights era racial ethos has become "common sense"; decades of advocacy of "colorblindness," diversity, and multiculturalism have taken their toll. Space is not available here for a full assessment of the conflicts and uncertainties besetting racial studies today, but it is at least possible to provide a glancing overview of the crisis. In what follows I first discuss *the changing meaning and political dynamics of race* at the start of the twenty-first century. Next I take note of *the centrality of racial studies in the curriculum.* I conclude with some notes, necessarily preliminary and sketchy, toward a new racial studies.

THE CHANGING MEANING AND POLITICAL DYNAMICS OF RACE

In the post–civil rights period, after decades of political and cultural conflict over the meaning of race and the persistence of structural racism in the U.S., the outlines of the country's twenty-first-century racial crisis are beginning to emerge. A new racial formation has developed from the processes of confrontation and accommodation, of conflict and reform that swept across much of the world over the past few decades. Changing racial dynamics are in part the effects of anti-racist movements and of the achievement of democratic reform in the latter half of the twentieth century. They are linked as well to new patterns of globalization, to the unsteady and unfulfilled postcolonial situation that obtains across the world's South, and to the tremendous international flows of people, capital, and information around the planet. Here, however, I propose a narrower "take" on the changing meaning of race, focused on what is to be taught and studied about race in the American university during the twenty-first century.

These changes have set off a crisis in racial pedagogy. Generally speaking, the crisis comes from two sources. The first of these proceeds from the politics of the post–civil rights era, from what I have called in other work "racial hegemony."[2] As the U.S. underwent a transition from the fairly explicit white supremacism and racial domination of the pre–civil rights era to the reform-based and incorporative logic of "colorblindness," diversity, etc. that had become the new racial "common sense" sometime in the 1970s, racial studies had also to confront the newly emergent, hegemonic situation. To be sure, the old issues that had spawned the movement still remained highly salient: discrimination and white privilege, structural and cultural racism, etc. But because reform had occurred, because the incorporation of movement demands (and persons) had taken place, racial studies were beset with a host of new challenges: pedagogical, empirical, and theoretical. Just as fierce debates took place across the country about the supposed "declining significance of race," so too conflicts engulfed numerous academic departments, both mainstream discipline- and ethnic studies–based, over curricular content.

The second source of crisis is linked to globalization. It may be seen in terms of national vs. transnational perspectives on race. This debate of course had a long history, stretching back to controversies over slavery, conquest, and colonialism, and touching upon such complex issues as pan-Africanism (and other panethnic movements), nationalism, dependency, world-systems theory, and migration. Here I can offer only the most schematic characterization of this complex question.

Briefly, the post-WWII world racial scene was shaped jointly by racial reform in the global North and decolonization in the global South, two processes that were themselves highly related. As this dual transition unfolded, racial politics became more global: a sustained period of nationalism linked anti-racist struggles in the U.S. to anti-colonial revolution, for example, and "internal colonialism" theories enjoyed a significant vogue. Later, while civil rights reforms marginalized racial radicals in the U.S., postcolonial regimes also lost favor because they descended into corruption, dictatorship, brutal civil war, and new forms of dependency and neocolonial subordination.[3] Complicating this huge transition in the U.S. was burgeoning immigration to that country after its 1965 immigration reform—which was itself an important and often neglected piece of civil rights legislation. Finally, the ever-expanding quest by the U.S. for global economic power—embodied in NAFTA, the WTO, and other forms of interventionism—began to cast transnational political economic issues in a newly racialized mold. This process reached new heights at the 2001 UN World Conference on Racism in Durban, South Africa, where the U.S. did its best to undermine and marginalize demands for global racial justice; new global racial politics have also inflected the Bush administration's "war on terrorism" and its Iraq intervention in various ways.

Advancing globalization tends in general to internationalize the racial curriculum. For example, teaching about various racial diasporas is heightened: African, Chinese, Filipino, Dominican, and others. Even Afrocentrism—which in my view is largely an inchoate and retro effort to revive the black cultural nationalism of the late 1960s—in some measure works to direct greater attention to diasporic issues. At the same time the internationalization of the racial curriculum disturbs and alienates more locally and nationally oriented scholars whose commitments to specific racially defined communities or to equality and justice are focused on domestic U.S. racial conditions. This pattern of divergence and debate isn't going away; it is driven by social structure itself. The U.S. increasingly throws its weight around in the big world: neo-imperialism is the name of the game. And it does this at a historical moment when its own demographics are more nonwhite, more replete with recent immigrants from the global South, more "diasporic" in short, than ever before. At the same time domestic racial discontent is rising, as the U.S. tears up its residual commitments to the welfare state, jams its prisons with more and more people of color, and exports poverty and unemployment as much as possible to the ghettos, barrios, and reservations.

All these tensions and conflicts flow inevitably into the racial curriculum. It seems apparent that these post-WWII racial transformations and upheavals, most centrally the reforms of the post–civil rights era and the onset of the racial ideology of "colorblindness," have unmoored the higher learning in America, racially speaking, leaving faculty, students, and administrators (even those specializing in this area) uncertain as to what should be taught, and what is to be learned, about race and racism. The significance of race ("declining" or increasing?), the interpretation of racial equality ("colorblind" or colorconscious?), the institutionalization of racial justice ("reverse discrimination" or affirmative action?), and the very categories—black, white, Latino/Hispanic, Asian American, and Native American—employed to classify racial groups have all been called into question over recent decades. The paradigmatic approaches to studying these issues—both in traditional academic disciplines (my main focus here is on the social sciences) and in the widespread interdisciplinary programs that may be grouped under the "ethnic studies" rubric—largely derive from sociopolitical and cultural conditions that have now been superseded, at least in part.

Exclusion of critical race-oriented problematics from the curriculum and the disciplinary canons has largely ended, reflecting the transformation of the university setting from an apparatus of racial domination to one of racial incorporation. By the 1980s, many universities and colleges had made watchwords of the terms "diversity" and "multiculturalism," although the practical meaning of this was debatable: as "diversity" was being celebrated, affirmative action programs were coming under attack and racially defined minority enrollments were decreasing. Did attention to racial and ethnic studies, whether proceeding from traditional disciplines or from the newer ethnic studies departments and programs, benefit from this new approbation, or was serious academic commitment to these areas of study being rendered symbolic in the newly dawning "post–civil rights," "color-blind" era?

More recently affirmative action has found new defenders, not in the relatively debilitated organizations and thinkers (myself included) who see themselves as carrying forward the movement's legacy, but in such mainstream and often conservative sectors as large corporations and the military, whose spokespeople have argued that "diversity" and upward mobility for racially defined minorities are crucial to their organizations' efforts to maintain market share and loyalty in the ranks.

This situation, in which formerly radical democratic demands now serve to undergird elite power, at first seems highly ironic. It calls forth cynicism, and perhaps even mockery, of the movement's legacy. But hold on there, my friends. When we look more deeply, we can see that every successful social movement realizes its goals by embedding them in the heart of the establishment, the power structure. That is what success means: lodging the arrows of your movement's demands in the bosom of your antagonist, most often the state but sometimes corporations, cultural elites, or other power-wielding groups. These elites and state administrators generally come to understand that honey works better than vinegar: moderate reform/hegemony are strategically more effective in maintaining consensual rule than intransigence, repression, or domination could ever be.[4]

At the same time, there is an implicit contradiction in the success that movements sometimes achieve. What Omi and I characterized as the political "trajectory" of racially based movements sets in here.[5] Achieving your goals as a movement involves becoming incorporated: again, within the state, the corporation, etc. Success means that "moderate" versions of movement demands are accepted and institutionalized, while more radical versions (and voices) are marginalized, or worse. Winning counts; winning reforms can mean accomplishing great transformations in patterns of social injustice; it can mean bringing the light of democracy to places where only the darkness of dictatorship existed before. But winning is also losing: it means that not only the state and power structure have made concessions, but that the movements that previously opposed them have compromised as well.

In the aftermath of intense political conflict, when reforms have become institutionalized and movement opposition has waned, the political "trajectory" reenters a period of abeyance. But during this period, uncertainty, doubt, and anger simmer: in cultural forums, in political organizations, in the "hood," and in the academy as well. How much did we (or previous generations) accomplish with all our movement blood, sweat, and tears? How much has changed, and how much remains the same? What new issues confront us now, in the age of "colorblindness" and multiculturalism?

THE CENTRALITY OF RACIAL STUDIES IN THE CURRICULUM

Whatever one's answer to those questions, the evidence remains strong that *approaches to teaching race and ethnicity have hewed closely to the political and cultural climate of the times.* There has always—always!—been some version of "racial and ethnic studies" in operation on American campuses. At one time there was racial theology; Drs. Morton and Agassiz were once prominent racial authorities; Herbert Spencer and E. A. Ross had their day. When racial segregation, quotas on Jews, and immigration restrictions were in place, the predominant view was white supremacist, restrictive, and given to eugenicism. For a long time—let us say until the aftermath of WWII—the study of race was almost entirely a conversation among whites. Only in a few places—notably the historically black colleges and universities—were racially defined minorities even present in any significant number. In the mainstream and elite universities, only an occasional scholar, often beleaguered and derided, could make his voice (and it was almost inevitably a male voice) heard.

Only in the 1960s, when students brought pressure on the universities to make changes—impelled by shifting demographics, social movements, and political changes at the national and even international levels—did the institutions finally respond. Only then were ethnic studies programs created and some measure of affirmative action instituted in hiring, admissions, etc. And often this came grudgingly and unevenly. Only in the 1970s, when ethnic studies programs were already in place and the problems of racial inequality and ethnic difference widely studied, did the histories, identities, and cultural varieties of the American "mosaic" even begin to be treated with any degree of respect across the curriculum.

What has happened in recent years? A notable stasis has developed: a gap may be opening up again, as has certainly occurred in the past. The teaching/learning strategies in place today at American institutions of higher learning developed in parallel with the racial and ethnic political and cultural milieux of the 1960s and 1970s. Now, more than three decades later, a new situation confronts this pedagogy, one for which it is unprepared. Such themes as hybridized identities, ethnically and racially based experience and "role-taking," generational shifts in specific groups and communities, global and national patterns of racial/ethnic stratification, ethnonationalism and ethnoglobality, race/gender/class "intersectionality," and overlap and antagonism between racially and ethnically based concepts of difference/identity/stratification, a new attentiveness toward "whiteness," and a resurgent interest in genocide and "ethnic cleansing" are just a few (!) of the many issues that confront teaching and learning strategies in this area, seem to call for new investigation and new responses.

Ironically, these new challenges are emerging at a moment when movement activity has waned, when "diversity" commitments are under attack, and when new claims of meritocratism, postraciality, and "colorblindness" are being advanced from numerous quarters (usually from the center-right, but sometimes even from the left or from liberal quarters, and sometimes from interventive courts and legislatures). It is no accident that debates over race/ethnicity on campus, conflict over the legacy of the civil rights movement, and discord within ethnic studies departments have become disturbingly familiar phenomena.

TOWARD A NEW RACIAL STUDIES

These large themes have been the subjects of a great deal of recent work, including my own.[6] It is not my intention to address them all in the context of a single chapter. Rather I offer a tentative list of emergent issues in racial studies. This is but a hint of some of the axes of promising new work being developed in "new racial studies." These are at least some of the issues given us by the new sociopolitical conditions we face in the twenty-first century.

Consider the following themes:

Diaspora/globality/migration as racialized processes: Here I am thinking of contested borders and citizenships; the racial continuity of the North-South divide, as expressed in debt peonage, unequal exchange, etc.

Micro-macro racial linkages: Here I mean the zone where the whole comparative/historical approach to race (the "macro" stuff) meets the whole experience-based, identity/difference dimension of race (the "micro" stuff). Race is a crossroads where social structure and identity/experience intersect.

Means of communication/media as racial phenomena: Here I mean the acceleration of culture contact as both (1) a diasporic (or if you prefer, "global") organized resistance phenomenon: hip-hop in São Paulo, Marrakesh, Berlin, and Bangkok, "one nation under a groove," the globalization of reggae, etc., as well as films, Internet connections, etc.; and (2) a means of cultural domination, "appropriation," delocalization, and thus disempowerment and suppression of people's expressive needs.

The legacies of conquest and slavery: These can be seen, for example, in labor processes and ideologies, concepts of "freedom," local/national/global divisions of labor, state form, mobilizational and political capacity, and concepts of personal identity. Two quick examples here: (1) Wage labor is never entirely free; it is only rented rather than owned. (2) Coercion (or the threat of coercion) is essential to all state action: it is no accident that the XIII amendment to the U.S. Constitution—which abolished slavery in 1865—explicitly excepted imprisonment.

Race and revolution: This is an evident but underexplored connection visible, for example, in the historical legacy of the Haitian revolution and in parallels between nineteenth-century decolonization in the Americas and twentieth-century decolonization in Africa and Asia. Few modern empires have fallen to revolutions in the absence of a significant call for racial emancipation and equality.

Race and capitalism: Here I mean the need for rethinking the world-system's development as a racially instituted process; even old Karl Marx denounced "the turning of Africa into a warren for the commercial hunting of blackskins." C.L.R. James's account of the sugar industry as foundational to industrialism, Du Bois's analysis of the U.S. Civil War/Reconstruction as a process of national (and global) realignment, Eric Williams's work on the centrality of racial slavery to the rise of the modern (capitalist) world-system, and the huge contemporary literature on the economics of race need to be reintegrated into the curriculum.[7]

Race and democracy: Patterson's concept of "freedom" is premised on a thorough (though problematic) analysis of slavery; abolitionism was a central factor in actualizing democracy and indeed propelling concepts of popular sovereignty forward.[8] Some signals of this complex of problems include Du Bois's account of the U.S. Civil War/Reconstruction as a failed attempt to break the world-historical democratic bottleneck; and the continuing presence of racial dictatorship in the form of structural racism, as evidenced in reparations controversies and lawsuits.[9] In general, continuing racial pluralism and the equalization of "life-chances" across racial lines are effective indices of the presence of democracy. Their absence reveals a democratic deficit in any given society.

Race/gender as co-constitutive in modernity: Here I mean sex-based enforcement of racial subjection and its consequences in colonial and slavery-based settings; this is revealed in the sexual exploitation of women through concubinage and trafficking, and in numerous other extremely common practices, as well as in continuing consternation about mixed-race identity or miscegenation. The generalized subjection of women's bodies in racial oppressions of the most varied type also carries forward in one way or another to the postcolonial, "emancipated" world. The racialized female body remains a primary site for sex-based resistance, as it has throughout the modern epoch.[10]

Whiteness as a central theme: What does it mean to think of whiteness as non-normalized? This is still a relatively new and difficult subject. What does it mean to see "white" as a *negative* category? To experience whiteness as a beleaguered identity? How should we understand ethnicity *within* whiteness? Are whites a racial group? Is there white subjectivity in the same sense as there is black or Latino subjectivity? In my view the utopianism of calls to "abolish" whiteness reveals a glaring need to reconceptualize whiteness as a form of Du Boisian "double consciousness." For example, where do the origins of white anti-racism lie? What are the threats it poses for the white psyche? What are the political wellsprings of transracial coalition politics?

Regarding ethnicity: When does it trump, and when does it get trumped by, race? Non-racialized subjects/groups are always racializable. Hitler's goons had to make my dad pull down his pants to check if he was a Jew (my dad became a refugee from his native Vienna, made it to the U.S., and thus survived the Holocaust), but the fact that the Nazis couldn't tell who was a Jew just by looking didn't keep the *Volkischer Beobachter* from printing a hook-nosed caricature of "the Jew" on every page. The Brits still racialize the Irish when they need to, and so did the Americans in the nineteenth century. The Bosnian Serbs racialized the Bosnian Muslims, reinterpreting an ostensibly religious distinction racially. The Hutus and Tutsis racialize each other; Jews and Arabs in Israel and Palestine (cousins whose languages and appearances deeply overlap) do the same. That's ethnicity: in the liberal (and some radical) versions of anti-racism, race will become ethnicity, a more benign version of difference, by and by, when the age of sweet tolerance arrives. But in the meantime, what do we do with the persistence of ethnicity *within* racial categories, as noted above? What do we do when ethnic divisions become quasi-racial chasms, as in Rwanda or Srebrenica?

A FINAL NOTE

This chapter is far from a fully worked-out program for the revitalization of the racial curriculum in the contemporary U.S. academy. Adequately to formulate a "new racial studies" pedagogy will require a much more systematic effort than is possible here. What is intended instead is an overview of at least some of the "thematic considerations" (as this chapter's title puts it) that would be involved in such an endeavor. I hope that this brief sketch will at least contribute to the effort to reinvent the racial curriculum as the twenty-first century advances. We must build on what we have accomplished thus far, and what our predecessors did in their time. But we cannot rest. Racial oppression is dynamic, ever-changing, adaptable, and absorptive. That is what hegemony, racial hegemony, means in the twenty-first century: the ability to incorporate opposition, to neutralize critique, to "get beyond"— and thus preserve—racism. Can we teach this to our students? Can we learn it ourselves?

NOTES

1. Of course, I don't mean this in the Arnoldian sense in which culture is seen as "the best that has been known and thought" (Matthew Arnold, "Preface," in Samuel Johnson, *Lives of the Poets*. London: Macmillan, 1921). What is best and even what is known are subject to continuous contention; people who are subject to racism learn a lot about it that no college course will ever teach. But the point that what is taught and learned in the university represents the general summa of intellectual life in a given society—including all the debates and controversies being explored—remains valid, it seems to me.

2. Michael Omi and Howard Winant, *Racial Formation in the United States: From the 1960s to the 1990s* (New York: Routledge, 1994).

3. A partial exception to this pattern was the belated but triumphant South African transition to racial democracy, but even this was fraught with difficulty.

4. Antonio Gramsci, *Selections from the Prison Notebooks of Antonio Gramsci* (New York: International Publishers, 1971), 182; Howard Winant, *Racial Conditions: Politics, Theory, Comparisons* (Minneapolis: University of Minnesota Press, 1994).

5. Omi and Winant 1994, 84–88.

6. Howard Winant, *The World Is a Ghetto: Race and Democracy Since World War II* (New York: Basic Books, 2001).

7. C.L.R. James, *The Black Jacobins: Toussaint L'Ouverture and the San Domingo Revolution,* 2nd ed. (New York: Vintage, 1989 [1938]); W.E.B. Du Bois, *Black Reconstruction: An Essay Toward a History of the Part which Black Folk Played in the Attempt to Reconstruct Democracy in America, 1860–1880* (New York: Atheneum, 1977 [1935]); Eric Williams, *Capitalism and Slavery* (Chapel Hill: University of North Carolina Press, 1994 [1944]).

8. Margaret E. Keck and Kathryn Sikkink, *Activists Beyond Borders: Advocacy Networks in International Politics* (Ithaca: Cornell University Press, 1998).

9. Du Bois 1977 (1935); Joe R. Feagin, *Racist America: Roots, Current Realities, and Future Reparations* (New York: Routledge, 2000).

10. Ann Laura Stoler, *Carnal Knowledge and Imperial Power: Race and the Intimate in Colonial Rule* (Berkeley: University of California Press, 2002).

2. Reinterpreting the Past: The New Black History

HERBERT APTHEKER

The Nature of African-American History

The basic character of African-American history and society is radical. Certainly there is another component to that history—that of acceptance, with an element of pleading. This acceptance is garnished with insistence on the alleged absence of viable alternatives. It is embroidered, too, with moments of alleviation or even improvement but always with acceptance of a subordinate position, a stance epitomized in the career of Booker T. Washington. It earned him accolades from political chiefs such as American presidents and support from economic tycoons such as Andrew Carnegie.

A third position, often adorned with blazing language, is withdrawal from a society that is allegedly hopelessly committed to racism.

Whatever the language, this supernationalist effort amounts to giving up the struggle for freedom. Precisely because this position is a blind alley, it obtains very extensive publicity.

Since the reality of African-American life has been and continues to be exploitation and enforced subordination, that reality is also fundamentally *resistance.*

In the centuries of enslavement, the historical essence was resistance in myriad forms—purchase of freedom (where and when permitted), suicide, assassination, infanticide (especially of female children), the use of poison (slaves prepared the food), arson (slaves provided the warmth), and flight—sometimes individual, sometimes collective, ever present, and involving many thousands.

Collective resistance permeated slavery's history. One form was the phenomenon of maroons—outlying, pugnacious groups of fugitives, offering a haven to those who would flee and constituting a persistent threat to slavery's stability. The

23

highest form of slavery's rejection was, of course, insurrection. Magnificent resistance to slavery by groups of the enslaved was a permanent feature of the slave system in the United States, from the successful uprising in 1526, in what became South Carolina, to the massive conspiracy to rebel in Mississippi that resulted in the execution of at least forty slaves in 1861.

The essence of this resistance is in the slogan emblazoned on the flags of Gabriel's rebels in 1800—"Liberty or Death." It is in the challenge hurled at his captors in 1831 by an enchained Nat Turner—"Was not Christ crucified?"

As Gabriel and Turner epitomized the heart of pre–Civil War black history, so did Douglass and Du Bois and King epitomize the heart of that history since slavery's end. They brilliantly challenged the dominators of society, and they succeeded in creating a tradition and a reality of rejecting the status quo and projecting a United States wherein the words of the founding Declaration would be reality rather than delusion.

In the twentieth century, rejecting the surface reforms that protect fundamental inequities has been the essence of a black radicalism that is the heart of the African-American reality. It is not Walter White with all his honors but Du Bois with all his heartbreak that represents the deepest reality of African-American experience. It is not Clarence Thomas with his Supreme Court robes but Paul Robeson with his enforced exile that represents the deepest reality of African-American experience. That reality challenges the United States as the nation enters a new century. Shall it become finally "one nation indivisible with liberty and justice for all"? Monumental effort has brought us to the point when that question may be propounded seriously.

One of the deeply hidden truths in the history of the slaves' resistance was the sympathy and even comradeship of some white people. The rebels who were tortured and executed in New York in 1741 were white as well as African-American; in New Orleans in 1811 a white man, Joseph Woods, was hanged for assisting slave rebels; in Virginia in 1816 George Boxley was in prison for conspiring with slaves and awaiting final judgment when with the aid of his wife, he escaped; in the great Vesey slave conspiracy in South Carolina in 1822 four white workingmen were sentenced to prison for avowing sympathy for the rebels; in 1831 the black insurrectionists led by Nat Turner carefully excluded poor whites from the list of victims. As the governor of Virginia wrote to the governor of North Carolina, those whites unharmed by Nat Turner were "no better than the slaves." The historic assault on the federal armory in Harper's Ferry in 1859 was made by a team of black and white revolutionaries. One of the former, John A. Copeland, on the way to the gallows, shouted (according to the *Baltimore Sun*), "If I am dying for freedom I could not die for a better cause—I had rather die than be a slave!" To his brother, Copeland wrote, "Nor could I die in a more noble cause . . . believe me when I tell you, that shut up in prison under sentence of death, I have spent some happy hours here. . . . Let me tell you that it is not the mere fact of having to meet death, which I should regret . . . but that such an unjust institution should exist as the one which demands my life."

In Richmond in 1860 fifteen people were imprisoned for assisting slaves to flee; of these, four were free black men, and eleven were white men, mostly native Southerners.[1]

It is certain that the idea of African-American placidity in the face of enslavement no longer has credence. But the idea of universality of racism among white people is false and as vicious as the earlier myth.[2]

When the twentieth century was very young Du Bois cried out,

> We appeal to the young men and women of this nation, to those whose nostrils are not yet befouled by greed and snobbery and racial narrowness: Stand up for the right, prove yourselves worthy of your heritage. . . . Courage brothers and sisters! The battle of humanity is not lost or losing. All across the skies sit signs of promise. . . . The morning breaks over blood-stained hills. We must not falter, we may not shrink.

Heaven knows he did neither. So must we now, at the close of this century and the birthing of a new one, neither falter nor shrink. Rather with tightened fist and clenched teeth we must renew and invigorate the battle for justice. Let the new century be one witnessing the fulfillment of Du Bois's call for righteousness!

NOTES

1. Of great value is the book *Slave Laws in Virginia* by Philip J. Schwarz (University of Georgia Press, 1996), from where this example is taken.

2. I made a beginning of unfolding this vital story of white sympathy for and assistance to black people in my *Antiracism in U.S. History: The First Two Hundred Years* (1992). If I have some additional years left I will complete a second volume, taking this story of the rejection of racism by white people to the post–Civil War period, ending in 1920.

∾

JEFFREY R. KERR-RITCHIE
Forty Acres, or, An Act of Bad Faith

> *. . . when we got freed we was going to get forty acres and a mule. Stead of that we didn't get nothing.*
> —Sally Dixon, 1938[1]

THE PROMISE

Most Americans have heard of "forty acres and a mule," but few can explain it. The debate over Reparations for Slavery has also revealed limited understanding. Opponents think it an insignificant footnote to the past; supporters use it without historical context. The following chapter offers a succinct account of the origins, nature, and legacy of Forty Acres and a Mule. An earlier talk and this publication aim to intellectually empower supporters, activists, and politicians committed to the Reparations Movement and broader struggles for social justice by people of African descent.

Scholars have long argued over Forty Acres and a Mule. Some maintain it was a foolish and impractical belief held by former slaves, encouraged by the misguided actions of the federal government. Others insist its origins cannot be established because of a confusing mix of hearsay, wartime expediency, and freedmen's wishes. Some historians of Reconstruction simply use the term without explanation.[2]

Most recent scholarship, however, supports the view that Forty Acres and a Mule emerged sometime during the critical year of 1865, as a consequence of Union military actions and congressional government policies. The two critical factors were General William T. Sherman's Special Field Order, together with the creation of the Freedmen's Bureau by Congress. Let us review each one briefly.

In early January 1865, General Sherman convened a special meeting with former slaves at his Headquarters Military Division of the Mississippi in the Field, at Savannah, Georgia. One of the freedpeople's leaders, the Reverend Garrison Frazier, a sixty-seven-year-old former slave and Baptist elder, provided an eloquent explanation of the difference between property-based and labor-based relations to the assembled Union officers and federal politicians:

> Slavery is, [*sic*] receiving by *irresistible power* the work of another man, and not by his *consent*. The freedom, as I understand it, promised by the proclamation [Lincoln's Emancipation Proclamation], is taking us from under the yoke of bondage, and placing us where we could reap the fruit of our own labor, take care of ourselves and assist the Government in maintaining our freedom.[3]

In response, General Sherman issued Special Field Order No. 15 on 16 January 1865. A coastal strip "thirty miles back from the sea" from Charleston, South Carolina, down to St. John's River, Florida, was "set apart for the settlement of the Negroes now made free by the acts of war and the proclamation of the President of the United States." Furthermore, no white person except Union military personnel was allowed to reside on the islands, where "the sole and exclusive management of affairs will be left to the freedpeoples [*sic*] themselves, subject only to the United States military authority, and the acts of Congress." In addition, "young and able-bodied Negroes" were encouraged to enlist as Union soldiers, their bounties to be used for purchasing "agricultural implements, seeds, tools, boots, clothing and other articles." Once "heads of families" had chosen their land, they were required to subdivide it, "so that each family shall have a plot of not more than forty acres of tillable ground." The military authorities agreed to protect the possessors of these forty-acre homesteads "until such time as they can protect themselves or until Congress shall regulate their title." The "possessory title" of these settlements would be furnished to "each head of family" by a general officer under the auspices of the federal government. General Sherman later authorized the army to loan these freed families mules to help them work their lands. By June 1865, some forty thousand freedpeople had settled on four hundred thousand acres of "Sherman land" along coastal South Carolina and Georgia.[4] Under the exigencies of war, the federal government had committed itself to a policy of emancipation, the civil rights of black soldiers, and the redistribution of land to freed families.

The other major factor behind Forty Acres and a Mule was the creation of the Freedmen's Bureau. On 3 March 1865, Congress funded the creation of the Bureau of Refugees, Freedmen, and Abandoned Lands (Freedmen's Bureau) under the auspices of the War Department. Its mandate was to provide rations for the destitute, to facilitate the transition of slaves into freedmen, and to redistribute land. At the time the federal government held some eight to nine hundred thousand acres consisting of "such tracts of land within the insurrectionary states as shall have been abandoned, or to which the United States shall have acquired title by confiscation or sale, or otherwise." From these lands, forty acres were to be assigned to every male citizen, whether refugee or freedman, for a three-year rental and eventual purchase with "such title as it could convey." Although limited—eight hundred thousand acres would only amount to twenty thousand freedpeople working forty-acre plots—this legislation pointed to the government's clear commitment to the establishment of a small peasantry in the postwar American South. As Professor Cox pointed out forty-five years ago, this congressional legislation "made in effect a promise of land ownership to the freed slave."[5]

Additional military and political commitments to the distribution and redistribution of land were made after Appomattox. Thomas Conway, Freedmen's Bureau Assistant Commissioner for Louisiana, leased over sixty thousand acres to freedpeople. General Rufus Saxton, Freedmen's Bureau Commissioner for South Carolina, Georgia, and Florida, announced his intention to provide freedmen with forty-acre homesteads along the lines suggested by General Sherman's Special Order. On 28 July 1865, General O. O. Howard, Freedmen's Bureau Commissioner, issued Circular Order No. 13 from his Washington, D.C., headquarters. Citing congressional legislation, General Howard ordered his Assistant Commissioners throughout the American South to "select and set apart such confiscated and abandoned lands and property as may be deemed necessary for the immediate use of Refugees and Freedmen, the specific division of which into lots, and rental or sale thereof according to the law establishing the Bureau."[6]

General Howard's order was rescinded in September 1865, but demands for confiscation and land redistribution to the freedmen continued. At Pennsylvania's Republican convention—held at Lancaster, Pennsylvania, in the same month—Thaddeus Stevens, radical Republican congressman and chair of the powerful

House Ways and Means Committee, called for government confiscation of 394 million acres owned by 70,000 white Southerners. Forty million acres would be broken into forty-acre lots and redistributed to freedmen heads of household much like "Sherman's land." The rest of the confiscated land would be divided into farms and sold to the highest bidder. "How can Republican institutions, free schools, free churches, free social intercourse," asked Stevens, "exist in a mingled community of nabobs and serfs?" "If the South is ever to be made a safe republic," the congressman decreed, "let her lands be cultivated by the toil of owners."[7]

Other Radical Republicans, including George W. Julian, Benjamin F. Butler, and Charles Sumner, repeatedly stressed the necessity for government confiscation and land redistribution. Prominent abolitionist activist Wendell Phillips called for the allocation of forty to eighty acres and a furnished cottage for each freed family. Apparently, this call became known as a "Wendell Phillips." Indeed, the advent of Congressional Reconstruction encouraged freedpeople in their belief that their Northern friends were fighting for their interests, including well-deserved property rights. This belief was strengthened by the circulation of Congressman Stevens's bill of 19 March 1867, which proposed the confiscation of 150 million Southern acres with each freed household obtaining forty acres. For one decade, this land would be inalienable, followed by the bestowal of absolute title.[8]

Thus, Forty Acres and a Mule emerged during 1865 as a key governmental policy concerned with land redistribution in order to facilitate the transition from slavery to freedom in the American South. The Union military and the Republican Congress set aside confiscated and abandoned lands, where the freedmen's settlements would be legally guaranteed. Some Republican politicians were even more adamant in demanding a fundamental agrarian revolution in land titles to punish the treasonable South, to break up its landowning monopoly, and to remake the region in the image of a more egalitarian national republic. Knowledge of Forty Acres was disseminated to the freedpeople through radical Republican speeches in pamphlet form, Freedmen's Bureau regulations and laws, homestead and confiscation acts, bureau agents, and Northern missionaries and teachers. The rumor mill also played its part.[9]

Although we can precisely date Forty Acres and a Mule, the *concept* was of an earlier provenance. This is crucial, because it supports the view that the freedpeople's belief in the government's commitment to the confiscation and redistribution of land was realistically rooted in wartime practice and policies. In other words, the idea was neither impractical nor wishful thinking, but grounded in material reality.

Much of this practice can be explained by the federal government's desperation to win a war against powerful Southern interests. On 6 August 1861 and 17 July 1862, the passage of Congressional Confiscation Acts made Confederate property liable to confiscation. The Direct Tax Act of June 1862 provided for governmental land confiscation where taxes were delinquent.

The rest was seized as "abandoned" or "captured" lands. In the process, Northern armies seized everything. Freedpeople heard about this federal policy from angry white Southerners, some of the letters dubbing it the work of Lincoln's thieves. Other freedmen saw Union troops engaged in confiscation activities and were easily persuaded that the property of rebel Southerners would soon be redistributed.[10]

This legislative confiscation had real meaning when Union troops occupied parts of the rebellious Southern states. The citizens in the parish of Terre Bonne, Louisiana, petitioned Major General Banks on 14 January 1862, concerning their "deplorable conditions." The cause was that "many of the Negroes led astray by designing persons, believe that the plantations and everything on them belong to them, the Negroes." After Union troops visited Jackson, Mississippi, in early 1863, the slaves "measured off land with a plow line making a fair apportionment among themselves, and also divided the cotton and farm implements." Although Confederate authorities subsequently called a halt to land redistribution, one local newspaper reported with alarm: "This is only one instance of the wholesome effects of Abolitionism. . . . Let the country be thus subjugated, and Lincoln's robbers will occupy every farm in the South." This concern was echoed elsewhere. The "more insolent Negroes actually passed over their former masters' lands, measuring with old ropes and pegs to mark the favorite tracts they designed taking possession of as soon as the word was given."[11]

In March 1863, thousands of acres along the South Carolina, Georgia, and Florida coast and sea islands were confiscated and sold at auction. Land was divided into lots ranging from twenty to forty acres. Land once worth $40 to $60 per acre in 1860 sold for $1.25 per acre three years later. As local whites fled the occupying Union army, freedpeople came into possession of land. Eventually, some fifteen hundred acres were sold to freedpeople.[12]

The creation of "Freedmen's Home Colonies" as government-run settlements further supported freedmen's belief in official land distribution. The estates of the former governor of Alabama and a prominent judge in Louisiana were parceled out among the freedpeople.[13] Similar schemes were pursued in Mississippi. General Ulysses S. Grant's successful Mississippi River campaign in the summer of 1863 resulted in the capture of six plantations owned by Jefferson and Joseph Davis about twenty-five miles south of Vicksburg in a fertile peninsula called Davis Bend. In 1864, seventy-five freedpeople working plots of five to one hundred acres showed profits of $500 to $1,000 at season's end. By 1865, freed families were raising an assortment of vegetables, including 12,000 bushels of corn, as well as 1,736 bales of cotton—all together worth $397,700. Minus disbursements, these freed families showed a profit of $159,200. The Davis Bend experiment, it should be emphasized, was guarded by a regiment of the United States Colored Troops (USCT).[14]

Early 1863 saw the creation of the Bureau of Negro Affairs in the War Department, with C. B. Wilder as superintendent for Hampton in southeastern Virginia. The proposal to settle freedpeople on abandoned farms was attractive to both the federal body and the freedpeople: For the government, it pointed to independent support rather than wasteful welfare; for former slaves, it offered socioeconomic autonomy. The former slaves were also persuaded that they would be able to keep the land once the war had been won. Settlements were established at

"Newtown" in York County, "Slabtown" in Elizabeth City County, and on scattered farms in Warwick County and around Norfolk. The land was divided into small plots of eight to ten acres, with each freed family farming independently. In other parts of the Virginia peninsula, former slaves squatted on abandoned lands and tried to eke out their newly found freedom.[15]

In other words, the policy the federal government pursued for settling former slaves on abandoned lands during the Civil War legitimized the idea of Forty Acres and a Mule. There was a familiarity to this policy, which, I would argue, explains both the subsequent military and congressional policy as well as the tenacity with which freedpeople held on to the idea of land distribution and redistribution as part of the government's obligations during Reconstruction.

The freedpeople's determination to obtain forty acres was especially evident in their defense of the right to the land. In June 1865, President Andrew Johnson issued his pardon and amnesty policy to the former Confederates, one consequence being the restoration of former property rights. Dispossessed landowners now demanded the return of their lands. Some freedpeople voiced opposition to their removal from land upon which they had recently settled. Freedman Bayley Wyat protested the injustice of Union eviction from land near Yorktown, Virginia:

> We has a right to the land where we are located. For why? I tell you. Our wives, our children, our husbands, has been sold over and over again to purchase the lands we now locates upon; for that reason we have a divine right to the land. . . . And den didn't we clear the land, and raise de crops ob corn, ob cotton, ob tobacco, ob rice, ob sugar, ob everything. And den didn't dem large cities in de North grow up on de cotton and de sugars and de rice dat we made? . . . I say dey has grown rich, and my people is poor.[16]

Wyat's protest amounted to a remarkable mixture of divine right based upon biblical reading together with a labor theory of surplus value similar to Reverend Frazier's explanation to General Sherman. These are the roots of the Reparations Movement.

Other freedpeople pursued more collective means of protest. In the South Carolina coastlands, freedpeople refused to vacate the land and instead armed themselves. Their actions were supported by the Freedmen's Bureau. Secretary Edwin Stanton and Freedmen's Bureau chief General Howard asserted freedmen "had been led to expect permanent possession of the lands, and to dispossess them would be an act of bad faith." Nevertheless, General Howard visited the region in October 1865, in an effort to persuade the freedpeople of the need to vacate the lands, as mandated by presidential policy. A compromise was struck whereby those who held possessory titles to twenty to forty acres from 1863 to 1865 could keep their land. But few freedpeople had legal title. This was partly because of the federal tax commission's refusal to recognize freedmen's land claims.[17] Similar armed resistance by the freedpeople occurred in Georgia's low country. At the end of 1865, Aaron A. Bradley, a militant local black leader, led efforts by the region's freedpeople to resist President

Johnson's order for land restoration. In December 1866, Bradley led armed resistance to land restoration on some Savannah River plantations, while in September 1867, he held a "confiscation-homestead" meeting in Savannah, Georgia.[18]

We should conclude this first section with the power of the gun. The government's promise of land was often tied directly to the mobilization of black men for service in the Union army. This policy was evident in General Sherman's military order, the protection of Davis Bend, and the presence of black Union soldiers in southeast Virginia. In local land disputes in Virginia, South Carolina, and Georgia, the role of USCT veterans was vital. It should come as no surprise, therefore, that reneging on this promise was preceded by the demobilization of black troops. In the fall of 1865, the War Department decided to disband all black regiments raised in the North. A year later, there were only 13,000 black troops left in the South, down from a total mobilization of nearly 85,000, or one-third of the entire occupation army.[19] The removal of this armed force did not end the struggle for land redistribution, but it did terminate a powerful potential force for its implementation at the grassroots level.

There was nothing mystical, confusing, or bewildering to the freedpeople about land and mules for making freedom work under the sponsorship of the federal government. Rather, land redistribution was a very *real* part of the landscape of Union victory, government policy, and freedpeople's expectations from past labors and present services. Freedpeople believed the federal government was committed to land redistribution, for it had done a great deal to demonstrate this through legislative acts of confiscation, military acts of resettlement, and postwar policies of reconstructing the American South. Indeed, one is left wondering how a war for the Union and Emancipation could *not* have entailed Forty Acres and a Mule.

THE FAILURE

There are numerous reasons to explain why land redistribution failed to occur in the aftermath of the American Civil War. One traditional argument is that the Republican Party's belief in the sanctity of private property made any attack on property rights unacceptable to Congress.[20] Without denying the U.S. republic's long-standing ideological commitment to life, liberty, and the pursuit of property, this explanation ignores the abolition of slavery as an attack on property rights. Two-thirds of the average slaveowner's wealth was held in slaves, while nearly half of Southern capital stock was invested in slavery.[21] Lincoln's Emancipation Proclamation and the Thirteenth Amendment to the U.S. Constitution rank as the largest confiscation acts in American history. Moreover, the context of political confrontation after a bloody civil war waged against secessionist traitors made agrarian reform and redistribution of property rights seem not so far-fetched after all. Similar property confiscation and redistribution had occurred during both the French and the Haitian revolutions.[22] Property rights were less sanctified than they might otherwise have been within the context of social revolution.

Another explanation for the failure of land redistribution was the absence of a clearly committed class leadership. According to one older account of Reconstruction, "the Negroes did not yet have a class among them capable of independently leading the agrarian revolution through to its end." More recently, one scholar expressed surprise that no "[black] convention debated the democratization of land proprietorship." In a well-researched study of black political leadership in Reconstruction South Carolina, another historian emphasized the opposition from some black legislators to land reform in spite of its popular demand by constituents. Thus, the absence of class leadership explains the failure of land redistribution among freedpeople.[23]

While it is true these black conventions were dominated by questions of civil and political rights, much of this agenda had to do with the limitations of coalition politics and issues of feasibility. Delegates to the Georgia State Convention equivocated on key issues of suffrage and land distribution because of their ties to Northern allies. The redistribution of land was not on the agenda of many Northern and Southern Unionist legislators working with freedmen legislators. Even some radical Republicans insisted upon the secondary significance of land distribution. "If I were a black man, with the chains just stricken from my limbs," said Congressman James M. Ashley, "and you should offer me the ballot, or a cabin and forty acres of cotton land, I would take the ballot."[24]

Moreover, we should not ignore those clear examples of class leadership on the land question. In a statement made to the U.S. Congress from the Colored People's Convention of South Carolina in November 1865, the "colored people" of the state requested "that a fair and impartial instruction be given to the pledges of the government to us concerning the land question."[25] In the first State Convention of Georgia, which freedpeople held in Augusta in January 1866, the delegates resolved for the disposition of government lands to the freedpeople at affordable rates rather than for free.[26] According to the Address of the Colored Convention to the People of Alabama in May 1867, one of the major reasons that nine-tenths of the state's colored people would vote the Republican ticket was that the Republican Party "passed new homestead laws, enabling the poor to obtain land."[27] At the 1867 State Constitutional Convention held in Richmond, Virginia, Buckingham County Representative Francis Moss was so insistent upon land redistribution that the Richmond press caricatured him as "Francis Forty-Acres-of-Land-and-a-Mule Moss." His constituents ignored these derogatory labels, electing Moss for terms in the Senate (1869–71) and the House of Delegates (1874–75).[28] Although many of these convention records no longer survive, future research in the local press, planter papers, and legal proceedings will likely reveal numerous other calls and struggles for the "democratization of land." Indeed, it would be surprising if this was not the case, given the preponderance of black political representatives from rural districts. Forty Acres was of central concern to their constituents. We have already seen the vigor with which freedpeople defended their newly won rights to the land at the local level.[29]

If the sanctity of property rights and the lack of class leadership do not explain why land confiscation failed, why was it that freedpeople did not receive their duly promised Forty Acres and a Mule? This historian is persuaded by three major reasons.

First, the meaning of freedom for the freedpeople clashed with the free-market dictates of Northern businessmen and Republican politicians. The primary interest of Northern business—whether mercantile, financial, or manufacturing—"was the restoration and expansion of cotton culture." This would give Northeastern manufacturers a share in the national and foreign markets in India and China. The United States could also recapture control of the world market for raw cotton production, which had been expanded by British imperial interests in Egypt and India as a result of the cotton embargo imposed during the Civil War. The resumption of cotton exports would help to increase foreign exchange, which would pay the huge public debt accrued as the price for winning the war. The free cotton economy would restore and extend the market for Northern products in the American South, creating a revitalized home market.[30]

One major obstacle to restoring the cotton economy was the freedpeople. They had a different understanding of freedom, which did not embrace cotton production because of its association with slavery. During the Civil War, Union-occupied areas such as South Carolina had revealed the contrasting ways that the former slaves understood their freedom. In an article on black farmers on government-controlled lands in South Carolina and on the Georgia Sea Islands, Boston lawyer Edward Pierce reported, "they were beginning to plant cotton in their patches, but were disinclined to plant cotton, regarding it as a badge of servitude." Boston reformer Edward Philbrick passed along the sentiments of the freedpeople on the sea islands in testimony to Congress in 1865:

> Cotton is no good for nigger. Corn good for nigger; ground nuts good for nigger; cotton good for massa; if massa want cotton he may make it himself, cotton do nigger no good; cotton make nigger perish.[31]

Moreover, the former slaves' distaste for cash crop production was already a familiar feature of other postemancipation societies such as independent Haiti and British Jamaica in which freedpeople had sought subsistence over cash crop economies. In those areas, it was noted, former slaves had accumulated land, thus becoming small peasant farmers.[32]

Hence, to redistribute land would not only jeopardize cash crop production in the South, but would deal a devastating blow to the Atlantic cotton economy. More broadly speaking, interest in the political economy of cotton profits in a global economy predominated over the moral economy of freedmen pursuing freedom. Freedpeople could not receive land because past experience suggested they were not interested in fulfilling the productive potential of that land with the production of cash crops. As Professor Cox succinctly put it: "There is no evidence of the direct influence of northern business leaders in the final formulation of the Freedmen's Bureau Act, but the desire for abundant cheap cotton helps to explain why Congress did not make a *gift* of land to the freedmen."[33] Underlying this notion of productive resources from land and labor lurks the key to understanding the bloody history of colonial slavery, the expropriation of lands away from Native Americans, and the imposition of bourgeois freedoms upon former slaves in post-slave societies. By the 1860s, the failure of Forty Acres was the latest act in a global drama of imperial domination.

The second explanation for the failure of land redistribution was the desire of Northern financiers to maximize the value of the lands in which they were investing. The system of slave labor had made Southern land valuable because of its massive human capital investment. Emancipation freed labor from the land, thus significantly reducing land prices. The value of Virginia real estate, for instance, fell by more than 25 percent during the 1860s. In the major slave tobacco regions of the Virginia southside, real estate prices fell from less than $13.00 per acre to less than $8.00 per acre during the decade. The depreciation in land values in the "cotton" South ranged from a 55 percent decline in Georgia to a 70 percent drop in Louisiana.[34]

Many white Southerners welcomed Northern investments after the Confederacy's surrender at Appomattox. Northerners purchased land, leased plantations, and formed partnerships with Southern planters. Some businessmen, along with many former soldiers, invested their savings in the South as a quick way to make a buck from the lucrative cotton. These "carpetbaggers" brought with them a belief in the superiority of free over slave labor. Needless to say, this included their management of the "Negroes." More importantly, the existence of speculative capital played a crucial role in maintaining the plantation system. Land values increased from this Northern investment as land titles did not change hands and cash crop production soon recommenced. Keeping the freedpeople propertyless further increased the value of these lands. Land redistribution would have kept property values down and scared away outside investment. As Professor Powell neatly summarizes: "At the very moment when Republicans in Congress were deliberating measures that would limit the power of the ex-slaveholders, northern investors were helping to rescue a land system that would limit the freedoms of the ex-slaves."[35]

The third major reason for the failure of land redistribution to freedpeople was the predominance of speculation and accumulation by Northern monopoly interests. In May 1862, the Thirty-seventh Congress, dominated by Republicans, passed the Homestead Act. It stipulated quarter sections of 160 acres of "unoccupied" land to homesteaders for a nominal fee after five years of residence. By June 1864, farmers had settled on over 1.2 million acres. To the poor, this act gave the illusion of land distribution. In actuality, between 1864 and 1869, speculators acquired nearly fifty million acres, much of it formerly inhabited by Native Americans.[36]

Immigrants and citizens were eligible, but not people of African descent, presumably because, according to the 1857 *Dred Scott* decision, they were not considered citizens. Inclusion of freedmen in homestead legislation came in 1866 through the passage of Indiana Congressman George W. Julian's Southern Homestead Act, which opened settlement of public lands in the South to freedmen and loyal whites. This did not lead to major land reform because the best land was owned by planters, while public lands were swampy and timbered, and had no link to transport hubs. Also, freedmen lacked capital, while federal land offices were sparse. Only four thousand freed families were registered by 1869: of these, three thousand lived in thinly populated Florida. Most public land went to lumber companies.[37] Indeed, Northern capitalists and Republican leaders were much more concerned with pursuing land speculations in the American West and South for railroad and mining companies than with distributing land to former slaves. One scholar estimates that the federal government provided more than 158 million acres to Western railroad promoters, of which 115 million acres were certified and patented. In this sense, American Reconstruction was not a revolution in land redistribution but a consolidation of bourgeois capital interests in the favorable climate of victorious Northern states.[38]

THE MEMORY

Having explained the origin, concept, and failure of Forty Acres and a Mule, let us conclude with the issue of its legacy. Most obviously, there was not an agrarian revolution in the postemancipation American South. The dictates of the cotton economy, Northern investors, and alternative speculations precluded the distribution and redistribution of land to the freedpeople. Despite the wartime policies of the federal government, together with the passage of important laws in the aftermath of Union victory, these promises of freedom went unfulfilled.

The failure of land redistribution after the Civil War, however, should not blind us to the fact that some freedpeople did obtain their forty acres. In Virginia, the amount of land owned by people of African descent increased tenfold, i.e., from one hundred thousand acres in the early 1870s to more than one million acres by 1900. In the sea islands adjacent to the South Carolina and Georgia coastline, former slaves enjoyed possessory title to the land for generations after the promise of "Sherman's land." It has recently been estimated that 15 percent of black households in Mississippi owned land in 1910.[39] It should be emphasized that this land accumulation had nothing to do with the federal government's failed promise of Forty Acres and a Mule. Freedpeople's landholdings—usually of less acreage than forty acres and of poor quality at that—resulted from a complex series of factors. These included an older generation's persistence to own the land; prolonged agricultural depression from 1873 through 1896, making land cheaper, less productive, and more available; and cash remittances from younger to older generations.[40]

Moreover, freedpeople never forgot their Forty Acres. Black voters supported some Reconstruction politicians because they promised forty acres. Swindlers preyed on the desires of former slaves through various duplicitous moneymaking schemes, including costly attorney's fees and bogus slave pensions. Some peddlers sold freedpeople wooden pegs, told them to stake out their land, and never returned. In 1871, the congressional joint committee on the Ku Klux Klan reported: "The Negroes heard and were inclined to believe [those reports] by their own sense of justice, which suggested that as their labor had produced the greater part of the property, they should have a portion. Hence, the idea was widespread and common among them that each head of a family would have 'forty acres and a mule.'" In researching his article on "forty acres and a mule" published in 1906, Professor Walter Fleming was "assured by old Negroes that a general topic of conversation in some Negro 'quarters' was the intention of the federals to confiscate the lands and divide them among the blacks." He reported that some blacks still believed a "homestead and the mule will be given over to them."[41] Meanwhile, General Sherman's memoirs, composed and published in the reactionary climate of the 1890s, falsely claimed that forty-acre homesteads had only been a temporary measure.[42]

During the 1930s, the federally funded Works Progress Administration (WPA) conducted a series of interviews with surviving former slaves. Some of their oral testimony suggests powerful memories of emancipation's failure—a failure no doubt enhanced by the decade's depressed conditions. Former slave Gabe Butler recalled: "Sum of de slaves sed when dey wud be sot free dey wud git forty acres uf land fum Mr. Lincoln an' sum sed dey wud git plenty uf good things to eat an' sum sed dey wudnt have to work any more, kaze Mr. Lincoln wud give dem everything." Turner Jacobs, another slave, observed that Lincoln "promise every nigger forty acres and a mule. We never did get dat mule or dose forty acres either, ceptin by hard work." Sally Dixon recalled being "told when we got freed we was going to get forty acres and a mule. Stead of that we didn't get nothing."[43] By the 1930s, "forty acres" had become a collective memory among older generations of former slaves, an indication of the failure of the federal government to fulfill its promise to make emancipation mean something tangible, material, and long-lasting.

Most recently, opponents of the Reparations Movement have challenged its premises: Modern moralities are being imposed upon a very different past. In contrast, this chapter argues that Forty Acres had less to do with morals than with war and postwar realities. Forty Acres was all about the federal government's failure to deliver on its promises and meet the reasonable expectations of the freedpeople. The redistribution of land concerned neither welfare relief nor handouts; rather it was rooted in centuries of uncompensated enslaved labor. Former slaves were not given their freedom; they died helping the Union to win its war against the secessionist South, and in the process secured their own freedom. (A fruitful analogy can be made with the national liberation struggle in Zimbabwe, the government's failure to redistribute land, and the present political fallout.) In the Union-occupied New Orleans of 1862, a pamphlet was found on the street signed by an anonymous "colored man": ". . . we heave been in it [the country] Slaves over two hundred And fifty years we have made the contry and So far Saved the union."[44] No more eloquent a case could be made for America's historical act of bad faith.

NOTES

1. "Interview with Sally Dixon," George P. Rawick, ed., *The American Slave: A Composite Autobiography* (Westport, CT: Greenwood, 1972), 629.

2. William A. Dunning, *Reconstruction, Political and Economic, 1865–1877* (O.P. 1907; New York: Harper, 1962), 46–7; Vernon Lane Wharton, *The Negro in Mississippi, 1865–1890* (O.P. 1947; New York: Harper, 1965), 59; John Hope Franklin, *Reconstruction after the Civil War* (Chicago: University of Chicago Press, 1961), 114.

3. Ira Berlin et al., *Freedom's Soldiers: The Black Military Experience in the Civil War* (Cambridge: Cambridge University Press, 1998), 149.

4. Eric Foner, *Reconstruction: America's Unfinished Revolution, 1863–1877* (New York: Harper & Row, 1988), 70; Kenneth Stampp, *The Era of Reconstruction, 1865–1877* (New York: Vintage, 1965), 125; Special Field Orders No. 15, from William T. Sherman, *Memoirs*, vol. 2, 250ff., reproduced in James S. Allen, *Reconstruction: The Battle for Democracy, 1865–1876* (New York: International Publishers, 1937), 225–7.

5. Foner, *Reconstruction*, 69–70; David Herbert Donald et al., *The Civil War and Reconstruction* (New York: Norton, 2001), 504–5; William S. McFeeley, *Yankee Stepfather: General O.O. Howard and the Freedmen* (New York: Norton, 1968), 104–5; Wanda Cox, "The Promise of Land for the Freedmen," *Mississippi Valley Historical Review 1005* (June 1958–March 1959): 413, 418.

6. McFeeley, *Yankee Stepfather*, 104–5.

7. W.E.B. Du Bois, *Black Reconstruction in America, 1860–1880* (O.P. 1935; New York: Atheneum, 1992), 198, 368.

8. Ibid.; Foner, *Reconstruction*, 236; Walter L. Fleming, "Forty Acres and a Mule," *The North American Review* 182 (1906): 731–3; C.L.R. James, *American Civilization* (Oxford: Blackwell, 1993), 96.

9. Fleming, "Forty Acres," 730; Steven Hahn, "'Extravagant Expectations' of Freedom: Rumor, Political Struggle, and the Christmas Insurrection Scare of 1865 in the American South," *Past and Present* 157 (November 1997): 122–158.

10. Fleming, "Forty Acres," 721–2; Ira Berlin et al., *Slaves No More: 3 Essays on Emancipation and the Civil War* (Cambridge: Cambridge University Press, 1992), 124.

11. Ira Berlin, Thavolia Glymph, Steven F. Miller, Joseph P. Reidy, Leslie S. Rowland, and Julie Saville, eds., *The Wartime Genesis of Free Labor: The Lower South*. Freedom: A Documentary History of Emancipation, series 1, vol. 3 (Cambridge, UK: Cambridge University Press, 1990), 408–9.

12. Fleming, "Forty Acres," 724.

13. Ibid.

14. Wharton, *Negro in Mississippi*, 38–41; Stampp, *Era of Reconstruction*, 125–6; Fleming, "Forty Acres," 724.

15. Robert F. Engs, *Freedom's First Generation: Black Hampton, Virginia, 1861–1890* (Philadelphia: University of Pennsylvania Press, 1979), 36–41; Allen, *Reconstruction*, 44; Fleming, "Forty Acres," 724; Berlin et al., *Slaves No More*, 109.

16. Foner, *Reconstruction*, 105.

17. Fleming, "Forty Acres," 726–8; Cox, "Promise," 428.

18. Eric Foner, *Freedom's Lawmakers: A Directory of Black Officeholders During Reconstruction* (Baton Rouge: Louisiana State University Press, 1993), 24; Joseph P. Reidy, "Aaron A. Bradley: Voice of Black Labor in the Georgia Low Country," in *Southern Black Leaders of*

the Reconstruction Era, ed. Howard N. Rabinowitz (Urbana: University of Illinois, 1982), 281–308.

19. Hahn, "'Extravagant Expectations,'" 131, 154, n.58.

20. Wharton, *Negro in Mississippi*, 41; Stampp, *Era of Reconstruction*, 130.

21. Gavin Wright, *Old South, New South: Revolutions in the Southern Economy Since the Civil War* (New York: Basic Books, 1986), 19; Roger L. Ransom and Richard Sutch, *One Kind of Freedom: The Economic Consequences of Emancipation* (Cambridge: Cambridge University Press, 1977), 52.

22. Allen, *Reconstruction*, 45; Alex Dupuy, *Haiti in the World Economy: Class, Race, and Underdevelopment Since 1700* (Boulder: Westview Press, 1989), chap. 4.

23. Allen, *Reconstruction*, 68; Leon F. Litwack, *Been in the Storm So Long: The Aftermath of Slavery* (New York: Vintage, 1979), 521; Thomas Holt, *Black over White: Negro Political Leadership in South Carolina during Reconstruction* (Urbana: University of Illinois, 1977), 17–18, 131.

24. Joseph P. Reidy, *From Slavery to Agrarian Capitalism in the Cotton Plantation South, Central Georgia, 1800–1880* (Chapel Hill: University of North Carolina Press, 1992), 180; Foner, *Reconstruction*, 236.

25. Quoted in Allen, *Reconstruction*, 228.

26. Reidy, *From Slavery to Agrarian Capitalism*, 179–80.

27. Appendix 5 in Allen, *Reconstruction*, 238.

28. Jeffrey R. Kerr-Ritchie, *Freedpeople in the Tobacco South, Virginia, 1860–1900* (Chapel Hill: University of North Carolina Press, 1999), 79.

29. See Endnotes 15–17, above.

30. Cox, "Promise," 435–7; Gerald D. Jaynes, *Branches Without Roots: Genesis of the Black Working Class in the American South, 1862–1882* (New York: Oxford University Press, 1986), 12–15.

31. Jaynes, *Branches Without Roots*, 13; Du Bois, *Black Reconstruction*, 368–9; Berlin et al., *Slaves No More*, 98–100.

32. Kerr-Ritchie, *Freedpeople*, 100–101; Dupuy, *Haiti*, 51–66.

33. Cox, "Promise," 437. My argument, of course, is that it was not a gift.

34. Kerr-Ritchie, *Freedpeople*, 94; Ransom and Sutch, *One Kind of Freedom*, 51.

35. Jaynes, *Branches Without Roots*, 23; Lawrence N. Powell, *New Masters: Northern Planters During the Civil War and Reconstruction* (New Haven: Yale University Press, 1980), 36, 49, 54.

36. Donald et al., *Civil War*, 285; Foner, *Reconstruction*, 21.

37. Foner, *Reconstruction*, 246.

38. Allen, *Reconstruction*, 70–71.

39. Kerr-Ritchie, *Freedpeople*, 211–12; Eric Foner, *Nothing but Freedom: Emancipation and Its Consequences* (Baton Rouge: Louisiana State University Press, 1983), chap. 3; Ted Ownby, *American Dreams in Mississippi: Consumers, Poverty, & Culture, 1830–1998* (Chapel Hill: University of North Carolina Press, 1999), 77.

40. Kerr-Ritchie, *Freedpeople*, chap. 7.

41. Fleming, "Forty Acres," 734–7, 730, 723, 720.

42. Quoted in Cox, "Promise," 429.

43. *The American Slave: A Composite Autobiography*, ed. George P. Rawick (Greenwood, CT: Greenwood, 1972) Series 1, Volume 6, No. 1, 323–4 (Gabe Butler); Volume 8, No. 3, 1119 (Turner Jacobs); Vol. 7, No. 2, 629 (Sally Dixon).

44. Ira Berlin et al., *Freedom's Soldiers: The Black Military Experience in the Civil War* (New York: Cambridge University Press, 1998), 110–111.

~

ROBIN D. G. KELLEY AND BETSY ESCH
Black Like Mao:
Red China and Black Revolution

This is the era of Mao Tse-Tung, the era of world revolution and the Afro-American's struggle for liberation is a part of an invincible world-wide movement. Chairman Mao was the first world leader to elevate our people's struggle to the fold of the world revolution.

—Robert Williams, 1967[1]

It seems as if Chairman Mao, at least in the symbolic realm, has been enjoying a resurgence in popularity among the youth. His image and ideas consistently turn up in a myriad of cultural and political contexts. The Coup, a popular San Francisco Bay Area hip-hop group, restored Mao Zedong to the pantheon of black radical heroes and in so doing placed the black freedom struggle in an international context. In a song simply called "Dig It" (1993), the Coup refers to its members as "the wretched of the earth," tells listeners to read *The Communist Manifesto,* and conjures up revolutionary icons such as Mao Zedong, Ho Chi Minh, Kwame Nkrumah, H. Rap Brown, Kenya's Mau Mau movement, and Geronimo Ji Jaga Pratt. In classical Maoist fashion, the group seizes on Mao's most famous quote and makes it its own: "We realize that power [is] nickel plated."[2] Even though members of the Coup were not even born during the heyday of black Maoism, "Dig It" captures the spirit of Mao in relation to the larger colonial world—a world that included African Americans. In Harlem in the late 1960s and early 1970s, it seemed as though everyone had a copy of *Quotations from Chairman Mao Tse-tung,*[3] better known as the "little red book." From time to time supporters of the Black Panther Party would be seen selling the little red book on street corners as a fund-raiser for the party. And it was not unheard of to see some young black radical strolling down the street dressed like a Chinese peasant—except for the Afro and sunglasses, of course.

Like Africa, China was on the move and there was a general sensibility that the Chinese supported the black struggle. Actually, it was more than a sensibility: There were real-life black folk calling for revolution in the name of Mao as well as Marx and Lenin. Countless black radicals of that era regarded China, not unlike

Cuba or Ghana or even Paris, as the land where true freedom might be had. China was not perfect, but it was much better than living in the belly of the beast. When the Black Panther leader Elaine Brown visited Beijing in the fall of 1970, she was pleasantly surprised by what the Chinese revolution achieved in improving people's lives. "Old and young would spontaneously give emotional testimonies, like Baptist converts, to the glories of socialism."[4] A year later, she returned with one of the Panther founders, Huey Newton, who described his experience in China as a "sensation of freedom—as if a great weight had been lifted from my soul and I was able to be myself, without defense or pretense or the need for explanation. I felt absolutely free for the first time in my life—completely free among my fellow men."[5]

More than a decade before Brown and Newton set foot on Chinese soil, W.E.B. Du Bois regarded China as the other sleeping giant poised to lead the colored races in the worldwide struggle against imperialism. He had first traveled there in 1936—before the war and the revolution—during an extended visit to the Soviet Union. Returning in 1959, when it was illegal to travel to China, Du Bois discovered a new country. He was struck by the transformation of the Chinese, in particular what he perceived as the emancipation of women, and left convinced that China would lead the underdeveloped nations on the road toward socialism. "China after long centuries," he told an audience of Chinese Communists attending his ninety-first birthday celebration, "has arisen to her feet and leapt forward. Africa arise, and stand straight, speak and think! Act! Turn from the West and your slavery and humiliation for the last 500 years and face the rising sun."[6]

How black radicals came to see China as the beacon of Third World revolution and Mao Zedong thought as the guidepost is a complicated and fascinating story involving literally dozens of organizations and covering much of the world— from the ghettos of North America to the African countryside. The following account, therefore, does not pretend to be comprehensive.[7] Nevertheless, we have set out in this chapter to explore the impact that Maoist thought, and the People's Republic of China more generally, had on black radical movements from the 1950s through at least the mid-1970s. We also explore how radical black nationalism has shaped debates within Maoist or "antirevisionist" organizations in the United States. It is our contention that China offered black radicals a "colored," or Third World, Marxist model that enabled them to challenge a white and Western vision of class struggle—a model they shaped and reshaped to suit their own cultural and political realities. Although China's role was contradictory and problematic in many respects, the fact that Chinese peasants, as opposed to the European proletariat, made a socialist revolution and carved out a position in world politics distinct from the Soviet and U.S. camps endowed black radicals with a deeper sense of revolutionary importance and power. Finally, Mao not only proved to black folks the world over that they need not wait for "objective conditions" to make revolution, but his elevation of the cultural struggle profoundly shaped debates surrounding black arts and politics.

THE LONG MARCH

Anyone familiar with Maoism knows that it was never a full-blown ideology meant to replace Marxism-Leninism. On the contrary, if anything, it marked a turn against the "revisionism" of the post-Stalin Soviet model. What Mao did contribute to Marxist thought grew directly out of the Chinese Revolution of 1949. Mao's insistence that the revolutionary capacity of the peasantry was not dependent on the urban proletariat was particularly attractive to black radicals skeptical of the idea that they must wait for the objective conditions to launch their revolution. Central to Maoism is the idea that Marxism can be (must be) reshaped to the requirements of time and place and that practical work, ideas, and leadership stem from the masses in movement, not from a theory created in the abstract or produced out of other struggles.[8] In practice, this meant that true revolutionaries must possess revolutionary will to win. The notion of revolutionary will cannot be underestimated, especially for those in movements that were isolated and attacked on all sides. Armed with the proper theory, the proper ethical behavior, and the will, revolutionaries, in Mao's words, can "move mountains."[9] Perhaps this is why the Chinese Communist leader Lin Biao could write in the foreword to the *Quotations,* "Once Mao Tse-Tung's thought is grasped by the broad masses, it becomes an inexhaustible source of strength and a spiritual atom bomb of infinite power."[10]

Both Mao and Lin Biao recognized that the source of this "atomic bomb" could be found in the struggles of Third World nationalists. In an age when the Cold War helped usher in the nonaligned movement, with leaders of the "colored" world converging in Bandung, Indonesia, in 1955 to try to chart an independent path toward development, the Chinese hoped to lead the former colonies on the road to socialism. The Chinese (backed by Lin Biao's theory of the "new democratic revolution") not only endowed nationalist struggles with revolutionary value, but they reached out specifically to Africa and people of African descent. Two years after the historic Bandung meeting of nonaligned nations, China formed the Afro-Asian People's Solidarity Organization. Mao not only invited W.E.B. Du Bois to spend his ninetieth birthday in China after he had been declared a public enemy by the U.S. state, but three weeks prior to the great March on Washington in 1963, Mao issued a statement criticizing American racism and casting the African-American freedom movement as part of the worldwide struggle against imperialism. "The evil system of colonialism and imperialism," Mao stated, "arose and throve with the enslavement of Negroes and the trade in Negroes, and it will surely come to its end with the complete emancipation of the black people."[11] A decade later, the novelist John Oliver Killens was impressed by the fact that several of his own books, as well as works by other black writers, had been translated into Chinese and were widely read by students. Everywhere he went, it seemed, Killens met young intellectuals and workers "tremendously interested in the black movement and in how the art and literature of black folks reflected that movement."[12]

Their status as people of color served as a powerful political tool in mobilizing support from Africans and African-descended people. In 1963, for example,

Chinese delegates in Moshi, Tanzania, proclaimed that the Russians had no business in Africa because they were white. The Chinese, on the other hand, were understood as being not only part of the colored world but also not complicit in the slave trade. Of course, most of these claims serve to facilitate alliance building. The fact is, African slaves could be found in Guangzhou during the twelfth century, and some African students in Communist China complained of racism. (Indeed, after Mao's death, racial clashes on college campuses occurred more frequently, notably in Shanghai in 1979, Nanjing in 1980, and Tianjin in 1986.)[13] Furthermore, Chinese foreign policy toward the black world was driven more by strategic considerations than by a commitment to Third World revolutionary movements, especially after the Sino-Soviet split. China's anti-Soviet position resulted in foreign policy decisions that ultimately undermined its standing with certain African liberation movements. In southern Africa, for example, the Chinese backed movements that also received support from the apartheid regime of South Africa.[14]

Yet, Mao's ideas still gained an audience among black radicals. Although Maoist projects in the United States never achieved the kind of following enjoyed by Soviet-identified Communist parties in the 1930s, they did take root in this country. And like a hundred flowers, they bloomed as a confusing mosaic of radical voices all seemingly at war with each other. Not surprising, at the center of their debate over the character of class struggle in the United States was the "Negro Question": What role will black folk play in world revolution?

THE WORLD BLACK REVOLUTION

People of the world, unite and defeat the U.S. aggressors and all their running dogs!
People of the world be courageous, dare to fight, defy difficulties and advance wave
upon wave. Then the whole world will belong to the people. Monsters of all kinds
shall be destroyed.
> —Mao Tse-tung, "Statement Supporting the People of the Congo
> against U.S. Aggression" (1964)[15]

All over Africa, Asia, South, Afro and Central America a revolution is haunting
and sweeping.
> —Revolutionary Action Movement, *The World Black Revolution*[16]

Maoism in the United States was not exported from China. If anything, for those Maoists schooled in the Old Left, its source can be found in Khrushchev's revelations at the Twentieth Congress of the Communist Party Soviet Union in 1956, which prompted an antirevisionist movement throughout the pro-Stalinist left. Out of the debates within the Communist Party USA (CPUSA) emerged several organizations pledging to push the Communists back into the Stalinist camp, including the Provisional Organizing Committee (POC, 1958), Hammer and Steel (1960), and the Progressive Labor Party (PLP, 1965).[17]

The PLP, an outgrowth of the Progressive Labor movement founded three years earlier, was initially led by ex-Communists who believed the Chinese had the correct position. Insisting that black workers were the "key revolutionary force" in the proletarian revolution, the PLP attracted a few outstanding black activists such as John Harris in Los Angeles and Bill Epton in Harlem. Epton had become somewhat of a cause célèbre after he had been arrested for "criminal anarchy" during the 1964 riots.[18] Two years later, the PLP helped organize a student strike to establish a black studies program at San Francisco State University and its Black Liberation Commission published a pamphlet titled *Black Liberation Now!* that attempted to place all of these urban rebellions in a global context. But by 1968, the PLP abandoned its support for "revolutionary" nationalism and concluded that all forms of nationalism are reactionary. As a result of its staunch antinationalism, the PLP opposed affirmative action and black and Latino trade union caucuses—positions that undermined the PLP's relationship with black community activists. In fact, the PLP's connections to the New Left in general were damaged in part because of its attack on the Black Panther Party and the black student movement. PLP members were thrown out of Students for a Democratic Society (SDS) in 1969 with the help of several radical nationalist groups, including the Panthers, the Young Lords, and the Brown Berets.[19]

Nevertheless, predominantly white Marxist-Leninist-Maoist parties were not the primary vehicle for the Maoist-inspired black left. Most black radicals of the late 1950s and early 1960s discovered China by way of anticolonial struggles in Africa and the Cuban Revolution. Ghana's independence in 1957 was cause to celebrate, and the CIA-sponsored assassination of Patrice Lumumba in the Congo inspired protest from all black activist circles. The Cuban Revolution and Fidel Castro's infamous residency at Harlem's Hotel Theresa during his visit to the U.N. brought black people face-to-face with an avowed socialist who extended a hand of solidarity to people of color the world over. Indeed, dozens of black radicals not only publicly defended the Cuban Revolution but visited Cuba with groups like the Fair Play for Cuba Committee.[20] One of these visitors was Harold Cruse, himself an ex-Communist still committed to Marxism. He believed the Cuban, Chinese, and African revolutions could revitalize radical thought because they demonstrated the revolutionary potential of nationalism. In a provocative essay published in the *New Leader* in 1962, Cruse wrote that the new generation is looking to the former colonial world for its leaders and insights, and among its heroes are Mao:

> Already they have a pantheon of modern heroes—Lumumba, Kwame Nkrumah, Sekou Toure in Africa; Fidel Castro in Latin America; Malcolm X, the Muslim leader, in New York; Robert Williams in the South; and Mao Tse-Tung in China. These men seem heroic to the Afro-Americans not because of their political philosophy, but because they were either former colonials who achieved complete independence, or because, like Malcolm X, they dared to look the white community in the face and say: "We don't think your civilization

is worth the effort of any black man to try to integrate into." This to many Afro-Americans is an act of defiance that is truly revolutionary.[21]

In another essay, which appeared in *Studies on the Left* in 1962, Cruse was even more explicit about the global character of revolutionary nationalism. He argued that black people in the United States were living under domestic colonialism and that their struggles must be seen as part of the worldwide anticolonial movement. "The failure of American Marxists," he wrote, "to understand the bond between the Negro and the colonial peoples of the world has led to their failure to develop theories that would be of value to Negroes in the United States." In his view, the former colonies were the vanguard of the revolution, and at the forefront of this new socialist revolution were Cuba and China.[22]

Revolutions in Cuba, Africa, and China had a similar effect on Amiri Baraka, who a decade and a half later would found the Maoist-inspired Revolutionary Communist League (RCL). Touched by his visit to Cuba and the assassination of Lumumba, Baraka began contributing essays to a new magazine called *African Revolution,* edited by the Algerian nationalist leader Ben Bella. As Baraka explained it,

> India and China had gotten their formal independence before the coming of the 50s, and by the time the 50s had ended, there were many independent African nations (though with varying degrees of neocolonialism). Ghana's Kwame Nkrumah had hoisted the black star over the statehouse in Accra, and Nkrumah's pronouncements and word of his deeds were glowing encouragement to colored people all over the world. When the Chinese exploded their first A-bomb I wrote a poem saying, in effect, that time for the colored peoples had rebegun.[23]

The Ghana-China matrix is perhaps best embodied in the career of Vicki Garvin, a stalwart radical who traveled in Harlem's black left circles during the postwar period. Raised in a black working-class family in New York, Garvin spent her summers working in the garment industry to supplement her family's income. As early as her high school years, she became active in black protest politics, supporting efforts by Adam Clayton Powell Jr. to obtain better-paying jobs for African Americans in Harlem and creating black history clubs dedicated to building library resources. After earning her B.A. in political science from Hunter College and M.A. in economics from Smith College in Northhampton, she spent the war years working for the National War Labor Board and continued on as an organizer for the United Office and Professional Workers of America (UOPWA)-CIO and national research director and cochair of the Fair Employment Practices Committee. During the postwar purges of the left in the CIO, Garvin was a strong voice of protest and a sharp critic of the CIO's failure to organize in the South. As executive secretary of the New York chapter of the National Negro Labor Council and vice president of the national organization, Garvin established close ties to Malcolm X and helped him arrange part of his tour of Africa.[24]

Garvin joined the black intellectual exodus to Nkrumah's Ghana, where she initially roomed with the poet Maya Angelou and eventually moved into a house next door to Du Bois. She spent two years in Accra, surrounded by several key black intellectuals and artists, including Julian Mayfield, the artist Tom Feelings, and the cartoonist Ollie Harrington. As a radical who taught conversational English to the Cuban, Algerian, and Chinese diplomatic core in Ghana, she would have had difficulty not developing a deep internationalist outlook. Conversations with Du Bois during his last days in Ghana only reinforced her internationalism and kindled her interest in the Chinese revolution. Indeed, through Du Bois Garvin got a job as a "polisher" for the English translations of the *Peking Review* and a teaching position at the Shanghai Foreign Language Institute. She remained in China from 1964 to 1970, building bridges between the black freedom struggle, African independence movements, and the Chinese Revolution.[25]

For Huey Newton, a future founder of the Black Panther Party, the African revolution seemed even less crucial than events in Cuba and China. As a student at Merritt College in the early 1960s, he read a little existentialism, began attending meetings sponsored by the Progressive Labor Party, and supported the Cuban Revolution. Not surprising, Newton began to read Marxist literature voraciously. Mao, in particular, left a lasting impression: "My conversion was complete when I read the four volumes of Mao Tse-Tung to learn more about the Chinese Revolution."[26] Thus, well before the founding of the Black Panther Party, Newton was steeped in Mao Zedong thought as well as the writings of Che Guevara and Frantz Fanon. "Mao and Fanon and Guevara all saw clearly that the people had been stripped of their birthright and their dignity, not by a philosophy or mere words, but at gunpoint. They had suffered a holdup by gangsters, and rape; for them, the only way to win freedom was to meet force with force."[27]

The Chinese and Cubans' willingness "to meet force with force" also made these revolutions attractive to black radicals in the age of nonviolent passive resistance. Of course, the era had its share of armed struggle in the South, with groups like the Deacons for Defense and Justice and Gloria Richardson's Cambridge movement defending nonviolent protesters when necessary. But the figure who best embodied black traditions of armed self-defense was Robert Williams, a hero to the new wave of black internationalists whose importance almost rivaled that of Malcolm X.[28] A former U.S. Marine with extensive military training, Williams earned notoriety in 1957 for forming armed self-defense groups in Monroe, North Carolina, to fight the Ku Klux Klan. Two years later, Williams's statement that black people must "meet violence with violence" as the only way to end injustice in an uncivilized South led to his suspension as president of the Monroe Chapter of the NAACP.

Williams's break with the NAACP and his open advocacy of armed self-defense pushed him further left, into the orbit of the Socialist Workers Party, the Workers World Party, and some members of the old CPUSA. By 1961, as a result of trumped-up kidnapping charges and a federal warrant for his arrest, Williams and his family were forced to flee the country and seek political asylum in Cuba.

During the next four years, Cuba became Williams's base for promoting black world revolution and elaborating an internationalist ideology that embraced black nationalism and Third World solidarity.

THE REVOLUTIONARY ACTION MOVEMENT

Williams's flight to Cuba partly inspired the creation of the Revolutionary Action Movement (RAM). In Ohio around 1961, black members of Students for a Democratic Society (SDS) as well as activists in the Student Nonviolent Coordinating Committee (SNCC) and the Congress of Racial Equality (CORE) met in a small group to discuss the significance of Williams's work in Monroe and his subsequent exile. Led by Donald Freeman, a black student at Case Western Reserve in Cleveland, the group's main core consisted of a newly formed organization made up of Central State College students at Wilberforce calling themselves Challenge. Members of Challenge were especially taken with Harold Cruse's essay, "Revolutionary Nationalism and the Afro-American,"[29] which was circulated widely among young black militants. Inspired by Cruse's interpretation of the global importance of the black freedom struggle, Freeman hoped to turn Challenge into a revolutionary nationalist movement akin to the Nation of Islam but using the direct action tactics of SNCC. After a lengthy debate, Challenge members decided to dissolve the organization in the spring of 1962 and form the Revolutionary Action Committee (RAM, originally called the "Reform" Action Movement so as not to scare the university administration), with its primary leaders being Freeman, Max Stanford, and Wanda Marshall. A few months later they moved their base to Philadelphia; began publishing a bimonthly paper called *black America* and a one-page newsletter called *RAM Speaks;* made plans to build a national movement oriented toward revolutionary nationalism, youth organizing, and armed self-defense; and recruited several Philadelphia activists to the group, including Ethel Johnson (who had worked with Robert Williams in Monroe), Stan Daniels, and Playthell Benjamin.[30]

RAM represented the first serious and sustained attempt in the postwar period to wed Marxism, black nationalism, and Third World internationalism into a coherent revolutionary program. In Max Stanford's view, RAM "attempted to apply Marxism-Leninism Mao Tse-Tung thought" to the conditions of black people and "advanced the theory that the black liberation movement in the U.S. was part of the vanguard of the world socialist revolution."[31] Besides looking to Robert Williams, young RAM militants sought political guidance from a number of black former Communists who had either been expelled for "ultraleftism" or "bourgeois nationalism" or bolted the party because of its "revisionism." Among this group of elders were Harold Cruse, Harry Haywood, Abner Berry, and "Queen Mother" Audley Moore. Moore would go on to become one of RAM's most important mentors on the East Coast, offering members training in black nationalist thought and Marxism. The Queen Mother's home, which she affectionately called Mount Addis Ababa, practically served as a school for a new generation of young black radicals.

She had founded the African-American Party of National Liberation in 1963, which formed a provisional government and elected Robert Williams as premier-in-exile.[32] RAM members also turned to Detroit's legendary ex-Trotskyists James and Grace Lee Boggs, former comrades of C.L.R. James, whose Marxist and Pan-Africanist writings greatly influenced RAM members as well as other New Left activists.[33]

As RAM grew, it developed a following in other parts of the country, though it continued to remain semi-underground and very loosely organized. Much like the African Blood Brotherhood of the 1920s or the group of radical intellectuals who published *Studies on the Left,* RAM made a contribution to the struggle that remained largely at the level of theory rather than practice. In the South, RAM built a small but significant following at Fisk University, the training ground for many leading SNCC activists. In May 1964, for example, RAM members held the first Afro-American Student Conference on black nationalism on Fisk's campus.[34] In Northern California, RAM grew primarily out of the Afro-American Association. Founded by Donald Warden in 1962, the Afro-American Association consisted of students from the University of California at Berkeley and Merritt College—many of whom, such as Leslie and Jim Lacy, Cedric Robinson, Ernest Allen, and Huey Newton, would go on to play important roles as radical activists/intellectuals. In Los Angeles, the president of the Afro-American Association was a young man named Ron Everett, who later changed his name to Ron Karenga and went on to found US Organization. The Afro-American Association quickly developed a reputation as a group of militant intellectuals willing to debate anyone. By challenging professors, debating groups such as the Young Socialist Alliance, and giving public lectures on black history and culture, these young men left a deep impression on fellow students as well as the black community. In the East Bay, where the tradition of soapbox speakers had died in the 1930s, except for individual campaigns led by the Communist-led Civil Rights Congress during the early 1950s, the Afro-American Association was walking and talking proof that a vibrant, highly visible militant intellectual culture could exist.

Meanwhile, Progressive Labor (PL) had begun sponsoring trips to Cuba and recruited several radical black students in the East Bay to go along. Among them was Ernest Allen, a U.C. Berkeley transfer from Merritt College who had been forced out of the Afro-American Association. A working-class kid from Oakland, Allen was part of a generation of black radicals whose dissatisfaction with the Civil Rights movement's strategy of nonviolent passive resistance drew them closer to Malcolm X and Third World liberation movements. Not surprising, through his trip to Cuba in 1964 Allen discovered RAM. Allen's travel companions included a contingent of black militants from Detroit: Luke Tripp, Charles ("Mao") Johnson, Charles Simmons, and General Baker. All were members of the student group Uhuru, and all went on to play key roles in the formation of the Dodge Revolutionary Union Movement (DRUM) and the League of Revolutionary Black Workers. Incredibly, Max Stanford was already on the island visiting Robert Williams. When it was time to go back to the States, Allen and the Detroit group were committed to building RAM. Allen stopped in Cleveland to meet with RAM members on his cross-country bus trip back to Oakland. Armed with copies of Robert Williams's *Crusader* magazine and related RAM material, Allen returned to Oakland intent on establishing RAM's presence in the East Bay. Never more than a handful of people—folks such as Isaac Moore, Kenn Freeman (Mamadou Lumumba), Bobby Seale (a future founder of the Black Panther Party), and Doug Allen (Ernie's brother)—the group established a base at Merritt College through the Soul Students Advisory Council. The group's intellectual and cultural presence, however, was broadly felt. Allen, Freeman, and others founded a journal called *Soulbook: The Revolutionary Journal of the Black World*, which published prose and poetry that is best described as left black nationalist in orientation. Freeman, in particular, was highly respected among RAM activists and widely read. He constantly pushed RAM members to think about black struggle in a global context. The editors of *Soulbook* also developed ties with Old Left black radicals, most notably the former Communist Harry Haywood, whose work they published in an early issue.[35]

Although RAM as a movement never received the glory or publicity bestowed on groups like the Black Panther Party, its influence far exceeded its numbers—not unlike the African Blood Brotherhood (ABB) four decades earlier. Indeed, like the ABB, RAM remained largely an underground organization that devoted more time to agitprop work than actual organizing. Leaders such as Max Stanford identified with the Chinese peasant rebels who led the Communist Party to victory. They seized on Mao's famous line: "The enemy advances, we retreat; the enemy camps, we harass; the enemy tires, we attack; the enemy retreats, we pursue."[36] And they took Mao quite literally, advocating armed insurrection and drawing inspiration and ideas directly from Robert Williams's theory of guerrilla warfare in the urban United States. RAM leaders actually believed such a war was not only possible but could be won in ninety days. The combination of mass chaos and revolutionary discipline was the key to victory. The fall 1964 issue of *black America* predicted Armageddon:

> Black men and women in the Armed Forces will defect and come over to join the Black Liberation forces. Whites who claim they want to help the revolution will be sent into the white communities to divide them, fight the fascists and frustrate the efforts of the counter-revolutionary forces. Chaos will be everywhere and with the breakdown of mass communications, mutiny will occur in great numbers in all facets of the oppressors' government. The stock market will fall; Wall Street will stop functioning; Washington, D.C. will be torn apart by riots. Officials everywhere will run—run for their lives. The George Lincoln Rockefellers, Kennedys, Vanderbilts, Hunts, Johnsons, Wallaces, Barnetts, etc., will be the first to go. The revolution will "strike by night and spare none." . . . The Black Revolution will use sabotage in the cities, knocking out the electrical power first, then transportation and guerrilla warfare in the countryside in the South. With the cities powerless, the oppressor will be helpless.[37]

The revolution was clearly seen as a man's job, since women barely figured in the equation. Indeed, one of the striking facts about the history of the antirevisionist left is how male dominated it remained. Although Wanda Marshall had been one of the founding members of RAM, she did not hold a national leadership post in 1964. Aside from promoting the creation of "women's leagues," the purpose of which would be "to organize black women who work in white homes," RAM remained relatively silent on women's liberation.

RAM's masculinist orientation has a lot to do with the fact that its leaders saw themselves as urban guerrillas, members of an all-black version of Mao's Red Army. Not all RAM members saw themselves this way, but those who did were deeply committed to a set of revolutionary ethics Mao laid down for his own party cadres and members of the People's Army. We see this very clearly in RAM's "Code of Cadres," a set of highly didactic rules of conduct members were expected to live by. Here are some examples:

- A revolutionary nationalist maintains the highest respect for all authority within the party.
- A revolutionary nationalist cannot be corrupted by money, honors or any other personal gains.
- A revolutionary nationalist will unhesitatingly subordinate his personal interest to those of the vanguard [without] hesitation.
- A revolutionary nationalist will maintain the highest level of morality and will never take as much as a needle or single piece of thread, from the masses—Brothers and Sisters will maintain the utmost respect for one another and will never misuse or take advantage of one another for personal gain—and will never misinterpret the doctrine of revolutionary nationalism for any reason.[38]

The similarities to *Quotations from Chairman Mao Tse-tung* are striking. The last example comes straight out of one of Mao's "Three Main Rules of Discipline," which urges cadres to "not take a single needle or piece of thread from the masses." Selflessness and total commitment to the masses is another theme that dominates the *Quotations*. Again, the comparisons are noteworthy: "At no time and in no circumstances," said Mao, "should a Communist place his personal interests first; he should subordinate them to the interests of the nation and of the masses. Hence, selfishness, slacking, corruption, seeking the limelight, and so on are most contemptible, while selflessness, working with all one's energy, whole-hearted devotion to public duty, and quiet hard work will command respect."[39]

Maoism's emphasis on revolutionary ethics and moral transformation, in theory at least, resonated with black religious traditions (as well as American Protestantism more generally), and like the Nation of Islam, black Maoists preached self-restraint, order, and discipline. It is quite possible that in the midst of a counterculture that embodied elements of hedonism and drug use, a new wave of student and working-class radicals found Maoist ethics attractive. On his return from

China, Robert Williams—in many respects RAM's founding father—insisted that all young black activists "undergo personal and moral transformation. There is a need for a stringent revolutionary code of moral ethics. Revolutionaries are instruments of righteousness."[40] For black revolutionaries, the moral and ethical dimension of Mao's thought centered on the notion of personal transformation. It was a familiar lesson, embodied in the lives of Malcolm X and (later) George Jackson: the idea that one possesses the revolutionary will to transform himself. (These narratives are almost exclusively male despite the growing number of memoirs by radical black women.) Whether or not RAM members lived by the "Code of Cadres," Maoist ethics ultimately served to reinforce Malcolm's status as a revolutionary role model.

RAM's twelve-point program called for the development of freedom schools, national black student organizations, rifle clubs, black farmer cooperatives—not just for economic development but to keep "community and guerrilla forces going for a while"—and a liberation guerrilla army made up of youth and unemployed. RAM placed special emphasis on internationalism, pledging support for national liberation movements in Africa, Asia, and Latin America as well as the adoption of "Pan-African socialism." In line with Cruse's seminal essay, "Revolutionary Nationalism and the Afro-American," RAM members saw themselves as colonial subjects fighting a "colonial war at home." As Stanford wrote in an internal document, titled "Projects and Problems of the Revolutionary Movement" (1964), "RAM's position is that the Afro-American is not a citizen of the U.S.A., denied his rights, but rather he is a colonial subject enslaved. This position says that the black people in the U.S.A. are a captive nation suppressed and that their fight is not for integration into the white community but one of national liberation."[41]

As colonial subjects with a right to self-determination, RAM saw Afro-America as a de facto member of the nonaligned nations. RAM members even identified themselves as part of the "Bandung world," going so far as to hold a conference in November 1964 in Nashville called "The Black Revolution's Relationship to the Bandung World." In a 1965 article published in RAM's journal *black America*, members started to develop a theory of "Bandung Humanism" or "Revolutionary Black Internationalism," which argued that the battle between Western imperialism and the Third World—more than the battle between labor and capital—represented the most fundamental contradiction in our time. They linked the African-American freedom struggle with what was happening in China, Zanzibar, Cuba, Vietnam, Indonesia, and Algeria, and they characterized their work as part of Mao's international strategy of encircling Western capitalist countries and challenging imperialism. After 1966, the term "Bandung Humanism" was dropped entirely and replaced with "Black Internationalism."

Precisely what "Black Internationalism" meant was laid out in an incredibly bold thirty-six-page pamphlet published by RAM in 1966, titled *The World Black Revolution.* Loosely patterned on the *Communist Manifesto,* the pamphlet identified strongly with China against both the capitalist West and the Soviet empire. The "emergence of Revolutionary China began to polarize caste and class contradictions within the world, in both the bourgeoisie [sic] imperialist camp and also in the

European bourgeois communist-socialist camp."[42] In other words, China was the wedge that sharpened contradictions between colonial peoples and the West. Rejecting the idea that socialist revolution will arise in the developed countries of the West, RAM insisted that the only true revolutionary solution is the "dictatorship of the world by the Black Underclass through World Black Revolution." Of course, the authors were not working from today's definitions; RAM used "underclass" to encompass all peoples of color in Asia, Latin American, Africa, and elsewhere; the "Black Underclass" was merely a synonym for the colonial world. China was in a bitter fight to defend its own freedom. Now the rest of the "black" world must follow suit:

> The Black Underclass has only one alternative to free itself of colonialism, imperialism, capitalism and neo-colonialism; that is to completely destroy Western (bourgeois) civilization (the cities of the world) through a World Black Revolution and establishing a Revolutionary World Black Dictatorship can bring about the end of exploitation of man by mankind and the new revolutionary world be created.[43]

To coordinate this revolution, RAM called for the creation of a Black International and the creation of a "People's Liberation Army on a world scale."

For all of its strident nationalism, *The World Black Revolution* concludes that black nationalism "is really internationalism." Only by demolishing white nationalism/white power can liberation be achieved for everyone. Not only will national boundaries be eliminated with the "dictatorship of the Black Underclass," but "the need for nationalism in its aggressive form will be eliminated."[44] This is a pretty remarkable statement given RAM's social and ideological roots. But rather than representing a unified position, the statement reflects various tensions that persisted throughout RAM's history. On one side were nationalists who felt that revolutionaries should fight for the black nation first and build socialism separate from the rest of the United States. On the other side were socialists like James and Grace Boggs who wanted to know who would rule the "white" nation and what such a presence would mean for black freedom. They also rejected efforts to resurrect the "Black Nation" thesis—the old Communist line that people in black-majority counties of the South (the "black belt") have a right to secede from the union. The Boggses contended that the real source of power lies in the cities, not the rural black belt. In January 1965, James Boggs resigned from his post as Ideological Chairman.

After years as an underground organization, RAM was identified in a series of "exposés" in *Life* magazine[45] and *Esquire*[46] as one of the leading extremist groups "plotting a War on 'Whitey.'" The "Peking-backed" group was considered not only armed and dangerous but "impressively well read in revolutionary literature—from Marat and Lenin to Mao, Che Guevara and Frantz Fanon." (The Harlem Branch of the Progressive Labor Party responded to the articles with a pamphlet titled *The Plot Against Black America*, which argued that China was not financing revolution, just setting a revolutionary example by its staunch anti-imperialism. The real causes of black rebellion, the pamphlet insisted, can be found in the conditions of ghetto life.)[47] Not surprising, these highly publicized articles were followed by a series of police raids on the homes of RAM members in Philadelphia and New York City. In June 1967, RAM members were rounded up and charged with conspiracy to instigate a riot, poison police officers with potassium cyanide, and assassinate Roy Wilkins and Whitney Young. A year later, under the repressive atmosphere of the FBI's Counter Intelligence Program (COINTELPRO), RAM transformed itself into the Black Liberation Party, or the African American Party of National Liberation. By 1969, RAM had pretty much dissolved, though its members opted to "melt back into the community and infiltrate existing black organizations," continue to push the twelve-point program, and develop study groups that focused on the "Science of Black Internationalism, and the thought of Chairman Rob [Robert] Williams."[48]

COINTELPRO operations only partly explain the dissolution of RAM. Some of its members moved on to other organizations, such as the Republic of New Africa and the Black Panther Party. But RAM's declining membership and ultimate demise can be partly attributed to strategic errors on its part. Indeed, its members' understanding of the current situation in the ghettos and their specific strategies of mobilization suggest that they were not very good Maoists after all. Mao's insistence on the protracted nature of revolution was not taken to heart; at one point RAM suggested that the war for liberation would probably take only ninety days. And because RAM leaders focused on confronting the state head-on and attacking black leaders they deemed reformists, they failed to build a strong base in black urban communities. Furthermore, despite their staunch internationalism, they did not reach out to other oppressed "nationalities" in the United States. Nevertheless, what RAM and Robert Williams did do was to elevate revolutionary black nationalism to a position of critical theoretical importance for the antirevisionist left in general. They provided an organizational and practical example of what Harold Cruse, Frantz Fanon, and Malcolm X were trying to advance in their writings and speeches. More important, they found theoretical justification for revolutionary black nationalism in Mao Zedong thought, especially after the launching of the Cultural Revolution in China.

RETURN OF THE BLACK BELT

No matter what one may think of the Cultural Revolution, it projected to the world—particularly to those sympathetic to China and to revolutionary movements generally—a vision of society where divisions between the powerful and powerless are blurred, where status and privilege do not necessarily distinguish leaders from the led. The socialists Paul Sweezey and Leo Huberman, editors of the independent socialist journal *Monthly Review,* recognized the huge implications such a revolution had for the urban poor in the United States: "Just imagine what would happen in the United States if a President were to invite the poor in this country, with special emphasis on the blacks in the urban ghettos, to win the war on poverty for themselves, promising them the protection of the army against reprisals!"[49] Of course, black people in the United States were not regarded by the state as "the people." Their problems were a drain on society and their ungrateful rioting and the proliferation of revolutionary organizations did not elicit much sympathy for the black poor.

For many in the New Left, African Americans were not only "the people" but the most revolutionary sector of the working class. The Cultural Revolution's emphasis on eliminating hierarchies and empowering the oppressed reinforced the idea that black liberation lay at the heart of the new American revolution. Mao Tse-tung himself gave credence to this view in his widely circulated April 1968 statement "In Support of the Afro-American Struggle Against Violent Repression." The statement was delivered during a massive demonstration in China protesting the assassination of Martin Luther King Jr., at which Robert Williams and Vicki Garvin were among the featured speakers. According to Garvin, "millions of Chinese demonstrators" marched in the pouring rain to denounce American racism.[50] Responding to the rebellions touched off by King's assassination, Mao characterized these urban uprisings as "a new clarion call to all the exploited and oppressed people of the United States to fight against the barbarous rule of the monopoly capitalist class."[51] Even more than his 1963 statement, Mao's words endowed the urban riots with historic importance in the world of revolutionary upheaval.

THE BLACK PANTHER PARTY

It was in the context of the urban rebellions that several streams of black radicalism, including RAM, converged and gave birth to the Black Panther Party for Self Defense in Oakland, California. Perhaps the most visible black organization promoting Mao Tse-tung thought, by some accounts the Panthers were probably the least serious about reading Marxist, Leninist, or Maoist writings and developing a revolutionary ideology. Founded by Huey Newton and Bobby Seale, a former RAM member, the party went well beyond the boundaries of Merritt College and recruited the "lumpen proletariat." Much of the rank and file engaged more in sloganeering than anything else, and their bible was the "little red book."

That the Panthers were, at least in rhetoric and program, Marxist was one of the sources of their dispute with Ron Karenga's US Organization and other groups they derisively dismissed as cultural nationalists. Of course, not only did the Panthers have their own cultural nationalist agenda but the so-called cultural nationalists were not a monolith or uniformly procapitalist. And the divisions between these groups were exacerbated by COINTELPRO. Still, there was a fundamental difference between the Panthers' evolving ideology of socialism and class struggle and that of black nationalist groups, even on the left. As Bobby Seale explained in a March 1969 interview,

We're talking about socialism. The cultural nationalists say that socialism won't do anything for us. There's the contradiction between the old and the new. Black people have no time to practice black racism and the masses of black people do not hate white people just because of the color of their skin. . . . [W]e're not going to go out foolishly and say there is no possibility of aligning with some righteous white revolutionaries, or other poor and oppressed peoples in this country who might come to see the light about the fact that it's the capitalist system they must get rid of.[52]

How the Panthers arrived at this position and the divisions within the party over their stance is a long and complicated story that we cannot address here. For our purposes, we want to make a few brief points about the party's embrace of Mao Zedong thought and its position vis-à-vis black self-determination. For Huey Newton, whose contribution to the party's ideology rivals that of Eldridge Cleaver and George Jackson, the source of the Panthers' Marxism was the Chinese and Cuban Revolutions precisely because their analysis grew out of their respective histories rather than from the pages of *Das Kapital*. The Chinese and Cuban examples, according to Newton, empowered the Panthers to develop their own unique program and to discard theoretical insights from Marx and Lenin that have little or no application to black reality.[53] Indeed, Malcolm X clearly exerted a strong ideological influence on the Panthers.

Eldridge Cleaver was a little more explicit about the role of Maoism and the thought of the Korean Communist leader Kim Il Sung in reshaping Marxism-Leninism for the benefit of national liberation struggles of Third World peoples. In a 1968 pamphlet titled *On the Ideology of the Black Panther Party* (Part 1), Cleaver made clear that the Panthers were a Marxist-Leninist party but added that neither Marx, Engels, Lenin, nor any of their contemporary followers offered much insight with regard to understanding and fighting racism. The lesson here was to adopt and alter what was useful and reject what was not. "With the founding of the Democratic People's Republic of Korea in 1948 and the People's Republic of China in 1949," Cleaver wrote,

something new was interjected into Marxism-Leninism, and it ceased to be just a narrow, exclusively European phenomenon. Comrade Kim Il Sung and Comrade Mao Tse-Tung applied the classical principles of Marxism-Leninism to the conditions of their own countries and thereby made the ideology into something useful for their people. But they rejected that part of the analysis that was not beneficial to them and had only to do with the welfare of Europe.[54]

In Cleaver's view, the sharpest critique of Western Marxism's blindness with regard to race came from Frantz Fanon.

Seeing themselves as part of a global national liberation movement, the Panthers also spoke of the black community as a colony with an inherent right to self-determination. Yet, unlike many other black or interracial Maoist groups, they never advocated secession or the creation of a separate state. Rather, describing black people as colonial subjects was a way of characterizing the materialist nature of racism; it was more of a metaphor than an analytical concept. Self-determination was understood to mean community control within the urban environment, not necessarily the establishment of a black nation.[55] In a paper delivered at the Peace and Freedom Party's founding convention in March 1968, Cleaver tried to clarify the relationship between interracial unity in the U.S. revolution and "National Liberation in the Black Colony." He essentially called for a dual approach in which, on the one hand, black and white radicals worked together to create coalitions of revolutionary organizations and develop that political and military machinery that could overthrow capitalism and imperialism. On the other hand, he called for a U.N.-sponsored plebiscite that would allow black people to determine whether they wished to integrate or separate. Such a plebiscite, he argued, would bring clarity to black people on the question of self-determination, just as first-wave independence movements in Africa had to decide whether they wanted to maintain some altered dominion status or achieve complete independence.[56]

Cleaver represented a wing of the party more interested in guerrilla warfare than rebuilding society or doing the hard work of grassroots organizing. The attraction to Mao, Kim Il Sung, Guevara, and for that matter Fanon was their writings on revolutionary violence and people's wars. Many self-styled Panther theoreticians focused so much on developing tactics to sustain the immanent revolution that they skipped over a good deal of Mao's writings. Recognizing the problem, Newton sought to move the party away from an emphasis on guerrilla warfare and violence to a deeper, richer discussion of what the party's vision for the future might entail. Shortly after his release from prison in August 1970, he proposed the creation of an "Ideological Institute" where participants actually read and taught what he regarded as the "classics"—Marx, Mao, and Lenin, as well as Aristotle, Plato, Rousseau, Kant, Kierkegaard, and Nietzsche. Unfortunately, the Ideological Institute did not amount to much; few party members saw the use of abstract theorizing or the relevance of some of these writings to revolution. The fact that *Quotations from Chairman Mao Tse-tung* read more or less like a handbook for guerrillas did not help matters much. Even Fanon was read pretty selectively, his chapter "Concerning Violence" being a perpetual favorite among militants. George Jackson contributed to the Panthers' theoretical emphasis on war, since much of his own writings, from *Soledad Brother*[57] to *Blood in My Eye*,[58] drew on Mao primarily to discuss armed resistance under fascism. Efforts to read the works of Marx, Lenin, or Mao beyond issues related to armed rebellion did not always find a willing audience among the Panthers. Sid Lemelle, then a radical activist at California State University in Los Angeles, recalls being in contact with a few Panthers who had joined a study group sponsored by the California Communist League. The reading, which included Mao's *Four Essays on Philosophy* and lengthy passages from Lenin's selected works, turned out to be too much and they eventually left the group amid a stormy debate.[59]

Perhaps the least read section of *Quotations from Chairman Mao Tse-tung*, at least by men, was the five-page chapter on women. At a time when the metaphors

for black liberation were increasingly masculinized and black men in the movement
not only ignored the struggle for women's liberation but perpetuated gender oppression, even the most Marxist of the black nationalist movements belittled the
"woman question." The Black Panther Party was certainly no exception. Indeed, it
was during the same historic meeting of the SDS in 1969, where the Panthers
invoked Marx, Lenin, and Mao to expel the PLP for its position on the national
question, that Panther Minister of Information Rufus Walls gave his infamous
speech about the need to have women in the movement because they possessed
"pussy power." Clearly a vernacular takeoff from Mao's line that "China's women
are a vast reserve of labour power [that] . . . should be tapped in the struggle to build
a great socialist country,"[60] Walls's statement turned out to be a profoundly antifem-
inist defense of women's participation.

Although China's own history on the woman question is pretty dismal, Mao's
dictum that "women hold up half the sky" as well as his brief writings on women's
equality and participation in the revolutionary process endowed women's liberation
with some revolutionary legitimacy on the left. Of course, Maoism did not make
the movement: The fact is, women's struggles within the New Left played the most
important role in reshaping left movements toward a feminist agenda or at least
putting feminism on the table. But for black women in the Panthers suspicious of
"white feminism," Mao's language on women's equality provided space within the
party to develop an incipient black feminist agenda. As the newly appointed Minister of Information, Panther Elaine Brown announced to a press conference soon
after returning from China in 1971, "The Black Panther Party acknowledges the
progressive leadership of our Chinese comrades in all areas of revolution. Specifically, we embrace China's correct recognition of the proper status of women as equal
to that of men."[61]

Even beyond the rhetoric, black women Panthers such as Lynn French,
Kathleen Cleaver, Erica Huggins, Akua Njere, and Assata Shakur (formerly Jo-
anne Chesimard) sustained the tradition of carving out free spaces within existing male-dominated organizations to challenge the multiple forms of exploitation
black working-class women faced daily. Through the Panthers' free breakfast and
educational programs, for example, black women devised strategies that, in varying degrees, challenged capitalism, racism, and patriarchy. Some African-American women radicals rose to positions of prominence and sometimes by sheer
example contributed toward developing a militant, class-conscious black feminist
perspective.

In some instances, the growing strength of a black left feminist perspective,
buttressed by certain Maoist slogans on the so-called woman question, shaped
future black Maoist formations. One obvious example is the Black Vanguard Party,
another Bay Area Maoist group active in the mid- to late 1970s; its publication
Juche! maintained a consistent socialist-feminist perspective. Michelle Gibbs (also
known as Michelle Russell, her married name at the time) promoted a black feminist ideology as a Detroit supporter of the League of Revolutionary Black Workers
and a member of the Black Workers Congress. A red diaper baby whose father, Ted

Gibbs, fought in the Spanish Civil War and who grew up in a household where Paul Robeson and the artist Elizabeth Catlett were occasional guests, Gibbs's black social-ist-feminist perspective flowed from her political experience; from the writings of black feminist writers; and from a panoply of radical thinkers ranging from Mal-colm, Fanon, and Amilcar Cabral to Marx, Lenin, and Mao.[62] Conversely, the pre-dominantly white radical feminist organization Redstockings was not only influenced by Mao's writings but modeled itself somewhat on the Black Power movement, particularly the movement's separatist strategies and identification with the Third World.[63]

Ironically, the Black Panther Party's greatest identification with China occurred at the very moment when China's status among the left began to decline worldwide. Mao's willingness to host President Nixon and China's support of the repressive governments of Pakistan and Sri Lanka left many Maoists in the United States and elsewhere disillusioned. Nevertheless, Newton and Elaine Brown not only visited China on the eve of Nixon's trip but announced that their entry into electoral politics was inspired by China's entry into the United Nations. Newton argued that the Black Panthers' shift toward reformist, electoral politics did not con-tradict "China's goal of toppling U.S. imperialism nor [was it] an abnegation of rev-olutionary principles. It was a tactic of socialist revolution."[64] Even more incredible was Newton's complete abandonment of black self-determination, which he explained in terms of developments in the world economy. In 1971, he concluded quite presciently that the globalization of capital rendered the idea of national sov-ereignty obsolete, even among the socialist countries. Thus, black demands for self-determination were no longer relevant; the only viable strategy was global revolution. "Blacks in the U.S. have a special duty to give up any claim to nation-hood now more than ever. The U.S. has never been our country; and realistically there's no territory for us to claim. Of all the oppressed people in the world, we are in the best position to inspire global revolution."[65]

In many respects, Newton's position on the national question was closer to Mao's than most of the self-proclaimed Maoist organizations that popped up in the early to late 1970s. Despite his own statements in support of national liberation movements and Lin Biao's "theory of democratic revolutions," Mao did not support independent organizations along nationalist lines. To him, black nationalism looked like ethnic/racial particularism. He was, after all, a Chinese nationalist attempting to unify peasants and proletarians and eliminate ethnic divisions within his own country. We might recall his 1957 statement in which he demanded that progres-sives in China "help unite the people of our various nationalities . . . not divide them."[66] Thus, although recognizing that racism is a product of colonialism and imperialism, his 1968 statement insisted that the "contradiction between the black masses in the United States and U.S. ruling circles is a class contradiction. . . . The black masses and the masses of white working people in the United States share common interests and have common objectives to struggle for."[67] In other words, the black struggle is bound to merge with the working-class movement and over-throw capitalism.

THE BLACK NATION

On the issue of black liberation, however, most U.S. Maoist organizations founded in the early to mid-1970s took their lead from Stalin, not Mao. Black people in the United States were not simply proletarians in black skin but a nation, or as Stalin put it, "a historically evolved, stable community of language, territory, economic life, and psychological make-up manifested in a community of culture."[68] Antirevisionist groups that embraced Stalin's definition of a nation, such as the Communist Labor Party (CLP) and the October League, also resurrected the old Communist Party's position that African Americans in the black-belt counties of the South constitute a nation and have a right to secede if they wish. On the other hand, groups like Progressive Labor—once an advocate of "revolutionary nationalism"—moved to a position repudiating all forms of nationalism by the start of the Cultural Revolution.

The CLP was perhaps the most consistent advocate of black self-determination among the antirevisionist movements. Founded in 1968 largely by African Americans and Latinos, the CLP's roots can be traced to the old Provisional Organizing Committee (POC)—itself an outgrowth of the 1956 split in the CPUSA that led to the creation of Hammer and Steel and the Progressive Labor movement. Ravaged by a decade of internal splits, the POC had become a predominantly black and Puerto Rican organization divided between New York and Los Angeles. In 1968, the New York leadership expelled their L.A. comrades for, among other things, refusing to denounce Stalin and Mao. In turn, the L.A. group, largely under the guidance of the veteran black Marxist Nelson Peery, founded the California Communist League that same year and began recruiting young black and Chicano radical workers and intellectuals. Peery's home in south central Los Angeles had already become somewhat of a hangout for young black radicals after the Watts uprising; he organized informal groups to study history, political economy, and classic works in Marxism–Leninism–Mao Zedong thought and entertained all sorts of activists, from Black Panthers to student activists from Cal State Los Angeles and L.A. Community College. The California Communist League subsequently merged with a group of SDS militants calling themselves the Marxist-Leninist Workers Association and formed the Communist League in 1970. Two years later the group changed its name again to the Communist Labor Party.[69]

Except for perhaps Harry Haywood's long essay, "Toward a Revolutionary Position on the Negro Question" (first circulated in 1957 and kept in circulation throughout the 1960s and 1970s),[70] Nelson Peery's pamphlet *The Negro National Colonial Question* (1972) was probably the most widely read defense of black self-determination in Marxist-Leninist-Maoist circles at the time. Peery was sharply criticized for his defense of the term "Negro," a difficult position to maintain in the midst of the Black Power movement. But Peery had a point: National identity was not about color. For him, the Negro nation was a historically evolved, stable community with its own unique culture, language (or rather, dialect), and territory—the black-belt counties and their surrounding areas, or essentially the thirteen states of the Old Confederacy. Because Southern whites shared with African Americans a common territory and by his account a common language and culture, they were also considered part of the "Negro nation." More precisely, Southern whites composed the "Anglo-American minority" within the Negro nation. As evidenced in soul music, spirituals, and rock-and-roll, what emerged in the South, Peery insisted, was a hybrid culture with strong African roots manifest in the form of slave folktales and female head wraps. Peery cited Jimi Hendrix and Sly and the Family Stone, as well as the white imitators Al Jolson, Elvis Presley, and Tom Jones, as examples of a shared culture. He even saw "soul" culture embedded in "the custom of eating pigs' feet, neck bones, black eyed peas, greens, yams, and chitterlings [which] are all associated with the region of the South, particularly the Negro Nation."[71]

Peery's positioning of Southern whites as part of the Negro nation was a stroke of genius, particularly since one of his intentions was to destabilize racial categories. His commitment to Stalin's definition of a nation weakened his argument, however. At the very moment when mass migration and urbanization depleted the rural South of its black population, Peery insisted that the black belt was the natural homeland of Negroes. He even attempted to prove that a black peasantry and stable rural proletariat still existed in the black belt. Because the land question was the foundation on which his understanding of self-determination was built, he wound up saying very little about the nationalization of industry or socialized production. Thus, he could write in 1972, "the Negro national colonial question can only be solved by a return of the land to the people who have toiled over it for centuries. In the Negro Nation this land redistribution will demand a combination of state farms and cooperative enterprises in order to best meet the needs of the people under the conditions of modern mechanized agriculture."[72]

The Communist Party (Marxist-Leninist) (CP[ML]) also promoted a version of the black-belt thesis, which it inherited from its earlier incarnation as the October League. The CP(ML) formed out of a merger between the October League, based mainly in Los Angeles, and the Georgia Communist League in 1972.[73] Many of its founding members came out of the Revolutionary Youth Movement II (a faction within SDS), and a handful were Old Left renegades like Harry Haywood and Otis Hyde. Haywood's presence in the CP(ML) is significant, since he is considered one of the architects of the original black-belt thesis formulated at the Sixth Congress of the Communist International in 1928. According to the updated CP(ML) formulation, Afro-Americans had the right to secede "to their historic homeland in the Black Belt South."[74] But the document added the caveat that recognition of the right of self-determination did not mean the group believed separation was the most appropriate solution. It also introduced the idea of regional autonomy (i.e., that urban concentrations of African Americans can also exercise self-determination in their own communities) and extended the slogan of self-determination to Chicanos, Puerto Ricans, Asian Americans, Native Americans, and indigenous people in U.S. colonies (Pacific Islands, Hawaii, Alaska, etc.). They were selective as to what sort of nationalist movements they would support, promising to back only revolutionary nationalism as opposed to reactionary nationalism.

The Revolutionary Union, an outgrowth of the Bay Area Revolutionary Union (BARU) founded in 1969 with support from ex-CPUSA members who had visited China, took the position that black people constituted "an oppressed nation of a new type."[75] Because black people were primarily workers concentrated in urban, industrial areas (what BARU called a "deformed class structure"), the group believed that self-determination should not take the form of secession. Instead, it should be realized through the fight against discrimination, exploitation, and police repression in the urban centers. In 1975, when the Revolutionary Union transformed itself into the Revolutionary Communist Party (RCP), it continued to embrace the idea that black people constituted a nation of a new type but began to uphold "the right of black people to return to claim their homeland."[76] Not surprising, these two contradictory lines created confusion, compelling RCP leaders to adopt an untenable position of defending the right of self-determination without advocating it. Two years later, they dropped the right of self-determination altogether and, like the PLP, waged war on all forms of "narrow" nationalism.

Unlike any of the Maoist-oriented organizations mentioned above, the Revolutionary Communist League (RCL)—founded and led by Amiri Baraka—grew directly out of the cultural nationalist movements of the late 1960s. To understand the shifting positions of the RCL (and its precursors) with regard to black liberation, we need to go back to 1966, when Baraka founded Spirit House in Newark, New Jersey, with the help of local activists as well as folks he had worked with in Harlem's Black Arts Repertory Theater. Although Spirit House artists were involved in local political organizing from the beginning, the police beating of Baraka and several other activists during the Newark uprising in 1967 politicized them even further. They helped organize a Black Power conference in Newark after the uprising that attracted several national black leaders, including Stokely Carmichael, H. Rap Brown, Huey P. Newton of the Black Panther Party, and Imari Obadele of the newly formed Republic of New Africa (partly an outgrowth of RAM). Shortly thereafter, Spirit House became the base for the Committee for a Unified Newark (CFUN), a new organization made up of United Brothers, Black Community Defense and Development, and Sisters of Black Culture. In addition to attracting black nationalists, Muslims, and even a few Marxist-Leninist-Maoists, CFUN bore the mark of Ron Karenga's US Organization. CFUN adopted Karenga's version of cultural nationalism and worked closely with him. Although tensions arose between Karenga and some of the Newark activists over his treatment of women and the overly centralized leadership structure CFUN had imported from the US Organization, the movement continued to grow. In 1970, Baraka renamed CFUN the Congress of African Peoples (CAP), transformed it into a national organization, and at its founding convention broke with Karenga. CAP leaders sharply criticized Karenga's cultural nationalism and passed resolutions that reflected a turn to the left—including a proposal to raise funds to help build the Tanzania-Zambia railroad.[77]

Several factors contributed to Baraka's left turn in this period. One has to do with the painful lesson he learned about the limitations of black "petty bourgeois" politicians. After playing a pivotal role in the 1970 election of Kenneth Gibson, Newark's first black mayor, Baraka witnessed an increase in police repression (including attacks on CAP demonstrators) and a failure on the part of Gibson to deliver what he had promised the African-American community. Feeling betrayed and disillusioned, Baraka broke with Gibson in 1974, though he did not give up entirely on the electoral process. His role in organizing the first National Black Political Assembly in 1972 reinforced in his mind the power of black independent politics and the potential strength of a black united front.[78]

An important influence on Baraka was the CLP East Coast regional coordinator William Watkins. Harlem born and raised, Watkins was among a group of radical black students at Cal State Los Angeles who helped found the Communist League. In 1974, he got to know Baraka. "We'd spend hours in his office," Watkins recalled, "discussing the basics—like surplus value." For about three months, Baraka met regularly with Watkins, who taught him the fundamentals of political economy and tried to expose the limitations of cultural nationalism. These meetings certainly influenced Baraka's leftward turn, but when Watkins and Nelson Peery asked Baraka to join the CLP, he refused. Although he had come to appreciate Marxism–Leninism–Mao Zedong thought, he was not ready to join a multiracial organization. The black struggle was first and foremost.[79]

It is fitting that the most important source of Baraka's radicalization came out of Africa. Just as his first left turn after 1960 was spurred on by the Cuban Revolution, the struggle in southern Africa prompted his post-1970 turn to the left. The key event was the creation of the African Liberation Support Committee in 1971. It originated with a group of black nationalists led by Owusu Sadaukai, director of Malcolm X Liberation University in Greensboro, North Carolina, who traveled to Mozambique under the aegis of the Front for the Liberation of Mozambique (FRELIMO). FRELIMO's president, Samora Machel (who, coincidentally, had been in China the same time as Huey Newton), and other militants persuaded Sadaukai and his colleagues that the most useful role African Americans could play in support of anticolonialism was to challenge U.S. capitalism from within and let the world know the truth about FRELIMO's just war against Portuguese domination.

The African Liberation Support Committee (ALSC) reflected the radical orientation of the liberation movements in Portuguese Africa. On May 27, 1972 (the anniversary of the founding of the Organization of African Unity), the ALSC held the first African Liberation Day (ALD) demonstration, drawing approximately 30,000 protesters in Washington, D.C., alone, and an estimated 30,000 more across the United States. The ALD Coordinating Committee consisted of representatives from several nationalist and black left organizations, including the Youth Organization for Black Unity (YOBU); the All-African People's Revolutionary Party (AAPRP), headed by Stokely Carmichael (Kwame Toure); the Pan-African People's Organization; and the Maoist-influenced Black Workers Congress.[80] Because the ALSC brought together such a broad range of black activists, it became an arena for debate over the creation of a black radical agenda. Although most ALSC organizers were actively anti-imperialist, the number of black Marxists in leadership positions turned out to be a point of contention. Aside from Sadaukai, who would go on to play a major role in the Maoist-oriented Revolutionary Workers League (RWL), the ALSC's main leaders included Nelson Johnson (future leader in the Communist Workers Party) and Abdul Alkalimat (a brilliant writer and founding member of the Revolutionary Union).

As early as 1973, splits occurred in the ALSC. Internal squabbling and sectarianism proved too much for the ALSC to handle, and Chinese foreign policy struck the final blow. China's support for UNITA during the 1975 Angola civil war and Vice-Premier Li Xiannian's suggestion that dialogue with white South Africa was better than armed insurrection placed black Maoists in the ALSC in a difficult position. Within three years the ALSC had utterly collapsed, bringing to an inauspicious close perhaps the most dynamic anti-imperialist organization of the decade.

Nevertheless, Baraka's experience in the ALSC profoundly altered his thinking. As he recalls in his autobiography, by the time of the first African Liberation Day demonstration in 1972, he was "going left, I was reading Nkrumah and Cabral and Mao." Within two years he was calling on CAP members to examine "the international revolutionary experience [namely the Russian and Chinese Revolutions] and integrate it with the practice of the Afrikan revolution."[81] Their study lists expanded to include works such as Mao Tse-tung's *Four Essays on Philosophy,* Stalin's *Foundations of Leninism,* and *History of the Communist Party Soviet Union* (Short Course).[82] By 1976, CAP had dispensed with all vestiges of nationalism, changed its name to the Revolutionary Communist League (RCL), and sought to remake itself into a multiracial Marxist-Leninist-Maoist movement. Perhaps as a way to establish its ideological moorings as an antirevisionist movement, the RCL followed in the noble tradition of resurrecting the black-belt thesis. In 1977, the RCL published a paper titled "The Black Nation"[83] that analyzed black liberation movements from a Marxist-Leninist-Maoist perspective and concluded that black people in the South and in large cities constitute a nation with an inherent right to self-determination. Although rejecting "bourgeois integration," the essay argued that the struggle for black political power was central to the fight for self-determination.

As a dyed-in-the-wool artist with deep roots in the black arts movement, Baraka persistently set his cultural and political sights on the contradictions of black life under capitalism, imperialism, and racism. For Baraka, as for many of the persons discussed here, this was not a simple matter of narrow nationalism. On the contrary, understanding the place of racist oppression and black revolution in the context of capitalism and imperialism was fundamental to the future of humanity. In the tradition of Du Bois, Fanon, and Cruse, Baraka insisted that the black (hence colonial) proletariat is the vanguard of world revolution "not because of some mystic chauvinism but because of our place in objective history. . . . We are the vanguard because we are at the bottom, and when we rise to stand up straight everything stacked upon us topples."[84] Moreover, despite his immersion in Marxist-Leninist-Maoist literature, his own cultural work suggests that he knew, as did most black radicals, that the question of whether black people constituted a nation was not going to be settled through reading Lenin or Stalin or resurrecting M. N. Roy. If it ever could be settled, the battles would take place, for better or for worse, on the terrain of culture. Although the black arts movement was the primary vehicle for black cultural revolution in the United States, it is hard to imagine what that revolution would have looked like without China. Black radicals seized the Great Proletarian Revolution by the horns and reshaped it in their own image.

THE GREAT (BLACK) PROLETARIAN CULTURAL REVOLUTION

> *There is in fact no such thing as art for art's sake, art that stands above classes, art that is detached from or independent of politics.*
> —Mao Tse-tung, "Talks at the Yenan Forum on
> Literature and Art" (May 1942)[85]

Less than a year into the Cultural Revolution, Robert Williams published an article in the *Crusader* titled "Reconstitute Afro-American Art to Remold Black Souls." Whereas Mao's call for a cultural revolution meant getting rid of the vestiges (cultural and otherwise) of the old order, Williams—not unlike the black arts movement in the United States—was talking about purging black culture of a "slave mentality." Although adopting some of the language of the Chinese Communist Party's (CCP) manifesto (the "Decision of the Central Committee of the Chinese Communist Party Concerning the Great Proletarian Cultural Revolution," published August 12, 1966, in the *Peking Review*), Williams sought in his essay to build on the idea rather than on the ideology of the Cultural Revolution. Like Mao, he called on black artists to cast off the shackles of the old traditions and only make art in the service of revolution:

> The Afro-American artist must make a resolute and conscious effort to reconstitute our art forms to remold new proud black and revolutionary soul. . . . It must create a new theory and direction and prepare our people for a more bitter, bloody and protracted struggle against racist tyranny and exploitation. Black art must serve the best interest of black people. It must become a powerful weapon in the arsenal of the Black Revolution.[86]

RAM leaders concurred. An internal RAM document circulated in 1967, titled "Some Questions Concerning the Present Period," called for a full-scale black cultural revolution in the United States, the purpose of which would be to destroy the conditioned white oppressive mores, attitudes, ways, customs, philosophies, habits, and so on. This meant a new revolutionary culture. It also meant an end to processed hair, skin lighteners, and other vestiges of the dominant culture. Indeed, the revolution targeted not only assimilated bourgeois Negroes but barbers and beauticians.

The conscious promotion of art as a weapon in black liberation is nothing new; we can go back at least to the left wing of the Harlem Renaissance, if not earlier. And the black arts movement in the United States, not to mention virtually every contemporary national liberation movement, took this idea very seriously. Fanon says as much in *The Wretched of the Earth,* the English translation of which was making the rounds like wildfire during this period.[87] Still, the Cultural Revolution in China loomed large. After all, many if not most black nationalists were familiar with China and had read Mao, and even if they did not acknowledge or make explicit the influence of Maoist ideas on the need for revolutionary art or the protracted nature of cultural revolution, the parallels are striking nonetheless. Consider Ron [Maulana] Karenga's 1968 manifesto, "Black Cultural Nationalism." First published in *Negro Digest,* the essay derived many of its ideas from Mao's "Talks at the Yenan Forum on Literature and Art." Like Mao, Karenga insisted that all art must be judged by two criteria—"artistic" and "social" ("political"); that revolutionary art must be for the masses; and that, in Karenga's own words, art "must be functional, that is useful, as we cannot accept the false doctrine of 'art for art's sake.'" One can definitely see the influence of Maoism on Karenga's efforts to create an alternative revolutionary culture. Indeed, the seven principles of Kwanzaa (the African-American holiday Karenga invented and first celebrated in 1967), namely unity, self-determination, collective work and responsibility, collective economics (socialism), creativity, purpose, and even faith, are about as consonant with Mao's ideas as with "traditional" African culture.[88] And it is not a coincidence, perhaps, that these seven principles were the basis of Tanzania's famous Arusha Declaration in 1964 under President Julius Nyerere—Tanzania being China's earliest and most important ally in Africa.

Although Karenga's debt to Mao went unacknowledged, the Progressive Labor Party took note. The PLP's newspaper, the *Challenge,* ran a scathing attack on the whole black arts movement and its theoreticians, titled "[LeRoi] Jones-Karenga Hustle: Cultural 'Rebels' Foul Us Up," which characterized Karenga as a "pseudo-intellectual" who "has thoroughly read Mao's Talks on Literature and Art." "'Cultural nationalism,'" the article continues, "is not only worshiping the most reactionary aspects of African history. It even goes so far as measuring one's revolutionary commitment by the clothes that are being worn! This is part of the 'black awareness.'"[89]

Of course, revolution did become a kind of art, or more precisely, a distinct style. Whether it was Afros and dashikis or leather jackets and berets, most black revolutionaries in the United States developed their own aesthetic criteria. In the publishing world, Mao's "little red book" made a tremendous impact on literary styles in black radical circles. The idea that a pocket-sized book of pithy quotes and aphorisms could address a range of subjects, including ethical behavior, revolutionary thought and practice, economic development, and philosophy, appealed to many black activists, irrespective of political allegiance. The "little red book" prompted a cottage industry of miniature books of quotations compiled expressly for black militants. *The Black Book,* edited by Earl Ofari Hutchinson (with assistance from Judy Davis) is a case in point.[90] Published by the Radical Education Project (circa 1970), *The Black Book* includes a compilation of brief quotes from W.E.B. Du Bois, Malcolm X, and Frantz Fanon that address a range of issues related to domestic and world revolution. The resemblance to *Quotations from Chairman Mao Tse-tung* is striking: Chapter titles include "Black Culture and Art," "Politics," "Imperialism," "Socialism," "Capitalism," "Youth," "The Third World," "Africa," "On America," and "Black Unity." Ofari's introduction placed black struggle in a global context and called for revolutionary ethics and "spiritual as well as physical unification of the Third World." "True blackness," he added, "is a collective life-style, a collective set of values and a common world perspective" that grow out of our distinct experiences in the West. *The Black Book* was not written as a defense of black nationalism against the encroachments of Maoism. On the contrary, Ofari closed by telling "freedom fighters everywhere, continue to read your red book, but place alongside of it the revolutionary BLACK BOOK. To win the coming battle, both are necessary."

Another popular text in this tradition was the *Axioms of Kwame Nkrumah: Freedom Fighters Edition,* which appeared in 1969—a year after China's Foreign Languages Press put out the first English edition of *Quotations from Chairman Mao Tse-tung.*[91] Bound in black leather with gold type, it opens with a line in the frontispiece underscoring the importance of revolutionary will: "The secret of life is to have no fear." And with the exception of its African focus, the chapters were virtually indistinguishable from the "little red book." Topics included "African Revolution," "Army," "Black Power," "Capitalism," "Imperialism," "People's Militia," "The People," "Propaganda," "Socialism," and "Women." Most of the quotes are vague or fail to transcend obvious sloganeering ("The foulest intellectual rubbish ever invented by man is that of racial superiority and inferiority," or "A revolutionary fails only if he surrenders.")[92] Many of Nkrumah's insights, however, could have come straight from Mao's pen, particularly those quotations dealing with the need for popular mobilization, the dialectical relationship between thought and action, and issues related to war and peace and imperialism.

On the question of culture, most Maoist and antirevisionist groups in the United States were less concerned with creating a new, revolutionary culture than with destroying the vestiges of the old or attacking what they regarded as a retrograde, bourgeois commercial culture. In this respect, they were in step with the Great Proletarian Cultural Revolution. In a fascinating review of the film *Superfly* published in the CP(ML) newspaper *The Call,* the writer seized the opportunity to criticize the counterculture's as well as the capitalists' role in promoting drug use in the black community. "Looking around at all the people overdosing on drugs, getting killed in gun fights among themselves, and getting shredded up in industrial accidents while stoned on the job, it's clear that dope is as big a killer as any armed cop." Why would a film marketed to black people glorify the drug culture? Because "the imperialists know the plain truth—if you're hooked on dope, you won't have time to think about revolution—you're too busy worrying about where the next shot is coming from!" The review also introduced a bit of Chinese history:

The British did everything they could to get the Chinese people strung out [on opium]. It was common for workers to get part of their wages in opium, turning them into addicts even quicker. It was only revolution that got rid of the cause of this misery. By taking their countries back, and turning their society into one that really served the people, there was no more need to escape into drugs.[93]

Maoist attacks were not limited to the most reactionary aspects of mass commercial culture. The black arts movement—a movement that, ironically, included figures very much inspired by developments in China and Cuba—came under intense scrutiny by the antirevisionist left. Groups like the PLP and the CP(ML), despite their many disagreements over the national question, did agree that the black arts movement and its attraction to African culture were misguided, if not downright counterrevolutionary. The PLP dismissed black cultural nationalists as petty bourgeois businessmen who sold the most retrograde aspects of African culture to the masses and "exploit[ed] black women—all in the name of 'African culture' and in the name of 'revolution.'" The same PLP editorial castigated the black arts movement for "teaching about African Kings and Queens, African 'empires.' There is no class approach—no notice that these Kings, etc., were oppressing the mass of African people."[94] Likewise, a 1973 editorial in *The Call* sharply criticized the black arts movement for "delegitimizing the genuine national aspirations of black people in the U.S. and . . . substituting African counter-culture for anti-imperialist struggle."[95]

Although these attacks were generally unfair, particularly in the way they lumped together a wide array of artists, a handful of black artists had come to similar conclusions about the direction of the black arts movement. For the novelist John Oliver Killens, the Chinese Cultural Revolution offered a model for transforming black cultural nationalism into a revolutionary force. As a result of his travels to China during the early 1970s, Killens published an important essay in *The Black World* praising the Cultural Revolution for being, in his view, a stunning success. In fact, he ostensibly went to China to find out why the Chinese revolution succeeded "while our own black cultural revolution, that bloomed so brightly during the Sixties, seems to be dying on the vine?"[96] By the time he was ready to return to the United States, he had reached several conclusions regarding the limitations of the black cultural revolution and the strength of the Maoist model. First, he recognized that all successful revolutions must be continuous—permanent and protracted. Second, cultural activism and political activism are not two different strategies for liberation but two sides of the same coin. The cultural revolution and the political revolution go hand in hand. Third, a revolutionary movement must be self-reliant; it must create self-sustaining cultural institutions. Of course, most radical nationalists in the black arts movement figured most of this out independently and Killens's article merely reinforced these lessons. But China taught Killens one other lesson that few male movement activists paid attention to at the time: "'Women hold up one-half of the world.'" "In some very vital and militant factions of the black cultural revolution, women were required to metaphorically 'sit in the back of the bus.' . . . This is backward thinking and divisive. Many women voted with their feet and went into Women's Lib. And some of the brothers seemed upset and surprised. We drove them to it."[97]

The other major black critic of the black arts movement's cultural nationalism who ended up embracing Maoism was Amiri Baraka, himself a central figure in the black cultural revolution and an early target for Maoist abuse. As the founder and leader of CAP and later the RCL, Baraka offered more than a critique; he built a movement that attempted to synthesize the stylistic and aesthetic innovations of the black arts movement with Marxism–Leninism–Mao Zedong thought and practice. Just as Baraka's odyssey from the world of the Beats to the Bandung world provides insight into Mao's impact on black radicalism in the United States, so does Baraka's transition from a cultural nationalist to committed Communist. More than any other Maoist or antirevisionist, Baraka and the RCL epitomized the most conscious and sustained effort to bring the Great Proletarian Cultural Revolution to the inner cities of the United States and to transform it in a manner that spoke to the black working class.

Having come out of the black arts movement in Harlem and Spirit House in Newark, Baraka was above all else a cultural worker. As he and the Congress of African Peoples moved from cultural nationalism to Marxism, this profound ideological shift manifested itself through changes in cultural practice. Dismissing the "black petty bourgeois primitive cultural nationalist" as unscientific and metaphysical, Baraka warned his comrades against "the cultural bias that might make us think that we can return to pre–slave trade Afrika, and the romance of feudalism."[98] CAP changed the name of its publication from *Black Newark* to *Unity and Struggle* to reflect its transition from a cultural nationalist perspective to a deeper understanding of "the dialectical requirements of revolution."[99] The Spirit House Movers (the organization's theater troupe) were now called the Afrikan Revolutionary Movers (ARM), and a group of cultural workers associated with Spirit House formed a singing group called the Anti-Imperialist Singers. They abandoned African dress as well as "male chauvinist practices that had been carried out as part of its 'African traditionalism' such as holding separate political education classes for men and women."[100] And CAP's official holiday, known as "Leo Baraka" for Baraka's birthday, became a day devoted entirely to studying Marxism–Leninism–Mao Zedong thought, the "woman question," and the problems of cadre development.[101]

By 1976, the year CAP reemerged as the Revolutionary Communist League, Baraka had come a long way since his alliance with Ron Karenga. In a poem in his collection *Hard Facts* titled "Today," Baraka's position on cultural nationalism vis-à-vis class struggle is unequivocal:

> Frauds in leopard skin, turbaned hustlers w/skin
> type rackets, colored capitalists, negro
> exploiters, Afro-American Embassy gamers
> who lurk about Afrikan embassies fightin for

airline tickets, reception guerrillas, whose
only connection w/a party is the Frankie Crocker kind.
Where is the revolution brothers and sisters?
Where is the mobilization of the masses led
by the advanced section of the working class?
Where is the unity criticism unity. The self criticism
& criticism? Where is the work & study. The
ideological clarity? Why only poses &
postures & subjective one sided non-theories
describing only yr petty bourgeois upbringing
Black saying might get you a lecture gig, "wise
man" but will not alone bring revolution.[102]

One might argue that *Hard Facts* was written as a kind of Marxist-Leninist-Maoist manifesto on revolutionary art. Like his former mentor Ron Karenga, Baraka built on Mao's oft-cited "Talks at the Yenan Forum on Art and Literature," though to very different ends. In his introduction to the book Baraka insists that revolutionary artists must study Marxism-Leninism; produce work that serves the people, not the exploiters; jettison petty bourgeois attitudes and learn from the people, taking ideas and experiences and reformulating them through Marxism-Leninism. No artist, he asserts, is above study or should produce his or her opinions unconnected to the struggle for socialism. As Mao put it, "Through the creative labour of revolutionary artists and writers the raw material of art and literature in the life of the people becomes art and literature in an ideological form in the service of the people."[103]

Baraka tried to put this manifesto in practice through intense community-based cultural work. One of the RCL's most successful projects was the Anti-Imperialist Cultural Union (AICU), a New York–based multinational cultural workers' organization founded in the late 1970s. In November 1978, the AICU sponsored the Festival of People's Culture, which drew some five hundred people to listen to poetry read by Askia Toure, Miguel Algarin, and Sylvia Jones and musical performances by an RCL-created group calling itself the Proletarian Ensemble. Through groups like the Proletarian Ensemble and the Advanced Workers (another musical ensemble formed by the RCL), RCL spread its message of proletarian revolution and black self-determination and its critique of capitalism to community groups and schoolchildren throughout black Newark, New York, and other cities on the Eastern seaboard.

Theater seemed to be Baraka's main avenue for the Black Proletarian Cultural Revolution. Among the AICU's many projects, the Yenan Theater Workshop clearly projected Mao's vision of revolutionary art. The Yenan Theater produced a number of Baraka's plays, including a memorable performance of *What Was the Lone Ranger's Relationship to the Means of Production?* In 1975 to 1976, Baraka wrote two new plays, *The Motion of History* and *S-1,* that perhaps represent the clearest expression of his shift, in his words, "from petty bourgeois radicalism (and its low point of bourgeois cultural nationalism) on through to finally grasping the science of revolution, Marxism–Leninism–Mao Tse-Tung Thought."[104]

The Motion of History is a long epic play that touches on just about everything under the sun, from slavery and slave revolts, industrial capitalism, civil rights and Black Power, to Irish immigration and white racism. And practically every revolutionary or reformist having something to do with the struggle for black freedom makes an appearance, including John Brown, H. Rap Brown, Lenin, Karenga, Harriet Tubman, Denmark Vesey, and Nat Turner. Through scenes of workers discussing politics on the shop floor or in Marxist study groups, the audience learns about the history of slavery, the rise of industrial capitalism, imperialism, surplus value, relative overproduction, and the day-to-day racist brutality to which African Americans and Latinos are subjected. In the spirit of proletarian literature, *The Motion of History* closes on an upbeat with a rousing meeting at which those present pledge their commitment to building a revolutionary multiracial, multiethnic, working-class party based on Marxist–Leninist–Mao Zedong thought.

S-1 shares many similarities with *The Motion of History*, although it focuses primarily on what Baraka and the RCL saw as the rise of fascism in the United States. A play about a Marxist-Leninist-Maoist group fighting antisedition legislation, it was written by Baraka in response to the Senate bill Criminal Justice Codification, Revision and Reform Act, known as S-1, which would enable the state to adopt extremely repressive measures to combat radical movements. S-1 gave police and the FBI greater freedom to search and seize materials from radical groups, as well as permission to wiretap suspects for forty-eight hours without court approval; it proposed mandatory executions for certain crimes; and it revived the Smith Act, subjecting any group or person advocating the "destruction of the government" to a possible fifteen-year prison sentence and fines up to $100,000. The most notorious aspect of the bill was the "Leading a Riot" provision, which allowed courts to sentence anyone promoting the assembly of five people with the intention of creating "a grave danger to Property" to three years in prison and a $100,000 fine.[105]

We do not know how activists and working people responded to Baraka's plays during the ultra-radical period of the AICU and the RCL, and most cultural critics act as if these works are not worthy of comment. No matter what one might think about these works as art, as propaganda, or as both, it is remarkable to think that in the late 1970s a handful of inner-city kids in Newark could watch performances that advocated revolution in the United States and tried to expose the rapaciousness of capitalism. And all this was going on in the midst of the so-called me generation, when allegedly there was no radical left to speak of. (Indeed, Reagan's election in 1980 is cited as evidence of the lack of a left political challenge as well as the reason for the brief resurrection of Marxist parties in the United States between 1980 and 1985.)

FAREWELL FOR MAO, THE PARTY'S OVER?

Depending on where you stand politically, and with whom, you could easily conclude that U.S. Maoism died when Mao did in 1976. But to say that Maoism somehow died on the vine is to overstate the case. Maoist organizations still exist in the United States. The Maoist Internationalist Movement maintains a web site, as does the Progressive Labor Party (though it can hardly be called "Maoist" today), and the RCP is as ubiquitous as ever. Indeed, there is some evidence to suggest that the RCP played a role in helping to draft the Bloods and Crips' post-L.A. rebellion manifesto, "Give Us the Hammer and the Nails and We Will Rebuild the City." The former CLP, now called the League of Revolutionaries, has a strong following in Chicago and includes the longtime radicals General Baker and Abdul Alkalimat. More important, even if we acknowledge that their numbers have dwindled substantially since the mid-1970s, the activists who stayed in those movements remained committed to black liberation, even if their strategies and tactics proved insensitive or wrongheaded. Anyone who knows anything about politics knows that Jesse Jackson's 1984 presidential campaign was overrun by a rainbow coalition of Maoists and that a variety of Maoist organizations were represented in the National Black Independent Political Party. In other words, now that so many American liberals are joining the backlash against poor black people and affirmative action, either by their active participation or by their silence, some of these self-proclaimed revolutionaries are still willing to "move mountains" in the service of black folk. The most tragic and heroic example comes from Greensboro, North Carolina, where five members of the Communist Workers Party (formerly the Workers Viewpoint Organization) were murdered by Klansmen and Nazis during an anti-Klan demonstration on November 3, 1979.

The fact remains, however, that the heyday of black Maoism has passed. The reasons are varied, having to do with the overall decline of black radicalism, the self-destructive nature of sectarian politics, and China's disastrous foreign policy decisions vis-à-vis Africa and the Third World. Besides, most of the self-described black Maoists in our story—at least the most honest ones—probably owe their greatest intellectual debt to Du Bois, Fanon, Malcolm X, Guevara, and Cruse. But Mao Tsetung and the Chinese Revolution left an indelible imprint on black radical politics—an imprint whose impact we have only begun to explore in this chapter. At a moment when a group of nonaligned countries sought to challenge the political binaries created by Cold War politics, when African nationalists tried to plan for a postcolonial future, when Fidel Castro and a handful of fatigue-clad militants did the impossible, when Southern lunch counters and Northern ghettos became theaters for a new revolution, there stood China—the most powerful "colored" nation on earth.

Mao's China, along with the Cuban Revolution and African nationalism, internationalized the black revolution in profound ways. Mao gave black radicals a non-Western model of Marxism that placed greater emphasis on local conditions and historical circumstances than canonical texts. China's Great Leap Forward challenged the idea that the march to socialism must take place in stages or that one must wait patiently for the proper objective conditions to move ahead. For many young radicals schooled in student-based social democracy, in antiracist politics, in feminism, or in all of these, "consciousness raising" in the Maoist style of criticism/self-criticism was a powerful alternative to bourgeois democracy. But consciousness raising was more than propaganda work; it was intellectual labor in the context of revolutionary practice. "All genuine knowledge originates in direct experience," Mao said in his widely read essay "On Practice" (1937).[106] The idea that knowledge derives from a dialectics of practice and theory empowered radicals to question the expertise of sociologists, psychologists, economists, and others whose grand pronouncements on the causes of poverty and racism often went unchallenged. Thus, in an age of liberal technocrats, Maoists—from black radical circles to the women's liberation movement—sought to overturn bourgeois notions of expertise. They developed analyses; debated; and published journals, newspapers, position papers, pamphlets, and even books, and although they rarely agreed with one another, they saw themselves as producers of new knowledge. They believed, as Mao put it, that "these ideas turn into a material force which changes society and changes the world."[107]

Ideas alone do not change the world, however. People do. And having the willingness and energy to change the world requires more than the correct analysis and direct engagement with the masses: It takes faith and will. Here Maoists have much in common with some very old black biblical traditions. After all, if little David can take Goliath with just a slingshot, certainly a "single spark can start a prairie fire."[108]

NOTES

The authors would like to thank Henry Louis Gates Jr. for proposing this article in the first place and Ernest Allen, Harold Cruse, Vicki Garvin, Michael Goldfield, Marc Higbee, Geoffrey Jacques, Sid Lemelle, Josh Lyons, Eric and Liann Mann, David Roediger, Tim Schermerhorn, Akinyele Umoja, Alan Wald, Billy Watkins, Komozi Woodard, and Marilyn Young for their insights, recollections, and/or advice. Finally, we wish to express our deepest gratitude to the staff at the Tamiment Library at NYU, especially Andrew Lee and Jane Latour.

1. *Crusader* 9, no. 1, July 1967, p. 1.

2. The Coup, "Dig It," *Kill My Landlord* (Wild Pitch Records, 1993).

3. Mao Tse-tung, *Quotations from Chairman Mao Tse-tung* (Peking: Foreign Languages Press, 1966).

4. Elaine Brown, *A Taste of Freedom* (New York: Doubleday Books, 1992), 231–232.

5. Huey Newton, *Revolutionary Suicide* (New York: Ballantine Books, 1973), 110.

6. W.E.B. Du Bois, *The Autobiography of W.E.B. Du Bois,* ed. Herbert Aptheker (New York: International Publishers, 1968), 404.

7. In fact, several organizations (e.g., Ray O. Light, the Communist Workers Party, the Black Vanguard Party, the Maoist Internationalist Movement, ad infinitum) are only

mentioned in passing or omitted altogether for lack of information. We recognize that only a book can do justice to this story.

8. A. Belden Fields, *Trotskyism and Maoism: Theory and Practice in France and the United States* (New York: Praeger, 1988), 16–19.

9. The allegory in *Quotations from Chairman Mao Tse-tung,* "The Foolish Old Man Who Removed the Mountains," instilled a missionary zeal in many radicals that enabled them to jump quickly to the question of guerrilla war, as if revolution were imminent. Of course, chapters of the "little red book" such as "People's War," "The People's Army," "Education and the Training of Troops," and "Revolutionary Heroism" certainly helped promote the idea that "political power grows out of the barrel of a gun," despite the fact that efforts to apply China's experience to the United States contradict Mao's own argument that each revolution must grow out of its own specific circumstances.

10. Mao Tse-tung, *Quotations,* iv.

11. Mao Tse-tung, *Statement Supporting the American Negroes in Their Just Struggle Against Racial Discrimination in the United States* (Peking: Foreign Languages Press, 1963), 2.

12. John Oliver Killens, *Black Man in the New China* (Los Angeles: U.S.-China People's Friendship Association, 1976), 10.

13. Philip Snow, "China and Africa: Consensus and Camouflage," in *Chinese Foreign Policy: Theory and Practice,* Thomas W. Robinson and David Shambaugh, eds. (New York and Oxford, UK: Clarendon Press, 1994), 285–299.

14. Fields, *Trotskyism and Maoism,* p. 213. Silber criticized Chinese policy in Angola where the Chinese were on the same side as the South African apartheid regime and the United States. Chinese foreign policy was a hindrance to American Maoists in a variety of contexts, not just southern Africa: China's reception of Nixon while U.S. bombs still dropped on Vietnam and support for Pinochet in Chile are two particularly striking examples.

15. Mao Tse-tung, *Quotations,* p. 82.

16. Revolutionary Action Movement, *The World Black Revolution,* pamphlet, 1966.

17. Vertical files on the Provisional Organizing Committee, Hammer and Steel, and the Progressive Labor Party, Tamiment Collection, Bobst Library, New York University.

18. Amiri Baraka, *The Autobiography of LeRoi Jones/Amiri Baraka* (New York: Freundlich Books, 1984), 220. Also, Fields, *Trotskyism and Maoism,* p. 185.

19. Fields, *Trotskyism and Maoism,* pp. 185–197. Also, Jim O'Brien, *American Leninism in the 1970s* (Somerville, MA: New England Free Press, n.d.).

20. Van Gosse, *Where the Boys Are: Cuba, Cold War America and the Making of a New Left* (London: Verso, 1993), 147–148.

21. Harold Cruse, "Negro Nationalism's New Wave," *New Leader* (1962); reprinted in his *Rebellion or Revolution?* (New York: Morrow, 1968), 73.

22. Harold Cruse, "Revolutionary Nationalism and the Afro-American," *Studies on the Left* (1962); reprinted in his *Rebellion or Revolution?* pp. 74–75.

23. Baraka, *The Autobiography,* p. 184; and see Komozi Woodard, *A Nation Within a Nation: Amiri Baraka (LeRoi Jones) and Black Power Politics* (Chapel Hill: University of North Carolina Press, 1998), 52–63; LeRoi Jones, "Cuba Libre," in his *Home: Social Essays* (1966; Hopewell, NJ: The Ecco Press, 1998), 11–62.

24. Interview with Vicki Garvin, conducted by the authors. Unpublished speech by Garvin in authors' possession.

25. Vertical file on Vicki Garvin, Tamiment Collection, Bobst Library, New York University.

26. Newton, *Revolutionary Suicide,* p. 70

27. Newton, *Revolutionary Suicide,* p. 111.

28. Sources on Robert Williams used are Robert F. Williams, *Negroes with Guns* (New York: Marzani and Munsell, 1962); Robert Williams, *Listen, Brother* (New York: World View Publishers, 1968); "Interview: Robert Williams," *Black Scholar* 1, no. 7, May 1970; Kalamu ya Salaam, "Robert Williams: Crusader for International Solidarity," *The Black Collegian* 8, no. 3, January-February 1978; Maxwell C. Stanford, "Revolutionary Action Movement: A Case Study of an Urban Revolutionary Movement in Western Capitalist Society," M.A. thesis, Atlanta University, 1986; Timothy B. Tyson, "Robert F. Williams, 'Black Power,' and the Roots of the African American Freedom Struggle," *Journal of American History* 85, no. 2, September 1998, pp. 540–570; Marcellus C. Barksdale, "Robert Williams and the Indigenous Civil Rights Movement in Monroe, North Carolina, 1961," *Journal of Negro History* 69, Spring 1984, pp. 73–89.

29. Cruse, *Rebellion or Revolution?* pp. 74–95.

30. Stanford, "Revolutionary Action Movement," pp. 75–80.

31. Stanford, "Revolutionary Action Movement," p. 197.

32. Interview with Tim Schermerhorm, conducted by Betsy Esch.

33. Stanford, "Revolutionary Action Movement," p. 40.

34. Stanford, "Revolutionary Action Movement," p. 91.

35. Interview with Ernest Allen, conducted by Robin D. G. Kelley.

36. Quoted in Stanford, "Revolutionary Action Movement," p. 92.

37. Cited in Stanford, "Revolutionary Action Movement," p.79.

38. Stanford, "Revolutionary Action Movement," p. 110.

39. Mao Tse-Tung, *Quotations,* pp. 256, 269.

40. "Interview: Robert Williams," *The Black Scholar* 1, no. 7, May 1970, p. 14.

41. "Revolutionary Action Movement," General File, Tamiment Collection, Bobst Library, New York University.

42. RAM, *The World Black Revolution,* p. 5. Echoing the Communist Manifesto, the pamphlet begins, "All over Africa, Asia, South, Afro and Central America a revolution is haunting and sweeping."

43. Harlem Branch of the Progressive Labor Party, *The Plot Against Black America,* pamphlet, 1965, p. 147.

44. RAM, *The World Black Revolution,* p. 9.

45. R. Sackett, "Plotting a War on Whitey: Extremists Set for Violence," *Life* 60, June 10, 1966, pp. 100–100B.

46. D. MacDonald, "Politics: Black Power," *Esquire* 65, October 1967, p.38; and G. Willis, "Second Civil War," *Esquire* 69, March 1968, pp. 71–78.

47. Harlem Branch of the Progressive Labor Party, *The Plot Against Black America,* Vertical File, Tamiment Collection.

48. Stanford, "Revolutionary Action Movement," p. 215.

49. Paul Sweezey and Leo Huberman, "The Cultural Revolution in China, " *Monthly Review,* January 1967, p. 17.

50. Interview with Vicki Garvin, conducted by the authors.

51. Mao Tse-tung, *Statement by Comrade Mao Tse-tung, Chairman of the Central Committee of the Communist Party of China, in Support of the Afro-American Struggle Against Violent Repression, April 16, 1968* (Peking: Foreign Languages Press, 1968).

52. Interview with Bobby Seale from Radical Education Project, "An Introduction to the Black Panther Party," (Ann Arbor, MI: Radical Education Project, 1969), pp. 26.

53. Newton, *Revolutionary Suicide,* p. 70.

54. Eldridge Cleaver, *On the Ideology of the Black Panther Party,* pamphlet, 1968, Black Panther Party, Organizational File, Tamiment Collection, Bobst Library, New York University.

55. Radical Education Project, "An Introduction to the Black Panther Party" (Ann Arbor, MI: Radical Education Project, 1969), pp. 19, 26.

56. Eldridge Cleaver, "National Liberation in the Black Colony," Black Panther Party, Organizational File, Tamiment Collection, Bobst Library, New York University.

57. George Jackson, *Soledad Brother: The Prison Letters of George Jackson* (New York: Coward-McCann, 1970).

58. George Jackson, *Blood in My Eye* (New York: Random House, 1972).

59. Interview with Sid Lemelle, conducted by Robin D. G. Kelley.

60. Mao Tse-tung, *Quotations,* p. 298.

61. Brown, *A Taste of Freedom,* p. 304.

62. Interview with Michelle Gibbs, conducted by Robin D. G. Kelley.

63. For this insight we are grateful to Rosalyn Baxandall.

64. Quoted in Brown, *A Taste of Freedom,* p. 313.

65. Brown, *A Taste of Freedom,* p. 281.

66. Mao Tse-tung, *Mao Tse-tung on Art and Literature* (Peking: Foreign Languages Press, 1960), p. 144.

67. Mao Tse-tung, S*tatement by Comrade Mao Tse-tung, Chairman of the Central Committee of the Communist Party of China, in Support of the Afro-American Struggle Against Violent Repression,* p. 2.

68. J. Stalin, *Marxism and the National Question* (Calcutta: New Book Centre, 1975), 11.

69. Interview with Sid Lemelle. Interview with William Watkins, conducted by Robin D. G. Kelley.

70. Harry Haywood, "Toward a Revolutionary Position on the Negro Question," mimeo (Provisional Organizing Committee for the Reconstruction of a Marxist-Leninist Party, 1959).

71. Nelson Peery, *The Negro National Colonial Question,* pamphlet, 1972.

72. Peery, *The Negro National Colonial Question.*

73. The Communist Party (Marxist-Leninist) and the October League, Vertical Files, Tamiment Collection, Bobst Library, New York University.

74. "The Negro National Question," founding document from the Communist Party–Marxist-Leninist Vertical File, Tamiment Collection, Bobst Library, New York University.

75. The Revolutionary Union, Vertical File, Tamiment Collection, Bobst Library, New York University.

76. Fields, *Trotskyism and Maoism,* p. 222.

77. *Forward: Journal of Marxism-Leninism-Mao- Zedong Thought* 3, January 1980, pp. 29–38; Woodard, *A Nation Within a Nation,* pp. 63–254.

78. *Forward,* pp. 89–90; Woodard, *A Nation Within a Nation,* pp. 219–254.

79. Interview with William Watkins, conducted by Robin D. G. Kelley.

80. *Forward,* pp. 80–81; Rod Bush, *We Are Not What We Seem: Black Nationalism and Class Struggle in the American Century* (New York: New York University Press, 1999), 211–213; Woodard, *A Nation Within a Nation,* pp. 173–180.

81. Baraka, *The Autobiography,* p. 298; Imamu Amiri Baraka, "Revolutionary Party: Revolutionary Ideology" (speech delivered at the Congress of Afrikan People Midwestern Conference, March 31, 1974), Vertical Files, Tamiment Collection, Bobst Library, New York University.

82. Interview with Komozi Woodard, conducted by Robin D. G. Kelley; *Forward,* p. 100.

83. *Forward,* p. 121.

84. Baraka, "Revolutionary Party," p. 5.

85. Quoted in Mao Tse-tung, *Quotations,* p. 299.

86. Robert Williams, "Reconstitute Afro-American Art to Remold Black Souls," *Crusader* 9, no. 1, July 1967.

87. Frantz Fanon, *The Wretched of the Earth* (New York: Grove Press, 1963).

88. Ron Karenga, "Black Cultural Nationalism," in Addison Gayle, ed., *The Black Aesthetic* (Garden City, NY: Anchor Books, 1971), 32.

89. "Jones-Karenga Hustle: Cultural 'Rebels' Foul Us Up," *Black Liberation (Articles by the Progressive Labor Party),* pamphlet, 1969, p. 47.

90. Radical Education Project, *The Black Book* (Ann Arbor, MI: Radical Education Project, ca. 1970).

91. Kwame Nkrumah, *Axioms of Kwame Nkrumah: Freedom Fighters Edition* (New York: International Publishers, 1969).

92. Kwame Nkrumah, *Axioms,* p. 114.

93. *The Call,* September 1972, p. 6.

94. "Jones-Karenga Hustle."

95. *The Call,* September 1973, p. 3.

96. Killens, *Black Man in the New China,* p. 18.

97. Killens, *Black Man in the New China,* p. 19.

98. Baraka, "Revolutionary Party," p. 2.

99. *Forward,* p. 94.

100. *Forward,* pp. 94–95; Baraka, *The Autobiography,* p. 301.

101. Baraka, *The Autobiography,* pp. 89–94, 298.

102. Amiri Baraka, *Hard Facts* (New York: Morrow, 1976), 15.

103. Mao Tse-tung, "Talks at the Yenan Forum on Art and Literature," in his *Art and Literature* (Peking: Foreign Languages Press, 1960), 100.

104. Amiri Baraka, *The Motion of History and Other Plays* (New York: William Morrow, 1978), pp. 13–14.

105. Baraka, *The Motion of History and Other Plays.*

106. Reprinted in Mao Tse-tung, *Quotations.*

107. Mao Tse-tung, *Quotations.*

108. Mao Tse-tung, *Quotations.*

3. Home to Harlem: Yesterday and Today

Losing Ground: Harlem, the War on Drugs, and the Prison Industrial Complex

Throughout much of the twentieth century, Harlem was unquestionably the symbolic capital of black America. Though it has been half a century since the community lost its designation as the most populous black urban center, Harlem remains the quintessential expression of the African-American cultural experience for much of the world. The community's significance, however, goes beyond the musicians, poets, and artists of the Harlem Renaissance. Harlem also anchored a unique political history. It was not only a place to which people of African descent from all over the world were drawn, but it was also a space where people made history through political struggle.

This chapter will explore some of the processes that constrained Harlem's history-making capacity in the 1980s and 1990s. We will discuss a community whipsawed by the drug epidemic and the so-called war on drugs, and the impacts of these events on sustained political movement. We conclude with a discussion of Harlem's potential to make history anew, whether its legacy of activism and community protest can be reinvigorated to once again push society at large toward more equitable structures.

HARLEM PAST

When I began a research project in Harlem in 1994,[1] I was struck by the widespread nostalgia for a "Harlem Past" that interviewees expressed. Residents spoke movingly of a past characterized by a sense of community. For example, one study participant described her childhood in Harlem as follows:

> I knew I was poor. . . . I didn't have what a lot of people had, but I never knew about like being poverty-stricken. . . .You know, we lived in a very family ori-ented-building. Everybody knew everybody. Everybody had each other's key. You know, people used to get robbed later on when drugs got bad, but I never wanted for anything. And I always had some place to go and eat if I was hungry or if I didn't want to eat at my mother's house like I didn't like what was for dinner, I could go next door and eat. I used to love going to my cousin's Barbara's house and eat 'cause they use to always have a lot of food.

Even in the mid-1990s, many residents continued to feel that Harlem retained an egalitarian spirit of community, and indeed, some middle-income peo-ple moved to Harlem for that very reason. One resident valued "the warm sense of your neighbors. Harlem is like . . . it's a little town. You know the people in a block. They . . . see me every day. I go to work and come home and feel more comfort-able." And yet, most residents we interviewed felt that Harlem had changed for the worse.

Memory is selective and often undependable, but other researchers working in Harlem have been confronted with this "tale of two cities." Columbia University professor of public health Mindy Fullilove contrasts "Harlem Lost" and "Harlem Present" as "the fractured landscape representing the conjunction of the grim pres-ent and the deeply mourned past."[2] This feeling is reflected in Fullilove's descrip-tion of participants' views:

> They spoke of Harlem with a mixture of pride in what the community once was and sadness for what existed today. In the past, they noted, there was a cohesive-ness that created a sense of stability and belonging. One focus group participant explained, "There was moral pride and moral dignity. It was something that moved around to everyone who was living here. It was electric. The network, it was a spiritual network. . . ."[3]

Why such a deep sense of loss? Though people speak of a changing commu-nity, inherent in these nostalgic memories is a sense of loss of history and hence of agency. Perhaps African political theorist Amilcar Cabral's description of colonial-ism has something to tell us. He describes the ways in which colonial rule disrupts the organic evolution and institutional integrity of societies. As individuals become disconnected from their past, they leave their own history and are forced to enter someone else's. Although Harlem was not a colony in the traditional sense, it has been subject to a war whose consequences have been devastating to the commu-nity's historical agency.

Harlem has historically been a focus of black political activism. Over three generations, major protest movements and personalities have found a base there. It was in Harlem that, in response to the epidemic of lynching following World War I, Marcus Garvey developed a mass movement for black empowerment and African-American liberation that involved as many as two million people at its height. During the Great Depression years, Unemployment Councils in Harlem demanded jobs, and, when marshals evicted renters for failure to pay rent, the councils organized community residents to move their possessions back into their homes. In 1945, Harlem residents were the first to elect a Communist, Benjamin Davis, to represent them in the New York City Council. Two years later, William Patterson and Paul Robeson, reflecting the internationalist consciousness of many Harlem residents, presented a petition to the United Nations charging the United States with genocide against African Americans.

In Harlem as in other parts of the country, the Civil Rights Movement spawned militant urban protests. In the 1960s and 1970s, the community was the home base of Malcolm X and the New York branch of the Nation of Islam, the Black Panther Party for Self Defense, and various other movements. Perhaps more than any other black community, Harlem has produced a variety of black leaders including David Dinkins, the former mayor of New York City; Charles Rangel, one of the most powerful Democrats in Congress; and Carl McCall, former New York state comptroller and recent candidate for governor of the state of New York.

Harlem's social protest movements reflected the broader African-American political struggle, which has in many ways been at the leading edge of the expansion of domestic human rights and therefore central to the construction of American democracy. The Civil Rights Movement stimulated a range of national reforms in the 1960s and 1970s including minority rights, women's equality, disabled persons' rights, democratization of immigration laws, and health care for the elderly. It quickly gave birth to such radical anticapitalist movements as the Panthers. The accumulated lived experience of nine generations of African Americans produced a logic of black political participation that emphasized the redistributive state, the public sphere, and the responsibility of government to its citizens. Such a perspective is fundamentally at odds with the decline of the welfare state and the rise of neoliberal ideology—processes that are characteristic of postindustrial, globalized capitalism.

For this reason, the tale of Harlem must be understood in the context of the global processes affecting Harlem and New York City. Two issues are particularly important here. First, the core elements of globalized capitalism—the relocation of domestic jobs overseas, significant cuts in social services, privatization of publicly funded institutions, repeal of union agreements about benefits and work conditions, and the abandonment of the state's responsibility to assist the truly disadvantaged—have had significant adverse effects on many Harlem residents. So much so that, in analyzing the consequences of globalization for urban areas in the United States, progressive theorists often depict racialized minorities, and African Americans in particular, as *marginal* as their labor becomes economically redundant.[4] This is accurate as far as it goes, but *marginality* as a descriptor misses a significant process involving black agency and the response to the black liberation struggle.

Analyses of black marginality fail to incorporate the second, and perhaps most important, issue: These global transformations imposed upon communities require new, harsher mechanisms to maintain order and control. African Americans, who have a history of protest against structures of inequality, pose a particular threat. Such dissent has often been criminalized, and the boundaries between protest and crime are shifted as the occasion demands. As far back as 1680, the Slave Codes of the Commonwealth of Virginia made public assemblies, bearing arms, traveling without a master's permission, and threatening whites a crime for black slaves. Indeed, Marc Mauer, assistant director of the Sentencing Project, a national non-profit organization that conducts research on criminal justice policy issues, dates the triumph of the "tough on crime" movement to the 1960s and Richard M. Nixon's campaign call for "law and order" in the wake of the Civil Rights Movement and urban rebellions protesting the assassination of Martin Luther King, Jr., and continuing structures of discrimination.[5] University of California, Berkeley, professor Ruth Wilson Gilmore, also argues that contemporary notions of disorder grew out of "the spontaneous and organized activism" of the 1960s and the need to interpret the turmoil as containable crime, rather than dissent.[6]

Harlem's location in upper Manhattan is also important. In the context of globalization, New York City has been described as a *world city* by virtue of its role as a preeminent financial capital.[7] A world city requires world-class order. New York City is an important testing ground for enforcing a global order "that reduces the power of individuals and peoples to shape their destinies through participation in democratic processes."[8] In the 1960s and 1970s, certain forms of dissent were managed through the welfare state. Subsequently, response to dissent has taken a very different form: incarceration. Today, there are two million U.S. citizens in prisons or jails, most for nonviolent offenses.[9] With 5 percent of the world's population, the United States has 25 percent of the world's prisoners. To illustrate the issue more dramatically and concretely, in 1956, the greater Youngstown, Ohio, area employed approximately 60,000 steelworkers. By 1997, it employed 15,000—a decrease of 45,000 steelworkers.[10] To revitalize the area, in 1997 Youngstown officials turned to the Corrections Corporation of America, and today, Youngstown's biggest business is incarceration, with approximately 48,000 inmates in correctional facilities in and around the city.[11] It is in this context that we explore the emergence of the prison industrial complex and its consequences for communities such as Harlem.

HARLEM PRESENT[12]

Central Harlem is a complex, diverse community populated by residents of all socioeconomic classes.[13] Harlem's complexity and heterogeneity stem from a history of settlement and economic change dating from its emergence as an African-American community in the 1800s. In the past quarter century, Harlem, along with the rest of New York City, has been deeply affected by global economic restructuring reflected in the shift from an industrial economy to an economy based on information and service.[14]

In New York City, this global economic shift resulted in a financial and economic crisis in the mid-1970s that led to drastic cuts in the city's budget—and slashed services. Loss of manufacturing jobs has also led to a decline in the unionized sector of the labor force, accompanied by a drop in wages and benefits for workers. From the early 1980s to the mid-1990s, wages stagnated. In the late 1990s, wages rose slightly as a result of high employment, low inflation, and a small increase in the minimum wage. Still, "the income gap between rich and poor remains wide and the ratio of black to white median family incomes (.56) was as low in 1996 as in 1972."[15] In fact, in 2000, New York state had the largest gap between rich and poor in the nation.[16] This was, in part, attributable to the types of occupations fostered by the postindustrial economy: a two-tiered structure with high-wage, information-based, highly skilled jobs at one end and low-wage, service-sector, part-time, and shift-work jobs at the other end. Downsizing by private industry further reduced the pool of jobs available for people with little postsecondary education or with moderate skills—a loss exacerbated by simultaneous cuts in job training programs.

During the 1980s, New York City, while losing 33 percent of its manufacturing jobs, began to emerge from the economic recession driven by the growth of the financial sector. Compared with previous economic booms, however, this one did not narrow the gap between rich and poor. In fact, the poverty rate increased from 15 percent of all households in 1975 to 23 percent in 1987.[17] By 1998 in New York state, the poorest families earned an average of $10,770, down $1,970 from 1988.[18]

Race and gender have intersected with these socioeconomic transformations in new ways. The civil rights and feminist movements of the 1960s and 1970s increased the opportunities available to African Americans and women. There has been a significant expansion of the black middle class overall (for example, nationally, black-owned businesses experienced a 46 percent growth from 1987 to 1992).[19] The distribution of occupations of the black middle class, however, is disproportionately concentrated in the public sphere and the social service sector of the economy—precisely the areas most affected by government disinvestment. The fastest-growing sector of the economy, the financial sector, is still dominated by white men.

The economic changes wrought by the transition to a postindustrial global economy were accompanied by social and demographic changes visible in the city's housing stock. New York's financial crisis of the mid-1970s led to a widespread collapse of housing markets and a major decrease in the availability of affordable housing. Most severely affected in New York were portions of the South Bronx and Brooklyn and most of northern Manhattan (including Harlem). As the economy recovered, people who could take advantage of the newly developing occupational structure escalated the demand for upscale housing and renovated old houses, abandoned warehouses, and industrial lofts. In some areas, this gentrification transformed the character of neighborhoods and created enclaves of young professionals living in renovated buildings amid neighborhoods generally mired in continued poverty and decay.

In 1989, a narrow majority of voters coalesced across racial lines to elect Democrat David Dinkins, an African American, as mayor of the city. The Dinkins administration allocated relatively greater resources to improving conditions for poor and low-income New Yorkers. City officials extended social services (particularly health care) and expanded entrepreneurial opportunities—most notably set-aside contracts for businesses owned by women and people of color. In Harlem, these policies encouraged a mini-revitalization: a small growth in retail and commercial outlets and services, construction of new housing and renovation of abandoned buildings, and moderate improvements in health care for residents.

In 1993, Mayor Dinkins was not reelected. Republican Rudolph Giuliani was elected on a platform that pledged to cut the city's budget in the face of a projected deficit and improve what he called residents' "quality of life." Soon after he took office, Giuliani decreased the budget for public education by $1 billion, initiated efforts to privatize public hospitals and public housing, and increased the budget for the police force. The Giuliani administration approved a citywide campaign to arrest "petty criminals" (i.e., subway turnstile violators, unlicensed street vendors, and others engaged in the informal economy) and street-level drug dealers, and it encouraged random stop-and-frisk police tactics that resulted in searches of tens of thousands of people of color.

Those years marked the beginning of a significant transition in Harlem, characterized simultaneously by increased neglect by the city and state governments, as reflected in the budget cuts and subsequent cutbacks in services, and an increase in investment by the private sector, particularly in high-end housing and new retail establishments. Economic transformations were accompanied by political interventions designed to create an environment in which the "global city" could flourish.

DRUGS: A WAR OF PACIFICATION?

It is in this economic context—characterized by the decline of economic opportunities and withdrawal of support for social services—that the informal and illegal sectors expand. In some instances, the sale of illegal substances became an important source of income for families. By 1982, a crack epidemic hit Los Angeles, San Diego, and Houston, and, by 1985, it was a serious problem in New York City. In 1986, *Newsweek* declared crack "an authentic national crisis," a pivotal issue for the media to examine as thoroughly as it examined the Civil Rights Movement, the Vietnam War, and Watergate.[20]

This chapter cannot do justice to the issue of how and why traffic in illegal drugs emerged as a major sector of the informal economy in inner-city communities or to the relationship of these communities to the global markets in drugs, arms, hot money, and criminal cartels. It is clear, however, that as Harlem became the contested terrain upon which drug wars were fought, there were long-standing, though often unsuccessful, community attempts to confront this intrusion. Residents attempted to intervene by patrolling neighborhoods, blocks, and buildings, among other approaches. At one point in 1995, the researchers noted a large banner hung across St. Nicholas Avenue near 155th Street. It read: "Drug dealer and buyers, get out—this is a drug watch neighborhood." In one very organized building, run by one of the more progressive Housing Preservation Department programs, the young people formed a junior tenant association to try to keep drugs out of the building. They designed their own community room in the basement and initiated activities to help young people stay in school and avoid drugs.

Harlem residents vocally complained that their community had become a marketplace for the international traffic in drugs, resulting in increased violence. In comments to ethnographers, community residents noted the frequent presence of outsiders with license plates from Connecticut, New Jersey, and other areas, speculating that the occupants of the cars intended to buy illegal drugs. During the mid-1990s, the many abandoned and deteriorating buildings in Harlem provided an optimal setting for the crack trade, as dealers set up so-called crack houses—24-hour centers for crack consumption, sale, and distribution. It was not uncommon for drugs to be sold openly on the streets as well.

Residents often attributed the drug proliferation in Harlem to a deliberate hostility toward its residents by outside forces. In the early 1990s, the director of a drug treatment center stated:

> Drugs were placed in the community as a conscious, political decision. The influx of drugs in the '50s did not do the job, so the effort expanded and became more sinister. The government can do anything except solve the drug problem. Drugs are allowed to proliferate in certain communities. A national emergency would be declared if white communities were experiencing what is happening here.

Another resident stated more mildly: "Years ago, racism and capitalism allowed drugs to take hold, and now it's out of control." A nurse practitioner/midwife asserted that "for the first time, women had been enticed into the use of illegal drugs" by the tobacco companies that had recently begun to target women through advertising, suggesting that there was a direct relationship between the rise of cigarette smoking by women and their use of illegal drugs.

Analyses along these lines were widespread in the Harlem community and were not inconsistent with the discovery by several mainstream journalists and researchers that, beginning after World War II and continuing through the Vietnam War and other wars of insurgency, sectors of the U.S. government formed strategic alliances with drug dealers throughout the world to protect U.S. corporate interests and fight communism.[21] For several years, the impact of these relationships on inner-city populations has been cause for speculation in the African-American popular media.

To many, there appeared to be a government-orchestrated conspiracy to expand illegal drugs in inner-city communities, either through neglect or with the intended consequence of destabilizing social institutions and political insurgency. The latter view was reflected in the 1995 movie *Panther,* starring Mario Van Peebles. Set in the San Francisco Bay Area during the late 1960s, the movie sympathetically portrays the rise of the Black Panther Party for Self Defense, under the leadership of Huey P. Newton and Bobby Seale, as a response to the harassment of the black community by the police. The movie chronicles the neutralization of the Panthers' movement in part as a result of internal struggles often instigated by police informants and exacerbated by the sudden overabundance of heroin in the ghettos of Oakland. The influx of illegal drugs is portrayed as organized by the Federal Bureau of Investigation in collaboration with organized crime. The movie, released in spring 1995, sparked a wave of vitriolic attacks by political commentator David Horowitz and other conservative and mainstream media. It was then quickly removed from mass distribution in American movie theaters.

In 1996, some of these issues were aired in the mainstream media. *San Jose Mercury News* Pulitzer Prize–winning investigative reporter Gary Webb reported that money had been raised for the illegal U.S.–sponsored Contra war against Nicaragua by the sale of cocaine. Most important to the black community, he implicated the Central Intelligence Agency in the importation of powder cocaine and in protecting its transport to largely black South Central Los Angeles, from where it spread to other inner cities in the 1980s.[22] Webb's three-part series was published in August 1996 and also posted on the Internet with supporting evidence. The allegations set off a barrage of protests among many in government and policy circles, protests echoed by mainstream media outlets, many of whom questioned the *Mercury News*'s credibility. In response to the mounting pressure, Jerry Ceppos, executive editor of the *Mercury News,* published a partial retraction.[23] Company officials at the newspaper also transferred Webb from Sacramento to Cupertino, eventually leading to his resignation. In months to come, major newspapers such as the *New York Times* and the *Los Angeles Times* discounted Webb's version of the government-cocaine connection. Subsequently, Webb wrote a book, *Dark Alliance,* detailing his research and the events surrounding the publication of the articles.[24]

Congresswoman Maxine Waters, whose district includes South Central Los Angeles, investigated Webb's allegations and held congressional hearings. In a foreword to *Dark Alliance,* she concludes:

> The time I spent investigating the allegations of the "Dark Alliance" series led me to the undeniable conclusion that the CIA, DEA [Drug Enforcement Agency], DIA [Defense Intelligence Agency] and FBI knew about drug trafficking in South Central Los Angeles. They were either part of the trafficking or turned a blind eye to it, in an effort to fund the Contra war.[25]

These findings were not contradicted by CIA testimony.[26] In 1999, a class action lawsuit alleging that CIA-involved narcotics trading caused harm to African Americans and others was filed in the Central District Court of California. Of interest is that the plaintiffs in the suit fall into two categories: inner-city residents, "largely African-American [who] experienced particular economic/physical and/or emotional injuries," and others "who experienced injuries suffered by the community as a whole, such as: lack of safety, overburdened social services, loss of local businesses and damage to the tax base."[27]

The crack epidemic coincided with a marked increase in the presence of firearms. Geoffrey Canada, director of the Rheedlan Foundation, a youth organization serving Harlem, discussed his frustration and "horror" upon learning that guns were being specifically marketed to youth by the firearms industry, which had a campaign to "expand the market beyond white males with the new targets being women and youth. A niche marketing plan was undertaken similar to that employed by cigarette and alcohol manufacturers."[28] In Harlem, the initial increasing violence was related primarily to conflicts around control of markets. This developed a dialectic of its own as more and more youth, who were not involved in the drug trade, felt it necessary to carry arms to protect themselves. The deadly effects of violence are evident in the urban memorials—walls decorated with flowers and the names and pictures of young victims—that came to dot the Harlem landscape. A neighborhood resident told one of our ethnographers that the pink and white wreaths across the street from her apartment commemorated the recent deaths of young men "not even a quarter of a century old." In the course of the research, one could encounter 14-year-old children planning their own funerals. The owner of a greeting card shop on 125th Street, Harlem's main thoroughfare, informed us that card wholesalers had congratulated her on selling more sympathy cards than any other card shop in New York City.

But if the crack epidemic, which peaked between 1985 and 1995, had a devastating effect on Harlem, unfortunately, the government's supposed cure was worse than the disease.

THE WAR ON DRUGS

The War on Drugs forseeably and unnecessarily blighted the lives of hundreds of thousands of young disadvantaged black Americans and undermined decades of effort to improve the life chances of members of the urban, black underclass."[29]

There is a strange disconnect between the drug epidemic and the war on drugs. In 1973, when Nelson Rockefeller, then-governor of New York state, declared that every illegal drug dealer should be punished with mandatory minimum prison sentences, the state's prison population had fallen to its lowest level since 1950.[30] Later that year, the legislature enacted the Rockefeller Drug Laws, which imposed a mandatory minimum sentence of fifteen-years-to-life for anyone possessing four ounces, or selling two ounces, of an illegal substance. By 1983, the Organized Crime Drug Enforcement Task Force of New York state had slackened its surveillance of traffickers and distribution networks, turning its attention to criminalizing the users.[31] Cocaine had begun to decline. The appearance of crack cocaine two years later, however, and a few celebrity deaths from cocaine overdosing, generated a national panic about drugs, resulting in a federal war on drugs and the appointment of a national "drug czar."

The war on drugs has been the single most important factor in the increase of the prison population. In the 164 years between 1817 and 1981, New York constructed 33 state prisons. But in the 17 years between 1982 and 1999, the state built—and went about filling—another 38. In 1971, the state's prison population was about 12,500; by 1999 it was over 71,000.[32] By that time, African Americans and Latinos, who comprise 25 percent of the state population, represented 83 percent of state prisoners and 94 percent of all individuals convicted of drug offenses.[33] Nationally, African Americans, who are 13 percent of the U.S. population, are approximately half of the 1.2 million state and federal prisoners.[34] As University of Minnesota Law School professor and nationally known criminal law scholar Michael Tonry argues,

> [T]he rising levels of black incarceration did not just happen; they were the foreseeable effects of deliberate policies spearheaded by the [Ronald] Reagan and [George H. W.] Bush administrations and implemented by many states. . . . Blacks in particular are arrested and imprisoned for drug crimes in numbers far out of line with their proportions of the general population, of drug users, and of drug traffickers.[35]

Tonry further points out that "arrest percentages by race bear no relationship to drug use percentages."[36] Based on Justice Department data, a study by the Sentencing Project found that although African Americans use drugs at approximately the same rate as whites—and thus constitute only 13 percent of all drug users in a given month—they are 35 percent of all those arrested for drug possession, 55 percent of all those convicted of drug possession, and 74 percent of all those incarcerated for drug possession.[37] This discriminatory pattern is evident at every level of the criminal justice system.[38] In April 2000, using data compiled by the FBI, the Justice Department and six leading foundations issued a study documenting racial discrimination throughout the juvenile justice process. Among youth who are arrested and charged with a crime, African-American youth are six times more likely to be assigned to prison than white youth offenders; among youth charged with drug offenses, African Americans are forty-eight times more likely than whites to be sentenced to juvenile prison.[39]

Communities such as Harlem have borne the brunt of these devastating realities. Prison activists Eve Goldberg and Linda Evans refer to the war on drugs as a "preemptive strike. . . . What drugs don't damage (in terms of intact communities, the ability to take actions to organize) the war on drugs and mass imprisonment will surely destroy."[40] The focus on users and the failure to provide treatment mean that inner-city areas often are targeted for sweeps and searches. In New York City, with the Zero Tolerance campaign instituted by Police Commissioner William Bratton under Giuliani in 1994, quality-of-life offenses such as panhandling, loitering, squeegee operators, graffiti, and prostitution were actively prosecuted. In the 1990s, there was a dramatic decline in crime, but many investigators attribute this to neighborhood policing first instituted under the Dinkins administration[41] rather than the police tactics of the Giuliani regime.

Most serious were the rising rates of police brutality and police murders. Between 1992 and 1996, the number of citizen complaints filed with the city's Civilian Complaint Review Board rose more than 60 percent. In 1996, African Americans, who are 29 percent of New York City's population, filed 53 percent of the complaints.[42] Police actions focused on communities such as Harlem. Between 1993 and 1996, complaints about police brutality in Manhattan north of Fifty-Ninth Street rose 38 percent; south of that street, the number was 8 percent.[43] The well-publicized murder of unarmed immigrant Amadou Diallo was only one of several lethal police actions that year.

Harlem residents did their best to negotiate between the need for protection on one hand and skepticism about police intent, corruption, and fear of police harassment and brutality on the other. We attended several meetings of the local police precincts with community members where such concerns were expressed. For example, at one meeting, the residents berated the police for spending time arresting people suspected of petty gambling—playing dice and "the numbers," an underground lottery prevalent throughout the community and used particularly by older residents. When the police captain defended these types of arrests, one woman commented that "gambling don't kill nobody," and she asked why the police were not focusing on more serious crimes. At the same meeting, several people complained that the police were arbitrarily detaining and searching people on the streets. The officers defended this as a tactic to find illegal weapons, but community members remained skeptical.

As we carried out research in Harlem, we began to note how many of our informants, across socioeconomic strata, were involved in the criminal justice system, either directly or through a family member, partner, or close friend. Several of the workers we interviewed, middle- and low-income, had been imprisoned for narcotics possession[44] and were in work release programs or on parole. Some women study participants who had been in stable relationships at the beginning of the study period were, by the time we completed the research, visiting their partners and the fathers of their children in prison.

The effects of this level of incarceration on individuals, families, and the local community have been enormous, and the full consequences will not become evident for some time. For the incarcerated individuals, the experience is increasingly inhuman. A recent prison innovation known as "special housing units" (SHUs), which prisoners generally call "The Box," consists of cells in which prisoners are confined for 23 hours a day for months and years. The two-person units are electronically monitored structures about 14 feet long and 8.5 feet wide, with approximately 60 square feet of usable space. All meals are served to prisoners through a slot in the steel door, and all toilet facilities are located in the cell.

Although Amnesty International and U.S. human rights groups have widely condemned SHUs, claiming that such forms of imprisonment constitute torture under international law, several states including New York have adopted them.[45] One man from Harlem, imprisoned in upstate New York and confined to an SHU, wrote in 2001:

> My confinement is "the functional equivalent of a dungeon." There is minimal outside contact and no educational programs, no psychiatric counseling or other opportunities for rehabilitation. As an SHU prisoner, if I complain, or don't follow the rules, I get additional time in The Box. As inmates in SHU we are treated as if we are less than human and our punishment of being kept in SHU for years on end borders on vengeance. . . . Once correctional officers put us, mostly black and Hispanics, into SHU we are locked away so tightly, that we have no voice. "Out of sight, out of mind" is politically attractive they believe.[46]

When ex-prisoners are released, they face serious obstacles in their attempts to find work and to reconstruct relationships. Furthermore, the demands of parole often interfere with the ability to reconstitute a normal life, and parolees return to prison more often for technical violations of parole than for new crimes.[47]

The incarceration of large numbers of men affects not only the individuals, but entire families and communities. One of the starkest features of the war on drugs and the prison industrial complex is the shortage of what Harvard sociologist William Julius Wilson calls "marriageable males"[48] and the increase of women raising children alone. In 1999, 57 percent of households in central Harlem were headed by women.[49]

The situation of women raising children alone, without economic support from partners, is made even more difficult by the lack of jobs and the declining redistributive functions of the state. The investment in prisons comes at the cost of disinvestment in social programs and other institutions, as money is shifted away from programs directed toward human needs and into the corrections budget. In a particularly cynical example of this, in 1982, then–New York state governor Mario Cuomo decided to use the Urban Development Corporation, a public agency created in 1968 to build low-income housing, to build prisons. Criminologist Elliot Currie sums this up: "We were, in effect, using the prisons to contain a growing social crisis concentrated in the bottom quarter of our population. . . . The prison *became* our employment policy, our drug policy, our mental health policy, in the vacuum left by the absence of more constructive efforts."[50]

In a focus group, community residents discussed the effects of deterioration of social services such as education. One said:

> If you look at what's going on in the schools, you know, our children are not being taught the way I guess we think they should be taught. And kids are dropping out of school left and right. I'm hearing young men talk about survival more

than anything else. And when they talk about survival, their focus is not, "Let me go to school and try to survive." When they're talking about survival, they're talking about being able to live an everyday life . . . and not be shot at. . . . And they don't care about dying. They're not afraid. Because they don't have anything to live for. They don't think that they have anything to live for.

Community residents frequently expressed their concerns about the effects of high levels of incarceration on children. One of the participants in a male focus group held in May 1995 remarked:

. . . [T]these kids are hungry for positive males . . . and they won't come out and say it, but . . . when I was in [a] school, I had four or five [young] guys follow me around. . . . They are starving for something. . . .

Ever inventive, Harlem residents developed strategies to care for children. Two participants in a focus group on women who head households discussed such strategies:

My daughter goes to daycare while I'm at work. I have a girlfriend and her husband, they pay some of the sitter's fee. And I have a neighbor that I braid her hair and I braid her daughter's hair once a week, and when I need to like go some place for a couple of hours, I leave my daughter there. So that's how we trade off.

Another said:

I braid hair. I braid my mother's hair, my sister's hair and I just drop him [my son] off. He irons his own clothes, he know how to fix sandwiches. He gets his own clothes together. He knows how to go to the store, but I don't send him because ever since . . . I heard of the man snatching kids and stuff I got to look out for my child.

Though women-centered networks are central to the care of Harlem's mothers and children, men also use male-centered networks to help care for their relatives, partners, and children while they are incarcerated. For example, some of our research participants reported that friends of their incarcerated partner or relative periodically stopped by to give them money.

Perhaps most disturbing are the long-term consequences of the prison industrial complex. Human rights lawyer Dorothy E. Roberts points out that the incarceration of parents puts children at risk for foster care, and placement in foster care puts children at risk of being committed to juvenile detention, as evidenced by the higher percentage of children leaving foster care who end up in prison: "[T]he prison system supplies children to the child welfare system when it incarcerates their parents. . . . [T]he child welfare system supplies young adults to the prison system when it abandons them after languishing in foster care."[51]

THE PRISON INDUSTRIAL COMPLEX: BEYOND HARLEM

> *For what can be the future of incarceration, when the underlying motive is profit?*
> *Under a regime where more bodies equal more profits, prisons take one big step*
> *closer to their historical ancestor, the slave pen.*
>
> —Mumia Abu-Jamal[52]

African-American communities such as Harlem have been the major victims of the international trade in illicit drugs, the war on drugs, and the escalating incarceration that results, but these levels of incarceration support other sectors of the society.[53] University of California, Santa Cruz, philosophy professor and prison activist Angela Davis suggests that the term *prison industrial complex*[54] is useful because it "take[s] account of the structural similarities and profitability of business-government linkages in military production and public punishment."[55] The prison industrial complex clearly provides profit, employment, and increased political representation for special interests. This includes transfer payments to private corporations for building prisons and supplying prison services, the exploitation of prison labor, a development strategy for stagnant rural communities, disenfranchisement of black and Latino voters, and enhancement of conservative voter blocks.

Although still accounting for only 5 percent of prison beds, private, for-profit companies increasingly build and operate prisons. During the mid-1990s the largest among them, the Corrections Corporation of America, was one of the top five performing companies on the New York State Stock Exchange,[56] and it is now expanding beyond the borders of the United States to become the largest multinational prison corporation in the world. In addition, private companies, including AT&T, Sprint, and MCI, contract to supply food and phone services to inmates. The phone services cost approximately six times the average long-distance rate.[57]

The hard-won Thirteenth Amendment to the U.S. Constitution reads, "Neither slavery nor involuntary servitude, except as a punishment for crime whereof the party shall have been duly convicted, shall exist within the United States, or any place subject to their jurisdiction." Although the use of prison labor at this point is not extensive, it is growing. In addition to government agencies, private companies such as TWA, Chevron, Starbucks, IBM, Motorola, Honeywell, Boeing, and Microsoft[58] use prison labor. Alabama, Florida, and Arizona have reinstituted the infamous chain gang. A 27 March 2002 article in the *New York Times* reported on the expanding use of state prison inmates by small towns for jobs once held by public employees, such as "tending cemeteries, cleaning courthouse restrooms, moving furniture, renovating municipal buildings and even running errands for the police."[59] As a labor force that works for a fraction of the minimum wage, does not (and cannot) demand benefits, and cannot organize, prison labor is ideal for maximizing profits. The issue is complicated by the fact that work is often a privilege for prisoners who otherwise lack access to income and the opportunity to leave their prison cells.

But the roles that prisons and prison labor increasingly fill in the consumer economy outweigh the importance of prison labor.[60] In this respect, benefits from the growth of prisons have not been limited to private corporations. One consequence of flexible accumulation, so integral to the current phase of global capitalism, has been the loss of jobs and livelihood in many rural areas of the United States. In New York state, as traditional industries such as mining, logging, farming, and manufacturing have declined, the prison boom has become a source of jobs in construction, corrections for local vendors, and a source of tax revenue. So much so that investigative journalist Eric Schlosser[61] notes that, in New York state, "the prison boom started transforming the economy of an entire region." Goldberg and Evans refer to prisons as "an essential component of the U.S. economy" and a "leading rural growth industry."[62]

The dialectic of benefit and deficit regarding prisons has a clear racial and political character. In 48 states, incarcerated individuals cannot vote, and in 10 states (excluding New York) ex-felons lose their right to vote after they are released. As of 1998, 13 percent of black adult males have lost the right to vote, and in some states that number is as high as 40 percent.[63] Ironically, for the purposes of political representation and other social benefits determined by Census tabulations, prisoners are counted alongside other residents in the counties where their prisons are located. In other words, communities with prisons reap state-determined benefits from their increased numbers, but the very prisoners being counted often are barred from voting when released. Between 1973 and 2000, 70 percent of New York state inmates came from New York City and its suburbs, but, of the 29 correctional facilities authorized by Governor Cuomo, 28 were built in upstate districts—largely Republican, white, conservative areas. Currently 93 percent of state penal institutions are located in Republican senate districts.[64] In fact, in some of these districts it is the addition of the incarcerated to an otherwise declining population that swells the population to the number needed to create a legislative district.[65] The prison industrial complex disenfranchises African Americans and Latinos while enhancing white Republican districts.

Though people of color are disproportionately victims of the prison industrial complex, and clearly some groups have benefited from the growth of prisons, in the long run, the effects of mass incarceration extend beyond the populations and communities primarily affected. Prison labor can replace or negatively impact workers who are not imprisoned by controlling and depressing their wages. Public money spent on the corrections system is shifted away from social services that have the potential to enhance the lives of all residents. For example, in New York state, there has been a nearly equal trade-off between money spent on public education and the construction and maintenance of prisons. Between 1988 and 1998, New York state decreased its support for public higher education (the State University of New York and City University of New York systems) by $615 million. In the same period, the Department of Correctional Services received a budget increase of $761 million.[66]

Furthermore, once order is achieved by force rather than consent, the rights of all citizens are curtailed. Warfare metaphors such as *war on crime* and *war on drugs* rationalize abuses and the suspension of rights for those who are demonized as the enemy. And they pave the way for the militarization of civil society—the suspension of constitutional safeguards protecting civil liberties and constitutional rights of all citizens. This rationale was clearly reflected in the USA-Patriot Act of 2002, which greatly expanded the category of crimes defined as *terrorism* by federal legislation and significantly increased the penalties for them.

Perhaps the larger and most important issue is the way in which the prison industrial complex serves to impede, for the majority population, a critical analysis of society. As American University philosopher and ethicist Jeffrey Reiman notes, society's treatment of crime "nudges middle Americans toward a *conservative* defense of . . . large disparities of wealth, power and opportunity." By fomenting mainstream discontent toward the poor, it obscures how the middle class is injured by "acts of the affluent," deflecting a "progressive demand for . . . an equitable distribution of wealth and power."[67] Race, racism, and racialization[68] play a central role in "undermining our ability to create a popular critical discourse to contest" the prison industrial complex.[69] Particularly insidious is the racialization of protest, and the blurring of the boundaries between dissent and disorder. For example, New York City residents peacefully demonstrating against budget cuts or police brutality or for peace have found themselves penned in by steel barricades. Even more ominous, in April 2003, the chair of Oregon's state senate judiciary committee, Republican John Minnis, wrote and submitted legislation identifying a terrorist as a person who "plans or participates in an act that is intended, by at least one of its participants, to disrupt" business, transportation, schools, government, or free assembly, and proposes automatic sentences of 25 years to life for the crime of terrorism.[70]

HARLEM FOUND

The war on drugs and the growth of the prison industrial complex have stifled critical discourse in the larger society and dampened the ability of local communities such as Harlem to continue and extend their protest stances. In addition to the disappearance—as a result of addiction, illness, death, murder, and incarceration—of untold numbers of young people who are often the vanguard of protest movements, the drug epidemic and the war on drugs severely disrupted the social relationships and networks that form the basis of social movements. Throughout the turmoil associated with post-industrial capitalism, the withdrawal of state support for human services and intensified policing in Harlem, grassroots organizations and movements for empowerment have continued—but their ability to organize effectively has been seriously weakened.

Over the past several years, in fits and starts, Harlem has been undergoing a gentrification process in which the black middle class is playing an active, though ambivalent, role.[71] Today, largely through the federal Empowerment Zone strategy of private-public investment, major corporate concerns including Chase Bank,

Modell's Sporting Goods, Magic Johnson Theatres, Old Navy, HMV Records, The Disney Store, Starbucks, The Body Shop, and New York Sport Club have set up shop on 125th Street. Harlem has become a major tourist destination. As is true in other areas of the city, such as the Lower East Side, it is almost as if the way for gentrification was paved by the prior devastation and excessive policing.

The rapidity with which these changes have occurred can be seen in what we might call "Two Tales of a City." In September 1994, a three-part series appeared on the front page of the *New York Times* describing one city block in central Harlem that coincidentally was one of our field sites. Entitled "Another America," it portrayed the residents of the block as "a world apart" from mainstream America, caught up in the hopelessness, dependency, and destitution of "the underclass."[72] It is important to note here that the residents of the block publicly protested the article, citing the many egregious inaccuracies and distortions. A year later, another series of articles in the *Times* portrayed the changes on the same block—including rehabilitation of 17 of the block's 35 buildings largely through privatization—as "extraordinary."[73]

Shortly after these articles were published, we returned to the block to locate some of the women who had participated in our research, but were told they had been forced to move. Although gentrification benefits some residents and may bring about the long-awaited cultural renaissance of "Harlem Lost," these processes do not replace political mobilization. Indeed, by displacing working-class and low-income residents, these transformations might well impede the development of political struggle. How extensively working-class Harlemites will be displaced depends partly on how well they can reclaim the grassroots protests of years past. At present, there are three overlapping levels of activity that are worthy of note.

On the level of individual empowerment, there is the rise of what we might term *revitalization movements*—a process of cultural and religious change—observed by anthropologists in various parts of the world. These often, but not always, involve charismatic leaders, whether Christian or Muslim. In Harlem, this direction was reflected in the extensive activities inspired by the Million Marches—the Million Man March, the Million Woman March, the Million Youth March. In these movements, individual empowerment clearly occurs within an institutional context. In Harlem, some of the major churches have been especially active in social services and real estate development, and President George W. Bush's faith-based initiatives may strengthen this trend. Although such strategies may be important for individual recovery and sustenance, they are not likely to effectively address the ravages of globalization discussed above.

On the household level, livelihood struggles through personal networks and individual actions are a major form of ensuring survival. People construct and utilize support systems, primarily women-centered, for garnering and redistributing material and social resources. For example, women spend an extraordinary amount of time attempting to retain shelter. In 1996, I carried out a participant observation in Housing Court, located in downtown Manhattan, where many Harlem women, in their struggle to retain decent shelter for themselves and their families, represent themselves in lawsuits against their landlords. These lone women often are left to their own devices to confront the landlords' *lawyers*. Over one-third of the respondents to our survey had taken their landlords to court, and two-thirds of those had represented themselves without the benefit of a lawyer. Among respondents to the survey, 39 percent participated in tenant's organizations and 33 percent in block associations. These household-level struggles shade into movements for community empowerment as people link individual problems in schools and housing to larger issues of the neglect of education and housing in Harlem.

On a community level, there are various actions sparked by specific social contradictions or events. With globalized capitalism, the rise of neoliberalism, and the decline of the welfare state, community organizations that once may have taken a more transformative approach now are forced to concern themselves with ensuring survival. Myriad community organizations focus on housing, health, education, and police brutality. Large-scale mobilizations may be centered on specific issues such as individual acts of police brutality, hospital closings, and school privatization efforts. Recent demonstrations against gentrification and displacement have drawn hundreds of protesters.

Although these activities may be directed at specific events and issues, they contain the seeds for broader action and wider analysis. Perhaps most encouraging were the events around the Giuliani administration's attempt to privatize five of the worst-performing public schools by turning over their management to the Edison Project, a private, for-profit company. In each of the five schools, all of which were in minority neighborhoods, the parents voted against this proposal. The most decisive defeat was in the Central Harlem school, where a significant majority of parents courageously voted against what may have been their short-term interests in order to preserve their rights as residents and citizens to quality public education. Their actions demonstrated recognition of the necessity to restructure democratic options and to demand the full rights of citizenship—in the face of neoliberalism and the ideology of unfettered markets.

Though overarching themes around human and citizens' rights, unifying the sites of resistance, and mobilizing networks of interlocking organizations do not yet exist to the extent they were present during the civil rights era, there are important signs that the movements of today could quickly incorporate broader concerns. In the six months between the end of 2000 and spring 2001, there were at least three major gatherings in Harlem that attracted hundreds of people who strategized around the slogan "Education Not Incarceration." Residents were consciously linking the struggle to defend public education with that against mass incarceration and mandatory sentencing. In addition, the East Coast Critical Resistance Conference held at Columbia University in 2001 attracted 3,000 young people, many of whom described the prison industrial complex as their generation's Vietnam. Since 2001, there have been annual rallies in Albany, the capital of New York, to protest the draconian Rockefeller drug laws: "Drop the Rock" is one popular slogan. These have likewise attracted thousands of young people, including Harlem residents. In August 2001, Harlem residents participated in the U.N. World Conference Against

Racism in Durban, South Africa. Speaking with delegates from all over the world, they and others organized workshops, presented petitions, and distributed information underscoring the global impact of the war on drugs and the prison industrial complex on people of color, urging the U.N. to include these issues in the conference concerns.

As a result of such actions, a critical discussion of the prison industrial complex has begun. Last year, in an op-ed for the *New York Times*, former New York state senator John Dunne wrote regarding the Rockefeller laws:

> I regret that as chairman of the State Senate Committee on Crime and Corrections, I was one of the original sponsors of these laws when they were proposed by Gov. Nelson Rockefeller. . . . I particularly regret the disproportionate impact the enforcement of these laws has had on minority communities. . . . I regret my own lack of foresight three decades ago, but surely there can be no excuse for not understanding the grim consequences of the drug laws now.[74]

Even in the era of globalization, politics are ultimately local. As Cabral reminds us in *Return to the Source,* by finding a way back, not to the past, but to the future of their *own* history, people reclaim the capacity to make history for themselves.[75] One cannot predict that, as Harlem goes, so go the possibilities for successful resistance to global inequality. Nevertheless, Harlem residents are fully aware that they have made history before. They expect to do so again.

NOTES

1. The Harlem Birthright Project, carried out between 1993 and 1996, explored the social context of health and reproduction. Methodological approaches included participation observation, focus groups, longitudinal case studies, and a random sample survey. A discussion of the methodology can be found in Leith Mullings et al., "Qualitative Methodologies and Community Participation in Examining Reproductive Experiences: The Harlem Birthright Project," *Maternal and Child Health Journal* 5, no. 2 (2001): 85–93. The findings on health are reported in a Final Report on Ethnographic Findings to the Center of Disease Control, 1996, and in Leith Mullings and Alaka Wali, *Stress and Resilience: The Social Context of Reproduction in Central Harlem* (New York: Kluwer Academic/Plenum Publishers, 2001).

2. Mindy Fullilove, Lesley Green, and Robert Fullilove, "Building Momentum: An Ethnographic Study of Inner-City Redevelopment," *American Journal of Public Health* 89, no. 6 (1999): 842.

3. Ibid., 842.

4. Saskia Sassen, *The Global City: New York, London, Tokyo* (Princeton, N.J.: Princeton University Press, 1991), Manuel Castells, *The Rise of the Network Society* (Oxford: Blackwell Publishers, 1996).

5. Marc Mauer, *Race to Incarcerate* (New York: The New Press, 1999).

6. Ruth Wilson Gilmore, "Globalization and U.S. Prison Growth: From Military Keynesianism to Post-Keynesian Militarism," *Race & Class* 40 (1998–99): 171–188.

7. Sassen, *Global City.*

8. Jeremy Brecher, Tim Costello, and Brendan Smith, *Globalization from Below: The Power of Solidarity* (Boston: South End Press, 2000), 8.

9. Jason Ziedenberg and Vincent Schiraldi, *The Punishing Decade: Prison and Jail Estimates at the Millennium* (Washington, D.C.: The Justice Policy Institute, 1999), 2.

10. Youngstown is situated in Trumbull and Mahoning counties. The number of steelworkers employed in "Primary Metal Industries" and "Fabricated Metal Industries" in Trumbull and Mahoning counties totaled 60,275 steelworkers in 1956 and 15,822 steelworkers in 1997. United States Census Bureau: County Business Patterns (Washington, D.C.: Office of Domestic Commerce, 1956 and 1997).

11. David Phinney, "Prisons Brought Jobs—and Murder to Youngstown," ABC, http://abcnews.go.com/sections/us/prison/prison_ youngstown.html. I would like to thank Joe Sims for pointing out this relationship.

12. This section adapted from Mullings and Wali, *Stress and Resilience.*

13. Cheryl Lynn Greenberg, *Or Does It Explode: Black Harlem in the Great Depression* (New York: Oxford University Press, 1991); Nathan I. Huggins, *Voices from the Harlem Renaissance* (New York: Oxford University Press, 1995); James Weldon Johnson, *Black Manhattan,* 1930 (New York: DaCapo Press, 1990); John L. Jackson Jr., *Harlem World: Doing Race and Class in Contemporary Black America* (Chicago: University of Chicago Press, 2001); Mullings and Wali, *Stress and Resilience;* Monique M. Taylor, *Harlem: Between Heaven and Hell* (Minneapolis: University of Minnesota Press, 2002).

14. John Mollenkopf and Manuel Castells, eds., *Dual City: Restructuring New York* (New York: Russell Sage, 1991); Sassen, *Global City;* N. Smith, *The New Urban Frontier: Gentrification and the Revanchist City* (New York: Routledge, 1997).

15. Cecilia A. Conrad and Malinda Lindquist, "Prosperity and Inequality on the Rise," *Focus* 26, no. 4 (May 1998): 11; jointcenter.org/focus/chron98.htm.

16. CBS, "Rich Get Richer, Poor Stagnate," CBS Online, http://www.cbsnews .com/stories/2000/01/18/national/main150545.shtml, 18 January 2000.

17. Mollenkopf and Castells, *Dual City,* 8.

18. CBS, "Rich Get Richer."

19. U.S. Census Bureau, 1997 Surveys of Minority- and Women-Owned Business Enterprises, 1992 Economic Census: Survey of Minority-Owned Business Enterprises, 5. http://www.census.gov/cssd/mwb/minorityp.html.

20. Richard M. Smith, "The Plague Among Us," *Newsweek,* 16 June 1986, 15.

21. Alexander Cockburn and Jeffrey St. Clair, *Whiteout: The CIA Drugs and the Press* (New York: Verso Press, 1998).

22. Gary Webb, "'Crack' Plague's Roots Are in Nicaraguan War," *San Jose Mercury News,* 18–20 August 1996, 1.

23. Jerry Ceppos, Editorial, *San Jose Mercury News,* 11 May 1997; http://www. cia.gov/cia/publications/cocaine/report/intro.html.

24. Gary Webb, *Dark Alliance: The CIA, the Contras, and the Crack Cocaine Explosion* (New York: Seven Stories Press, 1998).

25. Maxine Waters, foreword to Webb, *Dark Alliance,* ix–x.

26. Frederick P. Hitz, "Synopsis," in *CIA Inspector General's Investigation of Alleged Ties Between CIA, the Contras and Drug Trafficking,* unpublished paper, www.cia.gov, 1998. In testimony to a congressional committee, Hitz, inspector general of the CIA from 1990 to 1998, reported (p. 9), ". . . [D]uring the 1980s, CIA was aware of drug trafficking alle-

gations or information involving one Contra organization, 30 Contra-related individuals, and 21 other individuals supporting the Contra program. . . . [T]here were instances when CIA continued contact with Contra-related individuals after becoming aware of drug trafficking information or allegations." In defense of the CIA, he noted (p.19) that the agency is not legally required "to report narcotics allegations regarding non-employees." He added, "In the end, the objective of unseating the Sandinistas obscured the importance of properly dealing with potentially serious allegations against those with whom the CIA was necessarily working."

27. *Warren et al. v. CIA et al.*, Case No. 99-02603 U.S. District Court/Central District of California, 15 May 1999.

28. Geoffrey Canada, *Fish, Stick, Knife, Gun: A Personal History of Violence in America* (Boston: Beacon Press, 1995), 123. See also Mercer L. Sullivan and Barbara Miller, "Adolescent Violence, State Processes, and the Local Context of Moral Panic," in *States and Illegal Practices*, ed. Josiah C. Heyman (Oxford: Berg Publishers, 1999), 263. Sullivan and Miller note that despite the "moral panic" over youth violence, the proportion of young people engaged in violence has not changed, but what has changed is the levels of serious injury or death, a major cause of which is the possession and use of firearms. For a discussion of the increase in firearms, see Jeffrey Reiman, *The Rich Get Richer and the Poor Get Prison: Ideology, Class and Criminal Justice* (Boston: Allyn and Bacon, 1998), 31–32.

29. Michael Tonry, *Malign Neglect: Race, Crime, and Punishment in America* (New York: Oxford University Press, 1995), 82.

30. Eric Schlosser, "The Prison Industrial Complex," *Atlantic Monthly,* December 1998, 6; http://www.theatlantic.com/issues/98dec/prisons.htm.

31. Christian Parenti, *Lockdown America: Police and Prisons in the Age of Crisis* (New York: Verso, 1999), 47.

32. City Project, *Following the Dollars: Where New York State Spends Its Prison Moneys* (New York: City Project, 2000), 1.

33. Ibid., 6–7.

34. Marc Mauer, Cathy Potler, and Richard Wolf, *Gender and Justice: Women, Drugs, and Sentencing Policy* (Washington, D.C.: The Sentencing Project, 1999); www.sentenceproject.org.

35. Tonry, *Malign Neglect*, 4.

36. Ibid., 108.

37. Marc Mauer, *Intended and Unintended Consequences: State Racial Disparities in Imprisonment* (Washington, D.C.: The Sentencing Project, 1997); www.sentenceproject.org.

38. Jerome G. Miller, *Search and Destroy: African-American Males in the Criminal Justice System* (Cambridge: Cambridge University Press, 1996).

39. Youth Law Center, "And Justice for Some," in *Building Blocks for Youth*, Washington, D.C.; www.buildingblocksforyouth.org/justiceforsome.

40. Eve Goldberg and Linda Evans, *The Prison Industrial Complex and the Global Economy* (Berkeley: The Prison Activist Resource Center, 2000), 4; http://www.prisonactivist.org/crisis.

41. Mauer, *Race to Incarcerate*, 95.

42. Ibid., 98.

43. Ibid., 46.

44. See also Ansley Hamid, "Drug Patterns of Opportunity in the Inner-City: The Case of the Middle Aged, Middle Income Cocaine Smokers," in *Drugs, Crime, and Social*

Isolation, ed. A.V. Harrell and G. E. Peterson (Washington, D.C.: Urban Institute Press, 1992), 209–238.

45. Manning Marable, "Structural Racism and American Democracy," in *Souls: A Critical Journal of Black Politics, Culture, and Society* 3, no. 1 (2001): 6–24.

46. This letter was received by Manning Marable, then director of the Institute for Research in African-American Studies at Columbia University. He receives three to five such letters a month. For the protection of the prisoner, I have removed identifiers.

47. Joan Moore, "Bearing the Burden: How Incarceration Weakens Inner-City Communities," *1996 Oklahoma Criminal Justice Research Consortium Journal:* 5. http://www.doc.state.ok.us/DOCS/OCJRC/Ocjrc96/Ocjrc43.htm. Jagna Sharff, *King Kong on Fourth Street* (Boulder, Colo.: Westview Press, 1998).

48. William J. Wilson, *The Truly Disadvantaged: The Inner City, the Underclass, and Public Policy* (Chicago: University of Chicago Press, 1987). See also Tonry, who notes that among whites the number of employed men per 100 women has been stable or increasing for every age group. Among nonwhites, on the other hand, the number has been declining since 1960 for every age group, with sharpest declines among those under 25. Tonry, *Malign Neglect*, 6.

49. Of these households, female householders with no other household members comprised 23.0 percent; female householders with children under 18 only, 11.0 percent; female householders with no children under 18, 11.2 percent; female householders with other adults and children under 18, 11.8 percent (New York City Housing Vacancy Survey, *Central Harlem: Selected Characteristics by Year,* 1999).

50. Elliot Currie, *Crime and Punishment in America* (New York: Metropolitan Books, 1998), 32–33.

51. Dorothy E. Roberts, "Criminal Justice and Black Families: The Collateral Damage of Over-Enforcement," *U. C. Davis Law Review* 34, no. 929 (2001): 1005–1028.

52. Mumia Abu-Jamal, "Privatizing Pain," *Corporate Watch: The Watchdog on the Web,* 26 August 1999, http://www.corpwatch.org/feature/prisons/mumia.html.

53. This phenomenon is similar to the ways the informal sphere supports and maintains the formal sphere and the ways the existence of an economic underclass supports the ceiling on wages for the working class.

54. Paulette Thomas compares the prison situation to the military industrial complex: "[T]he defense establishment are cashing in too, sensing a logical new line of business to help them offset military cutbacks." Paulette Thomas, "Making Crime Pay: The Cold War of the '90s," *Wall Street Journal,* 12 May 1994, A1.

55. Angela Davis, "Masked Racism: Reflections on the Prison Industrial Complex," *Color Lines* 1, no. 3 (1998): 1.

56. Eric Bates, "Private Prisons: Over the Next 5 Years Analysts Expect the Private Share of the Prison 'Market' to More Than Double," *The Nation,* 4 May 1998, 2.

57. Goldberg and Evans, *Prison Industrial Complex.* http://www.prisonactivist.org/crisis/evansgoldberg.html.

58. See Parenti and various Internet sources for an expanded list of companies involved in building and administering prisons. Christian Parenti, "The Prison Industrial Complex: Crisis and Control," *Corporate Watch: The Watchdog on the Web,* http://www.corpwatch.org/feature/prisons/c-parenti.html, 1999.

59. Peter T. Kilborn, "Towns with Odd Jobs Galore Turn to Inmates," *New York Times,* 27 March 2002, A1.

60. See, for example, Gill Gardner, "Prisons and Capitalism: The New York State Prison Experience," in *Prison Crisis: Critical Readings*, ed. Edward P. Sbarbaro and Robert L. Keller (New York: Harrow and Heston, 1995), 16–33.

61. Eric Schlosser, "The Prison Industrial Complex," *Atlantic Monthly*, December 1998. http://www.theatlantic.com/issues/98dec/prisons.htm.

62. Goldberg and Evans, *Prison Industrial Complex*, 1–2. http://www.prisonactivist.org/crisis/evansgoldberg.html.

63. See James Fellner and Marc Mauer, *Losing the Vote: The Impact of Felony Disenfranchisment Laws in the United States*, Human Rights Watch Publications (October 1998), http://www.hrw.org/reports98/vote/.

64. City Project, *Following the Dollars: Where New York State Spends Its Prison Moneys* (New York: City Project, 2000), 1–7.

65. Peter Wagner, *Importing Constituents: Prisoners and Political Clout in New York* (Prison Policy Initiative Report, 22 April 2002), 6–7. http://www.prisonpolicy.org./importing/importing/shtml.

66. Robert Gangi, Vincent Shiraldi, and Jason Ziedenberg, *New York State of Mind?: Higher Education vs. Prison Funding in the Empire State, 1988–1998* (Washington, D.C.: The Justice Policy Institute, 1998). http://www.louisville.edu/journal/workplace/issue6/JPI.html.

67. Reiman, *Rich Get Richer*, 152.

68. Michael Omi and Howard Winant (*Racial Formation in the United States: From the 1960s to the 1980s* [New York: Routledge & Kegan Paul, 1986], 64) define *racialization* as a historically specific ideological process involving the extension of racial meaning to a previously unracialized category. Although crime and punishment have not been unmarked by notions of race, the events of the last decades solidified the relationship between criminal justice and race. Also see Tonry (*Malign Neglect*, 11), who reminds us that the conscious manipulation of racial imagery and crime has been national Republican policy since the campaign of Richard M. Nixon. A particularly egregious example was Lee Atwater's conscious manipulation of Willie Horton during the 1988 presidential election. Tonry provides an analysis of the success of this strategy in polarizing the population along racial lines, ensuring a Republican victory and prompting Lee Atwater's deathbed apology.

69. Davis, "Masked Racism," 1–5.

70. Lee Douglas, "Bill in Oregon Seeks to Jail Protestors as Terrorists," Reuters and *Boston Globe*, 4 April 2003, A6. Boston Globe online. http://www.commondreams.org/headlines/03/0404-05.htm.

71. See Neil Smith, *The New Urban Frontier: Gentrification and the Revanchist City* (New York: Routledge, 1997); Monique Taylor, "Gentrification in Harlem: Community, Culture and the Urban Redevelopment of the Black Ghetto," in *Research in Race and Ethnic Relations*, ed. R. M. Dennis (Greenwich: JAI Press Inc., 1994), 147–188.

72. Felicia Lee, "Another America," *New York Times*, 8 September 1994, A1.

73. Amy Waldman, "Beneath New Surface, an Undertow," *New York Times*, 19 February 2001, A1.

74. John R. Dunne, "When Will New York Correct Its Mistake?" *New York Times*, 10 May 2002, A35.

75. Amilcar Cabral, *Return to the Source* (New York: African Information Service, 1973).

John L. Jackson Jr.
Toward an Ethnography of
a Quotation-Marked-Off Place

I would argue that it makes some sense that in a time of elusive, yet emergent, cosmopolitanized identities, of sweatshop- and shantytown-spawning multinational corporations, of entry-level service-sector-only employment opportunities in Big City, U.S.A., an anthropologist attempting to write about the here-and-now of post–civil rights urban America might find it fruitful to begin, of all places, at that quintessential locale of global sameness called McDonald's.

That mythical space where identical memorized greetings ("Welcome to McDonald's, may I take your order, please?"—a capitalist command in the guise of a question) are offered up time and again by uniformed, minimum-wage-earning, secondary–labor market workers, each with that exact same perky yet disingenuous smile etched on an otherwise disgusted face. McDonald's, where the mass-produced logic of late capitalism duplicates itself, with ever-so-minor modifications, on nearly every strip mall or highway or street corner or college campus across the country. And most directly, the place where this particular story begins. On that fine line of evidential limbo separating the illuminatingly "ethnographic" from the merely "anecdotal." A line hardly different, conceptually speaking, from the one I was waiting in at a McDonald's restaurant on 125th Street when I first met Dexter, a young black male customer, arguing with Pam, the young woman trying patiently (but unsuccessfully) to take his order, please.

Dexter, dressed in white-and-black fatigues, held in the palm of his right hand a colorful coupon, in exchange for which he was supposed to receive a $.99 Big Mac in every part of the city (so read the fine print) "except the borough of Manhattan," where a Big Mac—with this same coupon—would cost him $1.39 instead. Well, hearing Pam repeat that important distinction, Dexter was outraged that he was being forced to pay $1.39 for his Big Mac sandwich. With only a dollar and a dime in his outstretched left hand (the $.10 was "for tax," he declared several times), Dexter made his case: "This is Harlem," he said, "not Manhattan! If they meant Harlem, if they meant Harlem, they should have written Harlem! Harlem is not Manhattan! So, I'm paying $1.10 for my Big Mac." Once Dexter finished his spiel and clunked the money on the counter, other customers lined up in front of cash registers all around him (along with the brown-and-red costumed McDonald's staff at work on the other side of the long silver counter) mostly chuckled, giggled, and shook their heads incredulously at his argument, an argument that, in its unabridged iteration, took over ten full minutes to play out. But Dexter didn't mind their smirks; he was adamant, determined—even though his half-smiling face and exaggeratedly playful body language clearly, if only indirectly, indicated he knew full well that Harlem was smack dab in the borough of a Manhattan Island where Big Macs (as a function of, say, higher-priced rental space and property taxes) simply cost $.40 more than in any other part of the city. On this particular day, however, Dexter would not and did not leave that crowded McDonald's restaurant until Pam, poised and patient behind her cash register, reluctantly snatched his dollar (and his dime) and handed him a Big Mac sandwich to go—a paper-bag-covered burger he was munching on greedily as I jogged out to catch up with his much heftier strides in the fast-food restaurant's wet and slippery parking lot.

Dexter's analysis served as the central frame and organizing principle through and around which I would toil for close to a year and a half. I was doing an ethnography of social solidarity in Harlem, but Dexter had hit on the complicatedly symbolic boundaries that I had to engage—before anything else. A Harlem in Manhattan, but then again not quite bound there. A Harlem thought (by both those who reside there and many more who wouldn't dare) to be a kind of world apart; a living, breathing space whose semiotic significances inform the boundaries between the supposedly black and white worlds of New York City. A place where the objective conditions of people's existence and their subjective responses to those conditions illustrate the elaborate relationships between structural marginalization, cultures of poverty, and individual agency in a postindustrial context rife with all manner of lucrative underground economies and devastatingly "savage" inequalities.

Hearing Dexter argue with Pam about the distinctly separate location of Harlem vis-à-vis Manhattan, of the impossibility of reducing Harlem to its geographical location, exposed my own facile assumptions about what—ethnographically speaking—made up Harlem and its borders.

According to the New York State Visitor and Convention Bureau, Harlem has the highest name recognition of any neighborhood in the entire state of New York, and for my argument, this tiny bit of trivia is quite substantial: the most famous neighborhood in the nation's most famous city is Harlem! It is known the world over. But for those who live there, who live with (and even off) that notoriety, what does Harlem mean? What and where is Harlem, really? One of my first ethnographic tasks, as I saw it, was to address just that: how field sites like Harlem, with reified names that far precede and exceed the stretches of land they designate, operate beyond easily demarcated and circumscribed ways; how places like Harlem are discursively and subjectively mobilized toward various ends; how a volitional rendering of place impacts and informs people's racialized identities and class(ed) positionalities.

It is possible to fall back on Benedict Anderson's notion of an imagined community as a means of vouchsafing access to arguments about the mystical constructedness of place and space and their impact on people's social identities. In Anderson, specific relations between literacy and industrialization helped spawn the discursive and extradiscursive foundations upon which contemporary nationalisms (and nation-state solidarities) were first made to stand. With the advent of mass-produced, print-culture capitalism, citizens became better able to imagine a connection to relatively unknown others across the daunting obstacles of both space and time. Andersonian assessments of created communities can speak most loudly and directly to a Harlem that not only uses various discursive modes to shore up the social and spatial parameters of its imagined home but also (and more important, I think) a Harlem possessing the uncanny ability to resituate itself in another time and space entirely. In Dexter's case, this relocation carries Harlem out of the borough of Manhattan altogether and into an area that he claims "is not Manhattan." Any ethnographic work conducted in Harlem, on the hard-core issues of the day (deindustrialization and its links to urban unemployment, institutionalized racism, welfare-to-workfare reforms, transgenerational cultural pathologies, and so forth), must take Dexter's cartography seriously.

This idea of "Harlem," a Harlem snuggled neatly within quotation marks, operates as a kind of place apart, functions as a geographic and iconographic space talked about with an almost mythical distinction, with an air of extraspecial signification. And an ethnographer working here must consciously and carefully wade through the mounds of excess meaning connected to a space imagined from within and without, by those who would use its name to either (1) index a sense of belonging or (2) scream at a black threat seeping down from uptown. Before writing a single word about the linkages between class stratification and racial identification in Harlem,[1] I first had to peel back the multilayered understandings of place and its connection to identity. Indeed, these understandings cloud and obstruct any attempt at writing race, class, and culture in a wonderfully mediated field site like Harlem, a Harlem where preconceived and continually reconfigured notions of "the real" simultaneously and contradictorily obscure yet illuminate what is most consequential about the place itself.

One of the first roads of inquiry into a quotation-marked-off Harlem has to do with Harlemites and their varying and prescient articulations of this place's taken-for-grantedness—that is, those articulations they choose to share with an anthropologist who asks. Danielle, a thirty-seven-year-old elementary school teacher who lives on a tree-lined street off Adam Clayton Powell/Seventh Avenue, just three blocks from where she teaches third graders, says that the "Harlem" she knows is nothing if not in a league all by itself:

Danielle: Harlem is special. It is a special place. I've been here fourteen years, and I know that I am lucky to be here. Because there is only one Harlem in the whole entire world. There is just one. So I'm lucky to be here, you know, to be making a way here, because it's easy not to make it. And there are plenty of people in Harlem who know that, you know, who live that. Who aren't as lucky as me. To be here and happy with their lives.

Asia, twenty-two, a third-generation Harlemite who lives on 104th and Lexington and works with Pam at the McDonald's restaurant where I first heard Dexter extract "Harlem" from Manhattan Island, offers a slightly different spin on Harlem's particularity:

Asia: Harlem to me is like the real nitty-gritty. Like hard and real and dangerous. I lived in Brooklyn before, for like two years, and my oldest sister lives in

Long Island with her boyfriend, but none of those spots is like Harlem. They just don't feel like Harlem.

John: What does Harlem feel like?

Asia: I don't know, but no other spot feels like it. I could close my eyes and you could take me anywhere and if you bring me back to Harlem, I would say, I'm back home. 'Cuz no place sounds and smells like here. Or is real and, I don't know, nitty-gritty, and rough and real like it. I can't really explain it. But I know I'm right.

Both Danielle's "special place" Harlem, the only one of its kind "in the whole entire world," and Asia's almost tactile, yet inexplicable "nitty-gritty" Harlem, a neighborhood that no other place quite "feels like," are significantly recurring strands of a common argument running through contemporary discussions about Harlem's embraceable distinctiveness. There are, in fact, many people (Harlem residents or not) with a highly vested interest in what this peculiarly "special" place looks like and reads like, how it is to be seen and represented.

People have a stake in the space's definition; they defend and police its meaning with a protective vengeance. Refracted through, say, social hierarchies, this place called "Harlem," this Harlem idea, can work as an important template for thinking not just about one's connections to place but also about one's relationships with others.

Cynthia, twenty-eight, a part-time security guard for an office building on 125th and Frederick Douglass/Eighth Avenue, was born in Virginia and has lived in New York City for the last twelve years:

Cynthia: When I see Harlem, you know, when I look at it, I don't see any welfare or crime or drugs. None of that nonsense. This is the Mecca. I mean, I don't see beggars and homeless people on the street. Or begging by the bank. When I see Harlem, I see, like, a perfect picture. It is just beautiful. That is Harlem.

Cynthia uses this "beautiful" version of Harlem to justify her criticism of what the social science literature would call "the underclass"—a group that is, according to Cynthia, tarnishing the shiny legacy of this "Mecca" of black America and, therefore, must be denied access (at least symbolically) to its most hallowed name. Cynthia's no-"nonsense" Harlem is asserted to the exclusion of stereotypical representations of urban America, stereotypes that foreground poverty, criminality, and drug use as emblematic and even constitutive of the place itself. Contrary to these many negative images and depictions of urban America, Cynthia's Harlem is a place "where you can just have fun and feel free. No racism and things like that. No. Just good lives. Like what it used to be."

Carl, thirty-one, more securely in the so-called black middle class than Cynthia, is a finance lawyer who has lived in Harlem for some fifteen years now. He grew up with "dirt-poor, broke parents" who moved here from the Caribbean in the 1950s, before he "was close to being born." Waving to a waitress as he whips out a credit card to cover our fried-chicken lunch at a new soul-food spot in midtown Manhattan, Carl offers a picture of "Harlem" that locates its validity and reality even more specifically in a past that, as Cynthia put it, "used to be":

Carl: Harlem is history. And I don't know a lot about all of it. I'm just starting to really know it. I've been focusing on my stuff, you know. I've seen some tours.
The grange. Not many, but that is Harlem. It is history, the history of an entire people. Sure there are bad things, but Harlem isn't just that. Troublemakers here are
people who don't know what Harlem should be like. That's all they've seen, you
know, the nastiness, the poverty. They haven't seen better and don't know no better.
Maybe if they knew more of that history, you know, they would try to fly right.

Ms. Joseph, fifty-five, a Seattle native who made collegiate pit stops in Southern California and Omaha, Nebraska, before settling into a Harlem brownstone
with her architect husband some twenty years ago, considers Harlem "the center of
the world."

John: Is it a bad place to live?

Ms. Joseph: It ain't bad at all. I mean, no worse than any place else, right?
The crime and stuff is not Harlem. If anything, that is gonna make Harlem not be
Harlem anymore. You know?

John: No. What do you mean?

Ms. Joseph: The more crime and violence and drugs . . . means we got less
and less of Harlem every day. Every time somebody gets killed or something,
Harlem is dying, too. That kind of thing is not Harlem. It's just killing Harlem—
little by little, bit by bit. It takes away from Harlem, like as if one day we'll wake up
and there won't be any Harlem anymore and people would be looking around asking, "What happened? what happened to it?" It would just be gone.

Ms. Joseph's Harlem, to be Harlem at all, presumes the exclusion of violent
death and crime. It is a Harlem that flies in the face of vicious murders and drugs,
the kinds of actions that don't just kill people, Ms. Joseph argues, but kill place as
well.

Ms. Joseph: I just get tired of all of it. Like when, when, when Jeffrey's sister—my husband, Jeffrey—got held up right around the corner, that wasn't more
than a month ago. I don't usually have no problems here. I see the people doing
what they doing, but I usually just go about my business. I go right past them like
they weren't there. Because for me, they are not there. I don't see them. They just
like ghosts: you know, the drug dealers and, and, and things. These people aren't
part of my community. They aren't from here.

John: Where are they from, do you think?

Ms. Joseph: I mean, maybe from the Bronx, or some other state, but even if
not, they still ain't from Harlem. Even if they from here, if they live here. Maybe
you could say they from upper Manhattan, or from 155th Street, but that don't
mean they from Harlem. That just mean they live on 155th Street. Not Harlem.
Not if they doing that kind of stuff. Harlem don't want them.

Ms. Joseph, too, has neighbors, like Cynthia's "beggars at the banks," who
may share the same physical surroundings but who are excluded from a valid social
place. Socioeconomic status functions as one of the criteria used to sift through the
social landscape and separate the legal/legitimate form of social citizenship from the
illegal/illegitimate. Just as Ms. Joseph and Cynthia can look down the socioeco-

nomic ladder at undesirables who don't belong, some "Harlemites" look up the social ladder to challenge their upper-class race mates' rights to call "Harlem" home.

"Harlem is what I know," says Sheila, twenty-seven, unemployed, and trying to get into a GED preparation program. We are walking and talking on Frederick Douglass Boulevard as she points out places she's lived in, or been to, or heard tall tales about:

Sheila: The people I know, the people who have to work and struggle to make it every day, we here and we real. Real life. There are people who want to come in here and don't have a clue, but they come 'cause it's cheap rents and stuff, and they want to be here and act like they better than any of us, but they really need to be someplace else. They not from here, not belonging here. They the ones that think they can do whatever they want up here, that they can do whatever they want and won't nobody do nothing. But that ain't true. And most of them gonna learn, too.

For Sheila, as for Cynthia and Ms. Joseph, there is vast space separating residency from really belonging. David, Sheila's twenty-year-old on-again, off-again boyfriend, talks emphatically about where Harlem "is really at":

David: Harlem is from the left side to the right side of Manhattan. Uptown. Period. Good and bad. Take it or leave it. Harlem is like a ghetto like everywhere else, where black people live and work and play and die. People kill each other and they go to church. And they, sometimes, some of them work, and some of them stay home and do drugs and wait for a welfare check and don't do nothing else except watch TV and movies. All of that is what is going on here every day. That's what's happening.

To hear David tell it, listening to him capture the series of divergent experiences during any average, ordinary day in a Harlem "where black people live," a "ghetto like anywhere else" (no more or less special and specific than any other neighborhood), we get a representation of Harlem's value as a sociological idea that becomes more and more complex and compelling. David's "Harlem" shows the ease with which a globally recognized Harlem-concept (that most famous neighborhood in all the United States) slides effortlessly back and forth between (1) black "Mecca" hyperspecificity and (2) an easy collapsibility into a stereotypical representation of contemporary black urbanity. Ms. Joseph's explicit exclusion of a 155th Street resident/drug dealer/crack addict from her pristine Harlem and Sheila's dismissal of the Buppie without-"a-clue" pragmatists who think they belong but really don't both speak to the subtle kinds of ways in which any community and its residents, not just those in Harlem, apply the litmus test of desirability to define locals/residents who are supposedly jeopardizing, in different ways, the sanctity and solidity of the collective social space.

All the understandings of this place called "Harlem" (and there are many more besides the few offered here) lead to one central point: that the importance with which "Harlem" is imbued does not negate its status as a stand-in for black America. Harlem can be both "special" and "ordinary" at one and the same time. But what does this mean for an anthropologist trying to make sense of the place itself? What should the ethnographic gaze behold when it casts its eyes upon a quotation-marked-off place like Harlem?

To answer this I want to backtrack a bit, to a genesis story of sorts. The early strands of the discipline's lineage are debatable, but in one origin story of anthropology's early years, there was an armchair. And in it sat the ethnologist, a person who supplied an analytical eye (or two) to the raw materials of others' observations. It was someone else who did the ethnographic dirty work (say, a traveling merchant with a trusty journal or a proselytizing missionary, diary in hand), and the masterful ethnologist pulled these sordid and motivated tales together into some universally explanatory schema. But this armchair brand of anthropological inquiry gave way as the discipline flung itself full swing into an institutional and accredited distinction between its methodologically honed scientific empiricism born of firsthand participant-observation versus what was considered the shoddy, grossly unscientific and relatively inadequate writings of nonanthropologists. The anthropologist's expertise came from a scientifically trained vision that could pierce through the many details of a seemingly incomprehensible culture and provide a scientific formula through which to make sense of it all—be it evolutionism, structural-functionalism, transmissionism, structuralism, cultural materialism, and so on.

The primitive's village became the site wherein rested the anthropologist's authority. A long visit to that "Promised land" as Roger Sanjek put it, coupled with a mastery of the native language, meant a scientifically holistic view of an entire people. But there is really so much more behind the scenes.

As many have argued, this perfect, scientistic picture of cultural critique elides as much as it illuminates. First of all, the "field" wasn't as isolated, discrete, and monolithic as (explicitly or implicitly) assumed. In fact, this reified field site, the empirical ground upon which the discipline stood, was even said to be a kind of fabricated region, a made-up space—and in more ways than one. A fabrication that resonates most directly with Dexter's attempts at dislodging Harlem from its Manhattan moorings. (Or even better, with Columbia University's pamphleteering two-step that maneuvers its thousands of dollars and tons of material in and out of "Harlem" into the sunnier site of "Morningside Heights"—except, of course, when recruiting students of color to its "home in Harlem.")[2]

The anthropologist can be said to create boundaries where there are none, to force and forge distinctions between here and there in an effort to pin down and circumscribe the space within which fieldwork will take place. In order to see "the other" better, the ethnographer has traditionally had to condense and downscale the amount that was to be seen. And that downsizing has often meant an overly rigid gerrymandering of social space. But for the anthropologist to see this in person, of course, was not the ultimate point, and the published monograph distilled the anthropological gaze into a narrative form that, according to Jim Clifford, solidified the ethnographer's unassailable authority while, as Johannes Fabian puts it, freezing the other into a perpetual past distinct from the Western world's much more modern present. And so, in that overly surefooted discursive field, a moment—a meta-ethnographic moment—opened up that would allow, using the tools of literary criticism, for ethnographic texts to be "looked at" as well as "looked through" to some overly reified and supposedly transparent other.

Critiques of the ethnography as a text abound. What ethnographers see and what they think they get are both fair game for critical engagement. Ethnographies, it is argued, are not just pure and unadulterated reflections of what has been observed but rather are crafted and constructed worlds that stand in for the jumbled reality from which often indecipherable field notes are alchemized into realist narrative accounts. And if that was true in the past for Bronislaw Malinowski's Western Pacific or Margaret Mead's Samoa (or, more self-consciously so, for Zora Neale Hurston's Eatonville), how much more so is it now? And even still, in a place like Harlem, "that Mecca of black America," the New World center of the fabled African diaspora, "the queen of all black belts." And how much more so in the here-and-now of the late twentieth century and its newfangled transnational trade agreements, international immigration shifts, and First World deindustrialization?

The head-in-the-sand, cultural-village anthropologist of yesteryear was a fiction (Clifford calls it an "allegory") created to, among other things, justify the discipline itself. Anthropologists must look up, out, and beyond what easy borders we are quick to create, beyond the arbitrary parameters we translate into and project onto our anthropological field sites. We must open up the ethnographic view to include international connections that link places through the flow of never-ending and mobile peoples and capital. And many theorists are arguing for just such an opening of the field site—for looking past our assumed, hard-and-fast boundaries. Jelan Paige asks for an ethnographic engagement with black people and cultures that takes mass media stereotyping seriously as obstructions to any ethnographic understanding of African Americans. Faye Harrison lobbies for an opening up of ethnographic inquiries and field sites into an analysis of how television, radio, and motion picture images inform and cocreate our perceptions of the world. Arjun Appadurrai pleads for a transnationalized, transculturally savvy understanding of societies that links the locally specific to its global context. Where they all agree is in the understanding that field sites must be opened up into other sites (even "multi-sited"). But how far open? And where does the opening end? Where does it close? Should we open the anthropological gaze into just other nearby neighborhoods? Into contiguous nations? Into a black Atlantic paradigm that recognizes the analytical bankruptcy of the nation-state's borders as valid cutoff points for social and cultural analyses? Even into Wallersteinian-influenced world-systems theories that ask for center-periphery models of the entire planet's players on the global stage? A Derridean invocation of signification means opening "the field" up into textuality and intertextuality, all of which could be interpreted with Geertzian-thick descriptions galore. I would say yes to these recommendations. But I want to go further, especially in a place like "Harlem." I want to argue for an opening up of the field site (as politically irresponsible as it might sound at first blush) into the ethnographic land of make-believe, into the ethnographic imaginary, where fact and fiction, true and false, chip away at the walls of demarcation that separate their shadowing and mutually constitutive worlds. An opening up into the ideas we hold and are taught to have about places like Harlem, places whose boundaries are magically malleable and whose people are stereotypically assumed.

Chuck, twenty-five, a part-time student at a community college in the middle of 125th Street, says that "Harlem is like a person you got to take the time to know. When you know Harlem, she will treat you right. And if you don't take the time to, she won't. She'll lie to you and you'll be stupid enough to believe it. 'Cause people do everyday. They think Harlem is this but it ain't. It's that. And they don't get it. And won't believe you when you tell them they wrong." Chuck's decidedly gendered Harlem is a place that, first and foremost, misrepresents itself. It is a Harlem that might be said to make itself up as it goes along. A Harlem able to fictionalize itself and keep its pursuers off its hidden tale.

And it is, of course, the artisans who are the first ones there in that make-believe, made-up land of a camouflaged, quotation-marked-off "Harlem" that "is not Manhattan." The artists. Particularly, the actors: the professional pretenders. The ones trained to recognize the inevitability of that constitutive intermingling of truth with falsehood when it comes to location and identity. As such, an ethnography of the cinematic is in order. Ethnographicus cinematicus. In this case, movie star Denzel Washington's carefully measured advice to rapper-turned-actor Will Smith—and the approach Denzel thinks Will should take to his role in the film *Six Degrees of Separation* (1993), where Smith plays Paul Poitier, a black, homosexual, Walter Benjamin–quoting con artist who lies his way into the home of a wealthy art dealer on Manhattan's Upper West Side by falsely claiming to be Sidney Poitier's son. Pretending to be the child of a black film icon, Paul is indeed Harlem's prodigal, if still unclaimed, offspring. In fact, Harlem, as a very character in the film, is right there (off-camera, of course) portentously in the background all the while—playing itself and providing the distant, aerial-shot backdrop to this tale of class-based posing, passing, and performativity. The separation point, the borderline, is an Upper West Side apartment of gullibility (an apartment off Central Park no less, that last landscaped border post protecting a posh middle-classness of double Kandinskys and English hand-blasted shoes from the presumed anarchy raging uptown).

But *Six Degrees* is based on only one real story made into a stage play and then adapted to the silver screen. The other real story, the other real-life story, has Denzel Washington, another icon, the next Sidney Poitier (some say), who's played many a Harlemite on-screen, passing on some acting wisdom to Will Smith: an arguably homophobic admonition that Smith not, as called for in the script, kiss a white, male actor on-screen; that Will feign the two kisses (one set in a Boston studio apartment, the other in a stagecoach riding through that very same Central Park borderland).[3] Denzel maintains that Will should obstruct the kiss from view, fake it (by turning his back away from the screen/the audience and pretending that he and his white, male costar's lips touch on the other side of the back of his head). Smith must conceal the act, Denzel argues, because the black audience wouldn't be able to read that action as just made up, wouldn't see the kiss as acting, couldn't distinguish between the "real" and the "make-believe" of the thing. Denzel's rather patronizing assessment of black people's mass-media decoding capabilities is a provocative and interesting (however condescending) model, I believe, for looking at an ethnographic field site, especially when that site is a place like Harlem, a place where the line between fiction and nonfiction, as people talk about the neighborhood they know, is fuzzy indeed. Maybe Denzel's point helps to unpack the truths and fictions of Cynthia's beggarless and Ms. Joseph's drug-dealerless Harlem, U.S.A. What if, Denzel's homophobia and provincialism notwithstanding, people in that black audience he talks about can't tell the difference between fact and fiction because they recognize the often equivalent effects of the shadow and its act? That is, they know a world where stereotyped unrealities have an impact on people's lives that disproves any easy argument for the power of some supposed real over the unreal. Indeed, the unreal assumptions about places like Harlem (assumptions that impact the decisions, say, of big businesses about whether to move there or that inform where people choose to eat, shop, and so on) have been powerfully determining factors in the very real lives of the people who reside there.

Moreover, in a place like Harlem, "What is 'real'" (what is Harlem, really?) becomes a tricky question. Margaret, thirty-three, goes to school at City College, fifteen minutes south, by foot, from where she lives with her mother, three sisters, a brother, and two nephews in a two-bedroom apartment. She offers yet another take on Harlem, a take very real in its unreality:

Margaret: Harlem is no poverty, no immigrants, no trash on streets. Harlem is not any of that. That is not what I think about. I don't. I don't at all. Harlem is nothing bad. Nothing bad like that. And nobody can't tell me any different. Nobody.

What people think about Harlem and its boundaries, whether true or not (even a trash-free Harlem xenophobically and unrealistically peopled, as Margaret asserts, without immigrants and the poor), has true enough consequences, especially when depictions of blacks, in or out of Harlem, carry the stereotypes of many generations on their backs.[4] As Dexter put it: "They come up here, they don't know us. Think they know Harlem; they think they do, but they don't. They could never know us. They just think they know us from what they been taught from TV and shit for all these years. Nothing but lies."

NOTES

1. This chapter was written for and presented at Columbia University's Institute for Research in African-American Studies during the spring of 1998 as part of a semester-long series on the Harlem community. This is an excerpt from a longer piece entitled "White Harlem: How to Do Ethnography with Your Eyes Closed."

2. I know from my own recruitment that Columbia University is strategic about when and where it mobilizes the quotation-marked-off notion of "Harlem" in its recruitment and admissions literature.

3. Will Smith has retold this story about Denzel Washington's advice many times, both in TV interviews and in print.

4. Ethnicity falls out of this equation, especially as ethnic differences are strained against the power of black overdeterminism in Harlem.

Part II. Old Constructs, New Contexts

4. *The New Racial Domain*

GEORGE DEREK MUSGROVE

"Good at the Game of Tricknology": Proposition 209 and the Struggle for the Historical Memory of the Civil Rights Movement

Good at the game of tricknology, but I have knowledge of myself, you're not foolin' me.

—Grand Puba[1]

Glenn Custred, a professor of anthropology at CalState Hayward, was by all measures a neoconservative academic. He subscribed to the idea of America as a melting pot in which all peoples can assimilate and find individual success. Thus, when multiculturalism appeared on Hayward's campus in the mid-1970s, Custred received it skeptically. Over the years, as multiculturalists moved into decisionmaking positions at Hayward and began to call for affirmative action policies and diversified curriculums, Custred's skepticism turned to open hostility. On many occasions, he could be found trying to organize his department against multicultural academic and policy reforms. Feeling outnumbered and outgunned at Hayward, Custred sought the company of other academics who still valued the Western canon on which he had been reared and on which he depended for his intellectual identity. In the late 1980s, this search led him to the National Association of Scholars, an organization of academics determined to resist the onslaught of multiculturalism.

Thomas Wood, a mid-1970s graduate of the Department of Philosophy at the University of California, Berkeley, had had no luck finding a full-time teaching position by 1984. The market for Ph.D.s was glutted in Wood's specialty, the philosophy of religion. That year, however, a position opened up at San Francisco State University. Because of his difficulty in finding a job, Wood's vita was not particularly impressive. He nonetheless believed that he was an excellent candidate for the position and sent in an application. After an interview which Wood acknowledges did not go well, he was turned down. He would later find out that an African-American woman received the post. Having no proof that he had been discriminated against, Wood decided that he had been turned down because he was a white male. "It didn't count that I was the most qualified," he grumbled.[2] By 1991, Wood had yet to find a full-time teaching position. He was exasperated, fully convinced that his bad luck had been the fault of African Americans, Chicanos, women, and the misguided affirmative action policies that had catapulted them into college teaching positions ahead of better-qualified white males like himself. After reading a *Newsweek* article highlighting a National Association of Scholars member's opposition to affirmative action at the University of Wisconsin, Wood contacted the California Association of Scholars, which Custred had helped to form just a few years earlier. By the end of 1991, the two had begun to share their ideas about multiculturalism and affirmative action.

Within a year, Custred and Wood produced the California Civil Rights Initiative (CCRI), a proposed state constitutional amendment that, if passed, would outlaw the use of "race, sex, color, ethnicity, or national origin" in California public life. In short, CCRI would end affirmative action. They presented CCRI to the state legislature for a vote in 1994. Amidst vigorous opposition, the bill died in the House. Disappointed but undaunted, Custred and Wood determined to "take it [CCRI] to the people" in the form of a statewide referendum in 1996. Immediately, they began collecting the thousands of signatures necessary to place their initiative on the ballot.[3]

In 1995, they received some unexpected help from Governor Pete Wilson (R). In order to secure reelection in 1994, Wilson had exploited the anti-immigrant feelings mobilized by Proposition 187, a draconian anti-immigrant initiative on the 1994 ballot. Wilson planned to run for president and believed the issue of affirmative action would enable him to distinguish himself from the pack in the 1996 Republican primaries.[4] Soon Custred and Wood, whose signature-gathering campaign had been floundering, were assisted by paid signature gatherers funded through the California Republican Party. Simultaneously, Wilson embarked on a campaign to end affirmative action at the University of California, seeking the media attention that such a controversial move might provide.[5] Here he found an eager ally in the U.C. Regent Ward Connerly.

Connerly, a black, conservative, multimillionaire housing consultant, was a longtime associate of the governor. He first entered California politics when Wilson appointed him as liaison to the legislature for the Department of Housing and Community Development. Wilson later appointed Connerly to the California Assembly's State Housing Committee, a position that helped him to amass the connections and insider knowledge needed to outperform his competition in the housing consulting business. Although affirmative action had been critical to Connerly's business success—Connerly had registered his housing consulting business as "minority" in order to obtain minority set-asides in state contracting—he was an outspoken opponent of the program.[6] In 1993, Wilson appointed Connerly to the Board of Regents. Not long after assuming his position on the Board, Connerly began to challenge the university system's use of affirmative action in its admissions processes. He charged that the University of California employed a system of unfair quotas that discriminated against Asian Americans and whites by privileging African Americans and Chicanos.[7] Coordinating his efforts with Wilson, Connerly introduced a proposal to end affirmative action in the U.C. system. The proposal passed the board by a vote of 14 to 10 in July 1995.

After Connerly's initial victory with the Board of Regents, Custred and Wood courted him for the top position in the campaign to pass the CCRI—now Proposition 209. Connerly accepted their offer, becoming the primary spokesman for "Yes on Proposition 209." Thus, the lives of two neoconservative academics and a black conservative converged in Wilson's unsuccessful bid for the Republican presidential nomination.

Despite Wilson's resounding defeat in the primaries and Democrat Bill Clinton's general election triumph in California, Proposition 209 passed by a margin of 54 to 46 percent, effectively ending affirmative action in state employment, education, and contracting. How did this happen? How did the most diverse state in the Union come to pass a constitutional amendment to end a program designed specifically to combat discrimination on the basis of race, ethnicity, gender, and disability in public life? The answers to these questions lie, to a large extent, in the anti–affirmative action movement's ability to manipulate Californians' historical memory of the civil rights movement.

> *History is important to this nation and its vision for the future.*
> —Ward Connerly[8]

> *The past is a ghost that can destroy our future. It is dangerous to dwell upon it. To focus on America's mistakes is to disregard its virtues.*
> —Ward Connerly[9]

During and after the November 1996 referendum on Prop. 209, a substantial segment of California voters were confused about what the measure stood for. Did it outlaw affirmative action? Was it pro– or anti–civil rights? Did it promote fairness, meritocracy, and equality of opportunity? This confusion was not the result of a lack of public debate. Affirmative action and Prop. 209 received heavy coverage by all news media in California and the nation in the run-up to the election. However, after two years of public debate over affirmative action and the ballot initiative itself, a substantial segment of the California electorate failed to understand the significance of Prop. 209. Lydia Chavez, author of *The Color Bind,* a detailed account of the campaign to pass Prop. 209, notes that in March 1995, "many voters failed to understand that in voting for CCRI they would be ending affirmative action."

In fact, many of these voters believed that "CCRI was a civil rights initiative." Nearly a year later in June 1996, polls showed that a majority of African Americans and Chicanos in Los Angeles, confused by the wording of the initiative, believed that it would strengthen civil rights protections and were prepared to support it. On election day, *Los Angeles Times* exit polls showed that a majority of voters favored affirmative action. These same voters had just voted to make Prop. 209 state law.[10]

The key to the anti–affirmative action movement's victory in California was its strategic use of a liberal civil rights discourse to appropriate the historical memory of the civil rights movement. To borrow a phrase made popular by many Afrocentric hip-hop artists, the anti–affirmative action movement relied on "tricknology" to pass Prop. 209. Supporters of the initiative employed three distinct tactics. First, the anti–affirmative action movement redefined affirmative action as quotas and preferences. Simultaneously, they appropriated the historical memory of the civil rights movement through liberal civil rights discourse—best represented by the phrases "color-blind society" and "equality of opportunity"—and the image of Martin Luther King Jr. Last, the anti–affirmative action movement camouflaged its own roots among white neoconservatives and the lily-white Republican Party. Although the vast majority of Californians who voted for Prop. 209 understood that it would do away with affirmative action, somewhere between 5 and 10 percent of those who supported the measure believed the opposite. It is this crucial group of confused voters who constituted the initiative's margin of victory.

Although the object of this study is political discourse, it would be unwise to ignore one of the more important factors in any political campaign—money. From the very beginning, the anti–affirmative action movement had more money than its opponents. During the campaign, Yes to Prop. 209, the largest anti–affirmative action organization, spent more than twice as much money as the largest pro–affirmative action group, Campaign to Defeat Prop. 209. Anti–affirmative action groups also received substantial support from the California Republican Party. The state Democratic Party, on the other hand, offered nothing comparable to the other side. Anti–affirmative action forces used their substantial financial edge to shape the public debate over Prop 209.[11] They defined the issues early and often.

> *They [the New Right] think they can change the name of "affirmative action" to "preferential treatment."*
>
> —Louis Harris[12]

On November 5, 1996, voters did not reject the use of affirmative action in California public life. They voted down the state's right to "discriminate against, or grant preferential treatment to, any individual or group on the basis of race, sex, color, ethnicity, or national origin." The text of Prop. 209 made absolutely no mention of affirmative action, yet based on the common legal definition of the program, the initiative outlawed it.[13] The same is true of the official ballot pamphlet for Prop. 209. The argument in support of the initiative, written by California Attorney General Dan Lungren (R), makes no mention of affirmative action. In it,

Lungren paints Prop. 209 as an attack on a system of preferences inherently unfair to whites and Asian Americans. He also alleges that affirmative action programs cost the taxpayers of California "$125 million annually"—a claim for which he provides no proof.[14]

Several polls show that language was the decisive factor in California voters' decision to end affirmative action. In two surveys, pollster Louis Harris discovered that if Californians had voted on the language of Prop. 209 in the fall of 1996, without outside debate or influence, they would have supported it by a margin of 78 to 16 percent. When those same voters were asked if they would favor the measure if it "outlaw[ed] all affirmative action measures for women and minorities," however, its approval rating dropped to 31 percent. A majority of 55 percent stated that they would oppose the measure. Polls conducted by the *Los Angeles Times* found similar results.[15] Harris argues that this enormous swing was the product of many Americans' belief that affirmative action and preferences were distinctly different things. In an autumn 1996 Harris poll, a majority of white Americans defined "preferential treatment" as "giving an unqualified black a job over a qualified white man." When the same group was asked what affirmative action meant to them, nearly 70 percent answered that it was "a program to help women and minorities who have not had an equal chance to have an equal opportunity in education or in a job."[16] Affirmative action, as far as Harris's respondents were concerned, was a remedial program designed to right contemporary and historic discrimination. Preferences, on the other hand, were perceived as being quite nearly the opposite.

Wood and Custred were aware of these numbers long before Harris published his findings. They had studied public opinion polls in the early 1990s and discovered a widespread tolerance for affirmative action among California whites. "Preferences," on the other hand, were roundly condemned by all Californians, regardless of race or sex. So the framers of the CCRI strategically manufactured a distinction between "preferences" and an imaginary form of affirmative action that did not take race, sex, color, ethnicity, or national origin into consideration.

The anti–affirmative action movement's attempt to manufacture this fictive distinction is illustrated in two lawsuits filed by Yes to Prop. 209 in July 1996. The official pamphlet for the ballot initiative contained arguments for and against Prop. 209. Although Wood and Custred had worked with Attorney General Lungren to write the argument for the initiative, they had no control over the counterargument contained in the pamphlet. Two sections of the pamphlet criticized the measure: "Rebuttal to Argument in Favor of Proposition 209" and "Argument Against Proposition 209." In both sections, the authors argued that Prop. 209 would end affirmative action in California public life. The first suit, filed in Sacramento County Superior Court, alleged that the author of "Rebuttal to Argument in Favor of Proposition 209" was misleading voters by "perpetuat[ing] the myth that Proposition 209 will ban all affirmative action programs." Lawyers for Yes on Prop. 209 went on to argue that "affirmative action" was not even a proper term to use in describing the initiative, "since the measure does not target all such programs and since it affects some unrelated areas." The second suit, filed against the authors of the "Argument Against Proposition 209," states that the authors were "intentionally misleading" when they alleged that Prop. 209 would prohibit some "nondiscriminatory and nonpreferential programs." Just what affirmative action programs the initiative would leave intact, Lawyers for Yes on Prop. 209 could not say. The presiding judge found the claims to be baseless and dismissed them.[17]

> *The American Civil Rights Institute [a national organization dedicated to ending affirmative action in America] should be regarded as the most accurate reflection of a man who looked forward to the day when you [Martin Luther King III], as one of his "four little children," would be judged not by the color of your skin, but by the content of your character.*
>
> —Ward Connerly[18]

> *I am merely acting on the basis of what he [Martin Luther King Jr.] said and giving literal meaning to his words.*
>
> —Ward Connerly[19]

Since the late 1960s, neoconservative activists and writers have used liberal civil rights discourse to attack affirmative action. They claim the sole purpose of the civil rights movement was the establishment of color-blind individual rights—an idea they often symbolize with the famous line from Martin Luther King Jr.'s "I Have a Dream" speech, "I have a dream, that one day my four little children will live in a world where they are judged not by the color of their skin but by the content of their character." Using this line of thought, they argue that race-conscious affirmative action programs have subverted the goals of the civil rights movement by creating a system of black privilege that is just as morally repugnant as the white supremacy that it has allegedly replaced.[20]

Taking the lead from these writers, the supporters of Prop. 209 linked themselves to the civil rights movement through sound bites of the last few lines of King's "I Have a Dream" speech. These activists seldom strayed beyond these few lines, for the goals of the civil rights movement were not limited to securing simple "equality of opportunity," and King repeatedly voiced his support for remedial racial policies like affirmative action throughout his career. No one in the anti–affirmative action camp was more energetic in using this one line to make a link between the anti–affirmative action movement and the civil rights movement than Ward Connerly.

In the quote at the beginning of this passage, Connerly makes a direct connection between the civil rights movement and the anti–affirmative action movement. He makes this connection through Martin Luther King Jr.'s "words": "the content of their character." During the battle over Prop. 209, Connerly exhibited an almost fanatical attachment to this single line of King's most famous speech. In an April 1996 speech to the U.S. Senate Committee on the Judiciary, Connerly claimed that his understanding of civil rights as "individual rights guaranteed by the Constitution against encroachment by the government" was the product of his exposure to Martin Luther King Jr.'s "voice . . . oratorical skills . . . [and] speeches."

Although Connerly implies a multiplicity of public statements by King, he would only reference the last paragraph of King's "I Have a Dream" speech.

Connerly's attempts to appropriate King's historical memory through this one phrase can best be seen in a commercial made by the California Republican Party in the later days of the campaign. In the spot, which was never aired due to disputes with the King family, King's famous musings on a world in which his children would be judged "not by the color of their skin, but by the content of their character" provide a ringing endorsement of Prop. 209. In the background an image of King standing before the Lincoln Memorial floats across the screen. Almost immediately, civil rights organizations and the King family voiced their protests. In the furor over the announcement of the ad, Connerly defended the anti–affirmative action movement's right to use King's image in its campaign: "I think it is outrageous for Jesse Jackson and all of those from the past, from the 1960s, to somehow suggest that it is inappropriate for any of us to use Dr. King's memory. . . . He belongs to all of us." By relegating Jackson and other civil rights activists to the "past," Connerly created a rhetorical space for himself as the 'present' of the civil rights movement. Individuals like Jackson, and even the King family, Connerly argued, had strayed from the true path of the civil rights movement. Despite these wayward civil rights activist protestations, Connerly defiantly proclaimed, he would continue to hold aloft the color-blind vision of the late Dr. King. "They [contemporary civil rights leaders] say 'How dare you,'" Connerly stated following the furor over the ad. "Well how dare them. . . . The words that he said are right. And from now on I am going to be using them with far more frequency."[21]

Connerly and the anti–affirmative action movement's elaborate reconceptualization of the civil rights movement could only be sustained if they were able to conceal Prop. 209's widespread support among the recognized opponents of black civil rights. Their efforts to accomplish this are most evident in Yes to Prop. 209's desperate attempts to dissociate itself from Louisiana white supremacist David Duke.

> [T]he face of Prop. 209 . . . is the face of David Duke.
>
> —Patricia Ewing[22]

Upon returning to school in the late summer of 1996, members of the student senate at CalState Northridge were worried about the upcoming vote on Prop. 209. Nearly one year before, the Board of Regents had voted to eliminate affirmative action in the university system. That fall, only one African-American student enrolled at the University of California Boalt Hall Law School—down from twenty the previous year. The same trend was likely to develop when the regents' ban on affirmative action was applied to undergraduate admissions in the fall of 1998.[23] The student senators suspected that Prop. 209 might affect the larger society in similar ways, and decided that a debate on the initiative by "big name" political figures would help to raise awareness of the issue and help students and members of the community to, in the words of student senate president Vladimir Cerna, "make an educated vote on Nov. 5." The senate invited several nationally known political figures and activists, among them David Duke, to debate the merits of the initiative on September 25. Duke, the founder and president of the National Association for the Advancement of White People and a former member of the Ku Klux Klan, was at the time embroiled in a race for the U.S. Senate in Louisiana. He gladly accepted the invitation and the $4,000 plus travel expenses offered him by the student senate, likely anticipating the free media coverage the event would offer him. Joe Hicks, a California civil rights activist, was booked to present the pro–affirmative action argument. Many of the better-known political figures invited to the debate declined to attend—thus the odd pairing of a Louisiana white supremacist and a local civil rights activist.[24]

Following the announcement of the participants, Connerly, acting in his role as a regent to the U.C. system, sent a letter to the president of CalState Northridge, Brenda Wilson, urging her to cancel the Duke-Hicks debate. In the letter, Connerly referred to Duke's invitation as a political ploy by the anti–Prop. 209 activists who were seeking to portray the initiative as racist. He warned Wilson to call off the debate, "unless it is your choice to dishonor your university and the integrity of the issue before us." Connerly also rejected the CalState Northridge student senate's invitation to appear alongside Duke in defense of Prop. 209, saying in the letter, "Duke and the Klan are despicable and I will not be part of giving them a forum to articulate their hatred." Wilson responded coolly to Connerly through the university's spokeswoman, stating that she was "proud of the fact the students are using their own funds and that the decision was reached through a democratic process."[25]

Duke arrived in California nearly two weeks before the Northridge debate. In the interim, he was featured on four local radio talk shows; several TV talk forums, at least two syndicated nationally; a CNN report; and in several national and regional newspapers. In his public appearances, Duke showed strong support for Prop. 209. He also exhibited the virulent racism that has made him so famous. On a Sacramento radio show, Duke alleged that "minority" men were raping white women "by the thousands."[26]

The week before the debate, Yes to Prop. 209 and Governor Wilson made a last-ditch effort to distance the anti–affirmative action movement from Duke. They claimed that Duke's appearance was engineered by opponents of Prop. 209 in an effort to discredit its supporters. Connerly denounced the debate as "political trickery" and claimed to have a source at CalState Northridge who could produce evidence of a conspiracy. Wilson repeated Connerly's charges soon after. Neither Connerly's source nor any evidence of a conspiracy ever surfaced. In an appearance on the *Tom Leykis Show*, Duke referred to Wilson's conspiracy theory as "stupid," stating that he had been invited by the students and no one else.[27]

Unable to stop the debate through political pressure, the anti–affirmative action movement took its case to the courts. During the week of September 25, Yes on Prop. 209 and several other anti–affirmative action groups requested a temporary restraining order on the debate from the Van Nuys Superior Court, alleging that the student senate was "using taxpayer funds to undermine the initiative." The presiding judge dismissed the suit without comment. Later in the week, anti–affirmative action activists were back in court, alleging that Duke's presence was the result of a conspiracy to undermine any "reasoned debate" about Prop. 209. Their suggested solution was a court-enforced cancellation of the debate and the replacement of Duke with a "qualified representative . . . first approved by the 'Yes on 209' committee." Again, the case was dismissed.[28]

Given all of the media attention and court activity surrounding the debate, the actual event was rather mundane. Duke and Hicks offered what one commentator referred to as "routine recitations" of the respective pro– and anti–affirmative action arguments. The overflow crowd in Northridge's student union was calm, amid tight security. Outside of the building, however, police wielding tear gas and exploding bullets violently dispersed students and pro–affirmative action protesters. Ten arrests were made, and at least one person was injured.[29]

In the weeks surrounding the debate, the Campaign to Defeat Prop. 209 and Stop Prop. 209—the two largest pro–affirmative action groups in the state— sought to capitalize on Duke's presence. After the announcement of the debate in early September, Patricia Ewing, head of Stop Prop. 209, began to mention Duke's support for Prop. 209 in media interviews. Only days after Duke left town, Campaign to Defeat Prop. 209 issued a press release revealing that Robert Thum, a financial supporter of Yes to Prop. 209, had contributed $500 to Duke's Senate campaign. Connerly, fearing yet another link between Duke and the anti–affirmative action movement, returned the $2,300 Thum had contributed to his organization. In a public statement about the affair, he stated, "I'm not suggesting he [Thum] is a bigot or Klansman, but I don't want there to be any doubt on what our campaign is standing for." Believing that it had found a winning strategy, Campaign to Defeat Prop. 209 continued to hammer home the Duke connection. On October 29, the organization débuted an anti–Prop. 209 television campaign that featured a burning cross and a white-robed image of Duke. Proponents of Prop. 209 were infuriated. Ward Connerly called the Duke ads a "despicable reversion to the discredited tactics of guilt by association." California Republican Party chairman John Herrington called the ads "flagrantly misleading" and warned that the voters of California would not be bullied by "scare tactics and intimidation attempts."[30]

The anti–affirmative action movement's reactions to the ads were an appropriate response to political mudslinging. They also revealed a deeper need to limit the debate surrounding Prop. 209. Duke, a symbol of white supremacy, complicated the anti–affirmative action movement's historical narrative of its origins. How could a former member of an organization that put a price on the head of Martin Luther King Jr. now support an initiative that claimed to advance his ideals? Even Connerly's conspiracy theory defied historical precedent. Why would a white supremacist help African Americans to sustain a system of black privilege? Duke contextualized Prop. 209. His presence was a threat to the labors of all of the anti–affirmative action activists who had skillfully constructed a historical myth for their movement.

Suppose it's just another clever Jedi mind trick.

—Mos Def [31]

Transparent as the anti–affirmative action movement's attempts to appropriate the historical memory of the civil rights movement might have been, they were successful. Anti–affirmative action activists were able to convince between 5 and 10 percent of the California population into believing that Prop. 209 would not end affirmative action. As this study was being completed, the politics of tricknology, exported to Washington state by Connerly and other anti–affirmative action activists, aided in the passage of another anti–affirmative action ballot initiative: I-200. I-200 contains near-identical language to that used in Prop. 209 and performs the same functions.[32] Affirmative action is now a thing of the past in Washington public life.

The narrative of American history propagated by these campaigns, in particular that of the civil rights movement, is a farce. Many of the voters of California and Washington accepted it, nonetheless. As political actors, Americans must become critical historians. In this time of sound-bite politics, professionally tailored political campaigns, and political spin, it is imperative that we entertain the political messages we encounter with the supposition that they could very well be "just another clever Jedi mind trick."

NOTES

Earlier versions of this chapter were reviewed in two seminars held by Lisa Duggan and Robin D. G. Kelley at New York University. I would like to thank all who participated for their insightful comments and encouragement.

1. Grand Puba, "Wake Up (Stimulated Dummies Mix)," on *One for All* (Elektra Entertainment, 1990).

2. A private letter from Wood states that he applied for the position after the final candidates had already been chosen and that the interview itself did not go well. Comments of the department head, James Syfers, refute Wood's claim that the department was looking for a diversity hire. "We were just looking for the best person we could find," recalls Syfers. See Dinesh D'Souza, *The End of Racism* (New York: Free Press, 1995), 10; and Lydia Chavez, *The Color Bind* (Berkeley: University of California Press, 1998), 13–14.

3. Terry Eastland, *Ending Affirmative Action* (New York: Basic Books, 1996), 173.

4. Proposition 209 did not get on the ballot because of overwhelming public support. Wood and Custred were only able to collect enough signatures to put the initiative on the November ballot after the Republican Party gave it the money to hire paid signature gatherers. This Republican support came not from a popular mandate within the party but from the political self-interest of Pete Wilson. See Chavez, *The Color Bind*, 57, 73–75.

5. The media frenzy created by the regents' vote on affirmative action was perceived as a boon by the Wilson camp. Prior to July, when the vote was taken, Wilson's campaign had been floundering—even in California. See Chavez, *The Color Bind*, 58.

6. Chavez, *The Color Bind*, 32.

7. See "Questions of Race Run Deep for Foe of Preferences," *New York Times*, July 27, 1997; and Michael Lynch, "Racial Preferences Are Dead," *Reason* 29.9 (February 1998): 32–33.

8. Ward Connerly, letter to Martin Luther King III, January 29, 1997.

9. Ward Connerly, testimony before the U.S. Senate Committee on the Judiciary, April 30, 1996.

10. Chavez, *The Color Bind*, 117–18, 152, 237.

11. Trevor Coleman, "Affirmative Action Wars," in *Emerge: Black America's News Magazine* (March 1998): 33; and Chavez, *The Color Bind*, 161.

12. Louis Harris, "The Future of Affirmative Action," in George Curry, ed., *The Affirmative Action Debate* (New York: Addison Wesley Publishing Co., 1996), 327.

13. Proposition 209, section A. The wording of Proposition 209 is nearly identical to that of the Civil Rights Act of 1964. Article A reads: "The state shall not discriminate against, or grant preferential treatment to, any individual or group on the basis of race, sex, color, ethnicity, or national origin in the operation of public employment, public education, or public contracting." Title VII of the Civil Rights Act of 1964 states that "any preference, limitation, specification, or discrimination based on race, color, religion, sex, or national origin" is unlawful.

The U.S. Civil Rights Commission defines affirmative action as any program "beyond simple termination of a disciplinary practice, which permits the consideration of race, national origin, sex, or disability along with other criteria, and which is adopted to provide opportunities to a class of qualified individuals who have either historically or actually been denied those opportunities, and to prevent the recurrence of discrimination in the future." Curry, *The Affirmative Action Debate*, xiv.

14. Ballot Pamphlet for Proposition 209. The two arguments against Proposition 209 in the ballot pamphlet mention affirmative action, as does the anti–affirmative action rebuttal to the second of those arguments.

15. Jesse Jackson Sr., "Race-Baiting and the 1996 Presidential Campaign," and Harris, "The Future of Affirmative Action," in Curry, ed., *The Affirmative Action Debate*, 297, 327–329.

16. Harris, "The Future of Affirmative Action," 328.

17. Ibid., 266.

18. Ward Connerly, letter to Martin Luther King III, January 29, 1997.

19. Ibid. My italics, Connerly's underline.

20. For examples of such writing, see the works of Shelby Steele, Nathan Glazer, Clarence Thomas, Steven Yates, Steve and Abigail Thernstrom, Clint Bolick, and Terry Eastland.

21. "Prop 209 Backer Defends Use of King in Ad," *Los Angeles Times*, October 24, 1996.

22. "TV Ads Close Gap in California's Vote on Racial Hiring," *Christian Science Monitor*, November 1, 1996.

23. "Black and Hispanic Admissions Off Sharply at U. of California," *New York Times*, April 1, 1998. The Northridge students' fears were realized in the fall of 1998. Admissions for African-American, Native American, and Chicano students fell by an average of 14 percent at the top University of California schools.

24. Former chairman of the Joint Chiefs of Staff Colin Powell and San Francisco mayor Willie Brown, among others, were invited to attend. They all declined. See "Judge Refuses to Bar Ex-Klansman from College Debate," in *Los Angeles Times*, September 24,

1996; and "Storm Rises over Ex-Klansman in Debate," *Los Angeles Times*, September 11, 1996.

25. "Rejection of Ex-Klan leader in Debate Urged," *Los Angeles Times*, September 6, 1996.

26. "Storm Rises over Ex-Klansman in Debate," *Los Angeles Times*, September 11, 1996.

27. Ibid.

28. "Judge Refuses to Bar Ex-Klansman from Debate," *Los Angeles Times*, September 24, 1996; and "Duke Debate Tickets Sell Out; Protests Rise," *Los Angeles Times*, September 25, 1996.

29. "Duke Debates California's Affirmative Action," *Boston Globe*, September 26, 1996.

30. "Storm Rises over Ex-Klansman in Debate," *Los Angeles Times*, September 11, 1996; "Ads Against Prop. 209 to Debut," *Los Angeles Times*, October 29, 1996; and "Furor over Latest Anti–209 Ad/TV Spots Feature Cross-Burnings, Hooded Klansmen," *San Francisco Chronicle*, November 1, 1996.

31. Mos Def, "Thieves in the Night," on *Mos Def and Talib Kweli Are Black Star* (Rawkus Records, 1998).

32. "Foes of Preferences Try a Referendum in Washington State," *Chronicle of Higher Education*, October 30, 1998.

~

NIKHIL SINGH

Notes on a National Report

> *Beware of those who speak of the spiral of history; they are preparing a boomerang. Keep a steel helmet handy.*
>
> —Ralph Ellison

It is difficult to comment upon *One America in the Twenty-First Century: Forging the Future*, without noticing that the "President's Initiative on Race" has been a relative nonevent. The so-called national conversation on race that it was supposed to spur simply has not taken place. Although the Advisory Board to the president, under the noble leadership of John Hope Franklin, pursued its charge with dignity and forthrightness, the report it has produced means very little in itself but takes its meaning from the context in which it has been disseminated and discussed. This context is marked by the sustained assault on "race" as a meaningful, or even an intelligible, political category. The orchestrated political campaign to wipe out state-based affirmative action, the academic impatience with anything smacking of "identity politics," the market-driven multiculturalism that turns the system of racial marks into apolitical figures of gift and variety, the disingenuous neo-leftism that "trumps" "race" with "class," and the new enclosures of the carceral state that redraw the color line behind a facade of steel and stone are all in various ways signs of these times.

The times for lack of a better word are "postmodern." Today, the virtual realities of the corporate media compete for our allegiances, and national-symbolic imperatives wane in importance, except when they cater to the spectacle. By "national-symbolic," I mean those signifying practices that enable us to locate ourselves and constitute the terms of our participation within (or exclusion from) the widest possible, public, political enterprise most of us are capable of imagining. The military enterprise remains preeminent in this regard ("as we take a station break for the bombing . . ."). Indeed, it is ironic the extent to which state violence has been a precondition and/or model for both the creation and the purported resolution of racial division and hierarchy, from our national origins in slavery and conquest, to the Civil War, to the beginnings of institutional desegregation at midcentury, to the various "wars" on poverty, crime, and drugs of our own time. That ineluctable relationship between "race" and violence, it would seem, must forever oscillate between a ruthlessly internalized exclusion and an explosive catharsis, both real and imaginary. (Had they called this fin-de-siècle initiative "the war on race," you can be sure there would have been some "national" conversation. Some silences at least must be counted a blessing.)

To continue in this vein, it is not an accident that the three major "race reports" published since 1940—the Carnegie/Myrdal Commission Report (1944), Truman's civil rights initiative *To Secure These Rights* (1948), and the Kerner Commission on Civil Disorders (1968), respectively—coincided with World War II, the onset of the cold war, and the escalation of the war in Vietnam. In each of these cases, the "race" question was elevated to an unprecedented national-symbolic centrality. Its inevitable resolution through the dismantling of Jim Crow, Gunnar Myrdal wrote, would only confirm the universality of the "American Creed," and legitimate, as Truman's appointees recognized a few years later, America's inherent national greatness and its leadership of "the free" world. Twenty years later, against the backdrop of a stalled civil rights movement, massive resistance, and civil insurgencies within the urban "black belt," the Kerner Commission threw a wrench into this favored, nationalist teleology, suggesting that "we" had become (at the very least) "two societies, one black, one white—separate and unequal." The urgent challenge of this austere social fact, presented without the soothing balm of premature or unilateral declarations of national unity and moral redemption, was quite simply never met.

In subsequent years, Nixonian "benign neglect" and neo-racist revanchism, culminating in Ronald Reagan's victorious electoral stance as a "state's righter," have left the nationalist teleology of racial reform in tatters. As an example, we might take note of the fact that the largest civil disturbance in the twentieth century, the L.A. riot/rebellion of 1992 (precipitated by the acquittal of the four police officers who bludgeoned speeding black motorist Rodney King), was processed less through any serious national public accounting such as might be signaled by "a race commission" than through the spectacular trial of one Orenthal James Simpson. As the O.J. trial filtered reality to us from channel zero to infinity, it modeled the contemporary race divide and disconnect. Split-screen scenes of black jubilation and white dejection told a tale not of "two nations" but of apparently incommensurable epistemological horizons and life-worlds.

To its credit, the Advisory Board's report acknowledges this situation, though primarily in the breach. It admits, for example, that perhaps the most disturbing aspect of the (post)modern racial regime is the fact that there now exist impossibly divergent beliefs and perceptions about how and why race matters, adding that a significant majority of so-called whites "believe . . . the problem of racial intolerance in this country has been solved and that further investigation is unwarranted and inappropriate." At the same time, the report acknowledges, I think correctly, what may be the obverse fact: that we are in a time of pronounced "racial transition," with dramatic shifts in racial demographics (due to new immigrant populations) and perhaps even more consequential changes in racial identification under way, "There are no easy metaphors or key slogans to describe what we are becoming," the report states. Yet rather than responding to the immense challenge posed by this insight, it instead falls into the worn groove of consensus, drawing upon an all-too-familiar repertoire: "bridging the gap," "forging the future," "redeeming the promise," "lifting the burden," "celebrating our differences," "searching for common ground," "one America," and so on, and on.

I am by no means suggesting that the contents and recommendations of the report are not in and of themselves entirely salutary. By itself, the report's call to reverse the gutting of federal civil rights enforcement under Reagan and Bush, if it were heeded, would go some distance toward reestablishing national-symbolic momentum toward racial equality. Similarly, its recommendations about restricting the widespread use of racial profiling by police and eliminating egregious drug sentencing disparities represent immediate, practical ways to begin chipping away at the racist criminal justice system. More cautiously, the report's promotion of universalist, social policies such as raising the minimum wage, targeting federal money for "urban revitalization," establishing job-training programs, expanding health-insurance coverage, and investing in K–12–through–higher education initiatives are clearly aimed at benefiting underserved, economically disadvantaged groups and communities. The push for interracial dialogue and transformation within affective relations of everyday life must also not be underestimated. In all these ways, the Advisory Board, at its best, tries to broadly resuscitate a liberal social policy agenda and civil rights ethic organized around antipoverty initiatives and nondiscrimination principles.

Given what now exists, it is hard to find fault with any of these recommendations. To see this, we need look no further than the statistical appendix to the report prepared by the board's Council of Economic Advisors. The appendix measures invidious racial disparities along economic, juridical, health, and educational axes to powerful effect. Even a cursory reading of the appendix shows what benign neglect has meant in practice for the nation's longest-standing minority groups, as the overall life chances of Indian peoples and peoples of African descent, as measured by the bulk of the statistical evidence, have either stagnated or declined since the early 1970s. Yet at the same time, statistics can be deceiving. The statistics on so-called whites, Hispanics, and Asians, for example, while expanding the scope of "race" as an analytic category, actually demonstrate how confusing this time of "racial transition" really is. Thus, the "racial" character of the "Hispanic" category (which the report notes is the fasting-growing statistical aggregate) is entirely unspecified, even as it remains coded in relation to white and black (with the latter two designated by the ubiquitous qualifier "non-Hispanic"). Meanwhile, the report shows the "Asian" category to be profoundly bifurcated, possessing both the highest rates of educational and occupational achievement and also the highest rates of indigence and poverty. Finally, the white category (the largest and, as I will suggest later, the most elastic of all) entirely occludes differentiation within itself, effectively obscuring the existence of anything we might want to term the "white" poor.

Do not misunderstand. I am not making the familiar argument, heard so often today, that our differences are "really" about "class" and material deprivation and have very little to do with "race." Our differences are certainly about class. The confusion of the categories, however, is at least in part the result of a bewilderingly complex, heterogeneous apartheid. Furthermore, I think we must note an ironic and perhaps unintended consequence of the production of race as a statistical aggregate. The effect of "race" as an aggregate works largely by suppressing salient internal differences within and across "racial" categories, whether they be of class, gender, or even "race" itself (not to mention age, sexuality, nationality, and region). Now, one might counter that this is precisely the kind of hairsplitting that must be avoided at all costs and that the valid purpose and valuable achievement of the Advisory Board's report is that it works to reestablish—in the face of a tremendous cultural and political assault on the legacies of antiracist struggle—the idea that invidious racial disparities exist and that they need to be investigated and remedied. In fact, the report acknowledges the dangers of statistics and emphasizes the need to establish and refine a lasting framework for data collection and analysis of these issues. Yet the problem remains: To gather statistical data on racial disparities, one must first presume the existence of well-defined, racially subordinated populations, precisely the idea that is under such intense social pressure and political scrutiny today.

Arguably, it is here that the Advisory Board's mission is clearest: to educate and even persuade the public as to how and why "race" matters. As Gunnar Myrdal noted over forty years ago, there has never been a sustained, systematic national effort to educate U.S. publics about the historical legacies and contemporary aspects of racism and racial formation. The so-called culture wars of the last two decades have in many respects revolved around precisely this issue, and the report comes down decisively in supporting greater public commitment to multicultural/multiracial democracy. Yet the pieties of multiculturalism and pronouncements of a putative "left" victory in the culture wars notwithstanding, it is difficult to evade the fact that we continue to wage a monumentally defensive struggle simply to hold the line against neo-racist social policy and what I call "post-racist" common sense. The problem in part is that the "race (still) matters" argument, as important as it is, is not supple or sophisticated enough to answer the attacks on the legitimacy or coherence of the categories. Nor is it able to provide compelling justification for, or direction to, progressive social and political action.

For evidence of this, we might look at the report's comments on affirmative action and so-called welfare reform, each of which is a "proxy" for a real, ongoing "national conversation on race." Significantly, the report has very little to say about welfare reform, only that more study is needed. Yet the fact is that Clinton's "ending of welfare as we know it" now has an almost untouchable, normative political salience, even as its devastating consequences, including quasi-forced, disposable labor (and laboring bodies), downward wage pressure, and intensified policing of poor, single women, proceed behind a veil of political platitudes about autonomy and self-worth and the temporary fortunes of a high-employment economy. With regard to affirmative action, the report is more decisive, expressing a commitment to what is an increasingly controversial and rapidly eroding public policy and calling for a new consensus highlighting its benefits in "promoting diversity" and "moving us to the goal of one America." The report argues further that a majority of Americans actually support affirmative action when they understand it as a means of overcoming racial discrimination. It mildly rebukes efforts to use it as a political "wedge issue" as misleading.

As with many of its recommendations, the Advisory Board ultimately defends affirmative action as one more "down payment on our future success as a multiracial, internally strong, globally competitive democracy." Yet, here above all, I want to flag how the report's reflexive lapse into nationalist teleology—the ritual appeal to "our common interests beyond race"—betrays us. According to this script, racial reform in the United States is paradoxically something that is always already accomplished, because our national principles are sound, and yet never quite complete, because our social practices still deviate from those principles. Yet the arguments against affirmative action have been successful precisely in their ability to draw upon and rewrite this national script as a story of fulfillment of the teleology—the effective end of (racial) history. What the anti–affirmative action momentum demonstrates is the ease with which universalism (especially juridical universalism) can become the mask worn by majoritarian (national) interests constituted as whiteness. This process has less to do with misinformation about the "real" extent of past or ongoing discrimination against people of color, or even with a regrettable moral lapse in judgment. Rather, it is about the calculated mobilization of a politics of white self-interest, or, more accurately, the mobilization of a political self-interest in "whiteness."

I do not have time to develop this argument further here, but I do want to stress that teleology or rationalization will not save us from this continuous and increasingly subtle reinvention of racism. The latter is above all a *political* project like any other and must be attacked as such, through alternative mobilizations. The kinds of mobilizations I have in mind are quite characteristically left out of the report's reassuring consensual lists of "promising practices" and "community heroes." I am thinking here of the Critical Resistance group, the Black Radical Congress, Race Traitor, and many others. I would add that the warning against teleology applies equally to the canard that surfaces prominently in the report, that the "face of America" is changing or that "we" are in the process of (slowly) becoming a majority minority (or nonwhite) country. Although this may be true within the terms of contemporary racial scripts and categories, it is precisely the elasticity of whiteness that should give us pause. As France Winddance Twine and Jonathan Warren point out, whiteness is an ever-expanding, constantly moving target. In this light, the report's own statistics on interracial marriage are revealing, suggesting that both blacks and whites are mostly endogamous, while immigrants are significantly less so but are much more likely to intermarry with whites than with blacks. (Blacks, by the way, marry nonblacks more often than whites marry nonwhites.) In light of my previous comments on the elasticity of whiteness, I want to suggest here that we need to acknowledge the degree to which blackness is a category of relative racial fixity in the modern United States (and perhaps in the world) and remains the functional template of a much wider societal differentiation. "Blackness," in this sense, is both the glue and the solvent of the body politic. "We" don't know what to do with it, and yet what would "we" be without it?

I am not saying that black and white are merely empty or arbitrary signifiers. Into these containers, very specific historical contents have been poured, mixed, and recombined. Being historical, indeed being at base a theory or philosophy of history, what Howard Winant (following Du Bois) calls "racial dualism" is our modernity's (and now postmodernity's) most uncanny time traveler. Through its magic, hierarchies are constructed and enforced, just as resistances are forged and won. Nonetheless, it is important, I think, to remain scrupulously nominalist about racial categories. They are the result of human practices of reduction, identification, domination, division, exploitation, and even affection, which have over time become an (illusory) account of those selfsame practices and, in turn, of distinct human populations we still call "races." To be nominalist, however, is not to believe that our task is simply to unmask or demystify racial categorization. As the complex, ramified, continuously remade "product" of an accumulated history, "race" continues to do its work as an insistent historical referent, cultural repertoire, and mechanism of social enclosure and prophylaxis.

Finally, by calling race an insistent historical referent, I also mean to suggest that race and racial division may be the only true "national" conversation that has ever existed in the United States. It is a conversation, consistent and interminable, about the nature of this "national" social reality, where we came from and where we are going. In the current conjuncture (the product of this accumulated history), "race" has come to represent the impossibility of stabilizing an interpretation of the nation as a guarantor of justice for all, and yet it remains the means by which we continue to gesture at that very possibility. This is one reason that *One America . . . Forging the Future* (and most of the rest of us) continues to speak a convoluted and self-contradictory rhetoric of race as burden and blight, as gift and variety.

Here one might recall Duke Ellington, who understood what this all meant for black people down at the charred bottom of the melting pot as well as anyone: "Race" is that *something apart that is also an integral part.* The only way to deal with it, he counseled, was to embrace "a strategy of dissonance." Today, I would suggest that strategy of dissonance requires us to cultivate skill with the politics and history of racial nominalism, while renewing our commitments to everyday communities of racial resistance. We need to understand the extent to which our postmodern racial regime is at once highly flexible and resistant to change, even as we try to develop new vocabularies with which to confront it, beyond the tired dichotomies of race versus class and the outworn teleologies of national transcendence. We must counter color-blind universalism with an insistent analysis of the *universal effects of racism,* the ways it shapes and energizes a wider social conservatism and authoritarian politics. Finally, we must refuse the real and imaginary politics of national (in)security that continues to organize the collective racial unconscious and keep trying to think differently about our unity.

≈

Gary Y. Okihiro
Cheap Talk, er, Dialogue

"Without substance," I thought to myself after having spent an hour with the staff of the Advisory Board to the President's Initiative on Race in October 1997. The staff members were at the time settling into their responsibilities and were open to advice, but mainly sought information from several quarters. I concluded, from their description of the board's mandate and from their queries, that the President's Initiative would simply provide a forum, even as the staff had made themselves available to us, a group of Asian-American educators, for a wide discussion on the subject of race without legislative agendas or programmatic outcomes. Like other incidental presidential initiatives, this one was to be limited to talk—politic, bloodless, and cheap.

And there was lots of it—talk—called "dialogue," from college conversations to community forums to statewide "days of dialogue." As described in the board's executive summary of its work, board members

> canvassed the country meeting with and listening to Americans who revealed how race and racism have impacted their lives. Board meetings focused on the role race plays in civil rights enforcement, education, poverty, employment, housing, stereotyping, and administration of justice, health care, and immigration. Members have convened forums with leaders from the religious and corporate sectors.[1]

And as put by its chair, John Hope Franklin, the board "traveled to many places, talked with countless Americans, heard many opinions and concerns," and served as the "eyes and ears" of the president on issues of race.[2]

To those of us in ethnic studies, such talk—focused, systematic, prodigious—has been constant and going on for years, in truth from the nation's founding, and across broad constituencies, indeed among all Americans. Some politicians and white Americans might have discovered race as a result of the President's Initiative, but scores of other Americans, especially racialized minorities, have long understood the sting and consequences of race in their daily lives. They not only talked about race; they experienced it. White privilege, too, was experienced, if unacknowledged.

I am herewith reminded, by way of contrast, of another presidential commission report written some thirty years earlier in the anxious aftermath of violent and widespread civil unrest in the United States. "This is our basic conclusion," the commissioners declared. "Our nation is moving toward two societies, one black, one white—separate and unequal." And of the distinction created by race consciousness, they wrote: "What white Americans have never fully understood—but what the Negro can never forget—is that white society is deeply implicated in the ghetto. White institutions created it, white institutions maintain it, and white society condones it."[3]

Those differences of race are documented in the more revealing addendum to the 1998 board's report, a statistical presentation of social and economic status by race.[4] In that document, we see the continuing separation, witnessed decades earlier, of America's peoples by race and its privileges and poverties. In 1995, for instance, poverty rates among African Americans hovered at 30 percent, while for whites, it stood at 10 percent; African-American unemployment among individuals sixteen years and older was more than twice that of whites, and greater percentages of whites than African Americans graduated from high school.[5]

But those statistics also show a greater complexity to the figures of race in America than those of thirty years earlier. If the nation of 1968 was polarized between black and white, the nation of 1998 was more diverse. African Americans made gains in education, employment, and income, although the gap between themselves and whites has remained essentially unchanged over those three decades.[6] Asians and Latinos, due in large part to immigration patterns, reveal very different and mixed profiles. Asians are among the most highly educated of all racialized groups and have higher median family incomes than whites, but they also have poverty rates that exceed that of whites by more than 50 percent.[7] And Latinos, as compared with African Americans, have considerably lower educational levels and slightly higher poverty rates but lower unemployment rates.[8]

Those contrasts under late capitalism point to a manifest conclusion about race in America—it was never a binary of white and black alone. And despite gestures toward a more inclusive universe of race, the 1998 board's report is mired in the racial binaries of white and black, white and nonwhite, both of which foreground and privilege the position of whiteness. The U.S. Census, instead, reported that in 1998, 73 percent of America's peoples were white; 12 percent, black; 11 percent,

Latino; 4 percent, Asian and Pacific; and 1 percent, Native American. But in 2050, if current trends continue, whites will drop to 53 percent; Latinos will increase to 25 percent, blacks to 14 percent, and Asian and Pacific to 8 percent; and Native Americans will remain at 1 percent. "The complexities, challenges, and opportunities that arise from our growing diversity point to the need for a new language," the board offered, "one that accurately reflects this diversity."[9]

Despite that insight, the report cites the white-black paradigm and in particular the enslavement of Africans as foundational to subsequent and apparently less important unfoldings of white-nonwhite relations. As Franklin remarked, "This country cut its eye teeth on racism in the black/white sphere. . . . [The country] learned how to [impose its racist policies on] . . . other people at other times . . . because [it had] already become an expert in this area."[10] The pattern was thus cut in black and white, then traced onto other, later cloths, according to that historical rendition. Further, as represented by the peculiar institution in the board's report, racism and racial subjugation were conceived of as exceptional and as aberrations in the nation's past or as "the darker side of our history,"[11] whereas another reading might generate the understanding that slavery was one among several forms of labor and racial bondage and exploitation and that a central and recurrent feature of America's history is that "darker side."

The board's notions of racism as largely an individual, and not a social, matter and of its eradication as a product of reaching a mutual understanding and thereby appreciation through dialogue surely influenced its readings of the past. As described in its report, the board strived to ignite "extensive dialogue" among Americans on how "problems of race have impinged on their lives and affected the Nation" and to therewith "refute stereotypes and provide opportunities for people to share their individual experiences and views, which may be different from others because of their race."[12] A parallel individuation is the largely correct, though also erroneous, view that each group has its own history and circumstance. Referring to Native Americans, board member Bob Thomas exclaimed: "Their history is unique, their relationship with our State and Federal governments is unique, and their current problems are unique." And as if racism could be measured or redress conferred, "While not large in numbers, their situation tugs at the heart."[13] Unique pasts and presents, although verities, are not the entirety. There are parallels and connections. Dillon S. Myer relocated, segregated, and sought to erase identities and cultures in his capacity as director of both the War Relocation Authority that held Japanese Americans captive during World War II and the Bureau of Indian Affairs when it instituted its termination policy toward American Indians and the reservations.[14] And African-American segregation upheld by the Supreme Court's *Plessy v. Ferguson* (1896) constituted the basis for school segregation of Asian-American children as affirmed by that same court in its 1927 decision in *Gong Lum v. Rice*.[15]

Those connections, it seems to me, enable a more comprehensive appreciation of racializations than that proposed by the board, along with their origins and natures and the means by which to transform them. And although I limit my examples to Asian-American history, the same case could be made for all of the other racialized groups and their social locations and articulations. Ignoring America's prerepublican past, one of the first and clearest racializations by the state was its 1790 Naturalization Act that defined citizenship for immigrants. Naturalization and, with it, rights and privileges accrued only to "free white persons," the act declared. That ability was extended to Africans in 1870. And although not envisioned by the founding fathers, their act denied Asian migrants naturalization for the most part from 1790 to 1952. Over the course of those years and in the challenges mounted by Asians to their racist exclusion, the very idea of race and racializations was contested, altered, and reinscribed, exemplifying not only the constructedness of race but also its profound and extended reach both within and beyond white and black.

Asians first tested America's racist definition of acquired citizenship in a California federal court in 1878 in the case *In re Ah Yup*. One of three litigants, Ah Yup, was joined by Li Huang and Leong Lan. The co-litigants claimed that Asians were included under the category "white," a strategy that was followed by all subsequent claims almost without exception, and Circuit Judge Lorenzo Sawyer, in his ruling against Chinese naturalization, employed the argument that formed the crux of later decisions that the Chinese, by everyday speech and scientific evidence, were "nonwhite."[16]

Between 1878 and 1909, American courts heard twelve naturalization cases that involved applicants from China, Japan, Burma, and Hawaii, along with two petitions from persons of mixed race, and one from a Mexican American. All claimed the cover of whiteness, and all were deemed to be nonwhite. Because of a treaty, however, the "pure-blooded Mexican" in Texas was allowed citizenship, despite the court's reasoning that science would define him as nonwhite. In contrast to the unanimity of the earlier period, the years 1909 to 1923 witnessed contradictory and confusing results. For the most part, in the twenty-five cases heard, courts continued to rule that Asians and mixed-race peoples were nonwhite. However, the distinction between white and nonwhite grew increasingly tenuous, especially in the light of disagreements over what constituted common speech and its divergences from scientific opinions, which themselves conflicted. Thus, Armenians were originally classed as Asians and hence nonwhite but were rendered whites by a court decision in 1909; Syrians were whites in 1909, 1910, and 1915, but nonwhites in 1913 and 1914; and Asian Indians were whites in 1910, 1913, 1919, and 1920, but nonwhite after 1923.[17]

Armenians were rendered white by the court based upon scientific evidence, but Syrians and Asian Indians, despite scientific opinion that they were white, were classed as nonwhite because of common knowledge. The 1923 U.S. Supreme Court decision in *United States v. Thind* codified that shift from both precedent and science in the matter of race. Bhagat Singh Thind was born in India, graduated from Punjab University, arrived in America in 1913, and served for six months in the U.S. Army. In 1920, Thind was granted naturalization by a district court based upon anthropologists' classification of Asian Indians as "Caucasians" and hence, in the court's opinion, "white." But upon appeal, that original ruling was overturned finally by the Supreme Court in a decision marked by a rejection of scientific evidence and an embrace of everyday speech. "It may be true that the blond Scandinavian and the brown Hindu have a common ancestor in the dim reaches of antiquity," wrote the Court in reference to scientific opinion, "but the average man knows perfectly well that there are unmistakable and profound differences between them today." The Court expanded upon its meaning: "What we now hold is that the words 'free white persons' are words of common speech, to be interpreted in accordance with the understanding of the common man, synonymous with the word 'Caucasian' only as that word is popularly understood."[18]

The capriciousness of race extended beyond the courtroom and into other venues of the state. Census workers in Louisiana, for example, classified Chinese Americans as whites in 1860 but as Chinese in 1870. They enumerated the children of Chinese men and non-Chinese women as Chinese in 1880, but they reclassified those biracial children as either blacks or whites; only those born in China or with two Chinese parents did they class as Chinese in 1890.[19] County clerks who issued marriage certificates, because of the state's miscegenation laws, had to determine the race of their applicants. Asian Indians were variously categorized as "brown," "black," or "white" by clerks who made those judgments based upon their perception of the applicant's skin color.[20] Racialization, as ruled by the Supreme Court, had indeed become the domain of the common man.

Asians, in their strivings for membership in the American community, tested the elasticity of the racialized category "white" and created the necessity for a classification that was neither white nor black. Caught in a racial binary, Asian Americans chose the mantle of whiteness instead of making a claim to blackness, both of which would have conferred naturalization rights after 1870. That calculated choice was understandable insofar as white supremacy ensured and limited guarantees and privileges to its members only. But it also revealed the workings of racializations between and among nonwhite groups that lie outside the compass of the black-white binary but are crucial to it.

Lai Chun-chuen, a prominent Chinese-American merchant, wrote to California governor John Bigler to protest the state's 1854 ruling, in *Hall v. the People*, that disallowed Asians, like American Indians and African Americans, from testifying in court for or against whites. In his letter, Lai took offense at that grouping and sought distance between Chinese and America's racialized minorities. "Your honorable people have established a new practice," Lai reminded Bigler. "They have come to the conclusion that we Chinese are the same as Indians and Negroes, and your courts will not allow us to bear witness. And yet these Indians know nothing about the relations of society; they know no mutual respect; they wear neither clothes nor shoes; they live in wild places and in caves."[21] Although perhaps a reflection of his economic class, Lai's sentiment appealed to racism and racialisms that emanated from Chinese ethnocentrism and from America's racial formation.

Similarly, Bhagat Singh Thind's argument before the U.S. Supreme Court asserted that people residing in many of the states of India, particularly in the north and north-west, including the Punjab, belong to the Aryan race. . . . The high-class Hindu regards the aboriginal Indian Mongoloid in the same manner as the American regards the negro, speaking from a matrimonial standpoint. The caste system prevails in India to a degree unsurpassed elsewhere.[22]

Thind's contention, accordingly, was that he was not only white but of the "Aryan race," that he was of "pure blood," that he was a member of a superior conquering group over primitive, indigenous peoples, and that he regarded the "aboriginal Indian Mongoloid" with the same disdain for inferiors that white Americans held toward African Americans.

Although some Asian Americans might have claimed whiteness on the basis of racial and cultural affinities, some African Americans sought distance from Asians on the basis of citizenship and history. "The Negro is an American citizen whose American residence and citizenry reach further back than the great majority of the white race," wrote Howard University professor Kelly Miller in 1924. "He has from the beginning contributed a full share of the glory and grandeur of America and his claims to patrimony are his just and rightful due. The Japanese, on the other hand, is the eleventh hour comer, and is claiming the privilege of those who have borne the heat and burden of the day."[23] Unlike the alien Japanese, Miller argued, African Americans deserved America's promise of equality as citizens and as their "just and rightful due."

Those separations among racialized minorities were assuredly accompanied by solidarities crafted across racialized divides, and those conflicts derived from and sustained the raced, gendered, sexualized, and classed social formation even as those unities resisted social hierarchies.[24] To forge a new future, as the President's Initiative on Race proposes, there must dawn this realization of racializations as constructions that uphold the relations of power and a determination to dismantle them. The 1967 commission came close to that when it proposed to attack "the continuing economic and social decay" that results in discontent and "threaten[s] democratic values fundamental to our progress as a free society."[25] It thus issued a call for "national action—compassionate, massive and sustained, backed by the will and resources of the most powerful and the richest nation on this earth"—to fulfill "our pledge of equality and to meet the fundamental needs of a democratic civilized society—domestic peace, social justice, and urban centers that are citadels of the human spirit."[26]

Perhaps the urgency has fled us. Perhaps the soaring vision is gone. Perhaps the failures of previous efforts have stymied us. Instead of a "massive and sustained" national campaign of will and resources directed at economic and racial inequality, the 1998 board recommends stricter enforcement of laws, better data collection, educational enhancements, more studies and testing, and support of existing initiatives and programs, among other things. And it calls on individual Americans "to become informed about people from other races and cultures," "to think about race," "to get to know people of other races," and so forth. The cure, considering the enormity of the crisis, can astonish.

NOTES

1. *One America in the 21st Century: Forging a New Future*, Advisory Board's Report to the President (Washington, DC: 1998), 1.

2. Ibid., i.

3. *Report of the National Advisory Commission on Civil Disorders* (New York: Bantam Books, 1968), 1, 2.

4. Council of Economic Advisers, *Changing America: Indicators of Social and Economic Well-Being by Race and Hispanic Origin*, September 1998.

5. Ibid., 21, 26, 36.

6. Ibid., 21, 23, 33.

7. Ibid., 20, 33, 36.

8. Ibid., 21, 26, 36.

9. *One America*, 3.

10. Ibid., 33.

11. Ibid., 36.

12. Ibid., 16.

13. Ibid., 38.

14. Richard Drinnon, *Keeper of Concentration Camps: Dillon S. Myer and American Racism* (Berkeley: University of California Press, 1987).

15. Gary Y. Okihiro, *Margins and Mainstreams: Asians in American History and Culture* (Seattle: University of Washington Press, 1994), 52–53, 58, 160, 162.

16. Charles J. McClain, *In Search of Equality: The Chinese Struggle Against Discrimination in Nineteenth-Century America* (Berkeley: University of California Press, 1994), 71–73; and Ian F. Haney Lopez, *White by Law: The Legal Construction of Race* (New York: New York University Press, 1996), 54–55.

17. Haney Lopez, *White by Law*, 61, 67, 203–207.

18. Ibid., 86–90.

19. Lucy M. Cohen, *Chinese in the Post–Civil War South: A People Without a History* (Baton Rouge: Louisiana State University Press, 1984), 167–168.

20. Karen Isaksen Leonard, *Making Ethnic Choices: California's Punjabi Mexican Americans* (Philadelphia: Temple University Press, 1992), 68.

21. Quoted in McClain, *In Search of Equality*, 22.

22. Haney Lopez, *White by Law*, 148–149.

23. Kelly Miller, *The Everlasting Stain* (Washington, DC: Associated Publishers, 1924), 163.

24. See, e.g., Okihiro, *Margins and Mainstreams*, especially chapter two.

25. *Report of the National Advisory Commission on Civil Disorders*, 410.

26. Ibid., 410, 413.

5. Black Feminist Studies: The New Politics of Gender

Michael Awkward

Black Feminism and the Challenge of Black Heterosexual Male Desire

After a brief respite in the 1970s and 1980s, when the socioeconomic plight of and the politics of artistically representing black women were at the forefront of our nationalist discourses, Afro-America has returned to a statistically justifiable emphasis on the topic that has been a preeminent concern throughout history: the victimized black male body, or what I have called elsewhere black-men-in-crisis. As we know all too well, although the percentages of black women in college and graduate and professional schools have increased significantly over the past two decades, these often-fatherless black males are only minimally more likely to pursue postsecondary education than they are to be relentlessly pursued by America's justice system in one form or another.

With few exceptions (particularly the work of some creative writers), generally self-described black feminist discourse remains unlikely to explore black masculinity except as a social, domestic, and intellectual force whose oppression of black women is energetic, self-conscious, and unremitting. Given the return of the black-male-in-crisis as preeminent concern, given Afro-America's historical (if sometimes ambivalent) fetishizing of black maleness, black feminism's capacity to impact black youth may be determined, in part, by how successfully it addresses the other side of the gender divide. Talk of "nonmonolithic masculinity," of a range of responses by individual or racialized men to patriarchal systems of oppression, is all the rage in mainstream feminism, which has branched out productively into the realm of "gender studies" or, more specifically, "masculinity studies." If its goals continue to include the improvement of black females' lives, lived overwhelmingly

137

alongside, and often dominated by, black men, black feminism might well come to see "nonmonolithic black masculinity" as a crucial topic and a way of encouraging potentially sympathetic men to live, work, and love in accordance with basic feminist principles. Three decades of contemporary black feminist writings and action have offered compelling insight into ways of assessing and, where necessary, moving beyond received myths about strong black women, about the emasculation of black men, and about the dangers to black people generally of embracing mainstream views and values wholeheartedly. Still, in the realm of popular culture, at least, and hence, in black youth culture, 1980s postfunk androgyny gave way to hip-hop machismo, legitimizing aggressively patriarchal ways of being and foregrounding sentiments about black male victimization at the hands of whites—and of black women—that culminated in the Million Man March. Certainly, black feminism hasn't failed to pay significant attention to these developments and to recognize them as reactions against black women's social and intellectual progress. But it might do well, in addition, to observe the rifts between putatively homogeneous black men that these events have demonstrated.

At this point in my life and career, my own black feminist practice is informed by beliefs I have articulated elsewhere and to which, for the sake of brevity, I will refer below. I have argued that a black male feminism must "be both self-reflective and at least minimally self-interested," must, that is to say, never lose sight "of both the benefits and the dangers of a situatedness in feminist discourse."[1] But despite— or maybe even because of—such recognition, it is my strong sense that "given the persistence of pejorative meanings attached to black male subjectivities, if a feminist discourse informed by an acute awareness of such perceptions is not a risky venture, its social and intellectual contributions will be, at best, negligible."[2] Recognizing what they may feel is the remarkably consistent devaluations of (forms of) black masculinity by both white hegemony and black feminists, young or potentially sympathetic black men encountering black feminism must be able to find in it the possibilities for self-validation and self-affirmation.

My own position as a black male in feminism has led me, perhaps inevitably, to question the possibilities of ideological purity and, indeed, whether embracing feminism is any easier for women than for men at this particular moment in our history. And although I recognize the rights of black females to view black feminism as an empowering political tool of their own, I believe that because it is such a crucial element of Afro-American culture, it is, or at least can become, through dint of hard, self-conscious labor, mine, also. Like any other collection of sociopolitical perspectives, feminism shapes and is shaped by the people who utilize it, including— in my own case—a black man. Hence, I believe that because it has so thoroughly illuminated aspects of black women's situatedness in America and elsewhere, certain versions of black feminism might profitably begin to interrogate the nuances of black masculinity. Using an underread moment in Zora Neale Hurston's *Their Eyes Were Watching God*,[3] I want to explore briefly one issue that black feminism might help us successfully to illuminate: representations of the politics of black male heterosexual desire.

But for me, as a literary critic by training, someone in love with words and their associative uses and possibilities in exploring a necessarily individualized version of a historical moment, there's another question that's crucial to address, also: Is there a way that we can turn—or return—to the art of the black text, to provocative uses of words and sounds whose meanings we have, if not abandoned, largely ignored in our efforts to tease the liberatory or complicitous politics out of the works we explore and help to re-create? Such a turn, obviously, need not be accompanied by a rejection of textual confrontations and encoding of politics—art for art's sake has always been a mindless, socially irresponsible endeavor—but may provide me with a way of contributing to twenty-first-century struggles to broaden the social impact of black feminist insights.

Their Eyes Were Watching God is one of the handful of novels men and women of my generation had to come to terms with to define and refine our critical selves. I want to use it similarly here to help me to interrogate what we might call, echoing influential takes on female sexuality and cinematic spectatorship, respectively, the pleasures and dangers of the black male gaze. The paragraph with which I am concerned is offered during the course of Hurston's description of Janie's return to Eatonville in the first scene of the novel after she had stood trial for murdering her third husband, Tea Cake, in self-defense. Here, Hurston introduces the theme of judgment that resonates so clearly with her protagonist's court appearance, where she is evaluated, officially, by an all-white male judicial body and, unofficially, by white women, who she imagines might be sympathetic to the plight of a woman forced to kill a rage-filled husband.

More important for my purposes here, however, is the fact that she is judged by members of the black community who, despite the Jim Crow segregation from the white evaluators that reinforces their sense of racial powerlessness, see her just as a rabid Tea Cake does before she is forced to shoot him before he shoots her: as an ungrateful, possibly adulterous woman who believes that because of her light skin, well-preserved Nordic beauty, and firmly middle-class status, she is too good for him, and thus, for them. Indeed, the associations between a jealous Tea Cake's diseased, murderous rage and this larger community's attitudes are underlined when Hurston insists that, in the courtroom, the "colored people" were all against Janie, "pelting her with dirty thoughts. They were there with their tongues cocked and loaded."[4]

To move, as I am doing here, from this moment of murderous intraracial judgment to the pejorative "zigaboo" evaluations of Janie that introduce the novel allows the reader to understand why Janie sees her place as necessarily apart from, rather than as a part of, "the people" whom she'd earlier sought to join physically, emotionally, and discursively through the act of storytelling on the porch of her second husband's store. Indeed, however self-protective her decision, her choice to confine herself to her house, to reject involvement with the Eatonville community, is a response to its strategically limited readings of her. Despite a common "envy" that led to a "mass cruelty" that transcended gendered boundaries, the resultant "burning statements" and the use of laughter as "killing tools" trained on Janie, she reenters communal lore in specifically gendered terms. As driven by their desire as the men overseeing her return about whom I am primarily concerned here, "the women" looked at her "faded shirt and muddy overalls and laid them away for remembrance," hoping "she might fall to their level someday."[5] In this aggressively heterosexual polarization of male and female responses, if the women's critical gaze is determined by petty anxieties, jealousies, and fear of not measuring up to Janie's monetary status and attitudinal self-possession, the men's examination of Janie emphasizes, almost exclusively, her striking, even luminous middle-aged figure: "The men noticed her firm buttocks like she had grapefruits in her hip pockets; the great rope of black hair swinging to her waist and unraveling in the wind like a plume; then her pugnacious breasts trying to bore holes in her shirt. They, the men, were saving with the mind what they lost with the eye."[6]

We see, in this passage, Hurston's metaphorizing of Janie's body, her strategic poeticizing of the male gaze. Certainly, it isn't the men who imagine grapefruits, plumes, and pugnacity. Hurston is simultaneously recording and translating masculine desire in a way that renders it if not more palatable, perhaps, to some readers, then more imaginative, more consistent with the rich black vernacular she constructs to record and reflect Janie's own discursive mastery despite the dictatorial mandates of her grandmother and second husband that she regard the black masses from a position "on high."[7] Unlike Nanny, however, Hurston is not protecting her protagonist from the often-dehumanizing effects of masculine desire, but offering an instance in which desire—female and male—is instantiated and in which the accompanying male desire is seen as no more problematic than the female contempt. Whatever we might say about female jealousy as it is manifested in the beginning of the novel, Hurston's is not merely—maybe not even primarily—a condemnatory representation of the black male gaze and, hence, black male heterosexual desire. Indeed, physical confinement proves unsuccessful as a way of containing, controlling, or constructing desire throughout the novel, because the imagination—in the case of the gendered gaze here—remains free and sufficiently lucid to pursue its own agenda. If Janie is confined in and by her clothes (and their imagined absence) to others' readings of her, those readings are, indeed, as potentially expansive as the sea, the horizon, and the pear tree, the central metaphors of *Their Eyes Were Watching God*.

In its concern with confinement and its escape, this scene recalls, with a difference, Joe Starks's forcing Janie to cover her "great rope of black hair":

> This business of the head-rag irked her endlessly. But Jody was set on it. Her hair was NOT going to show in the store. . . . Joe never told Janie how jealous he was. He never told her how often he had seen other men figuratively wallowing in it as she went about things in the store. And one night he had caught Walter standing behind Janie and brushing the back of his hand back and forth across the loose end of her braid ever so lightly so as to enjoy the feel of it without Janie knowing what he was doing. . . . He felt like rushing forth with the meat knife and chopping off the offending hand. That night he ordered Janie to tie up her

hair around the store. That was all. She was there in the store for him to look at, not those others.[8]

For Starks, Janie clearly isn't an expansive sign, an endlessly readable figure, but an object with which he can do whatever he desires, including dictating that she cover aspects of her appearance and slapping her to "assure himself in possession."[9]

But what does it mean that the contemporary reader on whom, like Pheoby, Hurston (and, by extension, Janie) seems to be depending for "a good thought"— and notice, again, the emphasis on judgment in Hurston's formulations of intraracial desire—is, in response to Janie's glorious reappearance in Eatonville, constructed as figuratively luxuriating over her attributes or, like Joe, desiring, metaphorically, at least, to protect Janie from the "dirty thoughts" that emanate from the imagination that produces the heterosexual black male gaze? What sorts of thinkers, of gender-inflected reading subjects, are we if those responses constitute the full range of our interrogations of black male desire?

Hurston insists that we—female and male readers—notice Janie, that we marvel at her well-preserved frame, her "firm"-ness, her freedom. She is free, in part, because she refuses to confine herself or see herself confined by others' limited interpretations of her expansive possibilities and, hence, meanings. We are not, in the capacity of expansive thinkers, doomed by our varied gendered, racialized, or class rage like Joe, who, in the scene where she rhetorically demasculinizes her second husband by insisting that he looks like "de change of life," figuratively "snatch[es] off part of [her] clothes while she wasn't looking and the streets were crowded."[10] Indeed, we can transcend, or at least incorporate into our ideological analyses, our own readings of Janie in ways that see her as more than we have ever imagined. To say simply that the heterosexual black male gaze is bad, that desire is oppressive, is, at this point, to move us nowhere. For black feminism to remain like Hurston's "movin' sea," which Hurston compares to love,[11] to be prepared for its contemporary challenges, including its much-stated desire for womanist racial wholeness, we need to acknowledge that desire and imagine metaphors, similes, ways of engaging it that make it what we need it to become, too. And in the face of black patriarchy's aggressive reemergence in the black popular culture that helps to shape the perspective of our students and our children, we must do so without reducing it to a single, static, self-confirming thing.

NOTES

1. Michael Awkward, "A Black Man's Place," in *Negotiating Difference: Race, Gender, and the Politics of Positionality* (Chicago: University of Chicago Press, 1995), p. 96.

2. Michael Awkward, *Scenes of Instruction: A Memoir* (Durham, N.C.: Duke University Press, 1999), p. 8.

3. Zora Neale Hurston, *Their Eyes Were Watching God* (1937; reprint New York: Perennial, 1991).

4. Ibid, p. 176.

5. Ibid., p. 2.
6. Ibid.
7. Ibid., p. 16.
8. Ibid., pp. 51–52.
9. Ibid., p. 67.
10. Ibid., p. 74.
11. Ibid., p. 182.

❧

BARBARA SMITH
Establishing Black Feminism

More than twenty years after some of the work in *Home Girls* was written, the primary question I want to examine is, how effective have black women been in establishing black feminism?[1] The answer depends on where one looks. Black feminism has probably been most successful in its impact on the academy, in its opening a space for courses, research, and publications about black women. Although black women's studies continues to be challenged by racism, misogyny, and general disrespect, scholarship in the field has flourished in the decades since *Home Girls* was published.

Not only is it possible to teach both graduate and undergraduate courses focusing on black and other women of color, but it is also possible to write dissertations in a variety of disciplines that focus on black women. Academic conferences about black and other women of color regularly occur all over the country, and sessions about black women are also presented at annual meetings of professional organizations. Hundreds if not thousands of books have been published that document black women's experience using the methodologies of history, the social sciences, and psychology. In the academy at least, black women are not nearly as invisible as we were when *Home Girls* first appeared. It is important to keep in mind, however, that discrimination continues to affect black women academics' salaries, opportunities for promotion, and daily working conditions.

When we search for black feminism outside the academy and ask how successful have we been in building a visible black feminist movement, the answer is not as clear. In reading my original introduction, I was struck by how many examples of organizing by women of color I could cite. When *Home Girls* was published in 1983 the feminist movement as a whole was still vital and widespread. Although the media loved to announce that feminism was dead, they had not yet concocted the 1990s myth of a "postfeminist" era in which all women's demands have supposedly been met and an organized movement is irrelevant. Reaganism was only a few years old, and it had not yet, in collaboration with an ever more powerful right wing, turned back the clock to eradicate many of the gains that had been made in the 1960s and 1970s toward racial, sexual, and economic justice. Now, much as in the beginning of this century, the end of the twentieth century is a time of lynchings, whether motivated by racism as in Jasper, Texas; by homophobia as in Laramie, Wyoming; by misogyny as in Yosemite, California; or by a lethal mix of hatreds as in Oklahoma City and Littleton, Colorado. Twenty years of conservative federal administrations and the U.S. populace's increasing move to the right have been detrimental to all progressive and leftist organizing, including the building of black feminism.

There are specific factors that make black feminist organizing even more difficult to accomplish than activism focused on other political concerns. Raising issues of oppression within already oppressed communities is as likely to be met with attacks and ostracism as with comprehension and readiness to change. To this day most black women are unwilling to jeopardize their racial credibility (as defined by black men) to address the reality of sexism. Even fewer are willing to bring up homophobia and heterosexism, which are of course inextricably linked to gender oppression.

Black feminist author Jill Nelson pointedly challenges the black community's reluctance to deal with sexual politics in her book *Straight, No Chaser: How I Became a Grown-up Black Woman.* She writes:

> As a group, black men and, heartbreakingly, many black women, refuse to acknowledge and confront violence toward women, or truth be told, any other issue that specifically affects black women. To be concerned with any gender issue is, by and large, still dismissed as a "white women's thing," as if black men in America, or anywhere else in the world, for that matter, have managed to avoid the contempt for women that is a fundamental element of living in a patriarchy. Even when lip service is given to sexism as a valid concern, it is at best a secondary issue. First and foremost is racism and the ways in which it impacts black men. It is the naïve belief that once racism is eradicated, sexism, and its unnatural outgrowth, violence toward women, will miraculously melt away, as if the abuse of women is solely an outgrowth of racism and racial oppression.[2]

Since *Home Girls* was published there has actually been an increase of overt sexism in some black circles as manifested by responses to the Anita Hill–Clarence Thomas Senate hearings, Mike Tyson's record of violence against women (and men), the O. J. Simpson trial, and the Million Man March. Some regressive elements of black popular culture are blatantly misogynist. Both black men and women have used the term "endangered species" to describe black men because of the verifiable rise in racism over the last two decades; yet despite simultaneous attacks on women, including black women who are also subjected to racism, black women are often portrayed as being virtually exempt from oppression and much better off than their male counterparts. It is mistaken to view black feminism as black "male bashing" or as a battle between black women and men for victim status, but as Nelson points out it has been extremely difficult to convince most in the black community to take black women's oppression seriously.

Twenty years ago I would have expected there to be at least a handful of nationally visible black feminist organizations and institutions by now. The cutbacks, right-wing repression, and virulent racism of this period have been devastating for the growth of our movement, but we must also look at our own practice. What if more of us had decided to build multi-issued grassroots organizations in our own communities that dealt with black women's basic survival issues and at the same time did not back away from raising issues of sexual politics? Some of the things I think of today as black feminist issues are universal access to quality health care; universal accessibility for people with disabilities; quality public education for all; a humane and nonpunitive system of support for poor women and children, that is, genuine welfare reform; job training and placement in real jobs that have a future; decent, affordable housing; and the eradication of violence of all kinds including police brutality. Of course, violence against women; reproductive freedom; equal employment opportunity; and lesbian, gay, bisexual, and transgender liberation still belong on any black feminist agenda.

Since the 1980s few groups have been willing to do the kind of black feminist organizing that the Combahee River Collective took on in Boston in the 1970s, which was to carry out an antiracist, feminist *practice* with a radical, anticapitalist analysis. It is not surprising that black feminism has seemed to be more successful in the more hospitable environment on campuses than on the streets of black communities, where besides all the other challenges, we would also need to deal with the class differences among us. To me black feminism has always encompassed basic bread-and-butter issues, which affect women of *all* economic groups. It is a mistake to characterize black feminism as only relevant to middle-class, educated women simply because black women who are currently middle-class have been committed to building the contemporary movement. From my own organizing experience I know that there are working-class and poor black women who not only relate to the basic principles of black feminism but who live them. I believe our movement will be very much stronger when we develop a variety of ways to bring black feminism home to the black communities from which it comes.[3]

In the present women of color of all races, nationalities, and ethnicities are leaders in labor organizing, immigration struggles, dismantling the prison industrial complex, challenging environmental racism, sovereignty struggles, and opposition to militarism and imperialism. Black feminists mobilized a remarkable national response to the Anita Hill–Clarence Thomas Senate hearings in 1991. Naming their effort "African American Women in Defense of Ourselves," they gathered more than sixteen hundred signatures for an incisive statement that appeared in the *New York Times* and in a number of black newspapers shortly after the hearings occurred.

Black feminists were centrally involved in organizing the highly successful Black Radical Congress (BRC), which took place in Chicago in June 1998. This gathering of two thousand activists marked the first time in the history of the African-American liberation movement that black feminist and black lesbian, gay, bisexual, and transgender issues were on the agenda from the outset. A black feminist caucus formed within the BRC before last June's meeting and is continuing its work.

Black feminists have also been active in the international struggle to free the political prisoner Mumia Abu-Jamal, who is currently on death row in Pennsylvania. The Millions for Mumia mobilization, which took place in Philadelphia on April 24, 1999, included a huge Rainbow Flags for Mumia contingent. This effort marked a first for significant, planned participation by the lesbian, gay, bisexual, and transgender community in a militant antiracist campaign. This participation in both the Black Radical Congress and the Millions for Mumia march did not occur without struggle. Not all the participants were on the same page in recognizing the necessity to challenge sexism and homophobia, and some did not even understand these to be critical political issues. But twenty years ago we most likely would not have been present, let alone part of the leadership of these two events. The success of these coalitions and others also indicates that there are some black men who work as committed allies to black feminists.

Within the lesbian, gay, bisexual, and transgender movement itself black lesbian feminists have been extremely active in the Ad Hoc Committee for an Open Process, the grassroots group that has successfully questioned the undemocratic, corporate, and tokenistic tactics of the proposed gay millennium rally in Washington in 2000. The Ad Hoc Committee has also been instrumental in initiating a dynamic national dialogue about the direction of the lesbian, gay, bisexual, and transgender movement, whose national leadership has distanced itself more and more from a commitment to economic and social justice.

Although the black feminist movement is not where I envisioned it might be during those first exciting days, it is obvious that our work has made a difference. Radical political change most often happens by increments rather than through dramatically swift events. Indeed, dramatic changes are made possible by the daily, unpublicized work of countless activists working on the ground. The fact that there is an audience for the writing in this collection, as a new century begins, indicates that *Home Girls* has made a difference as well, and that in itself is a sign of progress and hope.

NOTES

1. Reprint of the preface for the second edition of Barbara Smith, ed., *Home Girls: A Black Feminist Anthology* (New Brunswick, N.J.: Rutgers University Press, 1983, 2000), pp. xiii–xvii. Smith read excerpts from this preface at the Black Feminism Symposium.

2. Jill Nelson, *Straight, No Chaser: How I Became a Grown-up Black Woman* (New York: G. P. Putnam's Sons, 1997), p. 156.

3. A new anthology, *Still Lifting, Still Climbing: African American Women's Contemporary Activism*, edited by Kimberly Springer (New York: New York University Press, 1999), provides an excellent overview of black women's activism since the Civil Rights era.

∼

DANA-AIN DAVIS, ANA APARICIO, AUDREY JACOBS, AKEMI KOCHIYAMA, LEITH MULLINGS, ANDREA QUEELEY, AND BEVERLY THOMPSON[1]

Working It Off: Welfare Reform, Workfare, and Work Experience Programs in New York City

I've always worked. I worked all my life. I've worked for the Attorney General, the Manhattan Borough President's office, and now I work for the Census. I have a Bachelor's Degree. They [Social Services] want you to stop school. When they sent me to welfare, I made an appointment, you know, I kept it. So I bring my resume and everything. He (the caseworker) never once looked at my resume. He told me, "You're going to the parks." I said, "Excuse me, I'm standing up here in a suit, and you're telling me I'm going to the parks?" This is dead in the wintertime. He said, "You heard me, you're going to the parks." I said, "I don't think so. Why can't I be in an office or something?" He said, "No you're going to be out there with the rest of them . . ." He was so nasty. You can have your resume, skills, and everything . . . then they're going to put me to work in the parks or else cut off my benefits. They closed my case.

—Lorraine, 24 June 2002[2]

Lorraine, an African-American woman in her late forties, lives in Central Harlem with her asthmatic teenage son Michael. She not only has a work history, but also has a college degree. Lorraine's story exemplifies some reasons to reconsider the problems of welfare reform and the new work mandate. Her situation calls into question the roaring applause offered by policy pundits since changes in federal welfare rules were instituted seven years ago. Although the accolades reflect the interests of political elites who celebrate decreased enrollment in public benefits programs, for many people welfare reform is not the panacea it has been touted to be. This is especially true for many men and women of color who, along with advocates, vehemently argue that discrimination, poor access to education, and inadequate or inappropriate job training have made life under welfare reform harder for the poorest Americans. They also argue that its implementation is cruel because those in need must surmount tremendous barriers to access support.[3]

Life under welfare reform is not only harder than life pre-reform, but it can also be humiliating. People are forced to comply with work requirements that are often detrimental to the maintenance of their families and educational goals and do not capitalize on their prior work experience. As a result of welfare reform, a larger workforce has been generated, one that gluts the labor market, making it easier for employers to drop wages. Indeed, although the underlying assumption behind welfare reform is that poor people are lazy, in fact most people who receive benefits have worked in the past, but many find themselves unemployed, underemployed, or employed in jobs with wages so low they cannot survive. And because social service benefits are so meager, many recipients often supplement their income by working in the informal economy. Welfare reform discourages attainment of higher education and often steers people to inappropriate work assignments (as was the case with Lorraine). Rather than support people in developing and achieving long-term goals, welfare reform offers inadequate training that does not lead to permanent employment and a living wage. In fact, it often engenders antagonistic relations between government agencies and poor, working-class people.

This chapter describes experiences of welfare reform in New York City, specifically in Manhattan, and examines the effects of one aspect of this policy: work mandate and training programs. Through the voices of black and Latino men and women who are low-income and reside in several Manhattan neighborhoods, we learn that those whose lives are directly impacted by the changes in welfare legislation must confront new economic barriers face-to-face. Many programs do not prepare them to be engaged in the formal labor market. The men and women whose stories illustrate the effects of welfare reform are perched on a precarious economic ledge as the new welfare system compromises their life chances and personal choices.

WELFARE REFORM: AN OVERVIEW

In 1996, President Bill Clinton signed the Personal Responsibility and Work Opportunity Reconciliation Act (hereinafter PRWORA or the Act),[4] legislating changes that reflected "a politics of disgust"[5] that punishes the poor. The Act eliminated welfare assistance as a federal entitlement for all eligible families. Under PRWORA, welfare assistance is now a block grant program through which states receive a fixed amount of federal monies regardless of the number of people in need. Not surprisingly, this drives states to devise mechanisms to decrease their caseloads.

Title I of the PRWORA, known as Temporary Assistance for Needy Families (TANF), replaced the AFDC (Aid for Families with Dependent Children) program for women and children that had existed in various forms since the 1930s. The Act also replaced Home Relief, a program for childless single adults, Job Opportunities and Basic Skill Training Program (JOBS), and emergency assistance. The shift from entitlement to a block grant shredded much of the safety net, which had historically protected those most vulnerable against the vagaries and fluctuations of a market economy.

One of the most restrictive components of PRWORA is that it mandates that individuals may receive no more than five years of federal aid. Within these parameters, states may opt for a limit of less than five years or continue benefits after five years using state funds, but most do not. For example, despite the fact that 8 percent of the population live in poverty in the state of Connecticut, recipients may only receive TANF benefits for a lifetime limit of twenty-one months—even if they have dependent children.[6]

A second aspect of the new program, which has received much criticism, is the requirement that recipients meet increasing work participation rates and that all able-bodied welfare recipients work full-time after two years of receiving aid or risk losing their benefits. These two elements resulted in significant declines in the number of people receiving assistance. Between 1994 and 2001, there has been a national decline in the welfare rolls from 5.1 million to 2.9 million, as noted by Douglas J. Besharov, the Joseph J. and Violet Jacobs Scholar in social welfare studies at the American Enterprise Institute and a professor at the University of Maryland.[7] Although conservative and neo-liberal politicians continue to praise reforms for decreasing the number of people on welfare, when viewed through the lens of race, a different assessment clarifies the impact of welfare reform policy. Recent research such as that conducted by the New York State Scholar Practitioner Team[8] has pointed to the disproportionate impact of welfare reform policy on communities of color.[9] Race-based discrimination has long contributed to perpetual poverty, and welfare reform policy accentuates the racial imbalance of those who constitute the poor. For example, according to the U.S. Census Bureau, in 2001, the poverty rate among blacks was 22.7 percent and among Hispanics, 21.4 percent—more than double the rate for whites, of whom 9.9 percent were poor. (Among Asian Pacific Islanders, the rate was 10.2 percent.)[10] When seen in relation to the economic downturn and increasing unemployment rates in the United States, questions about the disparate impact of welfare reform on people of color and how they are faring must be raised.

In New York state, welfare reform began when Governor George Pataki signed the Welfare Reform Act of 1997. Political scientist and Distinguished Service Professor Emeritus of the State University of New York, Brockport, Sarah F. Liebschutz notes that the act had a twofold message: The message to recipients of public assistance was that they should work, not rely on welfare; to bureaucrats, the message was to emphasize workforce participation rather than welfare eligibility. The bureaucratic emphasis was hardly new. As early as 1988, former governor Mario Cuomo had promoted training and employment programs for public assistance recipients. In the early 1990s, he stressed the use of supportive programs to encourage persons receiving Home Relief to work through "job search, work experience or other assigned activities."[11] By 1994, Cuomo expanded the work-first policy beyond those receiving public assistance through Home Relief. The policy, which came to be known as the JobsFIRST initiative, preceded the New York Welfare Reform Act of 1997. But, unlike the Welfare Reform Act, people were not penalized if they did not work and they were able to attend school and obtain job training.

Meanwhile, downstate in New York City, Republican mayor Rudolph Giuliani was restructuring welfare. Giuliani had won the mayoral race just one year before Cuomo expanded the categories of JobsFIRST recipients. Although their approaches to increasing the rate of employment among recipients differed, Cuomo and Giuliani shared the goal of moving people off welfare. Indeed, increasingly, Democrats and Republicans nationwide shared this similar perspective regarding welfare policy: They viewed poor people as defective and seemed to believe that a job—any job—would automatically end poverty.

Giuliani's work-first approach was considered by welfare advocates as extraordinarily mean-spirited because it forced participants to search for work full-time though many had inadequate training to secure employment. In addition, the focus on work precluded meaningful educational attainment. A number of programs were developed to ensure attachment to work or work-related activities. The idea was that, if people were employed in private-sector jobs, they would no longer need welfare. Or at the very least, their need for public assistance would decrease as wages garnered in the formal labor market increased. In reality, however, participation in programs that placed people in the formal labor market did not offset the costs associated with work, such as having to pay for childcare, purchasing clothes, and increased transportation costs. Additionally, the jobs secured were often temporary. Nonetheless, benefits were reduced or terminated even though employment and income were tenuous.

WORKFARE IN NEW YORK CITY

In 1993, when Giuliani became mayor, New York City had more than 1.1 million public assistance recipients, making it the second-largest welfare system in the nation after California. His disdain for those on welfare was evident in a speech he gave when he took office: Something had to be done about the one-sixth of New Yorkers dependent upon the government, he said, and he promised to "end welfare by the end of the century."

According to the New York City Human Resources Administration (HRA), beginning in 1995 Giuliani led New York on a path to redesign its welfare policy.[12] The model used to facilitate the change was called New York WAY (Work Accountability You). The program's stated purpose was to encourage self-reliance and accountability, and the first step involved shifting the discourse about public assistance. No longer would a recipient go to a Welfare Center to apply for or receive benefits. By January 1998, the mayor announced that Welfare Centers would be renamed Job Centers.[13] To expedite moving from welfare to work, applicants and recipients would access job search and placement services, childcare information, and educational and training service information immediately at each Job Center.[14]

Theoretically, they would be assisted in exploring and pursuing working alternatives to welfare. The name change, however, resulted in confusion for many people. In its newsletter, *Welfare News,* the Welfare Law Center stated that Job Centers were refocused in such a way that *the fact that they provided public benefits was concealed.* In other words, some members of the public were no longer certain they could apply for or receive benefits at Job Centers. In fact, it was discovered that some Job Center staff routinely misled prospective applicants, denied them the right to apply for benefits during the first visit, pressured them into withdrawing applications, improperly denied food stamps and Medicaid when cash aid was denied, and failed to provide notice of the right to a fair hearing. Fair hearings are a process for challenging a determination of benefit denial, sanctions, or reinstatement of benefits. This diversionary strategy turned out to be successful, as many people missed their appointments and were dropped from the welfare rolls. But the tactics resulted in a lawsuit against Giuliani.[15]

The second step of the redesigned welfare system was the expansion of the workfare program, through which recipients would work off their monthly public assistance checks. This program was called the Work Experience Program (WEP). The administrative foot soldier who actualized Giuliani's vision was Jason Turner, HRA commissioner, whose office was responsible for the programmatic operation and compliance of social services. Turner, who was appointed in February 1998, won the position at least in part because he had reduced the number of public assistance recipients in Wisconsin. In New York City, Turner chipped away at the number of recipients receiving public assistance, and, over two years, city Human Resources Administration data showed that the number of single adults and those with dependents dropped more than 47 percent between 1998 and 2003. In February 1998, there were 791,884 recipients, and by February 2003, there were 418,700.[16]

Several core programs were designed to ensure rapid attachment to work. Those who did not find employment in the private job market and who opted to receive assistance were expected to participate in WEP, the rubric under which several programs are organized. Through WEP, each participant engages in structured work assignments and activities typically with government and not-for-profit agencies throughout New York City. These assignments are centered on the belief that people receiving public assistance do not value work and require training on how to follow directions and work cooperatively. Successful internalization of these objectives is supposed to lead to permanent employment in the private sector.

The Skills Assessment and Placement Program (SAP) is a four- to six-week program geared to new applicants for assistance—people not yet receiving benefits. Most Job Centers subcontract with one of four vendors who conduct assessments and place potential recipients in programs.[17] Vendors place case managers in the Job Centers to work with potential recipients when they first apply for public assistance to evaluate their so-called job readiness.

The Employment and Services Placement Program (ESP) is for those whose benefits have been recently activated. Recipients are placed in ESP for employment and job placement. Some ESP clients may be Family Assistance, Safety Net Assistance, or non–public assistance recipients (i.e., food stamp recipients or those who are low-income). Through ESP, job-related training and self-development workshops are incorporated into the job search effort for up to six months. Similarly to SAP, ESP services are subcontracted out to eleven vendors including the four that have SAP contracts. These contracts are performance-based, with payment linked to the number of clients placed in jobs, the level of work (e.g., full-time or part-time) a person secures, job retention, and case closures. The more successful subcontractors are in assisting individuals to leave and remain off public assistance altogether, the more money they receive.[18]

To meet the job-related needs of special populations, there are additional programs. One is the Begin Employment Gain Independence Now (BEGIN) Managed Programs. Through BEGIN, those with low basic education skills are targeted for assistance in accessing work assignments and training. For example, there are Adult Education, GED, and ESL (English as a Second Language) classes. Other programs include the Career and Services Training (CAST) program, which provides internships for high school graduates. Pregnant women——except those with high-risk pregnancies——are directed to the Perfect Opportunity for Individual Skills Development (POISED) program. Involvement in the POISED program is suspended from the eighth month of pregnancy until thirteen weeks after delivery, but after the newborn is thirteen weeks old, the mother resumes her work or work-related activities. There are also programs for those with medical limitations and substance abuse issues.

The Welfare to Work Program is a special WEP and Job Search program run by not-for-profit organizations that targets participants who have been on public assistance for two-and-a-half years or more, are ex-offenders, have a history of substance abuse, or have a history of mental or physical impairment. Those on welfare must take a job, any job, regardless of interest, skill level, type of job, or whether the job will lift the person out of poverty. As such, job placements and training are frequently menial. This was clear to the approximately forty thousand who were participating in workfare by August 1998,[19] many of whom equated workfare with slavery. Journalist and Columbia University journalism professor LynNell Hancock learned that, although some assignments were administrative, many people were forced to work picking up garbage in the parks, cleaning municipal buildings, and doing track work for the city's transit system.[20] If they did not comply, recipients risked being sanctioned, including having benefits denied or having their cases closed. The WEP assignments are not jobs, per se, since workers have neither benefits nor job protection. In spite of such pernicious exploitation, the HRA noted that New York City's WEP program was a tremendous benefit to the city because of the low associated labor costs. WEP workers receive approximately $1.80 per hour, representing the city's share of the welfare check.[21] Community Voices Heard, an activist group composed mostly of women either on or formerly on welfare, has argued that New York City's WEP uses welfare workers to do the same work as city workers, but the city pays them significantly less and undermines the employability of unionized workers.[22]

What concerns do people have about WEP, training, and their own employability? How are these policies contextualized by race?

GATHERING VOICES: METHODOLOGY

The New York State Scholar Practitioner Team conducted a two-year study that explored the impact of welfare reform on two New York City communities, Harlem and the Lower East Side.[23] Data for the study were collected using several methods: focus groups, in-depth interviews, surveys,[24] and Photo Voice.[25] The team conducted six focus groups, with a total of thirty-three participants, between June and November 2001, in collaboration with four community-based organizations and programs[26] designed to capture the range of experiences East and Central Harlem and Lower East Side residents had with welfare reform. Focus group members attended voluntarily, receiving $20 for their participation. The focus group interviews were semistructured, allowing participants to raise concerns they felt were most pertinent. During the focus groups, participants were asked if they were interested in a one-on-one interview for an additional $20. Those who agreed participated in interviews, which lasted one to two hours, that provided an opportunity for deeper discussion about experiences with and the effects of welfare reform.

Surveys were administered to two hundred individuals between October and December 2001 to capture a statistical picture of community residents' experiences under welfare reform. The team of surveyors approached individuals as they exited the eight HRA Job Centers in Manhattan.[27] Though the survey results represent a nonrandom sample of individuals applying for or receiving public assistance in New York,[28] the findings echo those of other studies exploring the effects of welfare reform, particularly studies focusing on people of color.[29]

Photo Voice allows people to capture the issues they feel are important in confronting their environment. Community residents and the staff of community-based programs were given still cameras and asked to photograph their communities and provide a narrative explaining how the images were representative of the impact of welfare reform. This approach enabled participants to record and reflect on their community's strengths and concerns. It also promoted critical dialogue and knowledge concerning personal and community issues through large- and small-group discussion of the photographs.

WORKING IT OFF: WORK EXPERIENCE PROGRAMS AND TRAINING

As a result of welfare reform, any individual receiving public assistance in New York City is expected to work it off, typically through participation in a WEP program, which is structured to simulate a 35-hour workweek. Generally, a person spends three days at work or at a WEP assignment and two days in an HRA-authorized activity such as job search, GED preparation, basic education, or job training.[30] In New York City, single parents must work twenty hours a week or be engaged in work-related activities, and adults in a two-parent family must work thirty hours per week. If people receiving assistance refuse to work or are unable to complete their assignments, they can be sanctioned—have their benefits terminated for a certain period of time or be cut off from receiving benefits altogether. Those working off a public assistance grant receive substantially less than a subsistence/minimum wage.

New York City's program is viewed as particularly restrictive by many, but is also held up by some as a shining example of all that is right with welfare reform and the work-first approach. In fact, the *Los Angeles Times* reported that President George W. Bush has been so impressed with New York City's workfare program that he wants it to become the national model.[31] The president's admiration may be related to the precipitous drop in the number of welfare recipients despite the nation's economic downturn. And, although the national unemployment rate had, by August 2002, increased by more than 20 percent in the previous six months, the rolls continued to drop.[32]

EXAGGERATED PRESUMPTIONS

During Giuliani's administration, Jason Turner often stated, "The best preparation for work is working."[33] The subtext of his comment is based on the presumption that people who receive welfare do not want to work, have never worked, or do not have the skills to work. People receiving assistance, however, do have a desire to work. Furthermore, they often had previous work experience. In fact, although less than 10 percent of survey respondents reported being employed at the time the survey was administered, 60.3 percent had been employed in the last five years. Having previous work histories should increase employability—*assuming jobs are available*. So why weren't people working in the formal wage labor sector? Many assume that they failed to embrace the work ethic. But were there a sufficient number of jobs available? What obstacles limited employment options?

Among the reasons given for unemployment, inability to find a job was the most frequently cited. Nearly 40 percent of survey respondents stated this was the reason for not working. Sheena is a case in point. A mother of one, Sheena lost her job five months before being interviewed for the survey in November 2001, and she had been unable to secure another job. In another instance, Linda, who was twenty-one years old, said she "could not find a job," but was willing to take "any job because [she didn't] want to live a life of boosting [stealing]." Finally, Hosea, who has twenty-two years' work experience, had been unemployed since March 2000. Yet, without formal employment, people had to find ways to make ends meet. According to the survey, 30 percent of all respondents did other work to survive, from braiding hair to babysitting to selling prepared food on the street.

These stories, which support analyses by other researchers,[34] contradict the images of opportunistic so-called welfare mothers and shiftless freeloaders—harmful stereotypes used to demonize poor and working-class people and manipulate the public into supporting legislation that further limits the possibility of true poverty reduction. The larger context of unemployment rates provides a lens through which individual cases can be understood. Although the rates are unreliable because they only include people who are actively looking for a job and exclude those who have stopped their job search, they can show that unemployment is not an aberration. The data confirm that securing employment is often extremely difficult. According to U.S. Department of Labor statistics,[35] between March 2000 and March 2001, when Hosea was jobless, the unemployment rate for the New York metropolitan area fluctuated between 4.7 percent and 5.8 percent. In March 2001, the rate was 5.2 percent, but a year later it was 7.1 percent. Unemployment rates in New York continued to rise, and as of January 2003, it was 8.3 percent, significantly higher than the national rate of 6.5 percent. Clearly, people lost jobs or were unable to secure employment, substantiating the claims made by research participants that unemployment was the result of an inability to find work.

Thirty-six percent of survey respondents and focus group members cited the presence of health conditions that prevented them from working. Carlos, an eighteen-year-old Puerto Rican man, suffered from chronic asthma and was injured, forcing him to depend on a cane and preventing him from securing employment. Rather than assist Carlos in securing appropriate rehabilitative training or educational activities that would allow him to engage in meaningful activities given his physical limitations, his caseworker continuously placed him in WEP assignments to work off the $368 in cash and $25 in food stamps he received each month. Rarely were the assignments desk jobs, and they usually involved some sort of physical exertion. Carlos's health condition limited his ability to work or participate in many work assignments. His health-related barrier to employment is a common reason for not working, reflecting findings in other studies. A recent study by Jamie Harris, a research analyst with the Alliance for Children and Families, and Thomas E. Lengyel, director of the Department of Research and Evaluation Services at the Alliance for Children and Families, found that one-third of the 106 participants in their study had a health condition that prevented them from working.[36] The federal government's own research identified health issues as a tremendous barrier to employment,[37] reporting that 44 percent of TANF recipients have work impairments or disabilities—a figure that was *three times that of the non-TANF population.* The New York State Scholar Practitioner Team's data revealed that people had a number of health concerns, including chronic asthma, physical limitations, diabetes, and drug addiction.

Poverty and joblessness are too often considered to be the fault of individuals and are frequently explained in human capital terms—that is, that people have no skills. Lack of skills will obviously hinder employability, and study participants affirmed the necessity of skills building. Only 14 percent of those who said they did not have a job, however, attributed their unemployment status to the lack of skills and work-related experience. Given that lawmakers and the media frame the reasons for poverty and welfare use as a personal rather than structural issue, this figure is less than one might expect. A human capital analysis does not encompass a critique of the structural barriers to employment; instead, it foregrounds behavioral deficits, directing the blame to the unemployed.

Emphasizing personal deficits obscures the structural explanations that contribute to unemployment, specifically those that lie along axes of race and gender. Racial distinctions were evident in employment patterns among the survey participants. Whites, for example, were twice as likely to be employed as blacks, and they reported the fewest work-related barriers to employment. Whites were also less likely to cite the lack of job skills or problems finding any job. Three times as many Latinos as whites said they could not find a job that pays enough, and when they were employed, 75 percent of blacks and Latinos had incomes of less than $5,000 per year compared with 42 percent of whites. The reported inability of blacks and Latinos to find jobs speaks to possible employer discrimination, which might explain the marked income differentials.

There are also gender distinctions in unemployment patterns. Overall, men and women reported similar reasons for their unemployment status, but there were three gender-specific barriers raised by women: Fifteen percent of women cited lack of childcare; 9 percent said there was domestic violence in their homes; and 8 percent said they were pregnant and, therefore, could not work. Women were also more likely than men to have to care for a sick child or to be unemployed due to lack of pre-school and after-school childcare. The latter suggests that some women do not have the supports to be employed during the typical nine-to-five workday. Additionally, some women indicated they *wanted* to stay at home, because they *preferred* to care for their children themselves.

When assessing why some women do not work, University of California, Santa Cruz, professor of politics Gwendolyn Mink argues that we cannot neglect the fact that historically the United States has expected domesticity, rather than wage-earning, from mothers. Thus, it is not unreasonable that some women desire to stay home.[38] Progressive, gender-sensitive social welfare policy in other countries such as Sweden, Norway, and Denmark sees domestic care as crucial to processes of social reproduction, and policies in these countries have offered greater support to those engaged in caregiving.[39] Gender-sensitive policies in those countries have centered on women's participation in part-time labor, allowing them to both work and care for their children.[40] Mink notes that, in the United States, the new welfare law presumes that if a caregiver is unmarried, market-based labor is better than caring for her own children.[41]

Lola, a mother of three, was penalized for choosing to stay home with her youngest child. Since she made the decision to have children, she said, she should be responsible for them, explaining that she worked for six months after her first two children were born and then left them with babysitters. But, when her third child was born, Lola wanted to stay home. Though she indicated she wanted to re-enter the workforce in the future, Lola preferred to return to work when she was ready—a determination she felt she alone should make depending on her child's development.

Women should be able to choose the model of motherhood that is most important to them. In its original conception in 1935, Aid to Dependent Children, as it was then called, was designed to support full-time caregiving. By the 1960s, employment was encouraged for some segments of the clientele, and by 1988, all AFDC parents with children three years of age and above were required to work or undergo training.[42] Forced employment among poor women reflects the growth of women's participation in the labor market since World War II. Reification of the mother load, that is, working and caregiving, is often carelessly linked to the positive and flexible experiences that white middle-class women have had. Walter Stafford, Diana Salas, and Melissa Mendez—policy analysts with the Roundtable of Institutions of People of Color, Women of Color Policy Network at New York University—point out that white women are the primary beneficiaries of such benefits as maternity leave and employer programs that offer flexible work options.[43] Their research found that, while the government is pushing poor women of color, like Lola, into the labor market, white women are increasingly staying home with infants before returning to work.

Given the expectation that women of color work, the issue of childcare becomes critical. The dearth of childcare options in some communities and the mandate to work have meant that younger and older women are caught in a web of mutual survival. Younger women must rely on older women's availability to care for their children in order to work, and older women are increasingly engaged in caretaking activities as their own benefits are at risk of being reduced or ended.

By focusing on alleged personal failings rather than factors such as race and gender discrimination and inadequate childcare supports, the public discussion about why people might need public assistance—since there are no government obligations to ensure employment—overlooks the very circumstances that might help us adequately understand this situation. The reality that there are too few jobs, especially those that pay living wages, and the myriad concerns specific to mothers belie the dependency discourse that surrounds welfare reform.

Beyond the mandated work hours, work-related activities include job skills training or education related to employment. The rubric of job skills training, however, is very broad, ranging from the acquisition of tangible skills such as computer, clerical, or other job-specific knowledge to so-called soft skills, such as resume writing, interviewing techniques, job searching, and appropriate demeanor with one's coworkers and supervisors. Since many study participants indicated they had not acquired hard skills, what do WEP experience and training programs teach them?

In a very limited number of cases, study participants reported positive assessments about their WEP assignments and training programs. LeAnn, for example, was a twenty-one-year-old African-American woman who reported she was given a good WEP assignment working as a receptionist at a New York City agency. She liked her job and stated, "If they have a position open, then maybe I can get a permanent job." Similarly, Lena, a Spanish-speaking woman in her twenties, said she had no problems at her training site after she was placed. She complied with all of the rules and successfully completed a training program. Unfortunately, LeAnn and

Lena were exceptional cases. Many more described profoundly negative encounters and, indeed, revealed that their hopes of permanent employment may not be realized through WEP.

DEAD-END SITUATIONS: WEP ASSIGNMENTS
AND TRAINING PROGRAMS

Overwhelmingly, WEP participants said they were required to do chore-focused assignments, often in the municipal system. Placements were frequently with the sanitation department and the New York City Department of Parks and Recreation, agencies that have been primary users of WEP workers in New York City. The parks department has aggressively utilized WEP labor,[44] as evidenced by the nearly six thousand workers assigned there in 1999.[45] In December 2000, the department had 3,852 WEP workers, more than any of the other 31 New York City agency WEP placement sites. At that time, the other 2 city agency WEP sites utilizing the labor of recipients were the Department of Sanitation, with 1,249 workers, and the Human Resources Administration, with 1,434. Some observers have argued that WEP employees' work has substantially improved the cleanliness of city parks during a time of stringent city budget constraints. Some study participants were aware of these constraints—and aware that they were assigned to work in departments in which the city has a hiring freeze. Between 1993 and 1998, their participation as a labor source neutralized the impact of cutbacks to the parks department.

One woman, Ivy, described the work assignments as "digging in the dirt," which minimized her chances to build transferable skills. The nature of placements factored strongly into participants' concerns about two issues: Many believed the scant training they received would not lead to permanent employment, and parents receiving assistance worried that their children would take note of their parents' menial work—work that offered no benefits, longevity, or potential for advancement—and would develop negative views of work in general. Ivy, who had three children, challenged the idea that nonworking parents are detrimental to the development of a child's future and their success, arguing that the *type* of work a child's parent does is also influential. "They want you to do sanitation . . . go in the parks and pick up the trash . . . walk around and pick up the trash," Ivy said. "What do I look like to you? You think that's all I want to do for the rest of my life is picking up trash? I don't want to teach my kids that. And I don't want them to be in the rut that I'm in. I'm struggling for them so they can have a better life when they grow up."

Given welfare reform's emphasis on formal work, most participants expected their six- to seven-month WEP assignments would lead to permanent employment. The city's own figures speak otherwise. Of the first 5,300 individuals who entered the job search program, only 5 percent were placed in permanent jobs, according to an HRA analysis.[46] A different study of individuals near or past their time limits recently found that, for 91 percent of respondents, their WEP assignments had not resulted in a permanent job.[47] Among survey participants, only 7 percent received such jobs. WEP has merely cut people off of welfare. It has not, however, helped most find jobs.[48]

Many expressed dismay and disappointment at this reality. Giselle, a young African American with an infant daughter, said, "Anytime they give you an assignment, you would think that . . . if you'd been there for six months, at least you would get hired." Giselle was exasperated because she was "tired of getting into dead[-end] situations." She explains, "They know that these city jobs have a freeze on them. And everywhere they have a freeze. That's why they put me there. And I'm tired of that. That needs to be stopped. My resume is pretty good. I want to go somewhere. If you place me [somewhere] for six months, put me in a situation where I know that the people are at least hiring. Don't put me in where there is a freeze. That's what pissed me off the most."

John, an African-American forty-seven-year-old, had a similar experience. Although he was one of the few people who enjoyed his WEP assignment—John was placed at a human rights organization—he acquired new skills, but it did not lead to a permanent job.

It may be argued that work assignments are supposed to assist in the acquisition of basic skills that lead to attachment to work, but most participants considered their placements bereft of opportunity because they rarely received substantive training. Although she was assigned to a training program, Ivy said, "I haven't seen a computer room, not a training place . . . I haven't seen it. And I haven't seen them really teaching us anything to benefit us. People that have one or two kids in their household need a lot of training." WEP and training programs would not help her secure employment that would enable her to support her family, Ivy said.

Furthermore, many WEP participants were placed in positions in which their prior skills and education were underutilized or ignored altogether. Lorraine, whose story is told at the beginning of this chapter, had some college education, but was not placed in a situation where her skills were put to use. Several people reported that caseworkers wanted them to participate in training programs or WEP assignments that were incongruent with their abilities. "How can you put a person out there to clean the street when some of them have an education? . . . [T]hey just put them in the street—even with a diploma—because that's all they have for now," said Ivy. The term *skills mismatch* comes to mind. Although generally used to describe an individual's dearth of skills, it also is apt to express the skill capital that some people said they possessed, but were unable to draw upon. In several instances, focus group participants reported that their skill level was higher than that required for their WEP placements. Some had lengthy work experience and/or higher education, as was the case with Lorraine, but had been unable to find a job. In these cases, rapid attachment to work and inappropriate placements in an effort to reduce welfare rolls succeed only in creating a dead-end situation.

We found that a greater percentage of blacks and Latinos were placed in WEP programs than whites. Thirty-one percent and 32 percent of blacks and Latinos, respectively, were in WEP programs, compared to no whites. The Applied Research Center conducted a study on welfare reform in various cities across the country, and their data suggest that there may be a racial dimension in relation to work-related activities. The Center found that more people of color were required to be engaged in work-related activities than whites. Thirty-three percent of African Americans and 37 percent of Latinos had to work for their welfare check rather than for wages, compared to 28 percent of whites.[49] Such patterns suggest that welfare reform policies may constitute government-funded racial stratification in employment opportunities.

"I JUST NEED HELP": HIGHER EDUCATION AND WORK EXPERIENCE PROGRAMS

"I want a better education. I'm on public assistance not because I want the government to support me. I just need help until I finish my degree and get ahead on my own," says Laura, a Latina woman who lives in upper Manhattan. Laura has a five-year-old child, is unemployed, and had just become pregnant when she was interviewed for the study. In spite of these challenges, she ambitiously enrolled in a four-year college program. To Laura's surprise, her self-initiated efforts were stunted when her caseworker informed her of her options if she wanted to continue receiving benefits: Although Laura was near the end of her semester, she was told that, effective immediately, she must attend night school so as not to interfere with her daytime WEP assignment. Or she could secure a full-time job. If she did neither, Laura would be sanctioned. The only other option, she was told, would be to attend a two-year college, even though she already possessed an associate's degree.

Discouraging people from educational attainment represents a shift from 1988, when the Family Support Act expanded educational options for welfare recipients. The act allowed recipients to attend two or four years of college, depending on state provisions, and it considered participation in higher education to be work. Prior to 1996, welfare recipients who were full-time students were exempt from work requirements.[50] But the 1996 federal welfare law does not permit four-year college programs to be counted as work. Making it difficult for participants to obtain higher education is illogical given that the potential return on investment in education is great.[51] One study published by the Educational Testing Service found that as little as one semester of full-time, post-secondary education can raise yearly earnings by as much as $10,000. Such barriers to educational success are fundamentally inconsistent with American values that posit the benefits of education. Welfare reform legislation seems to suggest that poor people should gain just enough work experience or educational achievement to be employed in menial labor. Challenging this limited educational access, advocates proposed a bill, Intro 93, to the New York City Council expanding educational and training opportunities for those receiving assistance. Seth Diamond, executive deputy commissioner for the Family Independence Administration of the Human Resources Administration for New York City, objected to the legislation. He stated at a council hearing that "allowing someone with a five-year federal limit on federal welfare to attend college only half-time as their only activity may not be the most appropriate way to move people toward self-sufficiency."[52]

Laura was not unlike others who recognized education as one key to success, but whose efforts were undermined by caseworkers promoting work above all else. Two other women, Vilma and Charlene, reported being forced to forego their self-initiated education goals as well. Vilma's caseworker told her to leave vocational school if she wanted to continue receiving her public assistance. Charlene's caseworker instructed her to leave the City University of New York and "take a WEP assignment, or else . . . [be] sanctioned." In New York City, the work-first mandate caused a precipitous drop in CUNY's enrollment among those receiving public assistance. Between 1995 and 1998, the enrollment for welfare recipients at CUNY went from twenty-eight thousand to fifteen thousand, according to Center for Community Change, an organization committed to reducing poverty and rebuilding communities.[53] Although the CUNY system created City University WEP in 2000 to accommodate TANF recipients—it allowed internships and work study to be used to satisfy their work requirements—state law does not allow students to enroll in non-vocational programs. Liberal arts curriculums were deemed unacceptable educational goals for those receiving assistance. To justify this tactic, some argue that taxpayers should not foot the bill for TANF recipients to attend school if those who don't receive TANF don't get the same help.[54] Further, they assert that education and training are not the best predictors of employment, but that work-oriented welfare reform programs are preferred over education and training.[55]

ON HOSTILE GROUND: CASE MANAGERS AND NON-WEP WORKERS

Welfare reform as presently administered inevitably promotes tensions between recipients and caseworkers, on the one hand, and between recipients and non-WEP workers at WEP sites on the other. Aisha was a young, married, African-American woman with two boys who had a third child on the way at the time of the study. She had been in school for the prior few years and cycled on and off welfare depending on her husband's employment status. Aisha followed all of the requirements in an attempt to make the system work for her, but it was hard. "I just want off . . . completely off," she said. "I can't deal with it. It's a heartache. You have to go constantly [to see caseworkers]. . . . The people at the centers are so nasty. . . . The supervisors don't help you, nobody does. It's like, it's really hard to get somebody [to help] . . . you have to run around for the little bit of public assistance they give you." Others, too, felt caseworkers were rude, lacked respect for clients, and were notoriously difficult to contact by telephone. Some were known to hang up on clients. Another measure of disrespect was caseworker inefficiency and inadequate monitoring of client progress. This resulted in improper handling of cases, sometimes to the point where a recipient was mistakenly sanctioned.

Antagonistic relations were not limited to interactions with social service staff. Study participants described the circumstances of working with non-WEP employees at their WEP sites. They explained the power non-WEP workers held over WEPs, and they argued that the distinctions between the two groups undermined collaboration and respect. Jay, an African-American man in his twenties, lived in a homeless shelter in West Harlem with his wife and two children. Jay was neither in a WEP program nor working due to health problems. But it was his perception that the WEP workers who worked in a park near his shelter, easily identified by their Day-Glo vests—did most of the work. Hostility between the two groups is not surprising given that WEP clearly undercuts the stability of non-WEP jobs. Non-WEP workers feel they can be replaced and WEP workers feel they do not get the same benefits or treatment as regular employees. Although federal law does not allow welfare recipients to substitute for paid workers, Gwendolyn Mink notes that some localities do not renew paid workers' expired employment contracts, therefore opening the way for new, cheaper workfare positions. In essence, then, workfare programs *can* displace paid workers.[56]

WEP workers' sense of vulnerability often was heightened by their supervisors' treatment—at best, lack of concern, and, at worst, passive hostility toward workfare workers—which compromised the receipt of benefits. Jenna, an African-American woman in her forties who lived on the Lower East Side, said the WEP supervisor at her assigned police station position routinely failed to submit her time sheets to her caseworker. The time sheets proved that Jenna had been at work; without that proof she was subject to sanction for alleged failure to show up—which is exactly what happened, as it had at a previous WEP site. Work-site supervisors, who serve as mediators for WEPs' compliance with attendance and work requirements, are supposed to report attendance biweekly.[57] As such, supervisors can wield great power over WEPs, which heightens the workers' sense of vulnerability. Unlike people in the formal wage market, WEP workers have little recourse in such circumstances. Many were forced to rectify such situations by going through a hearing. Reinstatement of benefits can take weeks, even months.

Aisha had been assigned to a BEGIN training program in which her trainer was supposed to submit weekly attendance sheets to Aisha's case manager. At one point, the sheets had not been submitted or were lost, and Aisha was sanctioned. She only discovered the sanction when her landlord warned her she would receive an eviction notice because social services had not forwarded her rent payment. Aisha, however, always kept copies of her time sheets. Describing the situation, she says, "[S]omeone did not put it on my file [that I was in the program], so I was not [considered to be] in compliance. And, lucky [for me], every time I go to the program, [I] have them sign a piece of paper and they stamp it. I don't like to be in a jam, you know, when I know that I was there. So I took those papers to have the sanction lifted." Even with the copies as proof, it took six months for her benefits to be reinstated. With difficulty, she managed to avoid being evicted.

WORK FOR PERMANENT LIFE IMPROVEMENTS

Welfare reform has forced many people onto an economic precipice with fewer options than ever for support in dire times. With rampant benefit reductions, sanctions, forced employment in jobs that do not lead to permanent paid employment, and lack of educational opportunity, overall quality of life for poor and working-class people is acutely compromised. The fabric of life is frayed. As welfare caseloads rise again due to the weak economy, the situation threatens to worsen.

Research participants reported that they often were unable to buy food, they skipped meals, and relied on food pantries. No matter their race or ethnicity, all survey respondents suffered from such food insecurity, but the rate of blacks being unable to buy food was nearly twice that of whites. One woman who once received $300 a month in food stamps was forced, under welfare reform, to buy food for her family of four with $70 in food stamps. Another woman living in a homeless shelter received $118 a month in food stamps for herself and her two daughters.

Respondents also reported increased challenges in meeting daily expenses and paying bills. Overall, 69 percent of survey-takers found paying bills harder in the previous year than in years past, and 58 percent said they had been unable to pay at least some bills at all. Blacks and Latinos reported having the hardest time paying bills—70 percent and 77 percent, respectively, compared to 46 percent of whites. One woman, when asked about paying bills, said, "What's a bill? I can't afford to make a bill. I don't buy new things. I only get $137 a month in cash assistance."

Welfare reform is up for reauthorization in 2004, and the issue of work participation rates and decreased access to education and training sit squarely at the center of the debate. What is not part of the debate are the voices of the people like those described above. Their stories magnify the nuances of policy as it is lived in Manhattan. Although they may not be representative of the nation's entire population of welfare recipients, they certainly express one reality about the effects of welfare reform that reaches far beyond the well-worn success stories.

Working off assistance does not represent a mutual exchange. How can it when workers are paid the equivalent of $1.80 an hour? How can it when the work people do and the training they receive cannot—and does not seem designed to—lift them out of poverty?

There is no single solution to the colossal challenges of poverty. There are, however, certainly better solutions than those found in welfare reform. The workfare concept shifts the focus away from the strategies that could truly assist people, such as earning a living wage through full employment. A policy of full employment would mean that nearly everyone who wants a job has one. It does not mean that the unemployment rate is zero, but rather that the supply of and demand for labor are in equilibrium and the labor force is fully utilized.[58] Full employment should provide people with meaningful jobs such as were found in the Works Progress Administration (WPA) implemented in the 1930s, and the Comprehensive Employment Training Act (CETA), which was passed in 1973. Both programs created jobs, and participants—and society in general—received numerous benefits. Some WPA programs resulted in the building of parks, roads, schools, and hospitals. Communities had access to school lunches, free theater, and public health services.[59] Though implementation of some of the New Deal projects did not pay sufficient attention to the consequences of race discrimination, President Franklin Delano Roosevelt's vision was that work should be "useful . . . in the sense that it affords permanent improvements in living conditions."[60] Although the WPA never provided jobs for all of the seven to eight million people who were unemployed, the two-and-a-half million it did employ worked in meaningful work projects. CETA created jobs for those who had been engaged in training programs with local community-based organizations. Sociologist Nancy Naples reports that CETA workers found employment in a variety of socially useful jobs, including battered women's shelters and neighborhood organizations, among others.[61]

According to Jared Bernstein, policy analyst with the Economic Policy Institute, and Dean Baker, co-director of the Center for Economic and Policy Research,[62] most labor market analysts argue that, in the new economy, the only thing that will help the least skilled is the acquisition of more schooling. Since it is known that subsidizing education will reduce unemployment, self-directed educational plans should be supported. Forcing participants to withdraw from such endeavors does a disservice to their attainment of personal goals, including self-sufficiency. People should certainly be permitted to engage in education, training, and job searches that will provide them with better-paying jobs at living wages—and this should be the mandate for all employers, not just among businesses that benefit from public money. Poverty-wage work should not be privileged in the interest of profit. Those who earn less than a living wage require food stamps, housing assistance, and other social services to survive. Minimum wage does not keep pace with inflation; nor does it close the gap between the rich and the poor.

Having to work off benefits is degrading and, in the long run, unproductive if the WEP assignments are not going to lead to permanent employment or help participants develop real skills. The United States, the world's richest country, should provide full employment at a living wage for those who can work. This should be at the forefront of domestic concerns.

NOTES

1. This chapter, which was drafted by Dana Davis, reports on the research of the New York State Scholar Team, one of five research groups across the country funded by the Kellogg Foundation's Devolution Initiative to examine, among other issues, racial disparities and welfare reform. The New York State team was based at the Graduate Center of the City University of New York and directed by Leith Mullings. Andrea Queeley coordinated the Photo Voice project. A more extensive discussion of the research findings can be found in *The Impact of Welfare Reform on Two Communities in New York City* (New York: New York State Scholar Practitioner Team, CUNY Graduate Center, 2002) and is available by contacting Dana Davis at danaain.davis@purchase.edu or Leith Mullings at LMullings@gc.cuny.edu.

2. The names of all individuals have been changed.

3. See Gordon Hurd, "Safety Net Sinking: Welfare Reform during Recession: Discrimination and Poor Access to Education and Job Training Make the Hard Times Harder," *Colorlines* (Summer 2002): 17–21; Rebecca Gordon, *Cruel and Usual: How Welfare "Reform" Punishes Poor People* (Oakland: Applied Research Center, 2001).

4. House of Representatives, Personal Responsibility and Work Opportunity Reconciliation Act, Public Law 104–193, 104th Congress, H.R. 3734, 22 August 1996 (*U.S. Statutes at Large* 110): 2105. The Act consists of nine sections addressing Aid to Families with Dependent Children (AFDC), benefits for legal immigrants, the Food Stamp Program, SSI for children, childcare, the Child Support Enforcement Program, modifications to the child nutrition program, and the Social Services Block Grant. The ninth section concerned miscellaneous issues such as the elimination of housing assistance to fugitive felons, sanctioning of those with positive drug tests, and national goals to prevent teenage pregnancy.

5. This term was used by Pennsylvania State University political scientist Ange-Marie Hancock, whose work elucidates the way political culture organizes the public identity of marginalized groups. Through distorted frames of public issues, consumers accept the hegemonic norms of elite representation. For example, Hancock argues that the disfigured image of black women on welfare, labeled "welfare queens," represented a "politics of disgust." Ange-Marie Hancock, *The Public Identity of the "Welfare Queen" and the Politics of Disgust* (forthcoming).

6. Bread for the World, "Facts for Connecticut," 2001. http://www.bread.org/issues/working_from_poverty_to_promise/state_facts/connecticut.html.

7. Douglas J. Besharov, "Welfare Rolls: On the Rise Again," *Washington Post*, 16 July 2002, A17.

8. Ana Aparicio, Dana Davis, Audrey Jacobs, and Leith Mullings, "Racial and Ethnic Disparities and Welfare Reform in New York State" (New York: City University of New York, 2000).

9. Other research focusing on the impact of welfare reform on women of color includes Linda Burnham, "Welfare Reform, Family Hardship and Women of Color," *The Annals of the American Academy of Political and Social Sciences* 577 (September 2001): 38–48; Dana Davis, "Surviving Welfare Reform: Battered Black Women's Experiences in Poughkeepsie, New York" (Ph.D. diss., Graduate Center, City University of New York, 2001).

10. Bernadette D. Proctor and Joseph Dalaker, *Poverty in the United States: 2001*, U.S. Census Bureau, Current Population Reports, Ser. P-60, No. 219 (Washington, D.C.: U.S. Government Printing Office, 2002).

11. Sarah F. Liebschutz, "Welfare Reform in New York: A Mixed Laboratory for Change," in *Managing Welfare Reform in Five States: The Challenge of Devolution*, ed. Sarah F. Liebschutz (Albany, N.Y.: The Rockefeller Institute Press, 2000), 57–76.

12. New York City Human Resources Administration, "Welfare to Work: New York City Welfare Reform Program, 'NYC WAY' Work Accountability You." http/www.nyc.gov.html/hra/html/serv_welfarework.html.

13. Ibid.

14. Ibid.

15. Welfare Law Center, "New York City Implements Major Changes in Manner in Which Applications for Food Stamps, Medicaid, and Cash Assistance Are Processed," *Welfare News* (April 1999). http://www.welfarelaw.org/nycimp.htm. The case, *Reynolds v. Giu-*

liani, challenged New York City Jobs Center practices that illegally denied access to Medicaid, food stamps, and cash benefits. This was the first case in the country challenging welfare reform implementation practices that illegally denied the right to apply for TANF, state-funded cash assistance, Medicaid, and food stamps. The court denied the state defendants' motion to dismiss the complaint, and ordered the city to comply with legal requirements protecting the rights of individuals to apply for assistance. The city defendants asked for an injunction, which was also denied in 2000. "*Reynolds vs. Giuliani.* Court Decisions," *New York Law Journal* (2000): 35.

16. New York City Human Resources Administration, "HRA Facts: February 1999" (March 1999); New York City Human Resources Administration, "HRA Facts: February 2000" (March 2000); "HRA Facts: July 2002" (August 2002) (New York: Data Analysis and Research Office of Policy and Program Analysis). http://www.ci.nyc.ny.us.

17. In 2001, the SAP vendors were Arbor, Federation Employment and Guidance Services (FEGS), Curtis and Associates, and Goodwill Industries of Greater New York.

18. Demetra Smith Nightingale, Nancy Pindus, Frederica D. Kramer, John Trutko, Kelly Mikelson, and Michael Egner, "Welfare and Work Reform in New York City During the Giuliani Administration: A Study of Program Implementation" (Washington, D.C.: The Urban Labor and Social Policy Center, July 2002).

19. Greg Butterfield, "Workfare Workers Plan Mass Jobs March in New York," *Workfairness* (press release, 22 August 1998). http://www.iacenter.org/Thursday.htm.

20. LynNell Hancock, *Hands to Work: The Stories of Three Families Racing the Welfare Clock* (New York: HarperCollins, 2002).

21. Committee on Social Welfare Law, "Welfare Reform in New York City: The Measure of Success" (New York: Association of the Bar of New York City, August 2001). http://www.abcny.org/currentarticle//welfare.html.

22. Andrew Stettmer, "Welfare to Work: Is it Working? The Failure to Move the Hardest to Employ into Jobs," New York Community Voices Heard, n.d. http://www.cvh action.org.

23. See Dana Davis, Ana Aparicio, Audrey Jacobs, Akemi Kochiyama, Leith Mullings, Andrea Queeley, and Beverly Thompson, *The Impact of Welfare Reform in Two Communities in New York City* (New York: Graduate Center, City University of New York Ph.D. Program in Anthropology, 2002).

24. The survey was developed in consultation with the Human Rights Project of the Urban Justice Center, which also conducted data analysis.

25. Photo Voice is a participatory action research strategy conceptualized by Caroline Wang. See Caroline C. Wang, "Photo Voice: A Participatory Action Research Strategy Applied to Women's Health," *Journal of Women's Health* 8, no. 20 (1999): 185–192.

26. Collaborating groups/programs were the Maternal Infant and Reproductive Health Program, a program of the New York City Department of Health; Union Settlement Association, which has worked to solve urban problems in East Harlem since 1895; Harlem Congregations for Community Improvement, an interdenominational consortium of city congregations in the Harlem community; and the Lower East Side Family Union (LESFU), a nonprofit neighborhood organization founded in 1974 to prevent the dissolution of families.

27. The eight Job Centers in Manhattan were Dyckman, East End, East Harlem, Hamilton, Riverview, St. Nicholas, Waverly, and Yorkville.

28. No statistical tests were run on the data, which are therefore not statistically significant.

29. See, for example, Susan T. Gooden, "All Things Not Being Equal: Differences in Caseworker Support Toward Black and White Welfare Clients," *Harvard Journal of African-American Public Policy* 4 (1998): 23–33; Gordon, *Cruel and Usual.*

30. Nightingale, Pindus, et al., "Welfare and Work Reform."

31. Margery Waller, "New York Program Wrong Model for U.S.," *Los Angeles Times,* 21 April 2002, M2.

32. Leslie Kaufmann, "Despite Slump Cities See Drop in Welfare Rolls," *New York Times,* 31 August 2002, A1.

33. Jason DeParle, "What Welfare-to-Work Really Means," *New York Times Magazine,* 20 December 1998, 50.

34. For example, see Kathryn Edin and Laura Lein, *Making Ends Meet: How Single Mothers Survive Welfare and Low-Wage Work* (New York: Russell Sage Foundation, 1997), and Leith Mullings and Alaka Wali, *Stress and Resilience: The Social Context of Reproduction in Central Harlem* (New York: Kluwer Academic/Plenum, 2001).

35. U.S. Department of Labor, Bureau of Labor Statistics, Local Area Unemployment Statistics. http://www.bls.gov.lau/home.htm.

36. Jamie Harris and Thomas E. Lengyel, "Ends That Don't Meet: Employment Under Welfare Reform," in *Faces of Change: Welfare Policy through the Lens of Personal Experience,* ed. Thomas E. Lengyel and David Campbell (Milwaukee, Wisc.: Alliance for Children and Families, 2002).

37. Government Accounting Office, *Welfare Reform: More Coordinated Federal Effort Could Help States and Localities Move TANF Recipients with Impairments Toward Employment* (Washington, D.C.: GAO, 2001). http://www.gao.gov/new.items/d0237.pdf.

38. Gwendolyn Mink, *Welfare's End* (Ithaca, N.Y.: Cornell University Press, 1998).

39. Ulrike Liebert, "Degendering Care and Engendering Freedom: Social Welfare in the European Union," in *Women and Welfare: Theory and Practice in the United States and Europe,* ed. Nancy J. Hirschmann and Ulrike Liebert (New Brunswick, N.J.: Rutgers University Press, 2001), 261–288.

40. Recent critiques of these policies argue that women work in low-wage, part-time employment and consequently experience occupational segregation and income disparity.

41. Mink, *Welfare's End,* 108.

42. Anna Shola Orloff, "Ending the Entitlements of Poor Single Mothers: Changing Social Policies, Women's Employment, and Caregiving in the Contemporary United States," in *Women and Welfare,* 138–159.

43. Walter Stafford, Diana Salas, and Melissa Mendez, "Race, Gender, and Welfare Reform: The Need for Targeted Support" (New York University, Robert F. Wagner School of Public Service, The Roundtable of Institutions of People of Color, Women of Color Policy Network, 2002).

44. Steven Cohen, *Managing Workfare: The Case of the Work Experience Program in the New York City Parks Department* (Columbia University School of International and Public Affairs, March 1999). http:// www.columbia.edu/~sc32/wep.html.

45. Nightingale, Pindus, et al., "Welfare and Work Reform," 40.

46. Stettmer, "Welfare to Work."

47. Meredith Ballew, *The Journey Toward Self-Sufficiency: Examining the Effects of Welfare Reform on New York City TANF Recipients Approaching Their Five-Year Time Limits* (New

York: New York University Robert F. Wagner Graduate School of Public Service and Community Voices Heard, forthcoming).

48. Stettmer, "Welfare to Work."

49. Gordon, *Cruel and Usual.*

50. Nightingale, Pindus, et al., "Welfare and Work Reform," 40.

51. Anthony P. Carnevale and Kathleen Reich, with Neal C. Johnson and Kathleen Sylvester, *A Piece of the Puzzle: How Education Is Making Welfare Reform Work in the States* (Princeton, N.J.: Educational Testing Service, 2000). http://www.span-online.org/puzzle.pdf.

52. The City Council passed the bill in February 2003, but it was vetoed by the current mayor, Michael R. Bloomberg. The council, in turn, overrode the mayor's veto in April 2003. See Seth Diamond, "Testimony of Seth Diamond, Executive Deputy Commissioner Family Independence Administration Human Resources Administration before the City Council Committee on General Welfare, Intro 93: Education and Training for Public Assistance Recipients" (City Hall, 17 April 2002). http://www.nyc.gov/html/hra/html/news_press4_18_02.html. Also see Leslie Kaufman and Nichole M. Christian, "Welfare Veto Is Overridden by Council," *New York Times,* 10 April 2003, D1.

53. Center for Community Change, "New York Welfare Rights Initiative" (Washington, D.C., 8 April 1998). http://www.communitychange.org/organizing/nywri8.htm.

54. Lawrence Mead, comments made at Bridging the Gap: Higher Education and Career-Centered Welfare Reform conference at Metropolitan College, New York City, 18 November 2002.

55. See, for example, James Riccio, Daniel Friedlander, and Stephen Freedman, *GAIN: Benefits, Costs, and Three-Year Impacts of a Welfare-to-Work Program* (New York: Manpower Demonstration Research Corporation, September 1994); Gayle Hamilton, Stephen Freedman, Lisa Gennetian, Charles Michalopoulos, et al., *National Evaluation of Welfare-to-Work Strategies: How Effective Are Different Welfare-to-Work Approaches? Five-Year Adult and Child Impacts for Eleven Programs* (New York: Manpower Demonstration Research Corporation, November 2001).

56. Mink, *Welfare's End.*

57. Nightingale, Pindus, et al., "Welfare and Work Reform," 39.

58. Jared Bernstein and Dean Baker, "Full Employment at Risk," *The American Prospect* 12, no. 19 (2001).

59. Frances Fox Piven and Richard A. Cloward, *Regulating the Poor: The Functions of Public Welfare* (New York: Vintage Books, 1993).

60. James T. Patterson, *America's Struggle Against Poverty 1900–1994* (Cambridge, Mass.: Harvard University Press, 1994).

61. Nancy A. Naples, "From Maximum Feasible Participation to Disenfranchisement," in *Whose Welfare,* ed. Gwendolyn Mink (Ithaca, N.Y.: Cornell University Press, 1999), 69.

62. Jared Bernstein and Dean Baker, "Full Employment, Don't Give Up without a Fight" (Washington, D.C.: Economic Policy Institute, Working Paper No. 122, January 2002).

～

DAPHNE A. BROOKS

"It's Not Right but It's Okay": Black Women's R & B and the House That Terry McMillan Built

Yo, R & B sucks! I mean, there's a couple of people who can flow, but the genre sucks! Just a bunch of people singing over rap records! Got an old rap record? Sing over it! Then everybody talk about their label. . . . Label this, label that! The Jacksons wasn't singin' about Epic, because nobody gave a fuck!

—Chris Rock[1]

From the cozy confines of our twenty-first century neo-soul universe, where guitar-picking earth goddesses India Arie and Lauryn Hill do battle with piano empress Alicia Keys and feisty wordsmith Jill Scott for the critical credibility throne, the era of mid- to late 1990s popular R & B threatens every day to fade into oblivion like the sour memory of a Mase–Puff Daddy B-side collaboration. But in 1997, the year of Puffy's meteoric rise to fame as a producer notorious for transforming past hits into slick aural wallpaper stunningly bereft of originality, Rock's churlishly blunt observations touched an all-too-familiar chord. Some years before Rock's vitriolic diatribe, *Village Voice* writer Nelson George declared the death of rhythm and blues. In his book of the same name,[2] George sought to expose the hollowness of the recording industry, which, over the past thirty years, he suggested, had eviscerated black musical innovation, transforming the presumed aesthetic backbone of contemporary popular music culture into transparent, market-driven product. Rock's comments, then, serve to reinforce George's claims regarding the state of rhythm and blues culture at the close of the twentieth century—that it was redundant and lacked invention, and it eschewed aesthetic innovation and creativity in favor of a relentless and unapologetic engagement with corporate, mainstream power structures.

More to the point still, Rock's critique here is perhaps indicative of an intense wave of contempt for the *popular* in 1990s African-American culture (though Rock, himself, is a creature of that very landscape). For just as that decade signaled the commercial rise and dominance of hip-hop music as well as the onset of a second wave of post–civil rights black filmmaking, one could argue that the 1990s also posed a fascinatingly new and disturbing crisis within black cultural criticism: how to discuss, analyze, and explore what one might call lowbrow, apolitical mass-market African-American expressive forms. Like 1990s R & B pop music, black popular literature of the period garnered similar disdain from cultural critics who seemed to struggle with the work of buppie pulp-fiction writers such as Terry McMillan.

Many of the literary and cultural critiques directed at novelist McMillan's work are, in fact, here summed up by Rock's observations: Her novels recycle the safe and culturally familiar, they market superficial narrative form and imagery in lieu of what many critics deem to be more gutsy and imaginative prose, and—as Albert Murray and many others have claimed—her fiction fails to register as legitimate literature in the grandest use of that term.

Curiously, however, although much has been made of the aesthetic shortcomings of black popular music and mass-market black literature, few have interrogated the striking cross-pollination of themes and imagery in black popular literature and the diva-dominated R & B of the 1990s. The juxtaposition of these two critical camps in mid-1990s contemporary culture is all the more provocative if one considers the gendered subtext of these debates. For every new scholarly study in the 1990s that interrogated the cultural and political currency of hip-hop as a subversive transformation of the African-American cultural landscape, and for every demand to forge a literature as brave and unapologetic as hip-hop itself, the push to discount the enormously successful genres of R & B and pop literature—forms that were dominated by women's voices—remains curiously undertheorized in cultural studies.

In this chapter, I suggest that we look closely at the complex relationship between the fiction of McMillan, one of the most financially successful African-American novelists of all time, and the booming industry of contemporary R & B recording. Specifically, I wish to illuminate the ways in which McMillan's *Waiting to Exhale*, her most successful novel to date, drastically influenced and informed the terrain of contemporary R & B culture in the past decade. The 1992 publication of that text had, by the time of its 1995 film adaptation, sold over 3 million copies. It marked a watershed moment in American culture as it announced and contributed to a shift in black popular cultural consciousness and production during the last decade of the twentieth century. Advantageously positioned in the aftermath of the Clarence Thomas–Anita Hill Senate hearings, *Exhale* dramatically extended and popularized for mass consumption the politics of a particular kind of heterosexual black middle-class conflict and desire.[3] Moreover, more than any other author and perhaps any other cultural figure save Oprah Winfrey, McMillan has contributed to the construction and visibility of a black middle-class female consumer, a comic transmutation of Toni Morrison's tragically rendered Hagar in *Song of Solomon*.[4]

McMillan's heroines—perhaps like many of the author's readers—express heartbreak, disappointment, loneliness, and sexual desire, and they participate as both creators and willing victims of American material culture. Further, her texts make visible for consumption a spectacularly derived image of black domestic, heterosexual-centered conflict that has become a staple of 1990s music, film, and (to a much lesser extent) television. Thus, I aim to recontextualize *Exhale*, resituating that novel within a broader network of pop cultural transmogrifications. Further, I trace the novel's influence on several successful R & B projects and on what I read as the popular construction and commodification of black women's discontent in contemporary pop. As I intend to demonstrate, by the close of the 1990s, it may have been impossible to hear two hugely successful R & B and pop crossover tracks—TLC's irreverently bawdy and playful "No Scrubs," which called for a ban on the jobless, status-less "scrub" who "hangs out the passenger's side of his best friend's ride trying to holler at me," and a teenage Destiny's Child's "Bills, Bills, Bills" bemoaning the situation where a "triflin', good for nothin' kinda brotha" can't pay his telephone bills—and not link them to McMillan's most successful novel.

WHAT'S THE 411? BLACK WOMEN'S POP CONFESSIONALS

Born on 18 October 1951 in Port Huron, Michigan, McMillan was raised by her mother after her parents divorced. She graduated from the University of California, Berkeley, in 1979. In 1987, after giving birth to a son and focusing her energies on single motherhood, McMillan published her first novel, *Mama*. Since then, she has published four novels, edited a literary anthology, and evolved into one of the more recognizable black female cultural icons of the past twenty years. *Exhale*, her third novel, rapidly became one of the top-selling works of fiction in 1992, spawning a film adaptation, a chart-topping soundtrack, and unprecedented attention to black literary culture. The cultural power and influence of McMillan's work became undeniable after the much-noted crossover success of the film adaptation. The 1995 Forest Whitaker–directed project remains the first and only film starring an all-black female cast to open at number one at the box office. With its popularity, along with that of the soundtrack, McMillan was able to garner a lucrative film deal for the adaptation of her follow-up novel, *How Stella Got Her Groove Back*.[5]

Exhale's popular appeal evolved as a result of its multiple narratives of intimacy and McMillan's lively and comic prose, which renders the trials and tribulations of four thirty-something, single black professional women living in Phoenix, Arizona. Each is on a personal quest for sexual fulfillment and lifelong partnership. Savannah Jackson, seemingly the critical and observatory core character of the narrative, is, when the novel opens, moving to Phoenix from Denver where, as she puts it, "the men are dead." A public relations executive, Savannah operates as the world-weary survivor who offers romantic advice to her friends, yet who, for herself, craves "peace of mind; a place I can call home; feeling important to somebody; and just trying to live a meaningful, significant, and positive life."[6] Savannah utters the now-famous phrase "waiting to exhale" as she "worries if she'll ever be able to exhale . . . if she'll ever be able to find the right man" (15). She speaks for the remaining characters in this regard. The faithful wife of a computer software company executive who has just left her for his white secretary, Bernadine Harris struggles to recover from her divorce, from "fitting into the blueprint of his life" (30). Flighty Robin Stokes, an insurance agent, finds herself addicted to unfaithful, emotionally bankrupt partners, "lying, sneaky, whorish" men, as she calls them. And Gloria Matthews struggles with self-esteem, a weight problem, and raising a teenage son alone while running a beauty salon.

Several interesting and occasionally overlooked critical points are worth noting regarding *Exhale*, particularly because critical discussions of it often seem to revolve around its sexual politics. The novel is, for instance, very much a narrative that thematically, culturally, and perhaps to a lesser extent structurally evokes the contemporary American West and specifically southwestern culture. Bernie and John have moved from Philly to Phoenix. Gloria has uprooted from her hometown of Oakland. Savannah is from Denver and Robin is a native of Arizona. The novel operates as a kind of nouveau migration narrative for middle-class, single black women. These women are in search of more hospitable climates (literally and figuratively), and they gravitate toward places of warmth, heat (passionate and otherwise), and the chance to enjoy a new landscape of spaciousness. *Exhale* is also very much a narrative of the desert, starting with nothing and working toward a fanciful oasis. This new landscape is largely built around an idealized notion of black women's friendships. Although some critics such as Janet Mason Ellerby and Rita B. Dandridge have argued that McMillan's work outlines the ways in which these characters free themselves "from the desire for the patriarchal family" and stress the importance of community, I suggest that these friendships seem tenuous.[7] What could be a true psychic and emotional interdependence among the four heroines is never fully realized, and the emphasis on heterosexual coupling suggests that lovers are ultimately valued over friends. The narrative also fails to explore the possibility of homosocial and/or homoerotic bonding altogether.

Perhaps the most curious aspect of *Exhale*, however, is its self-conscious temporality and its near-obsessive acknowledgement of the 1990s moment in which it is immersed. Deeply entrenched in the cultural media of 1990 and early 1991, it is a text with repeated references to the release of Nelson Mandela from prison, the governor of Arizona's refusal to endorse the Martin Luther King, Jr., holiday, and allusions to hit studio films such as *The War of the Roses* and *Steel Magnolias*.

The novel almost ritualistically references pop artists—from Luther Vandross and Bobby Brown to Paula Abdul and Prince—yet the narrative fails to mount an in-depth engagement with the significance, if any, of this environmental context in the characters' lives. The reason why Bernie would walk out of the misogynist divorce spectacle *The War of the Roses* or what kind of vicarious sexual pleasure Gloria derives from listening to a Vandross record in the dark are never fully explored. Rather, like brand names, these allusions function as empty signs of the times and as examples of the disposable consumption practices (sexual and material) that dominate these characters' day-to-day experiences.

In a 1990 *Village Voice* article, Thulani Davis expressed a wariness toward this "matter-of-fact" narrative style and found it characteristic, at the time, of what she viewed as a "new generation" of black novelists: McMillan, Melvin Dixon, Tina McElroy, Marita Golden. These writers, Davis argued, are "less interested in race and protest. . . . [T]heir books describe some part of the lonely, self-involved journey of the middle-class African American who has access to some little piece of the Dream and is as deeply ensconced in American mass culture as in our boisterous yet closely held black world." Writing at the dawn of this new decade of the (black) popular, Davis worried that as "we turn the corner of the century, the shared yearnings based on race, gender, generation, or family so common to black fiction could become inscrutable relics of the past, like the Motown records a Bup executive retrieves from the garbage in George Wolfe's play *The Colored Museum*."[8]

Outside of the "sankofa" impulse that, Tricia Rose argues, "is often used in contemporary black American culture" to suggest that "one must look backward before one can move forward," and clearly distanced from "emphasizing historically and culturally literate change and transformation," *Exhale* remains in an odd hypertemporal vacuum.[9] And this is perhaps the most disturbing aspect of McMillan's work: Her fiction's ephemerality and entrenchment in mass culture suggest the black experience is, on some level, disposable. As popular fiction, it recirculates the familiar, the literal, the safe, and self-conscious. As a text about the present, it seems uninterested in linking that present to the complexities of the historical past or the future. Instead, *Exhale* replaces historical depth with an affirming, fleeting engagement with the immediate. McMillan's fiction makes one question whether this sexy, shifting, and alluring thing called contemporary, popular blackness will go the way of a pair of Air Jordans—a flamboyant and flashy yet ultimately replaceable commodity.

Nevertheless, McMillan's work remains successful due, in part, to this very sense of cultural immediacy and contemporaneity with the lives of readers. *Exhale*, in particular, gained notoriety and cultural popularity not from lyrical and metaphorical prose reminiscent of a Morrison or a Gayl Jones, but from its affirmation of the literal, from its frank and occasionally ribald emphasis on black middle-class women's lack of fulfillment, their betrayal, their sexual and emotional frustration. Brimming with now-legendary tales of disastrous dates and explicit descriptions of sexual encounters gone sour (Savannah has such an unsatisfactory experience with a lover who performs oral sex that she says, "I didn't know what I was sleeping with: a man or a beast" (120) and Robin says with disappointment that one partner's penis feels more like a finger than a sexual organ), the fiction of McMillan and others such as Connie Briscoe and Bebe Moore Campbell "aim[s] squarely at the black middle class readers who are turned off by the relentless high-mindedness of say, Toni Morrison and who want to see more of their own experiences and aspirations reflected in the books they read."[10] Further, as Davis astutely observes, McMillan's work replaces political and literary protest with "homilies on how to survive."

Exhale also christened the popular embrace of a new genre of black women's confessional: Characters like Robin earnestly articulate a longing "to know what it's like to feel pampered, to not have to worry about how high the phone bill is or if the rent is going up" (52); and women like Savannah openly vent about men who "do not hold themselves accountable to anybody for anything. . . . And we let them. They lie to us without a conscience, they fuck as many of us at a time as they want to and then cry the 'I'm not ready for commitment' bullshit." Savannah firmly concludes that "I don't need a man to rescue me or take care of me financially—I can take care of myself" (12). This kind of declaratory content, which permeates the novel, is particularly distinct and significant. It is especially apparent as the text shifts between first, third, and even second person in passages in which the heroines address themselves in order to document the mistakes they've made in life and love. Indeed, consider the ways in which these lyrical patterns and structures reflect pop music and the singer-songwriter, sun-kissed, folk-pop genre of the seventies (to which McMillan may have been exposed during her years in Berkeley). McMillan essentially sparked the development of a mass-market black women's "confessional genre"—a space in popular fiction previously occupied almost solely in the sixties, seventies, and eighties by white female novelists, including Erica Jong and Judy Blume. A kind of black women's Lilith Fair, *Exhale* masters a format for conveying the intimate emotions of black middle-class, heterosexual women's self-involvement and conventional desires concerning sex and family. Thus, McMillan's third novel departs from the complex, swirling, blues and jazz notes and structures that Farah Griffin, Ann duCille, and other black feminist critics have convincingly identified in twentieth-century black women's fiction (e.g., Jessie Fauset, Morrison, and others).[11] Rather, it is a work of fiction that echoes the earnest outpourings of seventies folk and pop troubadours—less Joni Mitchell and Ricki Lee Jones, more Carole King and Stevie Nicks, Carly Simon and Janis Ian, Helen Reddy and Christine McVie.[12] Adding a hip-hop savvy element of urban vernacular, McMillan's work thus operates as a culturally hybrid, post–civil rights expression of black middle-class women's social and cultural desire.

OUT OF THE 'HOOD & INTO THE HOME: BE CAREFUL

McMillan has thus largely contributed to cultivating a popular discourse that presumably articulates the interior world of black women professionals in their thirties who are successful, alone, available, and unhappy. No doubt fueled in part by Oprah Winfrey's initial talk-show success in the 1980s and combined with McMillan's best-sellers, this trend of black women's confession manifested itself spectacularly in the pop R & B music of the past decade. Indeed, McMillan's work is tied very deeply to a shift away from the earnest harmonizing of black boy groups in the late 1980s and early 1990s, led by Boyz II Men, the New Edition revival, and the solo work of Johnny Gill, Ralph Tresvant, Al B. Sure, Christopher Williams, and Babyface. At that time, New Jack Swing epitomized by Guy and crafted by its architect Teddy Riley combined hip-hop soundscapes with 1970s pop balladeering, inflecting it with a more sexually aggressive, performative bravado. In turn, the raunchy R & B balladeer was born anew, owing as much to NWA as to Marvin Gaye.

Exhale thus opened the door to female R & B responses to this kind of black male pop braggadocio and to the black female pop consumer market. It was as though the book transformed into soap opera narrative black women's collective dismay after Guy lead singer Aaron Hall mumbled "dumb bitch" in the group's biggest single, "Piece of My Love." That 1989 hit declared, "You can have a piece of my love/It's waiting for you," an offer of no-strings-attached adulterous sex with a female lover. The song's New Jack Swing misogyny may have helped spark the 1990s rise of angry, defensive black female R & B responses to such burgeoning sexism. It is important to consider, however, that black women's R & B reactions collapsed, more often than not, into misinformed and misdirected constructions of liberation ideology for African-American female consumers—and *Exhale* had everything to do with this strategy of expression. Although Rita Dandridge suggests that McMillan's fiction demonstrates the ways that "black popular culture is group affirming and self-liberating," the music that McMillan's works have informed appears to be trapped in a vortex of alienation, betrayal, and a vaguely mapped blueprint of social independence. This is predicated on the spectacle of gender conflict and confrontation rather than social autonomy.[13]

Just as is the case with Terry McMillan's fiction, cultural critics have largely overlooked contemporary R & B—and particularly black women's R & B—in favor of a critical privileging of other forms. Viewed as the most politically salient popular music form, hip-hop is often perceived as the genre most worthy of cultural critique and political actualization. Black women's popular desire is thus depoliticized and disregarded for its reflections on domestic and socioeconomic politics and sexual fulfillment. What critics have failed to fully interrogate are the ways in which this subgenre also operates as a creative extension of hip-hop culture itself, while simultaneously offering a distinctive break from the art form. Indeed, although veteran singer Mary J. Blige has carried the dubious title of "the queen of hip-hop soul" since the release of her 1992 debut *What's the 411*, very few cultural pundits have unpacked the particularities of such a label. At its most challenging moments, hip-hop soul borrows from rap culture's sparring, braggadocio marathons, snaps, signifying, and verbal prowess. Although Blige's work on *411* would only hint at what she would produce in the following decade, it was that record that firmly relocated the R & B diva at the crossroads of urban, outdoor street energy and bedroom balladry. Although some of the work of Blige's peers harks back to the primitivist complexities of black female commodification that duCille explores in her work on blues songstresses, much of the material recorded by black female pop music artists in the 1990s extended the trope of emotional weariness and spiritual emaciation stylized by McMillan.[14] Profiles and confessionals of black women who are socially mobile, who have experienced great economic and professional success, but who go unfulfilled personally and romantically, abounded in 1990s R & B. Yet the candid expressions of loneliness are combined with *Exhale's* trademark hostility and disappointment in male partners. Blige and TLC beget Faith Evans, 702, and Destiny's Child—artists who rode the McMillan decade of discontent with much success.

In particular, the latter group built a steady crossover following based on a string of singles fueled by McMillanesque themes and narrative structural flourishes. "Bills, Bills, Bills," the first single on *The Writing's on the Wall*—the group's second album, released in 1997—recycles *Exhale* themes of material disillusionment and distrust.

At first we started out real cool/Taking me places I ain't never been/But now you're getting comfortable and ain't doing those things you did before/You're slowly making me pay for things your money should be handling/And now you asked to use my car/Drive it all day and don't fill up the tank/And you have the audacity to even come and step to me/And asked to ho' some money from me/Until you get your check next week/You triflin' good for nothin' type of brother/Silly me. Why haven't I found another/A baller. When times get hard someone to help me out/Instead of a scrub like you who don't know what a man's about/(Chorus) Can you pay my bills? Can you pay my telephone bills? Can you pay my automo bills? If you did then maybe we could chill/I don't think you do/So you and I are through![15]

Lead singer Beyoncé Knowles here takes her lover on a lengthy, detailed trip through the burgeoning stages of her distrust and disillusionment in their relationship. Backed by an airy, staccato rhythm section produced and arranged by She'k-spre Briggs and reminiscent of baroque melodies evocative of eighteenth-century parlor room culture, "Bills" stages a compressed comedy of manners in which a shiftless lover is chastised by a confrontational female protagonist. Teenagers at the time of this recording, the members of Destiny's Child utilized a familiar and marketable narrative structure made popular by McMillan and her characters to anchor the direction of the song. The sheer surfeiting lyrical content of each verse, its emphasis on vividly mundane plot development and imagery, and the song's insistence on relating the literal and quotidian reanimates McMillan's fiction in a pop music context. The familiar "ne'er do well" character lampooned and lambasted in *Exhale* has resurfaced here, only to be berated for failing to earn his own income, for depending on the material wealth of his girlfriend, driving her car, running up her cell phone bill, and generally refusing to assist and participate in the social mobility of the speaker. Like McMillan's characters, the speaker simultaneously chastises the "triflin' good for nothin' type of brother" and questions her own inadequacies for failing to find "another/A baller" willing and able to financially assist her in times of need. Destiny's Child thus redeploys the form and content of McMillan's fiction, transforming her popular style into 1997's number-one song on the R & B Billboard charts.

Most notable, however, it is Whitney Houston herself, one of the stars of the *Exhale* film, whose 1990s transformation reflects the popularity of this genre. The artist formerly-known-as-crossover-princess, whose traditional pop ballads ("Where Do Broken Hearts Go?" and "Saving All My Love for You") once got her famously booed at the Soul Train Music Awards, shrewdly extended her portrayal of Savannah on film into a 1998 studio recording, her first in eight years. In so doing, Houston's work perhaps best exemplifies the nexus between black pop fiction and music in the late 1990s. Entitled *My Love Is Your Love*, the album calls attention to how Houston's real-life turmoil—including well-publicized domestic squabbles and alleged drug dependencies—reflected McMillan's literary framework by including a narrative disclaimer: "[T]he events and characters depicted in this album are fictitious, and any similarity to actual persons living or dead, or to actual events, is purely coincidental."[16] *My Love* almost seamlessly created a bridge between Houston's characterization of an *Exhale* protagonist and the putatively fictional vignettes included on the album. In particular, its first single, "It's Not Right but It's Okay," fully embodies McMillan's aesthetics, which popularized relationship confrontation and vaguely defined gender empowerment predicated on the spectacle of domestic conflict.

> Friday night you and your boys went out to eat/Then they hung out but you come home around 3 am/If 6 of y'all went out, then 4 of you are really cheap/Cause only 2 of you had dinner/I found your credit card receipt/(Chorus) It's not right but it's okay/I'm gonna make it anyway/Pack your bags up and leave/Don't you dare come running back to me/(Repeat Chorus)/Close the door behind you/Leave your key/I'd rather be alone than unhappy/I'll pack your bags so you can leave home for a week.[17]

Lyrics admonishing a philandering lover and instructing him to "close the door," deposit his keys, and pack his bags so that he "can leave home for a week" expose the song's traditional blues cadences. I would argue, however, that the track's fixation on the literal and the minute—awkwardly cataloguing domestic details such as when a lover arrived at home versus the time that he was expected, narrating the discovery of a "credit card receipt" revealing a dinner for two and not six—situates the song most firmly within the McMillan oeuvre. As is the case with "Bills," the sheer verbosity of "It's Not Right" suggests the song's awkward positioning between explicit McMillan fiction and pop songwriting. Cowritten and produced by Rodney Jerkins, one of the more sought-after R & B producers of the mid-1990s, Houston's single articulates a familiar, Mary Tyler Moore, you're-gonna-make-it-after-all anthem of sorts—this time for black women. It removes our heroine from the arms of an insensitive lover, but fails to chart an alternative course for her. With its passive-aggressive chorus, "It's Not Right" emphasizes the protagonist's lack of fulfillment as a seeming raison d'être of her self-proclaimed new world existence. Rather than breaking free from this unsatisfying lover so as to cultivate her own autonomy, her empowerment appears to be rooted in this suffocating dynamic of speaking back to him. Within this narrowly conceived equation, liberation for Houston's "fictional character" remains tethered to the presence of an unfaithful partner.

This convention of having the R & B diva declare her independence from a philandering partner and an unfulfilling relationship yet simultaneously confining her performance to themes of contentiousness and desperation is evident in many of the tracks on the *Exhale* soundtrack, all of which were written by Atlanta-based songwriting mogul Babyface. On tracks such as Toni Braxton's "Let It Flow" and Blige's blockbuster "Not Gon' Cry," which includes the now-famous refrain "I shoulda left your ass a long time ago," these R & B heroines are positioned at the edge of a new day. They fail, however, much like the characters in McMillan's fiction, to tap the surface of the larger material and sociopolitical structures of oppression in which they are entrenched. Both the characters that the divas inhabit and the songs themselves lack a kind of interior analysis or awareness of these external obstacles that might challenge the protagonist and the listener to experience some kind of epistemological transformation. We, the listeners, are stuck—as they are—in a repetition of conflict and abandonment. Hence, what McMillan has made marketable and entertaining appears to diverge a bit from the "slag the black man" tendencies of which Stanley Crouch and others have famously accused other black female authors. Rather, McMillan has shifted the emphasis away from the problems of racism, sexism, and socioeconomic instability evident in landmark texts of the seventies such as Morrison's *The Bluest Eye*, Alice Walker's *The Third Life of Grange Copeland*, and Gayl Jones's *Corregidora* to focus almost exclusively on the sexual and material discontent of the middle-class contemporary black female consumer. McMillan redirects and recontextualizes the needs and concerns of these middle-class professional women's representations. She also sets the stage for the culture-wide spectacle of conflict buoyed equally by the popularity of Jerry Springer and WWF smackdowns. This latter trend is best exemplified by an enormously popular R & B duet from 1998 recorded by the former beautician to the stars, Sparkle. Produced by troubled recording artist R. Kelly—who also directed the video—Sparkle's single "Be Careful" pushed the envelope in displaying black women's confession and discontent in R & B pop culture.[18]

Depicting a song fueled by threat, warning, and veiled aggression between the sexes, the "Be Careful" video features the stereotypical construction of the unemployed and thus domesticated urban black male and the lying, cheating, equally irresponsible young black mother who enjoys partying more than parenting. Like "It's Not Right but It's Okay," the ending, which features a fur-adorned Sparkle leaving in a Range Rover with a female companion, offers a de rigueur notion of liberation for the 1990s black woman in this genre. With her scarf, sunglasses, and a final kiss from her female companion, à la *Thelma and Louise* (Sparkle denied the homoerotic implications of this scene in a 1998 interview with MTV News), it appears that heroines such as Sparkle are driving straight to oblivion. Penned by Kelly, "Be Careful," like the aforementioned Babyface and Jerkins projects, presents itself as a peculiar representation of black middle-class women's hostility and frustration toward their male partners. The song ends with a puzzling epilogue that proclaims in bold, Gothic letters: "There's no such thing as a no good woman. Every no good woman was made no good by a no good man." This perpetuation of a network of blame and oversimplification of gender conflict reflects a narrow mutation of resistance ideology that black male studio powerhouses successfully marketed.

Indeed, this period marked the peak of Kelly's popularity. He and Babyface evolved into the main architects of the movement to translate McMillan tropes and narrative machinations into pop-song phenomena. This is perhaps most evident in yet another Kelly-produced recording for the prodigious R & B and gospel singer Kelly Price. Her single, "Friend of Mine," features the ubiquitous Kelly and formidable R & B pioneer Ronald Isley. The video, directed by Hype Williams and featuring all three artists, reinforces one of the more popular and recurring themes—betrayal—in 1990s black women's pop music. The theme is troubling in these songs because each is often built lyrically on a profound distrust of both black male lovers as well as female friends. In the single and the video for the song, Price plays the deceived and heartbroken protagonist to Kelly's "creepin" husband, a partner who has betrayed Price by sleeping with the so-called friend of the title. In the video, however, the focal point is a dramatic confrontation between Isley's godfather character, "Mr. Biggs," and Kelly as the adulterous husband.[19] For although the song is ostensibly predicated on conflict between two female friends, the confrontation between Biggs and Kelly's character is ironic since it ultimately forces Price's female protagonist—bruised, betrayed, and broken—out of the video's frame entirely. Tellingly, in this McMillan-inspired universe in which black female heroines quest to confront and berate the men who have done them wrong, it is the men themselves, with their spectacular faults and foibles, who end up occupying the central space in the narrative.

Nevertheless, the visibility of Kelly and Isley—two "macho-lover" icons of distinct (and in the case of Kelly) dubious glory periods in R & B culture—should remind us here of the central and multiple ways that black male figures inevitably inform this pop cultural phenomenon. Beyond their obvious critical role as studio producers, stylists, and architects of McMillan pop, black men, black male iconography, and perhaps most important, the sociopolitical issues affecting the black male population of the 1990s provide a fitting backdrop to this pop-music subgenre. In 1994, in the midst of this cultural shift, Henry Louis Gates, Jr., wrote that when "we consider the plight of black males today in American society, we encounter the most horrible statistics, reflecting a nightmare reality for a large percentage of that half of the African-American community." Gates adds that in 1990 alone, "2,280,000 black boys and men were jailed or imprisoned, while 23,000 earned a college degree, a ratio of 99 to 1. . . . To this alarming fact, add the fact that every forty-six seconds of the school day, a black child drops out of school, every ninety-five seconds a black baby is born into poverty, and every four hours of every day in the year a black young adult, age twenty to twenty-four, is murdered, and one quickly realizes that the much discussed crisis of the black male is no idle fiction."[20] Hence, one could argue that the disillusionment that these songs catalogued with precision and (excessive) detail was a disturbingly displaced articulation of broad and deeply troubling issues facing black communities at the close of the twentieth century.

Indeed, as historians Robin D. G. Kelley and Earl Lewis have demonstrated, the post–civil rights era continues to present African Americans with extreme contrasts between progressive black class mobilization and increasing black poverty, drug abuse, and severe health obstacles in the 1990s. These contrasts are even more distinctly divided along gender lines in the 1990s as a disproportionate number of black women attended four-year colleges and universities while incarceration rates for both black men and women continued to rise.[21] Thus, it might do us well to consider the extent to which socioeconomic conflict and alienation, combined with gender divisions in 1990s African-American communities, did much to shape and inform the mass market R & B of the period. In other words, I would suggest that we consider how the domestic squabbles popularized on the music charts ultimately operate as allegories of the material and socioeconomic dissonance permeating urban spaces in the post–civil rights era. In the 1990s, as the penal-justice system continued to disrupt and render chaotic the lives and homes of poor to working-class families, as the Clinton administration's welfare-to-work program wreaked havoc on the working poor, and the rise of the AIDS epidemic and drug abuse in these same communities made absence, illness, and uncertainty recurring themes in the black popular consciousness of this period, hip-hop soul songstresses entered into McMillan's domestic spaces to obliquely articulate the intersecting issues of the urban personal and the political. There is, then, little doubt that this subgenre would, in its own diffuse way, speak to the broader fears and anxieties of a particular moment in African-American culture.[22]

The genre's obtuseness, however, may ultimately threaten its viability to function as a form of popular music capable of exacting social critique and transformation. With the recent deaths of TLC's Lisa "Left Eye" Lopes, hip-hop soul protégée and graceful songbird Aaliyah (whose work shortly before her death suggested a potential break from familiar forms), and the increasing crossover marketing of Knowles, the genre's potential for evolving into a more rigorous form of black feminist expression remains dubious.[23] Thus, where does this culture of confrontation, betrayal, and self-imposed isolation leave the black heroine of song in the millennium? All too often, the press and the public continue to christen these narratives of discontent as revisionary anthems for the new black middle-class woman professionals who are uncomfortable with the label "feminist" but who, nevertheless, long to transform their current social and cultural positioning.[24] The preponderance of the "moving on/don't look back" genre of black women's R & B ballads and up-tempo hits articulates a dissatisfaction with and an attempt to flee the conditions or current structure of one's life. But this concerted effort to disengage from the past is troubling since it suggests an inability to imagine a more specific and rehabilitative vision of the future. One almost gets the sense that even a youthful Brandy, who once sang a familiar chorus about packing her bags and moving on her way, is headed straight for a free fall. Where are these women going? And will wearing fur coats and driving sport utility vehicles (as nearly all of the women in the videos I have discussed here do) really alter their opportunity for fulfillment in this millennium? In the words of 702, the Las Vegas black female trio, in their 1999 summer club anthem: Where my girls at?

NOTES

1. Chris Rock, "Champagne," *Roll with the New* (Dreamworks Records, SKG 1997).

2. Nelson George, *The Death of Rhythm and Blues* (New York: Pantheon, 1988).

3. For an excellent study of the politics of black middle-class women's sexuality and desire, see Lisa B. Thompson, "Sex Talk: Sexual Politics and Black Middle Class Female

Desire in Contemporary African-American Fiction" (Ph.D. diss., Stanford University, 2001).

4. In Morrison's *Song of Solomon,* the character actor Hagar attempts to rebound from the trauma of unrequited love by immersing herself in the conspicuous consumption of beauty culture, only to face her own self-destruction. See Toni Morrison, *Song of Solomon* (New York: Plume, 1987). Susan Willis has argued that Morrison's depiction of Hagar demonstrates the ways in which "commodity culture mutilates black personhood." Susan Willis, "I Shop Therefore I Am: Is There a Place for Afro-American Culture in Commodity Culture?" in *Changing Our Own Words: Essays on Criticism, Theory, and Writing by Black Women,* ed. Cheryl A. Wall (New Brunswick, N.J.: Rutgers University Press, 1989), 179.

5. The film adaptation of *Waiting to Exhale* also sparked a short-lived studio fascination with developing films about the black middle class, as the "hood" genre began to wear out its shelf life in the mid-1990s. Other than Soul Food and the recent *Barbershop,* no other project of this kind has matched *Exhale's* crossover success. Indeed, the film version of *Dreamgirls* was scrapped, according to various trade journals, because of the inability of projects such as Why Do Fools Fall in Love to turn *Exhale*-like profits at the box office.

6. Terry McMillan, *Waiting to Exhale* (New York: Simon & Schuster, 1992), 3. All future references will be cited parenthetically.

7. Janet Mason Ellerby, "Deposing the Man of the House: Terry McMillan Rewrites the Family," *MELUS* 22, no. 2 (Summer 1997): 115. See also Rita B. Dandridge, "Debunking the Beauty Myth with Black Pop Culture in Terry McMillan's *Waiting to Exhale,*" in *Language, Rhythm, and Sound: Black Popular Cultures into the 21st Century,* ed. Joseph K. Adjaye and Adrianne R. Andrews (Pittsburgh, Pa.: University of Pittsburgh Press, 1997).

8. Thulani Davis, "Don't Worry, Be Buppie: Black Novelists Head for the Mainstream," *Village Voice Literary Supplement* 85 (May 1990): 26–27.

9. Tricia Rose, "Cultural Survivalisms and Marketplace Subversions: Black Popular Culture and Politics into the Twenty-first Century," in Adjaye and Andrews, eds., *Language, Rhythm, and Sound,* 264–265.

10. Dwight Garner, "Sistahood Is Lucrative," *Salon,* 18 April 1996, 2. http://archive .salon.com/weekly/blacklit960923.html.

11. See Farah Griffin, "Textual Healing: Claiming Black Women's Bodies, the Erotic and Resistance in Contemporary Novels of Slavery," *Callaloo: A Journal of African American and African Arts and Letters* 19, no. 2 (Spring 1996): 519–536. Ann duCille, *The Coupling Convention: Sex, Text, and Tradition in Black Women's Fiction* (New York: Oxford University Press, 1993).

12. While Mitchell, and to a lesser extent Jones, pioneered a new wave of songwriting craft that deftly combined lyrical confession with abstruse poetic flourishes, King and others dominated the 1970s pop charts with highly accessible anthems that articulated quotidian female heartache, desire, and longing for companionship.

13. Dandridge, "Beauty Myth," 123.

14. See Ann duCille, "Blues Notes on Black Sexuality: Sex and the Texts of Jessie Fauset and Nella Larsen," *Journal of the History of Sexuality* 3, no. 31 (1993): 418–443.

15. Destiny's Child, "Bills, Bills, Bills," lyrics by Kevin She'kspre Briggs, *The Writing's on the Wall* (Columbia Records, 1997).

16. Whitney Houston, album notes, *My Love Is Your Love* (Arista Records, 1998).

17. Whitney Houston, "It's Not Right but It's Okay," by R. Jerkins, F. Jerkins III, L. Daniels, I. Phillips, and T. Estes, *My Love.*

18. Sparkle and R. Kelly, "Be Careful," *Sparkle* (Interscope Records, 1998).

19. Kelly Price, "Friend of Mine," *Soul of a Woman* (Polygram Records, 1998).

20. Henry Louis Gates Jr., *Black Male: Representations of Masculinity in Contemporary American Art* (New York: Whitney Museum of Art, 1994), 13.

21. Kelley charts the simultaneous rise of the black middle class in the 1970s, 1980s, and 1990s coupled with increasing and dramatic black poverty, unemployment rates, drug abuse, and AIDS cases in the African-American community during this same period of time. See Robin D. G. Kelley, "Into the Fire: 1970 to the Present," in *To Make Our World Anew: A History of African Americans*, ed. Kelley and Earl Lewis (New York: Oxford University Press, 2000), 543–614.

22. More recently, in the twenty-first century, recording artists such as Alicia Keys, Angie Stone, Charli Baltimore with Ja Rule, novelist Asha Bandele, and slam poets Saul Williams and Sonja Sohn have narratives that examine the intersections of class, gender, incarceration, and black heterosexual desire with varying degrees of success. See for instance the video for Keys's ubiquitous "Fallin'," in which the singer portrays a protagonist visiting her incarcerated lover; Angie Stone's single "Brotha," in which she dedicates the track to her "brothers in lock down"; and the perplexing video for Charli Baltimore's duet with Ja Rule, "Down Chic," in which the former is sent to jail while Rule awaits her release. Alicia Keys, "Fallin'" (JRecords, 2001), video; Angie Stone, "Brotha," *Mahogany Soul* (JRecords, 2001); Charli Baltimore featuring Ja Rule, "Down Chic" (Murder Inc. Records, 2002), video. See also Bandele's controversial novel *The Prisoner's Wife* (2000) and the indie film *Slam*, starring recording artist Williams and poet Sohn, who spar over gender and incarceration politics. Asha Bandele, *The Prisoner's Wife: A Memoir* (New York: Pocket Books, 2000); *Slam*, dir. Marc Levin (Vidmark/Trimark, 1998), starring Saul Williams and Sonja Sohn.

23. Recently, Kelefa Sanneh has observed that the late Aaliyah Haughton "helped invent a style that might be called avant-garde R & B, and she did it by recording some of the least passionate love songs in recent memory—her favorite tools were grace and precision." See Kelefa Sanneh, "A Reminder of the Real Aaliyah," *New York Times*, 8 December 2001, 33.

24. This idea emerged in the summer of 1999 among a group of distinguished scholars during a roundtable session at the Black Women in the Academy Conference in Washington, D.C.

6. The Hip-Hop Nation: Black Youth Culture Today

ANDREA QUEELEY

Hip-Hop and the Aesthetics of Criminalization

In his essay, "Looking to Get Paid: How Some Black Youth Put Culture to Work," historian Robin D. G. Kelley explores the ways young people in economically depressed urban areas generate income from various forms of cultural play. He offers an interpretation of ghetto youth that counters the predominant depiction of them as menacing, lazy, immoral pleasure-seekers. Kelley suggests that sports, sex, and the creation of music, dance, and visual art are forms of play that constitute labor as resourceful young people transform practices of consumption into sites of production. Capitalism, Kelley writes, has come to be youth's greatest friend and greatest foe: Although the economic restructuring characteristic of post-industrial capitalism has led to permanent unemployment, the elimination of critical city services and public recreation space, the decimation of the public school system, and the militarization of the inner city, it has also created spaces for young people's "entrepreneurial imaginations and their 'symbolic work' to allow them to turn something of a profit, and to permit them to hone their skills and imagine getting paid."[1] Though he acknowledges that the opportunities for upward mobility through play-labor are limited, he asserts that it has "provided young people with a wider range of options for survival, space for creative expression, and at least a modicum of control over their own labor." Rather than police their play, Kelley asserts, we need to "change the streets themselves, the built environment, the economy, and the racist discourse that dominates popular perceptions of black youth."[2]

In this effort to reframe the practices of black youth as creative, labor-intensive strategies for survival in a society that has divested from their futures,

Kelley successfully challenges the pervasive and insidious antagonism harbored toward these youth, while illustrating the relationship between larger economic processes as they impact urban life and the dynamic (re)creation of black expressive culture. In framing his analysis of popular culture around the issues of labor, race, and class—as lived through gender—he demonstrates how popular culture and global economic restructuring are bound together by these interlocking issues. Indeed, further investigation into the historical context of play-labor as well as the fate of such strategies in today's rapidly changing urban landscape reveals the ruptures and continuities that occur within and among the intersecting and interdependent spheres of race, class, gender, and labor.

In 1970, at a triumphant moment of the worldwide national liberation struggles, Amilcar Cabral stated that "to take up arms to dominate a people is, above all, to take up arms to destroy, or at least to neutralize, to paralyze, its cultural life." He argued that there are "strong, dependent and reciprocal relationships existing between the cultural situation and the economic (and political) situation in the behavior of human societies."[3] Though, in the more contemporary context, popular global connections are increasingly defined by consumption, and liberation is measured by the extent to which one can participate in this practice, culture remains critical in the politics of domination and resistance. With the growing bifurcation in the labor force, the dismantling of the welfare system and rising incarceration rates among black and Latino men and women, young people have even more incentive to put their culture to work. At the same time, those who benefit from structural inequality have a growing interest in containing, if not eliminating, potential sites of resistance, intensifying such inequality.

Hip-hop[4] is one such site of resistance. The corporate appropriation of what began as a powerful expression of the black and Latino experience of urban poverty has significantly compromised its transformative potential as it has come to reinscribe the very racist discourse that Kelley urges his readers to combat. The recurrence of deeply embedded racist stereotypes coupled with the fixation on consumption characterizes corporate control of hip-hop and diminishes its position as a revolutionary art form and burgeoning mass social movement. The popularization of hip-hop has arguably created more economic opportunity for poor and working-class people who wish to develop and use their talents in labor that is both potentially lucrative and legal. Ironically, however, its entry into the mainstream has helped to calcify those conditions from which people are attempting to escape. More than simply not being "emancipatory, revolutionary or resistive,"[5] self-commodification in the context of corporate control fetters the creative process and indirectly narrows the economic options available to poor urbanites of color: Hip-hop now lives in the ghetto of the white imagination.

Characteristic of white supremacist patriarchal discourse, one of the primary mechanisms through which blackness[6] is subjugated is through uses and representations of the body, male and female. Record companies market rap as a profane, masculine music. The selling of the bodies of the performers is as important as the music itself.[7]

Kelley cogently analyzes the limitations that women face in their attempts to put their play to work. He asserts that, viewed through the prism of gender, the conversion of play into labor marginalizes female artists and results in the stigmatization of women who turn sexual play into work through prostitution. Presenting a case study of a young woman who enjoys sex and gets paid for it, he argues that prostitution is a way for women to resist their fate in "an increasingly service-oriented, low-wage economy with shrinking opportunities for working-class ghetto residents."[8] Unfortunately, he not only presents a somewhat problematic reading of prostitution, but he also neglects to explore how sex and the body are used in the context of hip-hop, particularly in music videos, the common visual complement to the sensory experience of hip-hop music. In the absence of any firsthand knowledge of behind-the-scenes sexual politics, it cannot be argued that the typical collection of aggressively attractive, often conspicuously light-skinned, long-haired women who provide the erotic backdrop to so many music videos are prostituting themselves. It is clear, however, that their "talent" and value to the industry lie in their sexuality, which is rampantly objectified and exploited. It is through music video performances that some women use sex to "get paid" and, in the process, provide a fantasized projection of female availability and disposability. Ironically, at the same time that such images have colonized the terrain of music videos, women's wage labor has become increasingly important to the growing service sector of a global economy that, according to anthropologist Faye Harrison, is dependent on the construction of women's labor and bodies as cheap, available, and easily controlled.[9]

Through rap music videos, the racialized body politics of the United States have now gone global. Since sex sells—or is sold—such politics are a critical component in the transformation brought about by the corporate appropriation of hip-hop culture. Black female sexuality and its representations have been central to the discourse on race in the United States, and every movement for black liberation in this society, whether reformist or radical, has had to formulate a counterhegemonic discourse of the body to effectively resist white supremacy.[10] Based on these premises, I hope to illuminate the limitations of and possibilities for cultural expression as resistance by looking at the historical and contemporary intersections of black performance, sexuality, and profit amid emerging manifestations of inequality. Furthermore, following music critic Mark Anthony Neal's suggestion to "examine the contexts and processes that produce the narratives commonly found in rap music,"[11] I propose to explore the historically rooted relationship between the representations of blackness most frequently found in hip-hop and the changing conditions in urban settings.

BLACK SELF-COMMODIFICATION AND "KEEPING IT REAL"

Jollity . . . is not an index of the expressive capacities of the enslaved but rather a means toward the enhancement of value, the emblem of coercion, and an incident of fungibility. Contrary to our expectations, gaiety articulates the brutal calculations

> *of the trade. The self-betrayal enacted by stepping it lively and enthusiastically assisting in one's sale underscores the affiliations of spectacle and sufferance. And, accordingly, fun and frolic become the vehicles of the slave's self-betrayal and survival.*
>
> —Saidiya Hartman, *Scenes of Subjection* [12]

Examining the history of black performance in the United States, several points emerge as particularly relevant to understand the meanings of corporate appropriation and self-commodification in black cultural expression. Despite the clear differences between contemporary and historical practices, and despite the significant transformations in U.S. society, it is particularly instructive to note the generation-spanning tenacity of certain dynamics. In her examination of black subject formation during slavery and the persistence of what she termed "unfreedom" in the post-Emancipation era, professor of English Saidiya Hartman turns away from the routine, shocking violence that constitutes a particular brand of coercion to consider "those scenes of terror that can hardly be discerned—slaves dancing in the quarters, the outrageous darky antics of the minstrel stage, the constitution of humanity in slave law, and the fashioning of the self-possessed individual." [13] In doing so, she reveals the complexities involved in the yoking of amusement and subjugation in the black experience.

Enslaved people were forced to dance on the slave ships to maintain their health—so they could ultimately fetch a good price—and to sing and play music on their way to being sold, for the enjoyment of the slaveowners. Such entertainment was interpreted as a sign of contentment. Furthermore, slaveowners sought to "cultivate hegemony, harness pleasure as a productive force, and regulate the modes of permitted expression. [They] managed amusements as they did labor, with a keen eye toward discipline." [14] Enjoyment and entertainment played a dual role in the lives of the enslaved. It was both a technique of discipline employed by slaveowners to construct and display the enslaved as willing participants in their own subjugation and a means by which the enslaved asserted their humanity.

Central to such complexities—and quite relevant in this discussion of the transformation of hip-hop culture—is the issue of performing blackness that is so obviously brought out by the tradition of minstrelsy. Although minstrelsy began with white performers putting shoe polish on their faces and acting out their distorted, obscene notions of blackness, black performers also performed blackness. Black performance of blackface was not simply self-mockery; it was also a mockery of those white people who initiated and patronized this tradition. Most important, it must be understood that black performers had no options. Their survival as performers was dependent on self-derision, and any portrayal of blackness that challenged the deeply racist beliefs around which the society was organized were prohibited. Indeed, whiteness was defined in opposition to all that was black, and thus its existence depended upon the recapitulation of blackness as deviant and grotesque. Thus, black performers have always been pressured to perform the blackness of the white imagination, and that blackness is most often in the service of white supremacy.

As has been documented particularly well in films such as *Ethnic Notions* by Marlon Riggs, *Hollywood Shuffle* by Robert Townsend, and, most recently, Spike Lee's *Bamboozled,* the types of characters that emerged out of slavery and the antebellum era still hold incredible purchase in the contemporary cultural life of the United States. From *Birth of a Nation* to *Amos 'n Andy* to *Good Times* to *Family Matters,* the television and film industries are notorious for disseminating stereotypical depictions of black people created by white writers and directors. What is interesting is that these depictions of black people in fictional accounts have found their complement in the real-life stories that came to be popularized in the '90s: Talk shows such as *Jerry Springer* and *Ricky Lake,* which are hugely popular spectacles, are actually color-blind in their malevolence toward working-class people, whereas on shows such as *Cops,* cameras trail police officers as they apprehend suspected criminals who are disproportionately of color.

The musical complement to these so-called real-life accounts—which actually present a distorted, narrow view of real life—can be found in the genre of "gangsta" rap. Evidence that "the performative has the power to produce the subject that it appears to express,"[15] this genre relies on the code of keepin' it real for its appeal. Keepin' it real, a term that indicates authenticity and an uncensored portrayal of experience, is now a market device used to project images of black youth as nihilistic, criminally minded, sexually promiscuous, irresponsible, and materialistic. Current notions of what is real are clearly distorted views of some aspects of black youth—distortions that are the fantasy of blackness to which the new majority of hip-hop consumers, that is, young white suburbanites, subscribe. All of these images serve to reinforce the racist discourse that was challenged by the Civil Rights Movement but has more recently reemerged in a subtle, more insidious manner, and this discourse is used to win elections, justify the prison industrial complex, dismantle welfare, and divest from public education. The history of black performance has, in part, been characterized by the insertion of disfiguring white perceptions; consequently, keepin' it real in hip-hop culture has serious implications for understanding and obscuring real conditions in contemporary urban America.

URBAN CRISIS AND THE GLOBALIZATION OF CULTURE

Like the conversion of play into labor, the appropriation and commodification of black cultural expression are certainly not a new phenomenon. What is new is the context in which this is taking place. With the economic transformations and technological advancements of the late twentieth century, cultural production has been globalized through television, film, videos, music, and style products. At the same time, the globalization of the economy has resulted in diminished possibilities for meaningful work for youth, who constitute an incredibly powerful consumer market. The transition from a manufacturing to a high-tech service economy has narrowed the prospects for reasonably well-paying, stable employment for many working-class young people while bifurcating the labor market, creating extremes of pay, skill, and stability.[16] Simultaneously, the frenzy toward privatization has dealt a blow to public education that threatens to be fatal, leaving poor and working-class youth, the children of persons who constitute the low-wage service sector, shamefully ill-prepared to fashion a future that is better than their parents'.

The other heavy artillery that has been unleashed in this war on the poor that began with the 1980 election of former president Ronald Reagan is the rising rate of incarceration. In *Newsweek*'s 13 November 2000 Special Report, journalists revealed that "at a time when the country enjoys record prosperity, when even many of those once on welfare are working, this is the America the good times have left behind: neighborhoods where prison time can seem as inevitable as rain, and only the lucky ones escape the storm."[17] Between 1980 and 1999, the number of Americans in jails and prisons rose 300 percent. Of the two million Americans incarcerated in federal and state prisons and local jails, more than half are African American. In 1991, 23 percent of all black men in their twenties were either in jail or prison, on parole, probation, or awaiting trial. Furthermore, children are increasingly treated as adults in the eyes of the legal system, and African Americans are nine times more likely than whites to be sentenced to juvenile prisons.[18]

Since 1980, the number of women in prison has increased at nearly double the rate for men, and there are now seven times as many women in federal and state prisons as there were two decades ago. This 573 percent rise in women prisoners is largely due to the so-called war on drugs, which has enshrined a set of law enforcement and sentencing policies and practices that have had a dramatic and disproportionate impact on low-income women of color, particularly regarding drug offenses: Between 1986 and 1995, 91 percent of the women sentenced in New York for drug offenses were black and Latina women. They constitute only 33 percent of the state's population.

At the same time, legislation has increasingly threatened the survival and well-being of women convicted of drug offenses. For instance, the 1996 Work and Personal Responsibility Act allowed states to prohibit women offenders from collecting welfare; the 1998 Higher Education Act delays or denies federal financial aid to any student convicted of a drug offense; and the Adoption and Safe Families Act of 1997 made it easier to strip women serving prison terms of their parental rights, increasingly pushing their children into foster care and adoption. Furthermore, although antidrug federal funding has increased, only one-third of it is allocated for prevention and treatment while two-thirds is spent on law enforcement and incarceration. Thus, as stiffer penalties for drug offenses have been implemented, public funding of drug treatment programs has been deprioritized. At the same time, the availability of living-wage and meaningful work has dwindled, welfare is being dismantled, and poor black and Latina women are increasingly caught in the web of the criminal justice system, while their children are funneled into permanent foster care.[19]

The United States continues to organize labor[20] along stark racial lines. As such, this boom in the prison industry, fueled by institutionalized racism, must be considered in the context of the recent revolution in the labor market. Although black unemployment rates appear to be at historically low levels and are cited as evidence of the nation's high-tech–inspired prosperity, black men's high rates of incarceration indicate that they have enjoyed no enduring recovery in employment.[21] The prison system is a mechanism by which people who have come to be viewed as redundant labor can be contained while creating employment for people who build and administer prisons. Furthermore, the dominant economic and social climate of privatization may begin to look to prisons to provide a labor force that is exploitable and expendable because it is literally captive.

The impact of the restructuring of the global labor force on black people who have historically occupied a position at the bottom of the labor hierarchy has been devastating. The revolving door between prisons and isolated, stigmatized neighborhoods brings a lack of social cohesion exacerbated by the growing incarceration rates.[22] These are the conditions that lead anthropologist Leith Mullings to assert that "African American women, and particularly poor women in communities such as Harlem, now face one of the greatest challenges since slavery."[23] Indeed, the transformations in the labor force, combined with rising incarceration and the assault on public education and social welfare programs, have created formidable obstacles for women, men, and children alike.

According to historian Manning Marable, "the driving ideological and cultural force that rationalizes and justifies mass incarceration is the white American public's stereotypical perceptions about race and crime."[24] At the same time that extreme poverty and incarceration rates are on the rise, there have been tremendous transformations in popular culture and in the implications and consequences of black youth putting culture to work. Rap music and hip-hop culture have migrated from the margins to the mainstream of popular culture. The marketplace has emerged as the dominant province of hip-hop expression.[25] Through the corporate takeover of hip-hop culture, multiconsumerism masquerades as multiculturalism and, in the process, white supremacist ideology has been rereleased onto a global terrain.

There is a clear connection among the appropriation of hip-hop culture, the representations of blackness that have come to dominate the visual landscape of hip-hop, and the unprecedented rates of incarceration that we are witnessing. Although conservative and misguided critics have argued that the violent and misogynist themes in much of mass-marketed hip-hop are responsible for increasing criminality, actually the increasing criminalization of poverty, particularly black poverty, through the manipulation of the legal system is far more culpable. The driving force propelling this legal and cultural manipulation is the continued profitability of racism. As Murray Forman, professor of communication studies at Northeastern University and author of *The 'Hood Comes First: Race, Space, and Place in Rap and Hip-Hop*, writes, "[I]t is important to recognize the ways in which images of gang warfare, pimping and drug dealing have been shrewdly manipulated in highly rationalized marketing campaigns."[26] Thus, it is critical to interrogate the macro-level structures and processes that both motivate and inform such actions.

CORPORATE CONTROL

In a 2000 article in the *Village Voice,* music critic Barry Walters observed that the American popular music scene is obstructed by the "Yank wall of UNI/WEA/BMG/EMI resistance." Corporate control over the music industry, he wrote, is responsible for the proliferation of cookie-cutter boy groups, test-market-research radio, and the artificial stability in the U.S. pop charts as compared to England, where new music groups regularly surface, gain popularity, and are displaced by other talent.[27] Mark Anthony Neal reports that 80 percent of the music recorded in the United States is controlled by six major corporate entities, and the power to control the rotation of music on radio stations is available to the highest corporate bidder.[28] Indeed, both Kevin Powell, hip-hop journalist and cultural critic, and Mos Def, one of the few conscious hip-hop artists to escape total marginalization in the music industry, note that the industry's failure to promote a diverse selection of music is a decisive weapon in the "battle for the soul of hip-hop."[29]

Though more—and more high profile—black people now are on the production end of the entertainment industry, Neal points out that "many of the artist/producers remain distanced from the real seats of power within their respective corporate homes—power that could be defined along the lines of joint or sole ownership of recording masters, control over production and promotional costs, and the authority to hire and replace internal staff members."[30]

Although this monopoly over the production and distribution of music clearly impacts all artists and shortchanges the North American listening audience, which has limited access to the existing range of music, it has particularly serious implications for people of color whose cultural life has for centuries been the object of European/European American assault. For them, corporate control over the lyrics and images selected to represent their experience is particularly problematic because it compromises the ability of cultural expression to help combat the effects of corporate control over other areas that shape material conditions. Powell believes that hip-hop has empowered more young, working-class black and Latino men than did the Civil Rights Movement. He writes: "Twenty years after the Reagan backlash on civil rights, the influx of crack and guns and the acceleration of a disturbing class divide in black America, hip-hop has come to symbolize a generation fragmented by integration, migration, abandonment, alienation and, yes, self-hatred. Thus, hip-hop, once vibrant, edgy, fresh and def, is now as materialistic, hedonistic, misogynistic, shallow and violent as some of the films and TV shows launched from Hollywood."[31] Unlike the films and television programs that feature whites in such dramatized destruction, however, the growing emphasis on violence and materialism in hip-hop has more serious repercussions as it pervades mainstream America and is thrust into the global market. The deteriorating content of hip-hop helps justify the growing rate of incarceration through reinforcing the naturalization of black criminality that is deeply rooted in the ideology and economy of the United States. It also obscures today's worsening urban conditions, which make fantasies of economic and sexual control embedded in both lyrics and music videos so appealing.

The corporate control of hip-hop has tremendous significance for Kelley's formulation of play-labor and the larger consequences and significance of putting culture to work. Although Kelley argues that the black youth who use hip-hop as a means to generate income are escaping the fate of their low-wage (and, I would add, their indebted middle-wage) counterparts, they actually occupy the same economic and social position in the context of the music industry. Yes, those who make it—which more often than not means enjoying just sixty seconds of fame—clearly have the opportunity to earn more money than they would in low-wage service-sector employment. Once inside the entertainment industry, however, they have far less power and fewer resources than owners, managers, and distributors and therefore remain in a subordinate position that is structurally parallel to the one from which they have allegedly escaped. And in the end play-labor has, for the most part, a very short life span: Aren't most of its participants among the ranks of the replaceable and therefore disposable laborers who are crowding the postindustrial capitalist landscape? In discussing black youth putting culture to work, it is important to keep in mind that those who commodify themselves are rarely the ones getting paid.

The consequences of corporate control reach beyond the unequal distribution of profits. As was the case with the integration of the popular music industry in the civil rights era, at issue here are the traditions of artistic integrity, creative autonomy, communal input, and aesthetic quality in black popular culture.[32] This is not to argue for an essentialized notion of black creative expression; hybridity and cross-fertilization of artistic style also are part of the black arts tradition. Rather, it is to highlight that the loss of black creative autonomy in a white supremacist, patriarchal society leaves black expressive culture vulnerable to strategic manipulation. Indeed, the case of hip-hop's wholesale cooptation by corporations in some ways mimics what eventually happened to soul music: The iconography of political struggle is separated from the organic sources and purposes of such struggle.[33] As Kevin Arlyck notes, the association with corporate America compromises rap's usefulness as a tool for rebuilding African-American civil society.[34]

This separation of meaning from iconography is evident in everything from the numerous music groups who perform a "straight outta Compton" identity when they themselves are "straight out of the suburbs" to advertisements featured in hip-hop magazines. For instance, in the November 2000 issue of *Vibe,* there is a double-page, black-and-white advertisement for UBO.com (Urban Box Office network) in which four men are pictured having their hair cornrowed. The young men are black, Latino, Asian, and white and are seated in that order, with the black man being closest to the camera/reader/viewer/consumer and the white man being farthest away. Each man is having his hair done by a black woman except the white man who is being serviced by a young black man. The caption for the advertisement reads "First Generation Urban." The suggestion is that the twenty-first-century urban experience, whether acquired by living in the city or by consuming the media depictions of this lifestyle, is the great equalizer.

The image of black people doing hair strikes a deep chord in the black experience: It signifies authenticity. The order of the men having their hair done clearly reflects the classical racial hierarchy in which white and black are at opposite extremes, while Latinos and Asians occupy a buffer zone, with Asians being closer to whites and Latinos closer to blacks. The wearing of cornrows by men began as a prison aesthetic and, with the growing purchase of a hardened, criminalized masculinity in society at large, has become popular beyond prison walls. Of course, the consumerism advocated by magazines such as *Vibe* masks the social context in which such ghetto iconography develops. Histories and contemporary realities become irrelevant. History and identity appear to be erased for the hip-hop generation. As this ad so vividly illustrates, however, corporate multicultural hip-hop features and relies on certain formulations of black cultural expression and everyday practice for commercial success. At the same time, it reinscribes a racialized social order even as it obscures that process of reinscription.

REPRESENTATIONS OF THE BODY AND
THE AESTHETICS OF CRIMINALIZATION

Though hip-hop magazines are certainly instruments integral to the annexation of hip-hop culture, the primary conduit of corporate constructions of blackness has been the ubiquitous music videos that help create and represent the urban aesthetic. As a form of advertising that appears not only on television, but also in movies, department stores, shopping malls, and clubs, music videos are a deterritorialized art form that has infiltrated public space and blurred the distinction between programs and commercials. Indeed, videos were in the "vanguard of reshaping the language of advertising" such that commercials for particular products have come to imitate videos and videos are always a "wall to wall advertisement for something."[35] Though music videos began to air when MTV was launched in 1981, they did not come to saturate the visual landscape until the '90s, when hip-hop gained widespread appeal. Indeed, hip-hop videos, which so graphically create and illustrate allegedly real life in the ghetto, undoubtedly helped popularize the music itself by relying on classic story lines and gendered images—often cultural stereotypes.[36]

Music videos have inspired much animosity by those who believe they exacerbate the damage inflicted by rap music's explicit lyrics. The videos have come to be as important as the songs themselves. In them, first-generation urban artists, regardless of their racial identities, perform blackness. This racialized performance illustrates the continuity of certain narratives of black people and, in particular, reveals that black male/female (hetero)sexuality remains a central vehicle through which white supremacist discourse is reinscribed. Although I do not believe the relationship between creative expression and lived conditions is causal, it seems clear that the emergence and promotion in hip-hop music and videos of what I term the aesthetics of criminalization and the performance of black sexuality are certainly related to the real-life crisis of incarceration and welfare reform.

For women, this aesthetic is linked to the popularization of the myth of the welfare queen and the images of lazy, predatory women whose sexuality and, more important for the discourse of white supremacy, whose fertility is out of control. As Leith Mulling states in an essay on female-headed households, "[F]or African Americans, the conflict over fertility has always been linked to the political economy. . . . [D]uring slavery, slave owners encouraged fertility among enslaved women to increase the labor force. In the contemporary economy, as African Americans resist confinement to the low-wage jobs of their parents and grandparents, they are increasingly considered a redundant population, an underclass that must be contained."[37] The political economy has always tried to control black fertility: Where slaveholders once encouraged it for profit, conservative voices now campaign for its reduction, citing the economic burden. Black women are alternately viewed as witless, irresponsible procreators and manipulative welfare mothers who purposely bear children to profit off the system. As professor of law Dorothy Roberts states, "modern-day racist ideology . . . seems to have shed the assumption that black people are entirely incapable of rational decision-making. . . . Black mothers are portrayed less as inept or reckless reproducers in need of moral supervision, and more as calculating parasites deserving of harsh discipline."[38] The media, elected officials, and academics alike have joined in the condemnation of black motherhood as pathological in an effort to justify dismantling welfare and rationalize the devastating effects of that process.

Ideologies that stigmatize women of color have been central to maintaining class, race, and gender inequality. The historical moments in which stereotypes about black women are most pervasive coincide with reactionary political climates—and the popular culture clearly reflects this. Sociologist Jessie Daniels, in her analysis of white supremacist literature and ideology, notes that the portrayal of black sexuality as deviant and out of control is directly related to the fear of the disappearance of whiteness as a racial category. "Black women's fertility," she states, "is at the heart of the welfare quagmire."[39] Evident in the current campaign to inject Norplant and Depo-Provera in the arms of black teenagers and welfare mothers,[40] black reproduction and, by implication, black female sexuality are criminalized. Again, one cannot but wonder at the connection between a myth whose power has fueled the dismantling of the welfare system—shredding the safety net for poor people—and the fact that most images of black women in hip-hop culture are highly sexualized. As neo-liberalism preaches personal responsibility and accountability for people who are economically marginalized and socially stigmatized, the corporations that this movement has unleashed on the world offer prominent representations of black women as sexually deviant.

Although there are certainly women hip-hop artists who can be considered conscious, feminist, and Afrocentric, female hip-hop pioneers have been squeezed out of much of musical production. Though they gained some recognition in the mid- to late '80s, by the early '90s, in the context of the Los Angeles uprising, rap became more deeply encoded as a male space. During that time the explosive violence of resistance overshadowed the systematic brutality and injustice to which African Americans were subjected, and the violence was broadcast throughout the country and the world. The white supremacist fantasy of the aggressive, egocentric, materialistic, sexually potent black brute was recycled and it emerged center stage to dominate rap music's popular image. Women artists were not considered by industry managers to have the same mettle as their male counterparts and many were forced to comply with the music industry's demands by doing love and romance raps.[41] Thus, women were, with few exceptions, part of the spectacle rather than the production process of hip-hop. Now, most women in the visual landscape of hip-hop are referred to as "video hos" and are critical to the creation of this spectacle. In the male-centered fantasy constructed by these videos, the every-day reality of young black men, in which sexuality is a process of negotiation, is sub-merged and, in its place, the fantasy of effortless sexual conquest is constructed. Tricia Rose, historian and expert on American cultural politics, argues that the misogyny in some rap music is actually the expression of hostility toward women who have the power to reject.[42] Kelley points out that, in some cases, the misogy-nist narratives are based on the rappers' experiences as performers whose status as cultural icons does indeed give them an enormous amount of sexual power.[43] Either way, it is undeniable that women's bodies are now indispensable in the production of the profane, masculine space of rap music videos. Like the white and platinum gold jewelry, the sales of which have, not coincidentally, risen 40 percent since Sean "P. Diddy" Combs—formerly Puff Daddy—became hip-hop's new don,[44] like the diamonds and designer clothing that project the image of success and control, beau-tiful women are transformed into another commodity used to create a fantasy. And, predictably, the media has fixated on the abundance of misogynist fantasy in hip-hop rather than investigating the reality of society's institutionalized and legitimized forms of misogyny, which are far more pernicious.

The hypersexualized performances in music videos reinforce multiple and contradictory stereotypes about black sexuality. In this genre of music video, there are often several different beautiful women who adorn the often average-looking, but conspicuously jeweled, male rapper(s). The women are presented to the viewer in a succession of mixed fast-paced and slow-motion frames that constitute a mobile collage of selectively sensual body parts. The camera stalks the swiveling hips, glazed legs, and plunging necklines that are offered regardless of the lyrical content of the song: They are clearly there to tell the viewer a sexual story. The videos reinforce the dismemberment of black women, who are valued only for their particular body parts. At the same time, black women are portrayed as aggressively sexual. The resulting narrative affirms the persistent myth of black hypermasculinity—the pimp narrative. Through the use of sexually provocative dance that is exaggerated to the point of being nearly comical, women convey their availability as sexual objects, but they do not assume a submissive, traditionally feminine role. Rather, they are the epitome of a black female sexuality that writer and professor bell hooks asserts is most poignantly articulated by Tina Turner's persona: wild and out of control even in the presence of hypermasculinity.[45] They are the object of the masculine gaze, dissected by the camera—the rear end having the most currency in the visual econ-omy—and occasionally fondled by the rappers who graze over them while main-taining eye contact with the camera, indicating that their real connection lies with the audience members, voyeurs of black sexual practice. These videos dramatize the psychohistories of white racism, which feature a tension between the black body as threatening—due to criminality and criminalized fertility—and the underlying eroticization of that threat as the black body is imagined to be the site of transgressive pleasure.

Kelley, as he considers gender in his essay on black youth getting paid, neglects the idea that the scantily clad women who appear in the endless strip club videos are getting paid to perform black female sexuality in a manner that reinforces the economic consequences of systemic racialized misogyny. As the women commodify themselves for either monetary reward or to advance their modeling, singing, or acting careers, women in music videos embody racist stereotypes— from the mulatta temptress to the dark-skinned exotic Other—in the interest of profit. Although some might argue that the women's use of sexuality is evidence of their liberation, the male-dominated power structure of the music industry debunks this assertion. As Tricia Rose reports, women rappers remark that this display and sexual exchange cannot be empowering when male rappers and executives have all the social and institutional power. Hotties, as they are called, are treated as expendable, and male desire controls every aspect of their presence and treatment in the videos.[46] Women in music videos are a classic example of how the black female body gains attention—and women gain power—only when they are accessible and deviant. Black women's sexuality is asserted only within the confines of colonized desire and racist/sexist imagery and practice, disabling women's sexual power.[47]

Women have long been reduced to mere objects of male desire. American entertainment is not known for its ability to wrestle with complexity, and it often depends on blatant racial stereotyping. These patterns are exacerbated by the globalization of culture, a culture increasingly dominated by American entertainment products. Upon entering the marketplace, these cultural practices are almost always divorced from the social struggles that inspired them and that they reflect. In this separation, the art form becomes a commodity, and it is made to represent an essentialized blackness: the blackness of the white imagination. Corporations project hip-hop images in the global market that do nothing to dismantle structural inequalities, the effects of which are romanticized, distorted, dramatized, and caricatured. Thus, in a gross departure from the roots of hip-hop, devastating social, political, and economic inequalities are relegated to the realm of fictional reality.

All the while, hip-hop is losing ground as a popular mechanism to articulate the pressing social and political realities brought about by transformations in the labor market, the globalization of finance capital, mass privatization, the destruction of public space, the development of the prison industrial complex, and welfare reform. Even as corporations use multicultural images to sell hip-hop culture, these conditions hardly affect all equally—society's disadvantaged remain disproportionately people of color. And so the cultural expression of blacks and Latinos, once vitally independent, is now being put in the service of their own persecution.

NOTES

1. Robin D. G. Kelley, "Looking to Get Paid: How Some Black Youth Put Culture to Work," in *Yo' Mama's Disfunktional! Fighting the Culture Wars in Urban America* (Boston: Beacon Press, 1998), 77.

2. Ibid., 76.

3. Amilcar Cabral, "National Liberation and Culture," in *Return to the Source* (New York: Africa Information Resource Service, 1973), 39, 40.

4. I use "hip-hop" to refer to the musical and aesthetic culture that emerged from the Bronx in the late 1970s and, as a result of commodification, has become integral if not synonymous with American youth culture.

5. Kelley, "Looking to Get Paid," 45.

6. This is of course true for other people of color. In the case of hip-hop, blackness is a particular representation that is prefigured but not confined by a black racial identity.

7. Robin Kelley, *Race Rebels: Culture, Politics and the Black Working Class* (New York: Free Press, 1994), 70.

8. Kelley, "Looking to Get Paid," 74.

9. Faye Harrison, "The Gendered Politics and Violence of Structural Adjustment," in *Situated Lives: Gender and Culture in Everyday Life*, Louis Lamphere, ed. (New York: Routledge, 1997).

10. bell hooks, "Feminism Inside: Toward a Black Body Politic," in *Black Male: Representations of Masculinity in Contemporary American Art*, Thelma Golden, ed. (New York: Whitney Museum of American Art, 1994).

11. Mark Neal, "Sold Out on Soul: The Corporate Annexation of Black Popular Music," *Popular Music and Society* (Fall 1997): 134.

12. Saidiya Hartman, *Scenes of Subjection: Terror, Slavery, and Self-Making in Nineteenth-Century America* (New York: Oxford University Press, 1997).

13. Ibid., 4.

14. Ibid., 44.

15. Ibid., 57.

16. Cindi Katz, "Disintegrating Developments: Global Economic Restructuring and the Eroding Ecologies of Youth," in *Cool Places: Geographies of Youth Culture*, Tracy Skelton and Gill Valentin, eds. (New York: Routledge, 1998), 131.

17. Ellis Cose, "The Prison Paradox," *Newsweek*, 13 November 2000, 42.

18. Manning Marable, "Racism, Prisons and the Future of Black America," http://www.zmag. org/rascismandblam.htm.

19. Marc Mauer, Cathy Potler, and Richard Wolf, "Gender and Justice: Women, Drugs and Sentencing Policy," Lindesmith Center–Drug Policy Foundation, http.//www .soros.org/sentencingproject.org.

20. Karen Brodkin, "Global Capitalism: What's Race Got to Do with It?" *American Ethnologist* 27, no. 2 (1998): 237–256.

21. Cose, 45.

22. Ibid., 44.

23. Leith Mullings, "Households Headed by Women: The Politics of Race, Class and Gender," in *On Our Own Terms: Race, Class and Gender in the Lives of African American Women* (New York: Routledge, 1997), 99.

24. Marable, "Racism, Prisons and the Future."

25. Neal, 130.

26. Murray Forman, "Moving Closer to an Independent Funk: Black Feminist Theory, Standpoint and Women in Rap," *Women's Studies* 23, no. 1 (1994): 35–55.

27. Barry Walters, "No Hype to Not Believe," *Village Voice*, 14 November 2000.

28. Neal, 131.

29. Allison Samuels, N. Gai Croal, and David Gates, "Battle for the Soul of Hip-Hop," *Newsweek*, 9 October 2000, 58.

30. Neal, 131.

31. Kevin Powell, "My Culture at the Crossroads: A Rap Devotee Watches Corporate Control and Apolitical Times Encroach on the Music He Has Loved All His Life," *Newsweek*, 9 October 2000, 66.

32. Neal, 123.

33. Ibid., 119.

34. Kevin Arlyck, "By All Means Necessary: Rapping and Resisting in Urban Black America," in *Globalization and Survival in the Black Diaspora: The New Urban Challenge*, Charles Green, ed. (Albany: State University of New York Press, 1997), 284.

35. Pat Aufderheider, "Music Videos: The Look of the Sound," *Journal of Communication* (Winter 1986): 53.

36. Ibid., 59.

37. Mullings, 87.

38. Dorothy Roberts, *Killing the Black Body: Race, Reproduction, and the Meaning of Liberty* (New York: Vintage Books, 1997), 18.

39. Jessie Daniels, *White Lies: Race, Class, Gender and Sexuality in White Supremacist Discourse* (New York: Routledge, 1996), 98.

40. Roberts, 4.

41. Forman, 35–55.

42. Tricia Rose, *Black Noise: Rap Music and Black Culture in Contemporary America* (Hanover, N.H.: Wesleyan University Press, 1994), 173.

43. Kelley, *Race Rebels*, 221.

44. Samuels, Croal, and Gates, 58; Powell, 66.

45. bell hooks, "Selling Hot Pussy: Representations of Black Sexuality in the Cultural Marketplace," in *Black Looks: Race and Representation* (Boston: South End Press, 1992), 66.

46. Rose, 170.

47. bell hooks, "Selling Hot Pussy," 75.

∽

TODD BOYD

From Elvis to Eminem:
Play That Funky Music, White Boy!

Shame on a nigga who try to run game on a nigga!
—Wu Tang Clan

I wonder how many people in the viewing audience at the 2000 Academy Awards presentation recognized the look on Denzel Washington's face when Kevin Spacey jacked him for his Best Actor Oscar. I did. And I'm sure that many of the black people who had tuned in that evening specifically for the purpose of seeing Denzel "get his," as it were, saw the same thing. Some hip white people saw it, too.

Washington would have been justified had his reaction fit in with the proverbial "angry black man" motif, but instead he simply flashed a quick tight-lipped smile and applauded sparingly, as if to say, "It's all good." But the look itself spoke volumes. We could see it. We could feel it. We know it all too well.

Denzel was certainly not the first black person to get jacked for his award, and, rest assured, he won't be the last. I am reminded of a similar story about Duke Ellington, when he was denied the Pulitzer Prize in music back in 1966. It was more than obvious to everyone that not only did he deserve the lousy prize, he deserved sainthood. But upon his rejection, Duke—so classy, so elegant—simply said, "I guess they don't want me to become too famous at such an early age." He was in his late sixties at the time.

Well, if Duke got jacked, then at least we can say that Denzel is in good company.

> *Where's my goddamn trophy?!*
> —Willie D. of The Geto Boys, "Trophy"

Don't get me wrong. It's not as though the Oscars are any objective measure of one's accomplishments. More than anything else, they are the industry's way of advertising itself, promoting its product. In the words of many a Brotha, at the end of the day, "It really ain't shit."

But, then again, maybe it is.

After all, Oscars translate to money. Oscars also translate to the so-called respect of one's peers, and maybe more than anything else, they represent one's full membership in "the club."

The only black man ever granted full membership to that club is the master thespian Sidney Poitier—and even that was a special dispensation due to the indirect influence of a man known as Martin Luther King. Though there have been other black actors and actresses to get love on a supporting tip—Denzel, Hattie McDaniel, Lou Gossett Jr., Whoopi Goldberg, and Cuba Gooding Jr.—none, with the exception of Mr. Tibbs, has gained that top honor.

Some may remember the comments Eddie Murphy made before he handed out the Oscar for Best Picture back in 1988. He said that considering the rather long time between blacks winning Oscars—there was about a twenty-five-year gap between successive winners—maybe he was on stage too soon. I understand that Cher was a bit peeved that Murphy took the spotlight on the occasion of her glory (for the film *Moonstruck*), using it to "play the race card." I also understand that Murphy couldn't care less.

Since the mid-nineties spectacle known as the O. J. Simpson trial, we have heard over and over again about people "playing the race card," as if race were a game, and one could choose to pursue this mere folly at one's leisure—as if we had some control, some real agency in the matter. Well, what happens when they play what I like to call the "nigga card"? I ponder this as an East Detroit 'hood rat known as Eminem reminds us that Elvis once did some jackin' of his own. Yet, Eminem is not Elvis, nor is he trying to be. Elvis jacked black culture when black culture was relegated to black people. It was underground in every sense of that word that Harriet Tubman helped make famous. It was dirty, grimy, and gritty. Elvis, Sam Phillips, and Colonel Tom Parker housed it and went straight to the bank. Black musicians had no choice in the matter other than to keep redefining the music and keep innovating so as to create the undisputed art form and cultural behemoth that the music is to this day.

> *The only thing a nigger can do for me is shine my shoes and buy my records.*
> —Elvis Presley

> *Nowadays everybody wanna talk like they got somethin' to say, but nothin' comes out when you move your lips, just a bunch of gibberish, and muthafuckas act like they forgot about Dre.*
> —Eminem on Dr. Dre's "Forget About Dre"

In today's world, in the world of hip-hop, white boys need entrance passes. The racially specific nature of hip-hop is indeed ghetto fabulous, and it suggests that even middle-class niggas need a ghetto pass. So a white boy can expect to either give it up or be held upside down out of a hotel window, like Big Red did homey in *The Five Heartbeats*.

We remember all too vividly Vanilla Ice, a charlatan if ever there was one. Vanilla Ice was associated with MC Hammer and, not surprising, neither of them is around anymore, except maybe as subjects on VH1's *Behind the Music*. Neither had street credibility, that most essential ingredient needed for true hip-hop acceptance.

Eminem's relationship with Dr. Dre is of central importance here, because it is Dre who extended Marshall Mathers a ghetto pass when he had no other way of gaining entrance. Elvis's rumored comments quoted above suggest that he lived in a time when there was nothing black people had that was of any use to him—except their music, of course. In other words, Eminem comes along at a time when the authenticity of the black experience is assumed, especially as it functions in hip-hop. Which stands in the way of any potential white performer trying to tell his story.

Pops (Louis Armstrong) once said that to be successful in America as a black man, you had to become "some White man's nigger." You needed white sponsorship. Not anymore, and definitely not in hip-hop. The story has been reversed. To the extent that America has accepted hip-hop as the authentic expression of ghetto existence, white folks need not apply.

I say all this, though, with the millennial reemergence of the white negro in full effect, as we speak. Leader of the pack, of course, is Eminem, but he has a crew,

however much he might like to think of himself as a solo act. Fellow Detroit sub-
urbanite Kid Rock has somehow managed to merge Johnny Cash with Too Short,
and Fred Durst, he of Limp Bizkit fame, has even found his way to Shaolin. Not to
mention cats like Jason Williams, "white chocolate" on the court, or Danny Hoch
and Upski, who are putting this phenomenon to critical scrutiny, while performing
its pathologies.

Even our own President Bill Clinton commented to the congressional Black
Caucus, after a previous meeting with the actor Chris Tucker—who is preparing to
play the first black president in an upcoming film—that Tucker was a little late, that
indeed, he, Slick Willie, had beat him to it. When the man on high is claimin'
Brothahood credentials, you know times have really changed. I have not forgotten
my recent acquaintance, Warren Beatty, who put this all before us a few years ago
in *Bulworth*. Can there be any question that Norman Mailer's late-fifties white
negro is back on the scene with a gangsta lean?

What do we make of all this? I single Eminem out because he is the only one
to have made his mark in the arena of black culture, as opposed to appropriating
blackness and sanitizing it for white audiences like many of the others. I am often
asked whether or not Eminem is like the return of Elvis. To this, I say a resounding
no. Yet this answer is not something one arrives at easily. First of all, Dr. Dre, as I
said, introduced Eminem to the world. Dre has not only produced many of
Eminem's tracks and appeared in his videos, but he's also the owner of Aftermath
Records, which distributes Eminem's records. In other words, Dre is making money
off of Eminem. Some have even argued that Dre is pimpin' the white boy, and that
it is about time that black people started making money off of white folks.

Eminem has not faced much opposition from the hip-hop community, either.
As a matter of fact, many other rappers eagerly embrace him as a legitimate figure.
They go overboard praising his lyrical skills and his overall prowess as an MC. This
is not unlike the days when Larry Bird played for the Celtics and many black NBA
players would bend over backward to tell you how good the white boy could play.

When you consider that Eminem came up within the genre of hip-hop, as
opposed to watching it from a distance, it underscores his effortless entry into the
culture. It's not like he's Michael Bolton or someone who tried to act like his work
had nothing to do with black culture. No, Eminem bows down accordingly, often
citing the work of his mentor, Dre, particularly work from Dre's NWA phase. It's
obvious to me that Eminem has totally absorbed all of those early NWA and Ice
Cube records, because his "I don't give a fuck" attitude, now a cliché in hip-hop, is
a carbon copy of what the Brothas from Compton put down back in the day.
Eminem has never tried to deny his debt to the culture.

This is not unlike the career of one Tina Marie, the white female singer who
was such an integral part of Rick James's world back in the late seventies and early
eighties, before the Superfreak got completely carried away. This was in a time
before music videos, when people heard Tina Marie sing before ever seeing her, and
most of the black community assumed she was black. It was certainly a shock to me
when I saw her for the first time. Yet, if you ask people who were listening at the

time, they will surely tell you that Tina Marie was a serious artist. She was embraced because she came up within the black culture. I have heard many people talk the same way about "Pistol" Pete Maravich, the late white NBA star from the seventies who was unanimously praised by the Brothas in regard to his highly stylized game.

Eminem's records are selling at a rate unparalleled in hip-hop—not a small task, when you consider that this is a genre that has consistently dominated the music charts in the past few years. His music is now being played on rock stations that never played hip-hop before. Again, there is a parallel to that phenomenon known as "white chocolate," white boy Jason Williams of the Sacramento Kings, whose NBA jersey is the best-selling jersey in the league. (This for a player who is now only in his third year, and who has yet to do anything really other than dominate the nightly sports show highlights.) Like Eminem's, Williams's popularity in an otherwise black arena represents a direct connection for white audience members should they choose to make it. But as much as we may talk about white people imitating black culture, there's also a point at which the prevalence of black culture is such that this imitation is unconscious. Here I would reference Donny Hoch's 1999 flick *White Boys,* which features a white character, Flip Dogg, who has so absorbed hip-hop's lifestyle lessons that he's convinced he is blacker than most black people. When this happens—when white audiences can feel an Eminem or a Jason Williams—is it because the middleman, or the black man, has been cut out? White audiences no longer have to put on blackface and parade around in knowing imitation. Now they can look to one of their own, whose anger, unmitigated rage, frustration, and anxiety are all now considered legitimate, even though the people from whom this rage originated are still struggling to be taken seriously.

I have always found it interesting the way that black men, when speaking among themselves, will often, if not always, refer to white men as "boys." The reduction of men to boys here speaks volumes—clearly it's an attempt to diminish the white man's masculinity. There is, of course, a reverse precedent to this, going back to when southerners publicly referred to black men as boys. But now, again, the script is being flipped.

I am so often reminded of my boys from back in the day at the University of Florida, future pro ball players who would talk all the time about how when they got drafted by the NFL or NBA, they were going to walk right up to the man and demand, "I want what's mine!" For many of them that day came true. For some of them, it did not. What these raised eyebrows around Eminem's rocketman-like success are all about is simply demanding some accountability for what looks on the surface to be much like the same old story, different decade.

To all concerned, I suggest, niggas might be a l'il less selfish when the cheese is spread a l'il mo equally; fo sho!

Part III. Beyond Traditional Boundaries

7. Beyond Black and White: Redefining Racialized Identities

LEE D. BAKER

Profit, Power, and Privilege: The Racial Politics of Ancestry

In March 2000, each adult residing in the United States was supposed to receive a census form—and was then confronted, once again, by those ominous racial boxes. This time you could check more than one box. Your ability to check more than one box was a compromise worked out by the Commerce Department and two opposing efforts to lobby the administration. One effort was launched by people who identify as biracial, or of mixed-race descent, and who wanted their own box. The other effort was led by the NAACP and the National Council of La Raza, who argued that the boxes should remain the same. Although virtually every Latino, black, or Native American person should go ahead and check "all of the above," the powerful biracial lobby did not want to force its constituents to choose between identifying with one ancestor and another. The NAACP and others argued that the census was about identification—not identity—and pressed the administration to make an accurate count of people who are identified as racial minorities in order to gain a better understanding of intercity demographics and to maintain the ability to demonstrate disparate impact. These organizations wanted to be able to account for all people identified as black, Hispanic, and so on. In this case, the biracial lobby viewed race as a proxy for ancestry, whereas the NAACP viewed race as a proxy for political status.

In February 2000, the U.S. Supreme Court ruled that the statewide election for the commissioners of the Office of Hawaiian Affairs, an agency that allocates resources set aside since Hawaii became a state in 1959, was not valid. Since these resources were for the explicit purpose of bettering "the conditions of Native

Hawaiians," previously only indigenous Hawaiians could vote for commissioners. The Court deemed the election unconstitutional, invoking the rarely used Fifteenth Amendment, which provides that the right to vote "shall not be denied or abridged by the United States or by any state on account of race, color, or previous conditions of servitude." Justice Anthony M. Kennedy explained in his majority opinion that "ancestry can be a proxy for race" and ruled the elections unconstitutional. But elections held by Indian tribes remained constitutional, Kennedy argued, because of their "unique political status."

A few years ago, the Lumbee Tribe of Pembroke, North Carolina, petitioned the U.S. Congress for federally designated tribal status. At stake was over $70 million in federal aid targeted for health and education. Although members of the Lumbee Tribe have made treaties with the federal government and some 40,000 are recognized as a tribe by the state of North Carolina and enjoy a very salient "political status," the federal government in 1994 refused to recognize their tribal status because they did not meet the stringent requirements imposed by the Bureau of Indian Affairs (BIA). BIA requirements include tracing descent from a "historic tribe." The Lumbees, however, have a mixed ancestry that includes earlier Hatteras and Cheraw groups. Unlike western tribes, the Lumbees have participated in the crosscurrents of culture since 1585 when Sir Walter Raleigh embarked on his ill-fated colony. For centuries, the Lumbees have absorbed the culture and people from neighboring black, white, and Indian populations, and today they are hard-pressed to meet the requirements set by the BIA that simply ignore processes of cultural change. In this case, the Lumbees viewed political status as a proxy for ancestry, but Congress did not.

Race and racism in the United States today are the historical end products of a gamy mix of social, political, and economic pressures grinding against each other. Like the tectonics of the earth's plates, the process is usually slow and certain, but one never knows when these forces will quake, forever changing the social landscape.

Although the outcomes of the cases I briefly described seem more like a game of "rock-paper-scissors," they fall within the slow racial tectonics. From the centuries-old "one-drop" rule to the complex equations used to claim tribal membership, race, culture, and heritage have always been used inconsistently in a struggle to define social, political, and economic relationships. As W. E. B. Du Bois once penned, the concept of race was "a group of contradictory forces, facts, and tendences."[1]

I have long thought that Du Bois's was one of the best definitions of race, but it does not get us very far. Anthropologists are supposed to identify patterns in process, but it is often difficult to do so when such salient modalities in American culture are used willy-nilly by even our most esteemed institutions. Although it appears in the above cases that race, ancestry, and political status are applied in a sort of catch-as-catch-can manner, there is a simple and usually predictable logic that shapes these "contradictory forces, facts, and tendencies"—profit, power, and privilege. Like the investigative reporter who "follows the money," a scholar is well served if he or she looks for the way people use race to acquire or protect any one of these three "Ps."

RACE AS ANCESTRY

The first and most recent case, regarding census categories, is perhaps the trickiest. The census has always been a politically charged exercise. Not only does the census serve to allocate billions of federal dollars and reapportion congressional districts, it accounts for who and how people in the United States view themselves as a nation. One can map the various permutations of racial categories throughout history by simply documenting how these categories change over time. Former categories included Hindu, mulatto, octoroon, and even "part Hawaiian." The administrators of this national rite have routinely added or subtracted categories as the political winds changed.

For the 2000 census, various groups joined together in an effort to add a category for people with parents who are of different races. Although the census is ultimately about identification—not identity—people view checking boxes as an important way to signify their identity and are understandably upset when their identity is not represented in the "official" count of all Americans. The countless newspaper and magazine articles documenting this effort usually got it wrong. The venerable NAACP, acting as the indomitable "soul patrol," was usually pitted against hapless children forced to choose between the identity of one and the other parent.

The stakes for the NAACP and La Raza were straightforward—-the contest was about power. The leaders and constituents of these organizations feared that muddying the waters, so to speak, with multiracial categories would adversely impact congressional redistricting, the number of race-based federal programs, and efforts to litigate against institutional racism by documenting racial disparity. The stakes on the other side of the debate are more complicated. These tech-savvy parents and their young adult kids mobilized through a network of grassroots and college organizations. Outraged that their identity was marginalized as "other," they advanced compelling arguments that resisted racial formation and questioned the foundations of the so-called one-drop rule. What was missing from both sides of the debate, however, was a sophisticated discussion about what race is and why the government wants to use it.

Individuals who yoke their identity to categories of race often miss the fact that most people stitch together an ethnic identity from various cultural heritages and that cultural identity has nothing to do with racial categories. This distinction between race and ethnicity was thrown into vivid relief when I used to walk out my back door and stroll down 125th Street—affectionately known as the "Heart of Harlem." The everyday lives of Puerto Ricans, Dominicans, Haitians, Nigerians, and African Americans commingle and converge in this community in a way that has transposed historic segregation into a form of congregation that exhibits the rich tapestry of the African diaspora.

The question remains, why does the mixed-race lobby insist on using ancestry as a proxy for race? I think the answer lies in the one argument I have not seen made by members of this lobbying effort. People advocating for a mixed-race category should also advocate that every racial minority check that box too. Barring recent immigrants, virtually no person today considered black, Indian, or Hawaiian can trace an uninterrupted genealogy back to Africa, Hawaii, or any ancestral group. Moreover, everyone with a mythical "Cherokee grandmother" should be encouraged to check that box.

In lieu of this argument, it appears that these advocates are trying to institutionalize a mixed-race category, which, in other countries at least, turns on a claim to white privilege. We can learn from South Africa, Jamaica, Haiti, and even Louisiana and South Carolina that efforts to institutionalize not a hybrid heritage but a mixed-race category actually advance racial injustice.

ANCESTRY AS RACE

The state of Hawaii has a complicated history. Native Hawaiians came from eastern Polynesia perhaps a thousand years ago. After the British explorer Captain James Cook arrived in 1778, the islands' ports became important way stations for ships trading with Asia. In 1810, King Kamehameha I unified the islands as the kingdom of Hawaii to stem the rising tide of colonial practices. The king staved off colonialism, in part, by brokering six agreements for peace and economic reciprocity with the United States. When Kamehameha I died in 1819, his son succeeded him, ushering in the so-called Great Awakening. Destabilized by epidemics of new infectious diseases, an influx of people, and new agricultural products, Native Hawaiians converted to Christianity in large numbers. Protestant missionaries began exerting enormous influence on Hawaiian society and politics, often using force to convert religion, morality, and lifestyle.

In 1839, the king's younger brother, Kamehameha II, assumed power and tried to stem the growing influence of foreign profiteers and missionaries by establishing a legislature and a constitution and declaring basic rights for his subjects. He remained, however, the sole title holder of land. Although he began to allow his people to own tracts of land, his land tenure reform spun out of control, and foreigners soon purchased most of the arable tracts. By the end of the nineteenth century, whites owned four times as much land as natives, planting sugarcane on nearly every acre.

An 1876 treaty enabled Hawaiian sugar to replace Southern cotton as king. Raw sugar could now enter the United States duty-free, and American investors chased the sweet profits. A veritable cane cartel emerged that aggressively "recruited" thousands of Chinese and Japanese laborers while usurping and concentrating the islands' economic and political power. With the blessings of their missionaries and the force of their militia, the cartel, in 1887, took control of the islands—all but deposing King David Kalakua. Like Captain Hook a century earlier, these captains of industry claimed Hawaii as their own. They imposed a new constitution that disenfranchised most Native Hawaiians and all Asian immigrants. When Queen Liliuokalani assumed the throne, she made a gallant last stand. By 1893, however, her efforts were crushed, and the sovereign kingdom of Hawaii was overthrown, thanks in part to the U.S. military. Five years later, the United States formally annexed Hawaii as a territory.

When Hawaii became a state in 1959, the federal government conveyed 1.4 million acres of land to the new state with the explicit understanding that a share of the revenues generated from this land go "for the betterment of the conditions of Native Hawaiians." Not until 1978 did the state fulfill its responsibility and allocate 20 percent of these revenues to the Office of Hawaiian Affairs (OHA). The OHA is governed by nine trustees of Native Hawaiian ancestry, and they are elected by people with Hawaiian ancestry. The office is charged with redressing the ills not only of the nineteenth century but those of the twentieth century too. From 1898 until 1959, when Hawaii became a state, Native Hawaiians were prohibited from speaking their language and discouraged from practicing their cultural traditions. Today, the more than 200,000 descendants of the original Polynesian population are at the bottom of the socioeconomic ladder, are 2.5 times more likely to be below the poverty level, and have an unemployment level almost twice that of any other group on the islands.

For the past twenty-two years, OHA has used its money to elevate the well-being of Native Hawaiians by providing job training, underwriting entrepreneurs, delivering health care, erecting housing, and promoting the use of the Hawaiian language. Moreover, the office has been an important impetus in a cultural renaissance that includes efforts to recover land, language, and self-determination. Perhaps the high-water mark of this renaissance was the 1993 apology rendered by Congress. Congress actually admitted that the overthrow of the kingdom of Hawaii violated international law and that the United States acquired the land "without the consent of or compensation to the native Hawaiian people of Hawaii or their sovereign government." Congress also apologized for the participation of its diplomatic corps and U.S. troops in the 1893 coup d'état and finally acknowledged that the United States deprived Native Hawaiians of "their inherent sovereignty as a people."[2]

These precepts articulated by the legislative branch stand in contradiction to precepts articulated last February by the judicial branch, in *Rice v. Cayetano* (2000), which found OHA elections to be in violation of the Fifteenth Amendment. This case was originally filed in federal district court in 1996 by Harold Rice, a white rancher on the Big Island who was denied the right to vote in the election for OHA commissioners. Although Rice's ancestors migrated to Hawaii in 1831, he does not claim to be indigenous and therefore could not vote in that election.

To qualify Native Hawaiians, the state legislature employed a cumbersome and indeed untenable definition that included a so-called blood quantum, and Harold Rice argued that he was being denied the right to vote on account of his race. The crux of the argument, however, turned on whether the Court should apply a "strict scrutiny test" or "rational basis review." The strict scrutiny test is required by *Adarand v. Peña* (1995), and the Court has used it to strike down affirmative action programs, majority-minority congressional districts, and contract set-aside programs. The more lenient rational basis review applies to legislation affecting American Indians under *Morton v. Mancari* (1974) and employs the notion of "political status"—as opposed to racial categories—to rationalize special programs and entitlements. The Supreme Court ultimately jettisoned the political status argument to fall back on the oft-cited color-blind mantra that has typified the Rehnquist Court, explaining that "it demeans the dignity and worth of a person to be judged by ancestry instead of by his or her merit," which motivated Justice Kennedy in his majority opinion to conclude that "ancestry can be a proxy for race," and thus OHA elections had violated the Fifteenth Amendment.[3]

Clearly OHA and its indigenous constituents were attempting to maintain their powers of self-determination and their right to control land revenues. The partisan polarity of this case becomes apparent when one peruses the many amicus briefs submitted by competing interests. Tribal governments, as well as Alaska's Inuit groups—who are not considered tribes but vote for representatives to native corporations—were compelled to weigh in on the side of OHA.

This case, however, became the latest cause célèbre for all of those "think tanks" and "action committees" that have fought so hard to maintain white privilege and right-wing conservative power by dismantling everything from affirmative action to bilingual education. The case was bankrolled by the Campaign for a Color Blind America (CCBA). Simply put, the case would never have been appealed if it were not for the deep pockets and the ardent support of conservative critics. The list of other supporters of Rice included a veritable who's who of Washington's most conservative think tanks: the American Enterprise Institute, the Pacific Legal Foundation, the United States Justice Foundation, and Americans Against Discrimination and Preference. As Robert Bork weighed in with a brief, George Will followed up with pithy punch lines in the *Wall Street Journal*, and newsletters and monthlies across the nation were littered with claims about the "racism" perpetuated by Native Hawaiians. In this case, it was the power of conservative Washington lobbyists that from many miles away erased the brutal history of indigenous Hawaiians to ensure their own ideal of a color-blind America, which turns a blind eye to white supremacy.

POLITICAL STATUS AS ANCESTRY

The Supreme Court decided that ancestry could not replace the unique political status of Native American tribes because it was cast in racial terms, but Congress has argued that ancestry cast in distinctly racial terms is a prerequisite for that political status. For years, the Lumbee Indians of Robeson County, North Carolina, have been struggling for federal recognition of their tribal status. In 1956, Congress passed the Lumbee Act, which recognized the Lumbee Tribe but did not grant it "tribal status." Although the state of North Carolina recognizes the Lumbee Indians as a tribe, they have been unable to meet the stringent requirements set up by the BIA to attain that coveted federal status, in large measure because they failed to meet the criteria promulgated in Title 25 of the Code of Federal Regulations, Section 83.7(e).

Approximately 40,000 Lumbee Indians live along the stretch of gray loam flatlands that straddle the North and South Carolina border. Concentrated in a ten-mile radius of Pembroke, North Carolina, the Lumbees' strong middle class of lawyers, tobacco growers, and businesspeople developed the powerful Lumbee Regional Development Association, which for years served as the de facto tribal government.

In 1994, the Lumbee Indians tried to bypass the BIA requirements for tribal status and appealed directly to Congress. Passed by the House, their legislation failed on the Senate floor, thanks in part to Jesse Helms, who sided with those Cherokees in the western part of the state who insisted on the same BIA processes that the Lumbees had already failed to satisfy. The Eastern Band of the Cherokee Nation did not want to be upstaged at the federal level by the Lumbees—the largest tribe east of the Mississippi. At stake was over $70 million in federal aid, and the Cherokees did not want to share the dwindling dollars allocated by the BIA. As the Lumbee petitions muddled through Congress, [Cherokee] Vice Chief Gerard Parker was quoted by the *Atlanta Journal and Constitution* as saying, "If they're Indian, where is the language? Where is the cultural background? I hope Congress won't be fooled." He went on to explain, "If they met the criteria to be Indian they should be Indians. But they don't; they don't even look like Indians."[4] Chief Parker is right: Lumbee Indians don't look like stereotypical braves-on-bareback—and that's part of the problem.

Part 83 of Title 25 of the Code of Federal Regulations outlines the mandatory criteria for federal acknowledgement of tribal status. Although most of the byzantine criteria involve history, culture, and political solidarity, Subsection 7(e) emerges as a very racialized criterion. Tribes must document "individuals who descend from a historical Indian tribe." The process of meeting this criterion becomes a percentage game, not unlike the blood quantum or fractions used in previous years. In a more recent case that mirrors the Lumbees' in important ways, the BIA denied tribal recognition to the Mobile-Washington (MOWA) County Band of Choctaw Indians of South Alabama because "there was no evidence in the substantial body of documentation submitted by the petitioner . . . to demonstrate Choctaw ancestry or any other Indian ancestry for 99 percent of the petitioner's membership. Thus, the petitioner fails to meet criterion (e), descent from a historical tribe."[5] In its final determination against federal acknowledgment,

> the BIA found that most of the records of the known MOWA ancestors did not document them as Indian, but described them racially or ethnically with ambiguous terms, such as: "Black," "Cajun," "Caucasian," "Creole," "French," "Mulatto," "Spanish," or "White." . . . None of the primary records revealed their documented known ancestors as "Native American or Indian."[6]

Like the MOWA Indians, the Lumbee Indians failed to gain recognition in the executive branch. The Lumbees also failed with the legislative branch because their racial ancestry was ostensibly not pure enough to warrant their claim to a "unique political status." Conversely, the judicial branch found the ancestry of Native Hawaiians too racial to warrant their claim to a "unique political status." Finally, the political status of the mixed-race lobby was powerful enough to warrant the executive branch changing the census forms. Again, it appears that we are back to that old game of rock-paper-scissors. But I hope you get a better understanding that it is not a game of chance but a life-and-death struggle between competing forces of profit, power, and privilege.

NOTES

1. W. E. B. Du Bois, "Dusk of Dawn: An Essay toward an Autobiography of a Race Concept," in his *Writings*, ed. Nathan Huggins (1940; New York: Library of America, 1986), p. 651.

2. Senate Joint Resolution 19, Congressional Record, 103rd Cong., H9627 (November 15, 1993).

3. *Rice v. Cayetano* (2000), opinion of Justice Kennedy, p. 20. Available at http:// supct.law.cornell.edu/supct/pdf/98_818P.ZO.

4. "Cherokee Objections," *Atlanta Journal and Constitution,* May 2, 1992, p. A1.

5. www.doi.gov/bia/mowa_not.htm.

6. www.doi.gov/bia/moanew.htm.

❧

NOEL IGNATIEV

The Politics of Studying Whiteness

As a matter of their own survival, the direct victims of white privilege have always studied this phenomenon. Afro-Americans in particular have long understood that the white race is not a biological formation, but a social one whose existence depends on its members' willingness to conform to the institutions and behavior patterns that reproduce it. Only after the Civil Rights Movement challenged race as a legal category did white academics begin to examine whiteness as a phenomenon.

The very process of defining an area of research, including settling on a name, is political. Whiteness studies recapitulates the experience of black studies, women's studies, and—if one cares to go back that far—Slavic studies. In each instance, academic entrepreneurs have attempted to hijack a field of study to dilute its subversive potential.

Those who study whiteness typically fall into two camps: the preservationists and the abolitionists. The preservationists mostly seek to identify aspects of whiteness that could exist without racial oppression and privilege. Some work to excavate elements of so-called white culture, although, given the mulatto character of American culture, they struggle mightily. Others acknowledge that whiteness is the product solely of privilege, but hold that it is too deeply embedded in the social structure to be done away with. Therefore, they argue, whiteness will have to be "reframed" or "rearticulated." Among the preservationists are white racial awareness trainers and professional diversity consultants, who must assume—as a condition of their work—the existence of a valid white identity. Such people remind me of doctors who secretly love the disease they claim to be fighting.

The abolitionists believe that whiteness is based solely on oppression and that it could no more exist without white supremacy than slaveholding could exist without slavery. They often use "white" the way the old Industrial Workers of the World used "citizen"—as a sneer—and propose not to "rearticulate" the white race but to abolish it as a social category.

Members of both groups who look critically at race and whiteness must face a crucial challenge: making sense of the "new immigrants" in quotes because many to whom this term is applied are neither new nor immigrants. People from the Caribbean and the Western Hemisphere south of the Rio Grande and people from Asia increasingly enjoy privileges in employment, schools, and housing once reserved for whites; and whoever heard of "driving while Asian"? Yet, when we at *Race Traitor,*[1] journal of the new abolitionism, suggested that immigrants from Asia and elsewhere may now be undergoing the whitening process, we were met with intense hostility and criticized for clinging to a traditional bipolar model of race, one not adequate to describe the current reality.

Of course some groups occupy intermediate positions, sociologically: everyone knows that even European American ethnic groups vary in wealth and status; what makes them all white is their social distance from those who are by definition oppressed. That social distance is whiteness. The U.S. may be multiethnic, but political stability has traditionally depended on a majority held together by racial definition. A racially privileged minority can rule only by naked force, as in pre–civil rights Alabama and apartheid South Africa, and as in the West Bank and Gaza today—an unstable and undesirable situation for those in power. The day the country has a functionally non-white (i.e., racially oppressed) majority is the day the Rodney King rebellion becomes permanent. One example of the pitfalls of a multiracial model is a recent book that hailed South Asian New York City cabdrivers as the vanguard of the struggle against racism in the city—just a few months before the Danny Glover incident revealed them to be a main force denying taxi service to black men. One might as well have hailed the 1863 New York City Irish as fighters against white supremacy for their determined opposition to nativist bigotry.

As in the nineteenth century, the white race is being recomposed, and as at that time, boundaries are not always clear. A great deal of the quarrel about "people of color" and "intermediate" races has to do with determining which groups will be socially white in the twenty-first century (however they may come to be called in popular parlance). Some things to investigate in this regard: marriage patterns of "Asians" and "Latins," the role of the Catholic Church in assimilating various groups, how ESL and other programs promote immigrants over Afro-Americans, the effects of immigration policy and the border, the labor market and the line between the official and the unofficial economy, and the effects of prisons and schools in channeling populations.

Of course, the evidence for recomposition can be read in several ways, and the outcome is not settled. A great deal depends on the actions of the "not-yet-white" (the phrase is David Roediger's) themselves; they may choose, as did many of South Africa's "Colored," to identify with the oppressed. But whatever the outcome, we must examine the issue without assuming the conclusion as a premise.

NOTE

1. Suscription information and sample articles are online at http://www.race traitor.org.

∽

ERIC KLINENBERG

The Political Economy of Whiteness Studies

In 1997, I joined a group of University of California, Berkeley, graduate students to organize a conference called "The Making and Unmaking of Whiteness." Faculty and funders loved the idea, and, without too much trouble, we had secured a substantial budget to create the first national forum for evaluating whiteness research. The media were fascinated. *USA Today* ran a brief story about the scholarly meeting in its list of important national events; the *New York Times, Washington Post, Wall Street Journal,* and even the *Times* of London covered the proceedings; major television networks and national radio stations invited the organizers on air. University presses heard the buzz, and, before long, several of the major publishers were competing to sign up the conference organizers to write a book.

Here was an important lesson: Unlike other race scholars, who fought long battles before they were taken seriously and given resources, academics who would focus on whiteness immediately got a platform, a voice, and a home in the academy. Whiteness studies is about uncovering and undoing racialized power and privilege. It also partakes in that power and privilege in ways worth investigating. The political economy of whiteness studies—which involves its disciplinary locations, its claims to public attention, its market value, and its place in elite academic publishing outlets—has been even more controversial than the research itself.

In the five years since the conference, there have been hundreds of academic and journalistic publications about whiteness, and the literature is still in an embryonic stage. Yet the most prominent proponents and opponents of whiteness studies ask too much of the project. Key figures in the field gained attention by claiming that their work would advance the abolition of whiteness, but they could not adequately explain how such an act would be possible at the individual or collective level. Others argued that whiteness is "the linchpin of racial inequality,"[1] and proclaimed that studying whiteness would suddenly make possible "the excavation of the foundations of all racial and cultural positionings."[2] Before whiteness studies, they implied or asserted, scholars of race had been missing the most important element. Their critics reacted in similarly impassioned language. According to labor historian Eric Arneson, "these startling claims have generated more historiographical smoke than fire. . . . After a decade of growing popularity . . . whiteness studies . . . remains a vague and intellectually incoherent enterprise."[3] Speaking to a *New York Times* reporter, historian Sean Wilentz dismissed the prominent whiteness scholars out of hand. "In their view whiteness is implicitly the racial category that is evil, and blackness is just a response to it. It's black nationalism by another means."[4]

It was not a productive way to advance scholarly debate. By foregoing intellectual modesty in favor of grandiose and revolutionary proclamations about their own contributions, the most prominent whiteness scholars set themselves up for ridicule, and they alienated potential sympathizers. For their part, the fiercest critics failed to recognize how whiteness studies would (and has) helped open an inquiry into the practices and policies used to produce and maintain racial inequality. As political scientist Adolph Reed has argued, "beneath faddishness and the novelty of buzzwords, the logic of academic subspecialization and the peculiarities of the current political climate," studies of whiteness help to make visible previously overlooked ways in which relationships among race, class, identity, and politics have organized American life. There is no question that earlier generations of historians—Reginald Horsman, Eric Foner, and Edmund Morgan, to name a few—recounted histories of race through scholarship of depth, rigor, and insight that is unmatched by most current research. By focusing on white privilege and the ways it is reproduced, however, whiteness studies offers a useful (though now mostly unused) perspective on the mechanics of racial domination. It would be foolish to abandon the inquiry because some of the inquirers have said foolish things.

Instead, scholars interested in whiteness and relational studies of race should look beyond the new abolitionism and shallow cultural criticism that have become such hot brands in academic publishing today. In the last decade (as in previous generations), anthropologists, historians, and sociologists who preferred not to use the term "whiteness" in their titles have produced a number of major books and articles that directly address the politics and culture of white privilege. The work of scholars such as Cheryl Harris, Linda Gordon, Micaela di Leonardo, Mel Oliver, Troy Duster, Douglas Massey, Nancy Denton, Arnold Hirsch, John Hartigan, Jr., Dalton Conley, and the late Michael Rogin makes clear that research on whiteness is more serious and significant than the skeptics acknowledge.

Take, for example, just two of the themes these authors take up in their work: segregation and wealth. In the twentieth century, white Americans did considerable work to create segregated cities and suburbs, which then became the geopolitical foundation for hoarding public goods and services. The segregating of America after Jim Crow was (to use sociologist Howard Winant's term) a purposeful but fiercely contested "white racial project." Pulling it off required vicious racial violence and rioting at the street level, elaborate restrictive covenants from neighborhood associations, discriminatory steering by realtors, and formal redlining by federal housing and lending agencies. There is significant white agency in the history of segregation, but recent books on the subject—among them Massey and Denton's *American Apartheid* and Hirsch's *Making the Second Ghetto*[5]—are more likely to appear in black studies courses than in seminars or conferences on whiteness. The burgeoning literature on racial inequalities in wealth, which also identifies specific social and political processes through which whites attained durable advantages, is similarly absent from whiteness studies today.

There is no theoretical reason why these issues should be excluded from a relational examination of racial domination. In fact, the activist camp of whiteness scholars should recognize the direct political relevance of research on segregation and wealth, which can be mobilized to support some of the major contests in the contemporary politics of race: campaigns for reparations, the defense of affirmative action, the fight for affordable, integrated housing, and criminal justice reform. In May 2002, for example, Neil Steinberg, a prominent Chicago newspaper columnist and author, announced in his column that, after learning the history of segregation, he had decided to change his position and support reparations. "What about the big black slums on the South and West sides of Chicago, and in every city in America? . . . What created that, and why is it still here? . . . I am beginning to suspect that it is the people demanding the issue of slavery be addressed who are the patriotic ones, the ones who believe in the grandeur of the United States and the sweep of history."[6]

The columnist's reaction was strong, but not unprecedented. When I teach courses on race and cities, my undergraduates are consistently surprised and outraged upon learning about America's history of segregation and suburbanization. White students, in particular, often report that such information forces them, for the first time, to confront the ways that race has shaped their own lives. Many appear uncomfortable, but it's a productive discomfort if it unsettles their presumption that America's race problem is not about them.

The critical question for the future of whiteness studies is whether the project is fundamentally about consciousness-raising—for students, columnists, or wider audiences—or about advancing new explanations and interpretations of racial differentiation and stratification. The answer will largely depend on who assumes intellectual leadership in the whiteness debates, and whether those scholars are capable of integrating contributors, concepts, and questions that are currently outside the inquiry. The abolitionists claim there is no conflict between their activist ambitions and their scholarship. In practice, however, many of them ignore or dismiss versions of whiteness studies that do not mesh with their agenda. In *Colored White,* for example, David Roediger identifies what he views as "healthy" studies of whiteness, but he excludes others—most notably the anthropology of John Hartigan, Jr., and the cultural criticism of Matt Wray—from his survey of the subfield.[7] According to cultural anthropologist Micaela di Leonardo, this narrow vision of whiteness studies and abolitionist politics has blocked recent scholarship from recognizing the white ethnic renaissance or the historical contributions of the literature on white ethnic identity.[8]

Whiteness studies—in both its political and scholastic incarnations—is an embryonic project whose future is difficult to predict. It is already losing its trendy status, and the standards for academic publishing on the topic will surely rise as editors become more discriminating. For the most part, contemporary scholars of whiteness no longer make the overblown claims that were so common in the middle and late 1990s. Soon, their critics will also become more moderate. I'll never teach a course on whiteness because, in my view, whiteness studies is just one part of the study of race, and it is best integrated into a broader set of questions about differentiation and domination. Nonetheless, I will not join the chorus that calls for its end or condemns it for failing to revise American history. Whiteness studies should never have aimed so high. Its critics, who have also had their day, should stop punching so low. Whether the project is political, scholastic, or a mix of the two, it's time to move on with the work.

NOTES

1. Quoted in Peter Goodman, "Conference Seeks to Clear Up What It Means to Be White; Berkeley Talks Draw High Turnout, TV Crews," *Washington Post,* 12 April 1997, A16.

2. Ruth Frankenberg, "Introduction: Local Whitenesses, Localizing Whiteness," in *Displacing Whiteness: Essays in Social and Cultural Criticism,* ed. Ruth Frankenberg (Durham: Duke University Press, 2001).

3. Eric Arneson, "A Paler Shade of White," *New Republic,* 24 June 2002.

4. Margaret Talbot, "Getting Credit for Being White," *New York Times Magazine,* 30 November 1997, 116–119.

5. Doug Massey and Nancy Denton, *American Apartheid: Segregation and the Making of the Underclass* (Cambridge, Mass.: Harvard University Press, 1993); and Arnold Hirsch, *Making the Second Ghetto: Race and Housing in Chicago, 1940–1960,* 2nd ed. (Chicago: University of Chicago Press, 1998).

6. Neil Steinberg, "Fighting Slavery's Legacy: Reparations Reconsidered," *Chicago Sun-Times,* 10 May 2002, 24.

7. David Roediger, *Colored White: Transcending the Racial Past* (Berkeley: University of California Press, 2002). Roediger's omission of Hartigan's work is especially strange, since he reviewed Hartigan's book, *Racial Situations,* favorably in the *Journal of American Ethnic History* (Spring 2001): 165–166.

8. Micaela di Leonardo, personal communication.

~

DAVID ROEDIGER

Defending Critical Studies of Whiteness but Not Whiteness Studies

During the U.S. Civil War, Karl Marx observed that the Confederate South was "not a country, but a battle cry." Allowing for the difference between tragedy and farce, such a remark might apply to whiteness studies today. Neither an interdisciplinary academic field nor a political project, whiteness studies lacks a single journal, book series, association, or regular conference. It exists only as a phantasm, a marketing niche, and a battle cry. The journal *Race Traitor,* the closest thing to an intellectual and activist center associated with recent critical scholarship on white supremacy and white consciousness, abjures all attempts to build anything called whiteness studies—and for excellent reasons. Similarly, none of the leading voices studying race and whiteness—not Toni Morrison, Cheryl Harris, Noel Ignatiev, Ted Allen, Karen Brodkin, Robert Lee, Maurice Berger, Cherríe Moraga, bell hooks, john powell, Neil Foley, or Ariela Gross, for example—have identified with anything as fanciful and narrow as whiteness studies. Thus, any assessment of the state of such studies must begin frankly: There is no such thing.

Matters cannot, however, quite end there. It is necessary to specify that the battle cry of whiteness studies has been forwarded not by those who are advancing the investigation of whiteness as a historical, moral, political, and social problem, but by opponents who deride such investigation and want to shut it down. Thus, in November 1997, the *New York Times Magazine*[1] ridiculed whiteness studies as the latest academic fad, the silly successor to porn studies and Madonna studies. Such a perspective makes it possible to dismiss the study of whiteness as a trendy, superficial phenomenon, unmoored from its distinguished predecessors. Premised on the falsehood that various fields of study are staffed only with academics from the group being studied—i.e., supposedly only African Americans participate in African-American studies—the label also makes the critical study of whiteness into a white project. Lost is the long tradition of inquiry by people of color—for whom whiteness has long been an urgent problem—into what it means to be white. This tradition stretches from slave folktales and American Indian traditions through W. E. B.

Du Bois, Ida B. Wells, Americo Paredes, and, above all, James Baldwin. The contributions of a handful of contemporary white scholars are aggrandized and then dismissed; the fact that scholars of color, often working within ethnic studies programs, have made seminal contributions to critical white studies—Morrison, Leslie Marmon Silko, Harris, Angie Chabram-Dernersesian, Moraga, hooks, and powell, among many others—is ignored entirely.

Within more academic venues, the same naming-then-trashing dynamic surrounds deployment of the term "whiteness studies." At a moment when important differences are emerging among those who study whiteness within the broad Du Boisian tradition of examining the material, public, and personal advantages that identity has conferred, only the fortunate few will happen onto radical historian Ted Allen's provocative recent discussion of those differences in the cyber journal *Cultural Logic*.[2] Distinguished scholars, none of whom centrally study whiteness, responded.[3] The label "whiteness studies" was used by Arnesen as it was in the *Times Magazine* piece. He portrayed whiteness studies as a largely white, recent, and goofy enterprise—the groundbreaking work of Cheryl Harris utterly eluded him, prompting sneers. In the section briefly acknowledging the field of study's longer roots, Arnesen offered a narrow and breathtakingly ill-informed inquiry into Du Bois's work, missing both its extent and import regarding whiteness and calling it "Marxism lite." Although none of the respondents, some of whom have claimed considerable indebtedness to Du Bois's Marxism, contested this matter, one suspects that somehow the Old Man's reputation will survive.

Scholars and writers cannot control how our work will be read and named, especially in the popular press. We ought, however, to be clear among ourselves. The critical study of whiteness is not whiteness studies. We should reject the term's implication that whites are just another group to be welcomed at the table of multiculturalism and instead continue to direct attention to who owns and designs the table. We should locate our work not in a burst of recent creativity, but in an enduring tradition of multiracial scholarship. We should recognize that much of that older scholarship—Baldwin!!—remains even now unparalleled in its risk-taking ability to consider whiteness, class, sexuality, gender, ethnicity, and what it means to be human all at once.

The critical study of whiteness, as Baldwin and the distinguished art scholar Maurice Berger show, can never be only about race. The most noticed recent work, such as that of Ignatiev, Allen, and myself, has concentrated on the intersection of race and class identity, but only recently, in the wonderful work of Venus Green and Bruce Nelson, has the connection of white privilege with labor processes been convincingly fleshed out.[4] The need is acute for more studies looking at gender and white identity, as per Louise Newman, Ruth Frankenberg, and Vron Ware. The relationship between whiteness and youth is also an oddly understudied topic, despite Pamela Perry's seminal *Shades of White*.[5] We know very little, for example, about how and why some white teenagers outgrow youthful attractions to (and mimicry of) African-American culture while others retain those attractions alongside decisions to live in segregated enclaves.

Such models as Baldwin's suggest that we need to ensure that young scholars have room to advance increasingly bolder inquiries into whiteness. They suggest that we should reject the insistence on purely empirical studies; the mandatory genuflection before (sub)disciplinary boundaries; the distrust of the study of language, literature, and popular culture; and the phobic reactions to psychoanalysis (and increasingly to Marxism) that accompany the most strident attempts to first inflate whiteness studies, and to then suffocate the critical study of whiteness.

NOTES

1. Margaret Talbot, "Getting Credit for Being White," *New York Times Magazine,* 30 November 1997, 116–118.
2. Theodore Allen, "On Roediger's Wages of Whiteness," *Cultural Logic* 4 (April 2002): 1.26 at http://eserver.org/clogic/4-2/4-2.html.
3. Eric Arnesen, "Scholarly Controversy: Whiteness and the Historians' Imagination," *International Labor and Working-Class History* 60 (Fall 2001): 3–32. Responses by James Barrett, David Brody, Barbara J. Fields, Eric Foner, Victoria Hattam, and Adolph Reed, Jr., follow the article.
4. Bruce Nelson, *Divided We Stand: American Workers and the Struggle for Black Equality* (Princeton and Oxford: Princeton University Press, 2001); Venus Green, *Race on the Line: Gender, Labor, and Technology in the Bell System* (Durham, N.C.: Duke University Press, 2001); Baldwin's most important writings on whiteness appear in his collection *The Price of the Ticket* (New York: St. Martin's Press, 1985); see also Maurice Berger, *White Lies: Race and the Myths of Whiteness* (New York: Farrar, Straus & Giroux, 1999).
5. Pamela Perry, *Shades of White: White Kids and Racial Identities in High School* (Durham, N.C.: Duke University Press, 2002).

~

JOHN HARTIGAN, JR.
The Difference between Whiteness and Whites

The great analytical power of the concept of whiteness is its broad attention to the practices and racial ideology that maintain whites' privileged social position. But this strength can be a liability in the difficult work of analyzing and intervening in the way whites experience and perceive race in daily contexts. The crux of the problem is that, as a concept, whiteness is an abstraction, a generalization that renders in overly broad strokes the subjects to which it is applied. As with any generalization about race, the use of "whiteness" as a term risks reproducing the polarizing characterizations that have long plagued racial thinking. Furthermore, such gener-alizations undermine the ability to address the specific circumstance of people's lives. At this moment, whiteness studies increasingly is split along these lines, either refining general analyses about whites or critically highlighting particular social cir-cumstances in which whites are racialized. Although the latter option opens onto ambiguous terrain, engaging the dimensions of daily cultural life helps move white studies from the general to the specific—and helps us develop a greater understand-ing of the ways whites think, perceive, and act racially.

The terrain of everyday life is the purview of ethnographers, and several recent ethnographies offer critical insight into the complexities of white racial iden-tification and modes of differentiation, globally and in the United States.[1] These works reveal the intensely local nature of social dynamics that shape whites' racial judgments and perceptions; they also underscore a critical disconnect between char-acterizations of whiteness as a national, hegemonic force and whiteness as it plays out in particular places. The overarching finding of these ethnographies is that local circumstances—racial demographics, popular cultures, political orders, and eco-nomic conditions—deeply inflect the significance of race and the processes by which racial matters are perceived and engaged. These works also raise a subtler and perhaps more profound question: How much of whiteness can be explained by racism versus other cultural forces?

Generally, those who view white identity primarily as an abstraction tend to treat it as virtually synonymous with racism. Certainly, antiracists seem convinced that white racialness is largely reducible to racism, which whites either reproduce or actively resist. My own ethnographic study of white residents in Detroit and my recent analysis of the social practices of antiracist workshops and forums, however, lead me to question the effectiveness of such emphatic assertions.[2] To be sure, racism among whites exists, and its impacts are profound. But the fact of racism does not explain everything about how and why race matters. In fact, an overre-liance on racism as an explanatory principle can obscure the fundamental ambiva-lence and ambiguity that characterize whites' understandings of race. Rather than simple conveyors of racism or as automatons dominated by a racial ideology, whites' engagement with race involves—as with any cultural dynamic—interpretive work. This work is made more or less precarious depending on the types of reinforcements provided by particular social settings. Key to understanding white identity, then, is understanding that racial interpretations are always competing with other interpre-tive prisms, such as class and gender and neighborhood and nation. Scholars must continue to investigate how a racial reading outweighs or is reinforced by compet-ing options for interpreting social circumstances. Pursuing such inquiries will pro-vide useful reminders that instances of white attitudes and behaviors that have racial consequences often are not only about race; instead, they result from multiple, over-lapping—at times mutually reinforcing or contradictory—frames of reference that inform social judgments and actions.

Early research in the field often asserted that whiteness was bereft of culture, that whiteness could be defined as a cultural vacuum.[3] On the contrary, the cultural density of whites' social circumstances enables them to invest in whiteness, and this cultural density actually creates widely divergent experiences of race that undermine generalizations about whiteness.[4] The key point here is that whiteness is not simply a racial ideology; rather, like any cultural artifact, it is constituted in daily life through symbols, images, discursive logics and interpretive repertoires, narrative genres, various forms of body work and discipline, and all the other arbitrary conventions that characterize cultural constructions. And it is the very arbitrariness of these forms that offers one of the best openings to deconstruct whiteness: Each mode of reinforcing whiteness is maintained through a tight correspondence with material, economic, and political structures that differ in specific locales. If any of these forms are altered, the tradition of racial interpretation that exists in that locale is undermined, as I found with whites in Detroit.

Once we recognize the cultural dimension of racial analysis, many subsequent points follow. First is the need to recognize the vast disparities of power and privilege within various white communities. Intense intraracial contests constantly shape and regulate participation in whiteness. Though so-called white skin privilege is a profound and telling concept, it has limits and can be severely curtailed through such boundary-marking terms as "white trash," "redneck," and "hillbilly."[5] We also must recognize the rapidly changing demographic and political circumstances that are reconfiguring racial formations in the United States. It is simply not the case that whites, particularly in the lower classes, in Detroit or Laredo, Miami or Houston, participate in a uniform order of racial dominance. The powers and privileges attributed to whites nationally are severely attenuated by certain local contexts, particularly the circumstances of minority-group status and the availability of limited social and economic resources or opportunities.[6] Though exceptional now, such local circumstances will become far more common, given the changing demographics of the United States.

Acknowledging the significance and diversity of these local circumstances leads to another point: We need to recognize that whites, too, are racial subjects. Though they are not subject to the same forms of racial domination or subordination as are peoples of color, they are in certain contexts and social situations confronted by the humiliations, hostilities, ambiguities, and charged discrepancies that constitute racial subjectivity. The advantage of this shift—from regarding whiteness to examining the racialization of whites in specific situations—is that it undercuts the current focus on white studies and the enshrinement of whiteness as a unique subject of study, which risks further inscribing the already deeply ghettoized status of race in academia.

Each of these points—the intraracial contests that constitute whiteness, the critical role of place in determining the significance of race, and the various circumstances through which whites are racialized—addresses, first, the need for analysis that distinguishes between racial dynamics at the national and local levels (and acknowledges their interrelations), and, second, the fundamental role culture plays in these matters. Culture, as an analytical perspective, treats matters of belonging and difference, the assigning of social meaning to arbitrary biological traits, the naturalization of certain orders of inequality or dominance, the forms of etiquette or decorum that discipline bodies and behaviors, and the styles of narrative that organize each of these into tangible forms of meaning that one then encounters in reinforcing or challenging circumstances.[7] This series of dynamics—observed intraracially as well as in interracial contexts—offers many opportunities for understanding and intervening in the reproduction of white racialness.

Antiracists—as scholars and activists—have great confidence in the ability of whiteness to articulate the real core of "the race problem." They use the concept to delineate how racism, whether "new" or "old," informs whites' social perceptions and actions. But if the sum of whites' experience of race is reducible only to racism, then this promising area of research and activism will achieve far from satisfactory results. The surge of critical attention to whiteness risks becoming stagnant, stymied by the vast gulf between the analytical clarity of the concept in articulating the operations of racial ideology and the far more muddled and mutable circumstances where whites are compelled to make sense out of race. We need to move now from reifying whiteness and proceed to use the resources of sociology, anthropology, history, and cultural studies to examine racialization in relation to whites more broadly.

In a sense, the easiest stage of studying whiteness is behind us. Now, those pursuing this line of analysis and critique are confronted with more daunting tasks of addressing specific circumstances with all their contradictory and ambiguous dimensions. Unless we engage these more confusing social settings, we risk losing a crucial audience: those whites who both recognize and live the profound chasm between whiteness as a conveyor of power and privilege and white racialness as a problematic, far from normative identity.

NOTES

1. See "Whiteness in the Field," a special issue of *Identities* 7(3), 2000; Lorraine Kenny, *Daughters of Suburbia: Growing Up White, Middle Class, and Female* (New Brunswick: Rutgers University Press, 2000); Pamela Perry, *Shades of White: White Kids and Racial Identities in High School* (Durham: Duke University Press, 2002); Roger Sanjeck, *The Future of Us All: Race and Neighborhood Politics in New York City* (Ithaca: Cornell University Press, 1998); Bridget Byrne, *White Lives: Gender, Race, and Class in Contemporary London* (Durham: Duke University Press, forthcoming).

2. John Hartigan, Jr., *Racial Situations: Class Predicaments of Whiteness in Detroit* (Princeton: Princeton University Press, 1999); and John Hartigan, Jr., "Object Lessons in Whiteness: Antiracism and the Study of White Folks," *Identities* 7(3), 2000: 373–406.

3. This claim is made by David Roediger in *Towards the Abolition of Whiteness: Essays on Race, Politics, and Working Class History* (London: Verso, 1993).

4. George Lipsitz, *The Possessive Investment in Whiteness: How White People Profit from Identity Politics* (Philadelphia: Temple University Press, 1998), and Leland Saito, *Race and Politics: Asian Americans, Latinos, and Whites in a Los Angeles Suburb* (Chicago: University of Illinois Press, 1998).

5. John Hartigan, "'Who Are These White People?': 'Rednecks,' 'Hillbillies,' and 'White Trash' as Marked Racial Subjects," in *Deconstructing Whiteness*, Eduard Bonilla-Silva, ed. (London: Routledge, forthcoming).

6. John Hartigan, "When Whites Are a Minority," in *Cultural Diversity in the United States*, Larry Naylor, ed. (Detroit, Mich.: Bergin and Garvey Press, 1997).

7. Anthropologists distinguish two senses of culture: one particular (e.g., American culture) and the other generic, referring to a common dimension of human behavior and belief. The lack of a cultural perspective on race today stems from the overemphasis on the former, as is evident in the debates from the 1960s to the1990s over the so-called culture of poverty or the "pathology" of "black culture." Regarding race today, I suggest the latter connotations of culture can provide great insight when paired with an understanding of the institutional and historical dimensions of race.

⁓

TIM WISE

Brilliance without Passion: Whiteness Scholarship and the Struggle against Racism

[T]his learned, civilized, intellectual-liberal debate cheerfully raged in its vacuum, while every hour brought more distress and confusion—and dishonor—to the country they claimed to love.

—James Baldwin, *No Name in the Street*

Sometimes I wish I had gone to graduate school and received an advanced degree. And then there are those moments when I thank God that I did no such thing. This is not meant to be a put-down of those with such accomplishments under their belts, but rather to make the point that knowledge comes from many places. For every truth uncovered and made more visible by professors and academics, there are other truths made infinitely more obscure.

Such is the case with the emerging discipline of whiteness studies, which, to the extent it has been turned into a discipline (mostly by whites, since people of color had long been studying white folks without getting paid for it), is a troubling concept.

I never took a whiteness studies class, but I learned plenty about whiteness from places where its impact was broadly felt: in the public housing projects of New Orleans, where I worked as a political organizer; and throughout Louisiana in the early 1990s, where white supremacy almost propelled former Klansman

David Duke to the United States Senate by winning him 60 percent of the white vote.

And I learned about whiteness by examining my own life—a nonacademic exercise requiring me to relinquish the impersonal tone of most intellectual discourse. Taking inventory of my personal privileges and the costs my family and I paid to obtain them did more to remove the veil that hid my whiteness from me than any postmodernist deconstruction of literature, media, or history could have done.

This begs the question: To what purpose whiteness scholarship?

Assuming that the purpose of whiteness scholarship is to make whiteness visible to white people (since it is already quite transparent to people of color), in the hopes that they may recognize the injustices that stem from its privileges and work to eradicate them, then it should be judged as a failure—or, at best, a marginally successful work-in-progress. There are at least two directions in which the discipline can improve. Unfortunately, much whiteness scholarship—though most certainly white—is only scholarly in the most inaccessible fashion. Many whiteness scholars spend so much time figuring out ways to use words that most folks have never heard—and, much to their credit, never use—that any applicability of their theories to the real world is lost in a casserole of intellectualism. Any scholarship that relies on such words as "epistemology" and "axiology" is every bit as dead as the language of the business class, what with their "thinking outside the box" and "capitalizing on our human assets" and "planned shrinkage." Since language is a key tool with which privileged persons maintain their status, it is the ultimate irony that those who claim to seek the eradication of unearned privilege themselves mystify common concepts by way of such wordplay.

James Baldwin said it best when he noted that intellectual activity, on its own, is a "masturbatory delusion and a wicked and dangerous fraud," since "brilliance without passion is nothing more than sterility." So too, much of whiteness scholarship. So long as the emphasis is on scholarship and not on active engagement with community and activism for institutional change, the field will be little more than a professional lifeline for the chattering class (what those who prefer big words might call the "cognitariat"). For proof of this problem, consider the words of a well-respected academic in this field, who has made important contributions to the scholarship of whiteness and racism, but who feels it necessary to include the following in a book with otherwise valuable insights: "The reiterative revisability of hybrid heterotopias confronts the command of homogeneity with the material and discursive conditions of its horizon. . . ." And it goes on. Masturbatory delusion indeed.

Until and unless whiteness scholars come down from the Ivory Tower—pun intended—and engage their ideas in common language, in communities where everyday white folks live, and in the journals and media relied upon by such folks, racism and white supremacy will remain unchallenged. It's a lesson I learned many years ago from the folks at the People's Institute for Survival and Beyond in New Orleans: Those striving for change in society must break down their complex ideas, say it plain, and be accountable to the wider community in their language and actions as antiracists. Otherwise, the gulf widens between the privileged few and those whose liberation is the first purpose of antiracism efforts.

For example, when I wrote the essay "School Shootings and White Denial" in 2001,[1] so as to confront whites with something readers of color already knew—that social dysfunction among whites is deracialized, unlike the same in communities of color—I didn't consider it whiteness scholarship so much as an obvious but relevant rant. Yet it spread around the Internet like a computer virus and was probably read by more people over a six-month period than any piece on whiteness ever written. This was not because it was particularly well scripted, but because it broke things down in a way that most academic discourse never does—and likely because it was published online, which made it easy to share.

After publication I received 8,000 e-mails from readers, including thousands of whites—teachers, PTA parents, even a sharpshooter on the Columbine SWAT team—most of whom said they had never before seen the racial aspect of school shootings, workplace murders, serial killings, or other forms of mostly white pathology. For many, the article had triggered more understanding of whiteness than thousands of pages of academic scholarship had ever done.

I say this not to toot my own horn, since the attention I received in the wake of this column was largely accidental (not to mention a function of my race and gender, which lent it more credibility in the eyes of whites than the same arguments put forth by people of color), but merely to say that even I had not fully appreciated the potential power of the situation until it happened.

I am also convinced that, if we hope to make whiteness visible so as to engage whites in a struggle to eradicate institutional racism, it will not suffice to merely rattle off or prove the litany of privileges afforded to those of us lacking melanin. As many an activist of color has said to me, "Sure, you can prove that whites have all these privileges; now tell me why in the hell they would want to give them up?" After all, simple awareness of one's privileges does not necessarily lead to the desire to relinquish them, especially given that our culture emphasizes self-interest over community-minded thinking. Unless we focus just as much attention on the harms and downsides of relative privilege, the best we can hope for is that altruism alone will motivate activism against racism.

From the loss of one's true ethnic and cultural heritage, to the loss of cross-racial friendships harmed by unequal institutional treatment, to the economic consequences of racial inequality for working people generally, to the consequences of the "white-blindness" that ruled the day in the "nice" white places where these school shootings happened, institutional racism and white privilege have deadly and destructive consequences even for most whites. Whiteness and its privileges create an unrealistic and unhealthy mentality of entitlement and expectation, an assumption of safety and security, all of which can be quickly undone by a layoff, a school shooting, or for that matter a deadly terrorist attack. After all, the vulnerability evidenced on September 11 was only a revelation to those who had always had the luxury of feeling safe, those who had never had to think or care about how others with fewer privileges viewed this nation.

Unless we are prepared to talk about what whites have had to lose to become and remain white in the first place, we will do little more than amuse ourselves with our own brilliance, as scholars sometimes do.

NOTE

1. Tim Wise, "School Shootings and White Denial," *AlterNet*, 6 March 2001. http://www.alternet.org/print.html?StoryID=10560.

∾

KAREN BRODKIN
Whiteness: A Mixed Bag

I have long been uneasy about embracing a project called "studying whiteness," instead of, say, "studying white racism." The naming of a concept is meaningful: It can shape its evolution, practice, and boundaries. In the early days of women's studies, for example, people mistook "studying women" for studying gender dynamics, culture, and social structure from feminist perspectives. People who hadn't a clue that society and culture institutionalized male dominance thought they were quite qualified to teach women's studies. Whiteness carries some of the same baggage, the same potential for confusion rooted partly in its terminology.

To name a subject "whiteness" can dissociate it from racism as a historical system of institutionalized political, economic, and ideological domination. It can wrongly separate whiteness studies from the wider intellectual heritage of antiracist scholarship, of which it is a part. It is crucial that the study of whiteness be linked to current scholarship that carries on that intellectual project—that is, critical race theory, ethnic studies, feminist theories, especially those formulated by women of color, and postcolonial feminist theories. Separating work on white racism from this radical heritage can limit its utility for analyzing racism today.

Not everyone would necessarily define the enterprise of studying whiteness this way. But this perspective does highlight two lines of debate implicit in recent criticisms of working-class whiteness scholarship: How do studies of whiteness treat the dialectic between structure and agency? If studying whiteness is part of a transformative project, what kind of project is it?

The structure-agency dialectic is a perennial tension, one not confined to studies of whiteness. On the one hand, one of the strengths of recent whiteness scholarship is that it illuminates the ways in which whites believe deeply in—and actively defend—their entitlement to institutionalized privileges. It unpacks whiteness as a political identity enacted in daily life and in collective action. On the other hand, such explorations often pay exclusive attention to the agency and identities of working-class, poor, and ethnic white people—an endeavor that risks disconnecting white racism from racism as a historically institutionalized system. This approach could boomerang and reinscribe the notion that white workers and their problems wholly embody the working class and its legitimate discontents.

There's also a kind of academic and political fatalism that may already be part of the fabric of whiteness studies. The academy encourages nuanced, complex scholarship that represents the world as it is—in all its racism, greed, and conservatism. Unfortunately, scholarship that also explores transformative potentials too often inspires charges of romanticism. If we merely analyze white racism, we risk perpetuating existing patterns, reinforcing the mainstream notion that racism, ethnocentrism, and xenophobia are natural and inevitable.

This inspires the question, Of what kind of transformative project is whiteness a part?[1] Eric Arnesen has charged that whiteness studies is an answer to why the working class hasn't united against capital.[2] This presumes that class is an essential and natural identity and that history has an inevitable trajectory. To the extent that studies of whiteness attend to social change (and not all do), they do it as part of a project shared with critical race theories, feminisms, queer theories, and Marxist perspectives. Each of these perspectives views political subjects as anything but predetermined or natural. They also presume identities to be works-in-progress, constituted on multiple axes, and part of a contradictory repertoire of possible identities. Studying whiteness this way directs our attention to whites' ambivalence about what racial privilege and entitlement may cost them. It raises the issue of what identities whites forgo because of the confines of their privilege. Likewise, understanding identities as constituted on multiple axes, including, say, the axis of gender, reveals hidden notions at the heart of whiteness about preserving a set of specifically white constructions of masculinity and femininity, which have undermined antiracist efforts.

Critical race/whiteness scholarship can analyze what has worked and what hasn't in building movements for interracial social justice. How have some movements unwittingly reproduced white privilege? What strategies work against doing this? What's going on racially now that the dynamics aren't just black and white? Are there identities and strategies that open wider visions of social justice? Whiteness scholarship has looked at these questions historically in situations where white racism wasn't "supposed to be," according to older progressive thinking—where white people were trying to overcome it or where they believed they already had, especially in the context of movements for social justice.

Los Angeles, for example, had a dynamic, Latino-led labor movement before September 11. Through HERE, the Hotel and Restaurant Workers Union, SEIU, and Justice for Janitors, new immigrant workers, mainly from Mexico and Central America, had revitalized labor and were beginning to build a community-based labor movement. Although economic recession and the decline of tourism in the wake of 9/11 affected these workers and their unions deeply, they continue to organize. Latino and Asian-American activists have initiated and led almost all of the progressive political activism among whites in Los Angeles. Community union-ism has mobilized white progressives, churches, and students from working- and middle-class backgrounds in a variety of local efforts involving HERE; SMART (Santa Monicans Allied for Responsible Tourism); the Bus Riders' Union, which brought a successful race discrimination suit against the city's mass transit system; and Communities for a Better Environment, an environmental justice group that blocked construction of a power plant in a predominantly Latina/o and highly pol-luted industrial area of Los Angeles County. I can think of no comparable white-initiated counterparts to these movements. The last visible one, the largely white feminist movement, has been silent since it drove the antiabortion Operation Res-cue out of town more than a decade ago.

Despite the successes achieved by local activist groups, race is at the center of grassroots politics too. Groups and movements among young people seem to have a greater repertoire for talking about race and privilege and about multiple axes of power more generally. Movements led by older generations, most notably the labor movement, have inherited a deeply race-avoidant culture and are struggling to think in new ways. They are seeking out organizers from among young activists across the racial and ethnic spectrum. How do young activists of color and white activists respond and contribute to the labor movement and to movements across the generational divide? What kinds of racial discourses and politics do they build in their own organizations? Embedded in groups and their political strategies are constructions of political actors, from colorless, genderless workers to a multiplic-ity of race-, class-, and gender-specific actors. The identities, or the ways groups present themselves as actors when they engage politically, shape more than the suc-cess of a particular struggle. They shape what issues can and can't be dealt with, who can and cannot participate, and what information can be shared. These are issues that Angeleno activists grapple with on a daily basis and where scholarly col-laboration can be helpful.

To do this, scholarship on whiteness needs to situate itself fully in the wider antiracist project and to analyze both the specific ways that whiteness deforms mul-tiracial resistance and the contradictions within whiteness that animate whites to support and join these movements.

NOTES

1. See Eric Arnesen, "Scholarly Controversy: Whiteness and the Historians' Imagina-tion," *International Labor and Working-Class History* 60 (Fall 2001).

2. Ibid., 3–32.

8.   Transnational Blackness: Africa and the African Diaspora, Asia, and Globalization

ASSATA SHAKUR

The Continuity of Struggle: An Interview

On May 2, 1973, three members of the Black Panther Party, including Assata Shakur, were stopped by state police officers on the New Jersey Turnpike. A gun battle ensued, leaving one state trooper and one Black Panther killed. According to Shakur, she was shot once with her hands in the air and was subsequently shot in the back while she was on the ground.

Shakur says, "Finally, when it was obvious that I was not going to die right then, I was taken to a hospital, where I was chained to a bed. I was beaten, tortured, kept incommunicado for four or five days, and I was denied any rights to see a lawyer." She was tried and found guilty of murder by an all-white jury, receiving a sentence of life, plus an additional thirty years and thirty days.

In all, Shakur spent a total of six years in U.S. prisons. During two of those years, she was held in solitary confinement inside a men's prison.

With outside assistance, Shakur managed to escape. After living underground for a time, she emerged in Cuba, where she was granted political asylum.

In 1998, the case of Assata Shakur returned to the headlines. New Jersey Republican governor Christine Todd Whitman launched a public relations campaign to "capture" Shakur and return her to the state to face imprisonment. Writing to the State Department, Governor Whitman requested that the U.S. government should refuse to "normalize" relations with Cuba so long as Shakur was permitted to live there. A bounty of $50,000 was offered by the State of New Jersey for anyone who could secure her return to the state.

Hundreds of African-American leaders and activists were outraged by the attempt to extradite Shakur from Cuba. In a public statement of support, a group of black supporters declared that

> the stellar example of Assata's commitment to the liberty of people of African descent in the United States places her in the company of not only Harriet Tubman but also Paul Robeson, Fannie Lou Hamer, Malcolm X, and the thousands of other known and unknown warriors in the fight for the liberation of black people in the United States. . . . Assata is our Sister and we stand in absolute solidarity with her right to live free from bondage in Cuba.

During the Columbia University African-American Studies delegation's visit to Cuba in June 1997, we had the opportunity to meet with Assata several times. The following interview was recorded late one evening, as part of a lively marathon conversation between Cubans and black Americans. What comes through in this transcript is the intelligence and creativity of an activist who retains a passionate commitment to social justice for her people.

—M. M.

ALL GO ON SURVIVAL: RACE AND REVOLUTION

When I came to Cuba, at first people were very reluctant to deal or to talk about race, to talk about racism. You could talk to anybody; they would say, "Well, there is no such thing. It's been eliminated." And what I think they meant was that all laws that upheld segregation in terms of housing and neighborhoods had been virtually eliminated. That doesn't mean that some historic segregation doesn't exist. In other words, old Havana had a huge number of African people and all of them have not moved to other areas. In areas that were historically black, there are still a lot of black people living there. But I think that the nature of neighborhoods has changed completely and areas that were completely white before are now very mixed.

Two seconds after the revolution took power, all hell broke loose, and they [revolutionary leaders] were under the gun on every side of the question. So the issue was unity. The consciousness that existed at that time was the consciousness that pretty well existed all around the world, the U.S. included. In terms of socialist theory at that time, you [would] give everybody the right health care, education, etc., [and] the conditions were going to make racism automatically disappear. Also, what was considered racism at that time was "White Only" signs [or] being forbidden from work in certain places. So, those things having been eliminated, there was this perception of "all Cubans." The national character of Cuba was never considered unmixed; it was considered that there's no Cuban that's all European and there's no Cuban that's all African. It was a popular saying here, the saying that there were no pure whites in Cuba.

Of course Cuba inherited a racist mentality of white supremacy that existed for hundreds of years. This was one of the last places were slavery was abolished, in 1886. All the racist ideas that upheld slavery, that justified slavery, were present here. There was a systematic whitening process that was institutionalized in the Spanish form of colonialism. You could buy, for [a] certain amount of [money], a paper that declared you white. If you wanted to be a don or a doña, someone who had power in the society, all you had to do was get a white father to say you didn't know who your mother was and you could buy a paper that purified your blood. Also, in order to work in certain areas if you were a so-called freed slave, you could work in [certain] areas if you had a paper that said you were white. And people bought those papers for their children so that their children could have a future.

Those attitudes did not disappear after the revolution. In fact, I think that many people felt that the revolution gave them more of a possibility. To many people, especially those who had college degrees, a white partner made them even much more of a contributor to the struggle against racism. I think that there was a whole sense of "Everything is going to be fine with Cubans together, white and black." [There was a feeling that] there were no differences until the Third Congress of the Cuban Communist Party, when Raúl and Fidel said that "look, number one, the power structures in the country have got to reflect the ratio of the composition of the country." They talked about race, they talked about gender, and they also talked about young people. And there were changes made in terms of people being promoted to vice ministers. There were a lot of black vice ministers—and when I say that I'm not saying it in a sarcastic way. I'm saying that the old guard, those who fought in the mountains, you don't get rid of those people easy. So it was a big shift, moving [black] people into positions [of power].

That movement, or that effort, was short-lived. It was short-lived in the sense that shortly thereafter the socialist camp in Europe started to crumble and the revolution was looking at basic, bare survival. It was life or death and they were up shit's creek without a paddle, between a rock and a hard place. That was the reality. [Cubans] lost like 80-something percent of their ability to import and their ability to export. There was not enough of anything. The price of sugar was in the pits and controlled completely by capitalist markets. The socialist camp did not honor trade agreements with Cuba. Not only did they not honor agreements, but diplomatically, economically, they became hostile toward Cuba. And every other place said, "We don't owe you anything. And those papers that we signed? That's your problem." And that's the position that Cuba found itself in. All of the focus of the revolution for three, four, five years at the beginning of the Special Period was on survival. The [official] position was: "We don't have time to argue about anything else. One percent of nothing is nothing. One hundred percent of nothing is nothing. So right now we've got to preserve our revolution." And the perception of black people in Cuba was the same. It was, like: All go on survival.

A BOXING RING, 24–7:
TOURISM AND CUBA IN THE GLOBAL ECONOMY

I don't think that any place in the history of the planet has ever built as many hotels, as many tourist installations, in the six years that we're talking about than Cuba has. Everything goes back on tourism. At the same time the focus on women, the focus on black people was, like, "That's not our problem. The problem is food, shelter, clothing." There was some discussion of affirmative action in the sense of "How do you have a policy of affirmative action when you don't have [anything]?" My position is that you can't. You cannot. If you do not have enough stuff for all the population, if you don't have enough food for the whole population, you cannot have an economic affirmative action program. But you can do things that make a difference. You can deal with the educational system. You can deal with the cultural aspects—what is on television, on radio. You can deal with how teachers, how professionals, are trained. There are things I believe that can be done.

As the tourist industry began to grow and prosper and as the joint ventures, the joint business ventures, began to become more and more common in Cuba, what I began to see was blondes in bikinis on all the travel brochures. The African people, when they were presented, were presented in the folklore mode, dressed up like *changó* with a knife between their teeth. There was a commercialization of the African religions. There was, and still is, a generalized perception by the public that corporations tend to have a preference for light-skinned Cubans. Tourism has brought all of these Europeans and South Americans and Mexicans with their racist ideas and the racist attitudes about the natives. And they come here, many of them, condoms in hand, looking for black pussy.

The Cuban government has really made an effort to try to promote what they call sane and healthy family tourism. Easier said than done. They have either tried to make regulations for the hotels where Cubans had prostitutes [so that prostitutes] would have difficulty going into hotels. They tried to have health tourism, ecology tourism, political tourism, healing tourism—all kinds of tourism to try to evade the money tourism. People come down here with big money, with big money attitudes, and no respect for the people, no respect for the revolution. They're coming down here for sun, sand, women and men, or whatever. And so the change is evident. It is evident in my opinion not only [in that] the tourism is there [but in] attitudes. You will find young women who are proud of going out with an Italian, Spaniard, whatever. [You find] people who want to know them, befriend them, who want to rediscover their Spanish roots: the resurrection of the Galician Association, the Catalonian Association, the Spanish Club. Because people say, "I may get some money in this. Let me reestablish my connections." So the tourism industry makes a kind of attitude that does not do anything but reinforce white supremacist values, mentality, relations, and power relations. You don't see a lot of black tourists come into Cuba. It's economic, so that power is associated with white people. Those that speed around Havana in fast cars are white people. [Cubans] look at television, they look at U.S. films, and they are affected by all this. You can't see all this around you and be unaffected by it. So there is the tendency for people to feel, "Well, maybe Europe isn't so bad. Maybe the States aren't so bad."

I think it is a mistake to think that the attitudes around race are totally separated from the attitudes around class, around gender. The resurgence of the woman as a sex object is more and more easy to see. When I came to Cuba, there was a national pride that was: "We're Socialists." I'm not saying that that national pride has disappeared or evaporated, but what I am saying is that the contradictions that are in the society are more evident. And you cannot have contradictions in how people live, what people see, without people having ideological problems, ideological questions. And the real bottom line is that when there are less crumbs on the table, the fight gets a little raunchy. The middle-management administrators in many cases tended to be white and not completely beyond helping each other at the expense of African people. I mean, they aren't going to come out and say that they're doing it. They try to hide it. They try to be slick about it. But there is in my opinion a group of white folks that look out for their own. Black folks are again observing, making sharper criticisms—and also in certain places dealing and saying, "Wait a minute. Hold on. There need to be changes. There need to be things that are addressed."

I believe that it would be historically impossible for this situation that I'm looking at now not to have occurred. I think it is historically inevitable because I think that when a country happens to put all its efforts on bare survival, they don't have time to rest. I mean, it's not like they're sitting there saying, "Oh my God, what do we talk about today?" This is basic survival with the raunchiest, most vicious enemy blockading you, trying to accelerate the blockade. You're trying to get a hand in but also at the same time trying to get an economic handle [and] that undermines the ideological, philosophical aspect of the revolution. Practically not one of the people investing in Cuba is doing so because they want to benefit and uphold the revolution. In a situation where [Cuba's] allies are the kind of allies that hang out with wolves and can barely make it to the UN to vote no on the blockade, it's been hard. This is no joke here. I mean, the U.S. has battered and bullied and knocked people down to the point that you got these whole little countries shaking in their boots. [These countries] will not even come out to make a [UN] vote unless everybody else has decided on it. In terms of economic integration, the English-speaking Caribbean is still running after the queen, and French Caribbeans think they're French men and women, so we have a real sick situation in terms of the worldwide vision. So Cuba has had to really be in a boxing ring 24–7. When you're in a boxing ring, it doesn't give you a lot of space and time to sit and concentrate on your internal problems and solve them.

OUR COMMUNITIES ARE SICK: HEALING ALIENATION

I hope that the revolution at this moment will pay more attention to not just serving the health system, the education system, but [to] dealing with the democratic functions in the country and relating that to what is going on in terms of race, in terms of gender, in terms of class. Saturday night in Cuba they see movies, and usually the movies come from the States. You have to put on whatever films you can put on. And 99 percent of what comes out of the States or out of Brazil is ideological poison. People think that this is how life is. Someone thirty years ago said, "Wow, I want a nice house and I want a house to have a bedroom, a bathroom." Now they want a kitchen with a little island in it, a sunken tub, a house with a deck. This is the image of what, materially, people should aspire to. And so [you find] the problems of ideological struggle in terms of just changing the whole focus of Eurocentrist fuckers that are part of every education system.

If you were to take every book you ever read and put them in piles and put the European pile on one hand and the Latin American, the Asian piles, you know what a distorted picture you would have. So can you imagine that even though socialism has been able to do something to reduce the Eurocentrism, it has not been able to accomplish that much? The Soviets claimed they knew everything. [They claimed] they had everything under control and had solved everything. Therefore, their line was "the line." And all this discussion about race was: You got a doctor, a free education and [racism] would evaporate. The Cubans got it from the West and they got it from the East. So that [now] they are faced with the task that every single country in the world with people of color [is] faced with: How can we de-Eurocentrize our system? Struggling against racism is I think very much connected to struggling to end Eurocentrism, [to end] the strict view that we can just take Marx and Engels and Lenin and have what they said become a coloring book—and we just color in the colors. I think that vision of social change is no longer applicable, if it ever was.

If we don't change the lifestyle that we are living right now—what we do in the morning to what we do at night, how we relate to other people, how our families are structured—I don't think we will be able to deal social justice. Because there's no way that this planet can offer a chicken in every pot, a computer in every den, a Mercedes-Benz in every garage. I don't think that the material reality exists on this planet for that. Our values and what we are fighting for have to change, and how we live and relate to each other has to change. The Cubans are looking at all this stuff. Anybody that is dealing with social change now better start looking at it. Because people are in a tremendous amount of pain, the pain is not just from not having enough food, not just [from not] having access to medical care. It is also because we have to live in [a] state of almost universal alienation. We do not have community. Our communities are sick. Our families are sick, and healing is needed in order for us to live in a society where we're not afraid to look somebody in the eyes and say good morning. We've got to change some real things other than material struggle. And so I think the world revolutionary movement, those who are struggling to make social justice on this planet, have got to rethink a lot of things about where we're going to go in the next millennium. I think we have to rethink our material focus. I think we have to think about how we see ourselves and what vision is our vision of liberation.

MONSTERISM: YOUTH AND THE CULTURE OF VIOLENCE

One of the problems I have with young people, they do not understand what we mean when we say we were fighting for freedom. A lot of times we cannot articulate what our vision of freedom is, so how can we expect them to continue something that we can't express? They're talking about the youth culture, the violence, and some people say that "well, rap creates violence." I think our consciousness creates what comes out of our mouths and what comes out of our mouths reflects our consciousness. Big business uses what comes out of young African people's mouths to pollute other young African people with ideas that are very capitalist. Most [rappers] are saying, "We want the shit, we want the sneakers, we want the gold, we want everything. You told us we can't have shit, so we're going to be gangsters." [They're] illegitimate capitalists. That is the only difference. They say, "You told us we could be capitalists, we could go to school. I can't get into school. I could barely make it in school, but I could sell these rocks out here and I could make it." You look at all the videos and you see models making $50 a day shaking their butts around a swimming pool in a big old house, somebody with their pants hanging down and drawers sticking out, and people think that's keeping it real. That is selling the capitalist dream to people who cannot even sniff at it. They're going to jail and can't even make commissary money. I spent big time in jail and I know what's in there. There ain't no Rockefellers or gangsters up there. But there is a dream that's being sold just like *The Godfather*.

We watch it on TV; we can't escape from it. Nor can we escape from monsterism. My daughter laughs at me because I'm scared. I look at some monster pictures and I get upset. I feel that these people who kill everybody just take over my consciousness for an hour and a half. And I'm, like, "Damn, how many monsters are these people going to create?" They got a human monster, animal monster, plant monster, mineral monster. It is a society that is innovative with monsters but is creating real live monsters. You know how little kids have baseball cards—you know, back in the old days, my day? Now they have mass murderer cards that kids trade. So the violence of the society is big business. And they're exporting it so that the Cubas of the world and any other process that wants to build a revolution has got not only to deal with the material—how you build a health clinic, how you do this— but: How do you build new values? How do you build new human relationships?

They talk about black women being with the families and stuff like that. And all I can think of is: If every guy walked off a video, if one day all these guys came talking, "Bitch, come get the money, ho, hood rat," etc., if all these guys walked off the videos and tried to marry somebody, can you imagine what the relationship would be like? Can you imagine that this is some way for human beings to live in and raise a family? I saw Snoop Doggy Dog, he was on video, and he had his little baby saying, "Hey, little motherfucker, pimp motherfucker." If we consider political change in more than a structural way, in more than a power way, I don't see how we're going to get social justice, 'cause who is going to live in the society of Snoop Doggy Dog?

ARE YOU PART WHATEVER?
THE LIMITS OF MULTICULTURALISM

I think social change can't be limited to the way that we have approached things in the past. I think it's got to be related to a lot of healing, 'cause we got people out there that are just too crazy to struggle. I'm serious. We got a lot of crazy people out there, people out of their minds. And dysfunctional families. I'm not talking about dysfunctional families in terms of African families. I'm talking about a dysfunctional world and how you raise a sane family in a dysfunctional world. The racism in the United States right now, everything is a code word. It is a racist agenda. It's saying to you, "Segregation for another hundred years. We [gave you] some affirmative action that was never very active or very affirmative, we gave you some rights that weren't too civil or too right, so what you got to complain about? You better get a job even though there aren't any." I mean, our future is a serious one. I mean, they got African people in England and in Holland, they represent a small percentage of the population, and they've become the number one enemy. They have a country like Denmark where they have two Africans, and one of them has got a suitcase on the way out—and you got people there convinced that those two Africans are the problem!

So in the States what's happening now with the multiculturalism, everybody's talking about, "I'm part Egyptian and part whatever." And I appreciate people discovering that about themselves and discovering aspects of who they are. But that is not political activity. The police are not going to ask you as they shoot you down, "Oh, are you part whatever?" The census is not going to change the district 'cause you are one-fifth Cherokee or whatever.

I think that we have to take a new look at what globalization means in terms of gender issues, in terms of race issues, and to rethink very seriously the kinds of not only structures that we deal with in terms of building social justice but the kinds of lives we live and the kinds of examples we're setting for those people who follow us. Because unless we make our lives as people who are dedicated to social change attractive so people are attracted to it, they feel good, they feel warm, they feel a sense of community, we're going to lose a majority of our youth. Because I think that in our style of political work, political activism has left a lot to be desired. I think a lot of people struggled for a lot of years without forming some kind of family or creating warm relationships. I think this has meaning. [Without this], I think we haven't discovered a new way of humanity.

RELATING POLITICALLY AND PERSONALLY:
TOWARD A NEW STYLE OF POLITICS

It's almost impossible for us not to have a double consciousness in terms of class, in terms of gender, our vision of family. Most of us go for what we know, and what we know is some historical model that is not applicable today. But we haven't been able to substitute all of it. We've substituted part of it. I mean, I can read whoever—Marx, this, that, and the other—then say, "Damn, I wish I was near a swimming pool." There is a bourgeois side to our consciousness because we were raised in a bourgeois society. I remember in the Seventies after we finished dissing everyone, we started talking about humanism and unity and democracy. Not only were we imitating Europeans—that's one thing—but we were unaware completely about our double consciousness, our internal contradictions, and of the pact we had individually of fighting against those things. Because you cannot fight against something that you don't talk about and you don't admit. [Back then], everybody was more revolutionary than everybody else and everybody's mind was more correct than everybody else's. I think that this time if we talk about the things that shaped us, our values, etc., and they are full of contradiction, then we can start to go somewhere else and move to somewhere else. But the arrogance, the dishonesty that so many of us have had . . .

I don't mean we're bad people because of it, because I think it was a political style that we inherited. I thought being a good revolutionary was being like that or trying to be a talking head or . . . I had millions of powerful images of what being active in a movement for social change meant. Now I'm in another place in my life—and maybe this is a touchy-feely stage that I'm going through—but I like the idea of people relating politically and relating personally, of communion, coming together, having picnics, of people talking about themselves as human beings and not just about social change in the abstract. Because I think that what happens when you talk about social change in the abstract, what happens is that you see the social being in the theoretical phase as one type of being. [But] the diversity of the social being is almost infinite. And in order to take into consideration those small people who had different visions, who have different needs, who have different whatever from the big picture, we have to stop and sympathize in terms of the social relationships we're trying to create. Because I don't think that the general is enough.

CHANGE IS A WAY OF LIFE: LOOKING TO THE FUTURE

I also feel very optimistic. I think a lot of dead weight has been removed from the back of social change. Creativity is part of the struggle—it is one of the most important parts. When people talk about sacrifice—you know, sacrifices that people made in the Sixties—I feel almost very weird. Had I not become involved in the struggle, I would be tagging along with some kind of needle stuck somewhere or some fate worse than that. So I think that the movement has done much more for me than I'll ever be able to do for the movement. [Even] with all of the boring, terrible, miserable experiences I've had, this has been a lifesaving experience intellectually, spiritually, socially. I don't think I would've met the kind of beautiful people I've been lucky enough to have met in life. So I feel very fortunate to have not *chosen* this path—but to have stumbled, fallen, into it.

I think the continuity of struggle is something we pay a lot more attention to in terms of being aware of people that struggled before. I think we have sometimes forgotten the continuity, thought that the struggle was going to be five minutes and, after, we could all go to the movies. I think that when we understand the world is not going to change in five minutes, we can be part of that change, and being part of that change is a way of life. It is something that I like. I look at the Clintons and, I mean, these are grotesque people. They really are. I just don't like them.

I'm one of those people who had to piece my life together with Band-Aids. And I mean that physically, mentally, and every other way. So I don't look at the U.S. as being my country. Maybe my daughter or my grand-something will look at it another way. I'm one of those people that has been alienated. I am a victim. I feel like Malcolm. And until there is another "Savior," my attitude is going to be the same. But I understand that this is a process, and what's going on with us has to become connected with what's going on in Africa, what's going on in the Caribbean. Because I do see us winning, not by ourselves and not with just looking at the United States as this isolated place, but looking at our African ancestors—whether they are in Cuba, whether they are here—and our spiritual ancestors, who-ever they may be.

~

Bill Fletcher Jr.

The New South Africa and the Process of Transformation

I arrived in South Africa twenty days after the second democratic national election and six days following the inauguration of the African National Congress (ANC)–led government of Thabo Mbeki. There were three things that I immedi-ately noticed: the beauty of the land, the continued impact of colonialism and apartheid, and the pervasiveness of crime.

I actually had expected the first two, but there was nothing that could have prepared me for the ever-present existence of crime—guarded and gated communi-ties with walls around them topped by barbed wire; in some of the more upscale neighborhoods, electrified fences; warnings to me by my hosts that I needed to be *very* careful in walking around, even in daylight.

In the streets of Johannesburg, Cape Town, and Durban, there are individu-als who wear orange vests who "guard" parked cars. I asked about this and was told that it was a step by the government to give jobs and responsibility to those who in the past often robbed cars. When one parks or when one leaves a parking space, one gives a tip to the "guard."

In Johannesburg, all shops close promptly at 5 P.M. and everyone leaves for the day. There appear to be no after-work parties or evening shopping sales.

Many white South Africans cannot stop talking about crime and about what they see as the deteriorating conditions since the end of apartheid. In fact, in the last election, the slogan of the so-called Democratic Party (which appears to have become the major opposition party to the ANC and is a white party) was "Fight back!" a slogan normally advanced by the left, but in the South African context takes on an entirely different meaning. Many of those white South Africans who have chosen to emigrate cite crime as symptomatic of the deterioration of conditions.

Yet what is missed by this are the underlying conditions. Cunningham Ngcukana, general secretary of the National Council of Trade Unions (NACTU, the smallest of the three trade union federations and the one that emerged largely out of the Black Consciousness and Africanist movements), stated to me forthrightly, "When the government talks about having a summit on crime, I'm not interested. I am interested in any discussion on job creation!"

Ngcukana's statement is not a rhetorical ploy. South Africa has an unemployment rate estimated at 30 to 37 percent. This dwarfs the level of unemployment during the Great Depression in the United States, which was around 25 percent. The crime problem in South Africa is directly related to economic conditions and the complete distortion of economic relations, which are holdovers from years of colonial rule and apartheid.

Riding along the shore in Cape Town, one sees a very different South Africa. Perhaps one of the most beautiful geographical locations on Earth, the area is dotted with wealthy estates and communities virtually secluded from the realities of the day-to-day existence of the black majority. The distribution of wealth in South Africa is very evidently among the worst on this planet, and one needs only contrast such idyllic communities with those one sees on the road to the Cape Town International Airport, where latrines back onto creeks and shantytowns seem to grow out of the ground like marsh foliage. This contrast illustrates the fundamental challenge facing the progressive forces in South Africa: Can what they reference as the national democratic revolution be completed, or is this a revolution stalled?

ONE PART OF THE MASS MOVEMENT

What came to be known as the independent black trade union movement, which arose in South Africa during the 1980s, played a major role in the bringing down of apartheid. This movement expressed the different ideological currents arising from the South African liberation movement. Two of the three current federations—the Congress of South African Trade Unions (COSATU, the largest of the three federations) and NACTU—represent a direct line from earlier formations that emerged in the 1980s. Although both formations advance a "nonracial/ antiracist" approach, COSATU soon after its formation in 1985 chose to align itself with the ANC and the South African Communist Party (SACP). NACTU, on the other hand, although associated with the Pan-Africanist Congress of Azania (PAC) and the Azanian People's Organization (AZAPO), chose to remain nonaligned while advancing a set of politics that was essentially derived from the Black Consciousness and Africanist movements. The third federation, the Federation of Unions of South Africa (FEDUSA), is approximately 60 percent white and tends to be more conservative in its politics than the other two federations.

COSATU and NACTU, by their own admission, played a dual role in the anti-apartheid struggle. They organized a burgeoning trade union movement to fight for workers' rights, but they additionally played a key role in the political struggle against the apartheid system. A high degree of political education and discussion took place within the ranks of both federations, and they consciously saw themselves as part of the mass movement to oppose the racist system.

With the end of apartheid and the assumption of power by Nelson Mandela and the ANC, the role of the trade union movement began to change, first in subtle and then in more dramatic ways. COSATU faced an immediate challenge in 1994 when many of its top leaders and staff were chosen to run—under the banner of the ANC—for elected office. This was soon supplemented by those who left the union movement to work in government or business (e.g., the onetime National Union of Mineworkers' leader Cyril Ramaphosa, who is now a prominent businessman). This drain put immediate pressure on COSATU to bring forward new leaders. Although this may have, in some respects, been inevitable, it nevertheless forced a changing of the guard at precisely the moment when veteran strategists were needed to address the newly emerging conditions of the post-apartheid era.

NACTU faced other challenges. During the anti-apartheid struggle, and particularly during the tail end of the Cold War, U.S.-influenced and -directed forces attempted to utilize NACTU and its predecessor organizations against COSATU (and its predecessors) because of the developing relationship that COSATU had with the ANC and the SACP. There were immense ironies here, given that the NACTU tendency contained within it anti-imperialist and revolutionary Marxist forces, albeit not aligned with the SACP. In any case, the tension created between these forces was exacerbated by the activities of many U.S. trade unionists of the AFL-CIO, then led by the arch–Cold Warrior Lane Kirkland. The residue of this relationship carries through to this day.

The COSATU/NACTU differences, although remaining, have receded in their most dramatic aspects. Particularly since the Mandela win in 1994, the significance and influence of the Black Consciousness and Africanist forces have declined dramatically. In the 1999 election, the PAC performed terribly, seeming to be on the verge of oblivion. This trend was discernable in 1994 and forced some rethinking within the NACTU ranks.

1999: EXHILARATION AND CONCERN

Despite the fact of Nelson Mandela's heroic status during his tenure as South Africa's president, struggle began to unfold within the popular movement over the direction of politics and economics. The issue, on the surface, was that of economic development. The Alliance (ANC, COSATU, and SACP) had advanced a platform for economic development known as the Reconstruction and Development Programme (RDP). This was a comprehensive attempt to overhaul South Africa and transform it from its apartheid days. There is considerable argument as to whether the RDP was ever fully implemented, because during the Mandela presidency another approach was advanced by the government, which earned the wrath of the popular movements—the Growth, Equity and Reconstruction (GEAR) program, which emphasizes private investment, and specifically privatization.

The struggle around GEAR represented the continuation of a battle that began in the early 1990s within the ANC: the battle between "TINA" and "THEMBA." "TINA"—"There is no alternative" (as articulated notoriously by former British Prime Minister Margaret Thatcher)—was the view of those forces that sought an accommodation with neoliberal global capital. In essence, the view held that there is no viable alternative to cutting the best deal with global capital, particularly in light of the collapse of the Soviet bloc and the evolution of capitalist relations in China. "THEMBA"—"There must be an alternative"—was the view of those forces that were attempting to rearticulate an anticapitalist/prosocialist vision for the future of South Africa.

The TINA/THEMBA battle has seen itself unfold in several countries following national liberation. The battle in South Africa was situated in the context of an incomplete national democratic revolution, the term used by the Alliance to describe the period of the anti-apartheid/anti-imperialist struggle. Political power was largely won by the popular democratic forces led by the ANC, yet economic power remained largely in the hands of white, apartheid-era capitalists. Even those capitalists who recognized that apartheid must come to an end were not necessarily prepared to accept the verdict of a fully enforced national democratic revolution.

There were many nuances to the struggle around GEAR, but fundamentally the issue came down to whether the ANC-led government would play a major role in the economic development of the country and redress the gross injustices that remain or, in the alternative, whether the development of the country would largely be left to the private sector.

Added to this battle was the strengthening role of global capital. In many respects, apartheid-era South African capitalism had shielded itself from the global market. Ironically, with the end of apartheid, the ANC-led government in many respects opened up South Africa, thus challenging the domestic producers who had to face international competition. Many of the same features of global capitalism we are witnessing in the United States became evident in South Africa—plant closings, runaway shops, contingent workforce, growth in capital-intensive production—at precisely the moment when the new South Africa desperately needed job creation and a redistribution of the wealth.

Thus, in the months leading up to the June 1999 election, there were hot debates in the popular democratic movements surrounding the question of what stand to take vis-à-vis the ANC. Forces, within both COSATU and SACP, not to mention in nonaligned organizations, questioned the continued viability of an alliance. This question was the source of important debates. As just one example, at the SACP's congress in June 1998 the delegates were treated to harsh words from both Mandela and Mbeki, who questioned the stand taken by some SACP members and leaders in opposition to the ANC-led government's policies.

Nevertheless, both the COSATU and the SACP decided to uphold the Alliance and throw everything into the election. The level of mobilization conducted by these forces and the ANC led to a dramatic victory in June.

Two-thirds of the parliament is either ANC or aligned with the ANC. Important provincial posts have been retained or captured by the ANC. And not insignificant, the ANC has retained its alliance with former foe Chief Buthelezi, leader of the KwaZulu-based Inkatha Freedom Party.

Despite the elation resulting from the election victory, the popular democratic forces remain on edge. COSATU and NACTU activists have been looking for a clear sign from the government that it is committed to a pro-people economic development approach, rather than one favoring the free market. In Mbeki's opening address to parliament, he seemed to signal a commitment to stand firm against neoliberal capital when he spoke out against those who attack the South African labor relations system as too rigid (by which is meant that the system is allegedly too proworker) and needing greater flexibility. Mbeki challenged these critics, saying instead that the system was sufficiently flexible, and then went on to address job creation. This address was well received by the COSATU leadership, although it was obvious that concern remains within the ranks.

THE QUESTION OF THE FRAMEWORK

June 30–July 2, 1999, the coastal city of Durban witnessed the twelfth annual Labour Law Conference, a gathering bringing together trade unionists, labor lawyers, and academics to review current questions in the arena of labor/management relations. The 1999 theme was "Regulated Flexibility: Labour law, the South African Labour Market, and the Global Economy." Many of the tensions of post-apartheid-era South Africa emerged in this gathering.

Although trade unionists constituted a significant percentage of the delegates, they were far from a majority, a fact that led to a decision to hold a preconference workshop directed specifically at trade unionists. In this preconference workshop, the issue of labor market flexibility was hotly debated as well as the impact of global capitalism on the new South Africa.

It might be useful to step back for one moment and clarify terms. This issue of "labor market flexibility" actually refers to the ability of capital to restructure the workforce and work process to advance its own interests. The nice-sounding term "flexibility" hides the real intent: the ability of capital to rid itself of government regulations and union restrictions to increase profits. The voices of business regularly announce that restrictions on their ability to restructure the workforce hurt their profits and, ipso facto, hurt the national economy. These voices in recent years have risen in volume in South Africa, and murmurings were heard in the Labour Law Conference as well.

In the preconference workshops, trade unionists debated the implications of global capitalism for South Africa's development. They closely examined the question of whether post-apartheid labor law changes have actually benefited or impeded the advance of the working class. They also began looking at the implications of all of this for working-class organization and power.

The actual conference was a bit more formal, albeit with very well-attended and -organized workshops. Nevertheless, many trade unionists began to express reservations about what they perceived to be the dominant tone of the conference: the implicit need for greater levels of workplace flexibility and the onus being on the trade unions to build and strengthen a partnership with the government and business.

The context of this debate is quite different from that in the United States.

The ANC-led government took steps to engage popular involvement in various levels of decisionmaking. One key arena was the economy, where the government established the National Economic Development and Labour Council (NEDLAC), a tripartite body of representatives from labor (all three federations), business, and government. The notion of tripartite involvement, practiced in many social democratic–run or –influenced countries in Europe, is largely unknown in the United States for a variety of historical reasons. Nevertheless, in South Africa, a legitimate role has been established for the union movement beyond (or in addition to) the basic issues of workplace wages, hours, and working conditions. The underlying question in the conference was the extent to which the three components of NEDLAC—business, labor, and government—were equally committed to the notion of a "social partnership."

An indirect debate ensued at the conference, held as often in the conference's halls between sessions as during the full sessions, over the nature of South Africa's future and the terms and conditions under which a social partnership could be put into place. Two experiences stood in dramatic contrast, presented separately at the conference. The Republic of Ireland, which since the late 1980s has witnessed a dramatic turn of economic events, in part influenced by an arrangement between the union movement, government, and business, was presented as a positive example from which South Africa should learn and that it should implicitly follow. Later that same day, a presentation was offered regarding the situation in the United States, where workers have witnessed a rather one-sided class war against them by business, and where, with relatively little power, there has been no interest by capital in anything approaching a social partnership.

What was particularly striking about the contrast in experiences was the reaction of the participants. Many of the labor lawyers and academics were thrilled with the presentation of the Irish experience and appeared to be convinced that this was a viable route for the South African movement. Trade unionists from all three federations expressed varying degrees of discomfort about the Irish experience and were not sure that it had much in the way of applicability to the South African situation. By contrast, the presentation of the U.S. experience resonated for the trade unionists, who saw real parallels in the actions and intentions of South African capital. Many of the lawyers and academics were irritated by the presentation of the U.S. experience, seeing it as unnecessarily provocative.

It is also worth noting that many of the trade unionists who came to the conference expressed no opinion because they had to leave early. In Durban, the blacks continue to live, for the most part, outside of the city. Their absence from the discussion was a reflection of how much and how little has changed in the past several years since the toppling of the apartheid regime.

The tension witnessed in the conference was symptomatic of the larger tension in the popular democratic movement. It is not a simple counterposing of positions. In a situation where there has been an incomplete national democratic revolution and where capitalism is very much alive and well, what steps does a progressive-led movement take to advance a popular democratic model of development? What connection is there between structural reforms that are advanced in the interests of the popular democratic movement and an end to capitalism? These questions confront the popular democratic movement, and they are the subject of almost constant debate in the trade union movement.

TRANSFORMATION AND THE "S" WORD

The leaderships of both COSATU and NACTU have, broadly speaking, advanced the need for a socialist future for South Africa. By "socialist," they generally mean a radical expansion of democracy and popular control, where the working class leads the economy and the economy responds to and addresses the needs of its people. For some, socialism is clearly no more than rhetoric; for others, it is clearly their life's blood.

Nevertheless, for the movement the question of the connection between the current situation and the socialist future remains a bit unclear. The movement, and particularly the labor movement, is, quite understandably, focused on the immediate needs of the people, most especially job creation. One of the most important debates revolves around whether the South African economy, as currently structured, will produce more jobs (on its own) or, on the contrary, whether additional steps will need to be taken to address this. One aspect to this is whether economic development in South Africa must stress an export-driven approach to advance South Africa's world competitiveness.

One must say that at the moment all the votes have not been counted toward resolving this debate. Until the recent Asian economic crisis, the export-driven model for economic development appeared to be a viable direction within the framework of capitalism, irrespective of the downside to the Asian experiences. With the Asian crisis, a number of questions have begun to emerge, including whether national economic development necessitates a greater level of concern about the expansion and responsiveness to the domestic market, rather than going all out for exports. There is also some concern that the entire notion of what has come to be known as "progressive competitiveness," that is, whether a progressive-led approach to developing the economic competitiveness of the national industries is a workable direction given global overcapacity in so many sectors and the bases upon which most competitiveness models are situated—lower labor costs.

Perhaps one of the most exciting features to the current debate is over a regional approach to economic development. Within the leadership of COSATU, there seems to be a growing realization that South Africa's economic future cannot realistically be separated from that of other southern African states. Thus, the question of focusing on domestic needs takes on a new and actually broader definition. "Domestic" may mean South Africa *and* the other southern African states.

Two significant problems remain, even if/when this debate is resolved. One concerns the matter of jobs; the other concerns wealth redistribution. A recent study commissioned by COSATU and conducted by its research arm (NALEDI— National Labour & Economic Development Institute) determined that the major manufacturers in South Africa have no plans for greater levels of job creation. Specifically, these manufacturers are planning on greater use of capital-intensive production (i.e., greater levels of labor-saving technology). Thus, the South African government, and the labor movement, even with a resolution of economic development direction(s), cannot rely on the private sector to produce the number and type of jobs necessary to address the depression-level unemployment problems.

Within COSATU, this problem has led to discussions of alternative economic strategies. This discussion is far from over, but it includes thought as to the use of industrial cooperatives and greater levels of government investment in public-sector work, what can probably be described as a neo-Keynesian or structural Keynesian approach to the economic picture.

The other problem haunting the country is the wealth polarization. South Africa is a very wealthy country, but the wealth levels are so distorted as to make a mockery of democracy. To complete the national democratic revolution that the ANC set out to achieve, wealth redistribution will have to take place. This is no easy task since rather than being an economic question, it is actually more of a political problem. The incomplete national democratic revolution and the end of apartheid were the results of popular mobilizations, armed struggle, and ultimately negotiations. To deprive the superrich of the booty that they accumulated over the course of the colonial and apartheid era, a renewed popular mobilization and pressure will be necessary.

This point cannot be exaggerated, since any steps to wealth redistribution will be fought vehemently, not only by domestic right-wing forces but also by global capital, which would see such steps as taking South Africa away from an economic course on which the International Monetary Fund and the World Bank would look favorably.

In some respects, the issues of wealth redistribution and job creation are related to a third matter under debate in South Africa: affirmative action. It is hard to believe that with the stark polarization that exists that there could be any debate on the need for affirmative action in South Africa. Nevertheless, there is such a debate and opposition from whites as well as some so-called coloureds who believe that such steps, taken to redress years of oppression, are unfair.

What all three issues have in common is that they relate to a reinterpretation of the question of "democracy." In the period since the mid-1980s and through the end of the Cold War to today, the notion of democracy has been reinterpreted by global capital very narrowly. Whether one was looking at the Philippines, Haiti, Eastern Europe, or South Africa, the spokespersons for global capital have defined democracy as the existence of elections and formal representative government.

What is both interesting and challenging in the South African experience is that the popular democratic forces, particularly those in the labor movement, are struggling to rearticulate democracy in a much broader manner, a manner that they believe is consistent with developing a road to socialism. That is, democratic rule cannot exist with 37 percent unemployment; it cannot exist with vast polarizations of wealth; it cannot exist with a dismantled apartheid yet clear workforce stratification. Democracy, or people's power, must exist through a dramatic restructuring of society to meet the needs of its majority. This is what the prosocialist, popular democratic forces appear to believe to be the actual conditions that will lay the basis for a successful, and indeed, revolutionary transformation of South African society.

BY WAY OF CONCLUSION

The level of popular mobilization in South Africa remains astounding, yet it is not something that can be sustained. Every movement goes through periods of ebbs and flows. Believing that one can sustain high levels of popular mobilization is a recipe for problems, because there remains a pull on the masses "back" to their regular lives.

The South African trade union movement is attempting to come to grips with this problem as it grapples with the need to keep the pressure on the ANC-led government. It is obvious to the trade unionists that there is pressure from South Africa's right wing and from global capital to bend the ANC-led government to its wishes. The trade unionists are attempting to grapple with how to continue to truly represent workers (and not solely their current membership) while at the same time collaborating with the ANC in advancing its agenda, an agenda that flows out of a hard-fought national liberation struggle.

All of this brought to mind a story I heard on National Public Radio (NPR) in the United States concerning a very different part of the globe. When the progressive Mexican political leader Cuauhtémoc Cardenas was elected mayor of Mexico City, NPR interviewed progressive and left-wing activists from Mexico City about the victory and about their involvement in the campaign. Prior to the Cardenas mayoral campaign, many of these groups and individuals had never taken part in electoral politics, but in this case they decided to become active. NPR asked them whether they were going to now demobilize. Their response was instructive. They stated that they could not afford to demobilize, because they knew that the right wing would be mobilizing to pressure Cardenas to back away from his campaign pledges and that if they (progressives) did not offer a countervailing pressure, there was no question in their minds but that Cardenas would falter, regardless of his best intentions.

The future for true South African democracy rests in the hands of the popular democratic forces such as the trade union movement. The extent to which they keep the pressure on the government and remember that there is a fundamental difference between access and power when it comes to politics will be the extent to which South Africa completes or aborts its efforts at a great transformation.

∿

JULIA SUDBURY

Globalized Punishment, Localized Resistance: Prisons, Neoliberalism, and Empire

In September 1998, activists, students, scholars, prisoners and their families came together at the first Critical Resistance conference in Berkeley to plan an international grassroots movement against the prison-industrial complex. In the following months, Critical Resistance (CR) became a new social movement, establishing chapters and affiliates in New York, Western Massachusetts, New Haven, Washington, D.C., Kentucky, Los Angeles, and Oakland, creating an analysis of the prison-industrial complex and disseminating a model of grassroots activism against mass incarceration throughout the nation and, to a lesser extent, beyond U.S. borders.[1] In March 2001, a second conference in New York was organized by the Critical Resistance East chapter. Subsequently, in April 2003, Critical Resistance South, the third CR conference, took place in April 2003 in the Tremé, a historic black neighborhood in New Orleans, bringing together two thousand former prisoners, family members, students, community members, and scholars from thirteen states to share strategies for dismantling the prison-industrial complex in the South.

In the past half decade, several organizations have emerged to oppose the prison-building boom, including Families Against Mandatory Minimums, Schools Not Jails, and Prison Moratorium Projects in New York, California, and Arizona. The Africana Criminal Justice Project thus exists in conjunction with and as an off-shoot of a vibrant movement which locates the abolition of prisons at the center of a vision of liberation and a struggle for social justice. The ultimate goal of the radical prison movement is not to create racially balanced or anti-racist prisons, or even to give two million prisoners the vote, but to bring prisoners home, to heal their families, and to rebuild our communities.

As we seek to develop a field of Africana Studies Against Criminal Injustice, we must be vigilant about silences and erasures within the discipline of Africana Studies. We need to challenge the tendency for African-American Studies to become the study of black men,[2] we need to actively counter the nationalism that creeps into even our most progressive movements and prevents us from seeing beyond U.S. borders, and we need to resist pressures to become an academic discipline detached from communities of resistance and from our radical roots.[3] We can do this by building on the radical internationalist tradition in Africana political thought such as that of Claudia Jones, a diasporic intellectual with roots in Trinidad who was active in anti-racist, feminist, communist, anti-imperialist, and anti-war organizing in both the United States and Britain.[4]

Jones's outspoken membership in the Communist Party, her trenchant critiques of racism and segregation, and her efforts to encourage African Americans to join the internationalist opposition to capitalism and militarism were particularly threatening to the U.S. government. In 1948, she was arrested and convicted under the Smith Act, or Alien Registration Act of 1940, of being "an alien who believes in, advocates, and teaches the overthrow, by force or violence of the Government of the United States."[5] While incarcerated in a federal penitentiary, she wrote in a letter to the United Nations:

> [I]f we (immigrants) can be denied all rights and incarcerated in concentration camps, then trade unionists are next; then the Negro people; then the Jewish people, all foreign born, and progressives who love peace and cherish freedom. . . . Our fate is the fate of the American people. Our fight is the fight of all opponents to fascist barbarism, of all who abhor war and desire peace.[6]

Jones's predictions about the U.S. penal system, thirty-three years before the Reagan administration embarked on the present prison-building binge, and over fifty years before the federal government began rounding up over eighty thousand Middle Eastern immigrants and asylum seekers, are frighteningly accurate.[7] Claudia Jones's praxis was also visionary in other ways: long before academics started theorizing about intersectionality, she argued that racism could not be eradicated without also ending the specific forms of sexism assailing black women.[8] She was a vigorous advocate of multiracial coalition-building between people of color, something she practiced as co-founder and chair of the Confederation of Afro-Asian-

Caribbean Organizations in England. Jones's analysis of the connections among global capitalism, imperialism, militarism, and racism provided an important radical foundation for international solidarity between African Americans and colonized peoples worldwide. Her radical, anti-imperialist, transnational feminism can serve as a model for our own efforts to challenge criminal injustice at this time of war and renewed U.S. empire-building.

CENTERING WOMEN'S NARRATIVES

The stories of two women in particular will illuminate the connections between neoliberal globalization and the rise of the prison-industrial complex. Accounts of mass incarceration tend to reduce prisoners to nameless statistics and to produce criminogenic typologies that enhance the state's ability to develop efficient and impersonal punishment regimes. In addition, women's imprisonment is rendered invisible when women prisoners, as frequently happens, are dismissed as "too few to count."[9] A counter-criminological analysis, to borrow a term from Nigerian scholar Biko Agozino,[10] one that centers on social justice, not punitive efficacy, must begin with the personal. Women's narratives are case studies that provide a deep, textured counterpoint to statistical data. They link struggles with addiction and self-esteem; relationships between mothers and daughters and women and their lovers; with systems of exploitation based on racism, class, and gender; and with social policy and the political economy of prisons.[11]

Marta is a Jamaican woman in her mid-thirties serving a five-year sentence for importation of drugs. I met Marta at HMP Westhill, originally the young offender annex of a large Victorian male prison in the picturesque town of Winchester in the South of England. During the 1990s, when the women's prison population began to increase faster than men's, the annex was painted pink and reopened as a women's medium-security prison. While Winchester's general population is predominantly white, approximately 40 percent of the women at HMP Westhill are black. Many, like Marta, are non-citizens from Africa or the Caribbean, who will be deported at the end of their sentence. Most, like Marta, have children whom they have not seen for many years.

Diane is a biracial African Canadian twenty-five-year-old serving a five-year sentence for importation of criminalized drugs in Toronto. Diane served most of her sentence at the Grand Valley Federal Prison for Women in Kitchener, Ontario, one of five new "women-centered" federal prisons built by the Canadian government in the late 1990s. As a teen, Diane left home and moved into a women's shelter because of an abusive relationship with her father. While there, she began a relationship with a Caribbean immigrant who was subsequently incarcerated for selling drugs. Shortly after his release, she gave up her job and started importing for him, not knowing at the time that his previous courier, a prior girlfriend, had been arrested and incarcerated. During the first few days of her sentence, she met and shared experiences with her husband's prior girlfriend and also learned that he had already moved in with another woman. Nevertheless, when offered a shorter sentence in return for information about who supplied the drugs, she refused out of a continued sense of loyalty.

GLOBALIZATION OF THE PRISON-INDUSTRIAL COMPLEX

Marta's and Diane's stories tell us that mass incarceration is not only a U.S. phenomenon. Prison populations throughout the global north have risen exponentially in the past twenty-five years, leading to massive overcrowding and a worldwide prison-building boom[12] characterized by three elements: it is fuelled by the criminalization of African diasporic, indigenous, and immigrant populations; it is marked by the exponential rate of growth of women's imprisonment, which in most nations has outstripped men's; and it has generated (and has been fuelled by) a transnational prison-industrial complex—a symbiotic relationship between the state and the private sector that translates prison expansion into corporate profits, campaign donations, and electoral victories.

Scholars working in a radical tradition of prison studies, such as Ruth Wilson Gilmore, Angela Y. Davis, and Christian Parenti, have analyzed the relationship between neoliberal globalization and the explosion in incarceration in advanced industrial nations.[13] Free trade and open borders for some have increasingly made working-class people of color in North America, Europe, and Australia surplus labor in the global economy. As corporations relocate their manufacturing operations to Taiwan, Haiti, or the Philippines in search of ever lower costs, cheap, non-unionized third world women have become the exploitable labor force of choice. Penal warehousing, which combines physical immobilization with political disenfranchisement, has become the state's solution to the "surplus populations" left behind. This solution is part of a broader shift from the welfare state to the "law and order" state embraced by neoconservatives and third-way liberals alike. Hence the well-documented transfer of public spending from education, health, and welfare, to policing and prisons, and tax breaks benefiting corporations and wealthy individuals. The feminization of poverty created by neoliberal economic restructuring combines with patriarchal gender relations to make women of color particularly vulnerable. Diane's story demonstrates that the incarceration of women is often the culmination of years of gender violence and exploitation, reminding us that the criminalization of surplus labor works in specifically gendered ways, often taking as its starting point the abuse of women and children by men in our communities.[14]

The transnational prison-industrial complex is not just about surplus labor, it is also, as Ruth Wilson Gilmore has pointed out, about surplus land.[15] "Industrialized punishment" has become a key economic development strategy for rural towns devastated by the economic restructuring brought about by globalization. Timber, steel, and paper factories, forced into bankruptcy under the new regime of unfettered free trade, have been replaced by the steel and concrete of new prisons. Farmland, vacated by family farms gone bust under competition with multinational agribusiness, has become profitable once more when used to warehouse criminalized bodies. The rise of industrialized punishment has birthed a rural prison lobby in Canada and Australia as well as in the U.S., which through town councils, business and realtor associations, and organizations like the Association of California Cities Allied with Prisons clamors for new prisons in place of productive forms of economic revitalization. It has woven mass incarceration into the fabric of the global economy.

CAPITALIST PUNISHMENT

Nowhere is this more evident than in the transnational spread of the private prison industry. While the private prison industry was birthed in the U.S. it has become a multinational entity with even greater significance outside of the U.S. Within the U.S., the industry has been plagued by vocal opponents, highly public human rights abuses, escapes, scandals, and overbuilding leading to expensive empty beds and troubled stock valuations.[16] Elsewhere, however, it has successfully positioned itself as a helpmate and "partner" to state correctional agencies, and the answer to a whole host of problems. In Britain, it has been embraced as a panacea for crumbling Victorian prisons, a rigid prison guards union, and—bizarrely—institutionalized racism. Despite initially opposing the privatization of prisons, the Labour government has announced that all new prisons will be put out to competitive tender and that "failing" prisons will be privatized.[17] In Chile, Mexico, and South Africa, foreign private prison corporations have been celebrated as a solution to inhumane conditions, overcrowding, human rights abuses, and government corruption.[18] For neoliberal Latin American governments, new high-tech steel and concrete penal warehouses with eighteen-year lease-purchase contracts have replaced housing, hospitals, and universities as signs of modernization and development.[19]

The emergence of shiny new prisons alongside the shantytowns and slums of the southern hemisphere is a reminder of the hollow promise of trickle-down development offered by proponents of neoliberal globalization. Even as governments are being forced to rein in spending on health, housing, clean water, and other basic necessities, they are also under pressure to embark on a U.S.-style war on drugs and law-and-order buildup. For example, the Inter-American Development Bank (IDB) is currently working to promote "justice reform" in Latin America and the Caribbean. In 1993, the IDB organized a conference in which its borrower nations were encouraged to modernize their justice systems. Since the conference, the IDB has spent $460 million in criminal justice loans and technical assistance in twenty-one countries. The IDB's interest in justice reform is driven by corporate executives, who, according to a recent report, are concerned that struggling criminal justice systems in the region, quote, "present a major problem for their business operations."[20] The IDB's focus on the criminal justice system demonstrates the connection between the neoliberal development agenda and the politics of law and order. When kidnappings of business executives, popular uprisings, and property-driven crime threaten investments, controlling disenfranchised and insurgent populations becomes a priority. In this context, strengthening criminal justice systems becomes an alternative to government funding for programs to redistribute wealth and reduce income disparity, poverty, and landlessness, exemplified by the popular socialist transformations spearheaded by Lula Da Silva's Workers Party in Brazil.

ECONOMIC RESTRUCTURING IN THE GLOBAL SOUTH

Third world women and men are not only increasingly at risk of incarceration in new private U.S.-style prisons at home, they are also filling the cells of penal warehouses throughout the global north. In the U.S. federal system, for example, 29 percent of those detained on criminal charges are non-citizens, while 9 percent of the British prison population are non-citizens.[21] Marta's story provides some insight into the rise in cross-border incarcerations. Speaking of her decision to import drugs, Marta told me:

> Things in Jamaica is very expensive. It's hard for a single woman with kids, especially anywhere over three kids, to get by without a good support or a steady job. It doesn't mean that I didn't have an income. I did have an income, but having four kids and an ex-husband who doesn't really care much. I had to keep paying school fees and the money kept going down. I did need some kind of support. That's why I did what I did. We don't get child support in Jamaica, three quarters of the things that this country offers for mothers here we don't have it. This country gives you a house, they give you benefits, we get nothing in Jamaica. We have to pay for hospital, not even education is free. Primary school used to be free under one government hand, but under another government it has been taken away. You're talking about high school, you're talking about fifteen up to twenty thousand dollars a term, for one kid to go to high school. It's difficult in Jamaica.

Since the mid-1980s, the Jamaican Labour Party (JLP), in unequal partnership with the U.S., the International Monetary Fund (IMF), and the World Bank, has undertaken a radical restructuring of the economy. Following the so-called Washington consensus, the JLP has slashed public-sector employment; scaled back local government services, health, and education; sold state-owned companies to the private sector; and reduced tariffs on imported goods. The result has been a sharp increase in the cost of living, the decimation of local farms and businesses, and a dramatic decline in real wages. These cuts have hit women particularly hard as they seek to fill the vacuum left by the vanishing welfare state.[22]

While the state has cut back its role in social welfare, it has stepped up its role in subsidizing foreign and domestic capital. Free Trade Zones established in Kingston and Montego Bay offer foreign garment, electronic, and communications companies equipped factory space; tax exemptions; a cheap female workforce; and, for the busy executive, weekends of sun, sea, and sex. Foreign-owned agribusiness and mining companies have also been encouraged, displacing traditional subsistence farming and causing migration from rural areas to the cities, which now host 50 percent of the Jamaican population. As the economy has shifted, women working in the informal economy as farmers and petty traders, popularly known as "higglers," like Marta, find themselves unable to keep up with the rising costs of survival. While younger women may find employment in the tourist industry as maids, entertainers, or prostitutes, or within the Free Trade Zones assembling clothes or computers for Western markets, working-class women in their thirties and older have fewer options.

Marta's experience exemplifies the increasing economic pressures facing women in the global south under free trade and IMF-led structural adjustment. The failure of the global economy to provide legal means for third world women to support themselves and their children guarantees a pool of low-level disposable workers for the criminalized drug industry and the global sex trade, and a continual supply of criminalized bodies for the prison-industrial complex.

DIRECTIONS FOR FUTURE ACTIVISM

The globalization of capital is driving prison expansion in four ways. It produces surplus populations—black, Latino, indigenous, immigrant, and working-class communities in North America, Europe, and Australia—who are immobilized and disenfranchised in penal warehouses in the global north. It produces surplus land that in the absence of other economic development opportunities generates local demand for new prison construction. It globalizes the private prison industry, spreading the U.S. model of high-tech mass incarceration throughout the world, and offering global south governments the mirage of modernity via mass incarceration. Finally, the neoliberal economic restructuring foisted by the IMF and the World Bank is undermining traditional survival strategies and decimating government services, driving women and men in the global south into the criminalized drug industry and fuelling cross-border incarceration.

What does this mean for the research and praxis of scholars and activists? A great deal more work needs to be done to unravel the complex interconnections between mass incarceration and the global economy. As activists at the heart of the "American Empire" our priority should be to make connections with prison activists outside of the U.S. We must begin to develop cross-border activism to challenge the transnational prison-industrial complex along the lines of the anti-sweatshop activism against Wal-Mart and Nike. The International Conference on Penal Abolition, which met in Lagos, Nigeria, in August 2002, is a model for such cross-border work. The 2002 meeting was important in that it brought together prison activists from numerous West African countries for the first time to focus on decolonizing criminal justice systems in the region. We have a great deal to learn from traditional African models of justice and conflict resolution. We also need to build alliances to prevent the spread of U.S.-style private prisons from South Africa through the rest of the continent.

As we seek to challenge the global forces that fuel incarceration, we should not lose sight of the individual stories that make up the prison crisis. A movement that will liberate us must have at its center the voices of the most marginalized and invisible. One way to achieve this is to promote movement-building among former prisoners and their families. I am struck by the words of All of Us or None, an emerging civil rights movement which aims to mobilize the thirty million former prisoners and felons in the U.S.:

> Nationally, there have been a number of former prisoners who have managed to involve themselves in organizations, agencies and on boards of directors in an effort to engage the policy makers, foundations, and society at large. For the most part we are invited as minority voices, we sit on panels to give them the appearance of legitimacy, and we are invited not to set the agenda but to respond to it. Even if that agenda is about our life and our families, we remain the subject and not the solution. . . . There are those among us who have had the privilege of meeting in rooms and discussing the problems that face us as former prisoners and felons. The atmosphere was electric and we walked away not committed to crime but to changing society. The notion that if we get together with each other we will return to crime is a cynical myth, designed to isolate us from each other. We were able to see that in spite of all odds many of us had changed our lives. We could see the common scars of incarceration. We could recognize that our experiences made us the best kind of experts. We could see the absence of a national plan that could reintegrate us back into society. We could see the financial profits that drive the prison building boom and could see the absolute need to organize ourselves to resist this oppression.[23]

Academics can play an important role by providing resources to organizations like All of Us or None and the Nu-Leadership Group, which are developing an autonomous collective political voice of those most directly affected by the prison-industrial complex. At the same time, we must develop better strategies for building horizontal solidarity with those currently behind bars, despite the efforts of prison authorities to keep us at arm's length.

We must also develop coalitions with the anti-globalization movement, both in the U.S. and internationally. The World Social Forum (WSF) is an important venue where critiques of and alternatives to free trade, imperialism, and neoliberalism are developed. We need to infuse the politics of the WSF with an analysis of the role of the prison-industrial complex in bolstering global capitalism. At the same time, our movement to abolish prisons can learn from the unprecedented successes of popular movements in the global south such as the Movimento Sim Terra in Brazil and the Ruta Pacífica in Colombia. These movements are broad-based, involving organized labor, feminists, the homeless, students, and indigenous communities. They have developed a sophisticated intersectional analysis of globalization, imperialism, and militarism as well as race, gender, and class. And most importantly, they have been successful in generating mass mobilizations by generating a viable alternative to the Washington model, by prioritizing people and the environment over corporations and profits.

Central to an anti-imperialist critique of the prison-industrial complex must be an analysis of the connections between militarism and prisons. If prison abolitionism is to continue to have relevance at a time when bombs are falling and Iraqis—or in the coming months, perhaps North Koreans, Palestinians, Saudi Arabians, Syrians, or Pakistanis—are dying, we must develop an integrated analysis of war, imperialism, and mass incarceration. The war on terror is not about ridding the world of the threat of terrorism. It is not even only about oil. It is about establishing a new world order based on neoliberal globalization. It is about expanding the reach of U.S. corporate interests at a time of recession and heightened international opposition to globalization, and replacing any regime hostile to the vision of a world dominated by these interests with puppet regimes friendly to the U.S. Bush's National Security Strategy spells out this administration's military goals. The U.S., it declares, will "ignite a new era of global economic growth through free markets and free trade."[24] Indeed, as the reconstruction of Iraq continues, "Operation Iraqi Freedom" will perhaps come to be relabeled "Operation Iraqi Free Trade." For, as Naomi Klein points out, Iraq has become "a blank slate on which the most ideological Washington neo-liberals can design their dream economy: fully privatized, foreign-owned and open for business."[25] Iraqi protestors taking to the streets shortly after the fall of Baghdad were more succinct. Their banners reading "We will not sell out our country" suggested that the Iraqi people were at risk of being both "sold out" and "sold off." U.S. corporations, many with senior political connections to the Bush administration, are the major beneficiaries of the reconstruction effort. Just as the war itself boosted the stock of the U.S. arms industry and private military companies, the rebuilding of Iraq has generated multimillion-dollar contracts for U.S. oil and manufacturing companies. While the Bush administration has rejected the idea of a long-term colonial presence in Iraq, this is hardly necessary for the neoliberal transformation of Iraq. With U.S.-headquartered multinationals receiving a monopoly on rebuilding roads, bridges, water and sewage plants, communications systems, and other infrastructure, it is clear that Iraq will have become a neocolonial outpost long before the last U.S. troops are withdrawn.[26]

The war on Iraq, and the war on terror in general, reflects a decision by the Bush administration to use military force to do what the Clinton regime and the IMF and World Trade Organization were doing through diplomacy, free trade agreements, and the carrot and stick of third world debt—creating new markets for the U.S. capitalist elite. In this sense, regime change in Iraq is the first step toward establishing a free trade area sympathetic to the U.S. in the region. This "U.S.–Middle East Free Trade Area" would join NAFTA and the much contested FTAA in remaking the world for U.S. multinational capital.[27] Penal warehouses for people of African descent, immigrants, indigenous people, and the global poor are central to this new world order. That is why even as "small government" has been promoted as a prerequisite for competitiveness in the global market, "corrections" budgets have continued to skyrocket. That is also why prison abolition remains of vital importance in this time of endless war. During the war on Iraq, "Bring them Home" became a popular anti-war slogan, countering the pro-war logic of those claiming to "Support our Troops." Our new movement for peace and social justice needs to bring all of our sisters and brothers home—not just from the battlefield, but from the prisons, jails, detention centers, and juvenile halls.

NOTES

1. Critical Resistance Editorial Collective, Critical Resistance to the Prison-Industrial Complex, *Social Justice,* Special Issue 27, no. 3 (2000). See also http://www.criticalresistance.org.

2. Hazel Carby, *Race Men* (Cambridge, MA: Harvard University Press, 1998).

3. Joy James, "The Future of Black Studies: Political Communities and the 'Talented Tenth,'" in *Dispatches from the Ebony Tower: Intellectuals Confront the African American Experience,* ed. Manning Marable (New York: Columbia University Press, 2000).

4. Marika Sherwood, *Claudia Jones: A Life in Exile* (London: Lawrence and Wishart, 1999).

5. FBI Files on Claudia Jones, quoted in Carole Boyce Davies, "Deportable Subjects: U.S. Immigration Laws and the Criminalizing of Communism," *The South Atlantic Quarterly* 100, no. 4 (Fall 2001): 949–966, 956. The Smith and Walter McCarran Acts were the legal basis for the Communist witchhunts carried out by the House Un-American Activities Committee from the 1950s. In 1950, Jones was issued a deportation order under the Walter McCarran Act and was subsequently removed to England.

6. Claudia Jones, Letter to United Nations, quoted in Sherwood 1999.

7. As of March 2003, the INS had registered 42,954 individuals at ports of entry and 46,035 individuals at domestic INS offices under a Special Alien Registration Program targeting nationals of nineteen predominantly Muslim countries and North Korea. Of these, 1,745 were detained, many for minor immigration violations. A nationwide class action lawsuit has been filed by those affected by the roundups. American Immigration Law Foundation. http://www.ailf.org/lac.

8. Claudia Jones, "An End to the Neglect of the Problems of Negro Women," in *Words of Fire: An Anthology of African-American Feminist Thought,* ed. Beverly Guy Sheftall (New York: The New Press, 1995).

9. Ellen Adelberg and Claudia Currie, eds., *Too Few to Count: Canadian Women in Conflict with the Law* (Vancouver: Press Gang Publishers, 1987).

10. Biko Agozino, *Counter-Colonial Criminology: A Critique of Imperialist Reason* (Ann Arbor: University of Michigan Press, 2003).

11. The personal narratives are part of a larger research project in which I have carried out semi-structured interviews with women of color and indigenous women in prisons and halfway houses in the U.S., Canada, and England.

12. Julia Sudbury, "Celling Black Bodies: Black Women in the Global Prison Industrial Complex," *Feminist Review* 70 (2002): 57–74.

13. Angela Y. Davis, "Race and Criminalization: Black Americans and the Punishment Industry," in *The Angela Y. Davis Reader,* ed. J. James (Malden: Blackwell Publishers, 2001); Christian Parenti, *Lockdown America: Police and Prisons in the Age of Crisis* (London and New York: Verso, 1999); Ruth Wilson Gilmore, "Globalisation and U.S. Prison Growth," *Race and Class* 40, nos. 2/3 (1998): 171–188.

14. For a detailed analysis of the complex relationship among violence against women, racism, and criminalization, see Beth Richie, *Compelled to Crime: The Gender Entrapment of Battered Black Women* (London and New York: Routledge, 1996).

15. Gilmore 1998 and *Golden Gulag: Labor, Land, State, and Opposition in Globalizing California* (Berkeley: University of California Press, forthcoming).

16. Judith Greene, "Bailing Out Private Jails," *The American Prospect* 12, no. 6 (September 10, 2001).

17. Julia Sudbury, "Transatlantic Visions: Resisting the Globalization of Mass Incarceration," *Social Justice* 27, no. 3 (Fall 2000): 133–150.

18. Stephen Nathan, "The Prison Industry Goes Global," *Yes* 15 (Fall 2000).

19. Gendarmería de Chile, "Establecimientos Concesionados" (2002), available online at http://www.gendarmería.cl/penitenciaria; Tessie Borden, "Mexico Will Try Private Prisons," *Arizona Republic*, September 19, 2002.

20. Christina Biebesheimer and J. Mark Payne, *IDB Experience in Justice Reform* (Washington D.C.: Inter-American Development Bank, 2001), i.

21. Federal Bureau of Prisons, "Quick Facts," May 2002, available online at www.bop.gov; HM Prison Service, "Prison Life," 2003, available online at http://www.hm prisonservice.gov.uk.

22. Faye Harrison, "Women in Jamaica's Urban Informal Economy," in *Third World Women and the Politics of Feminism*, ed. C. T. Mohanty, A. Russo, and L. Torres (Bloomington: Indiana University Press, 1991).

23. All of Us or None, "A Proposed National Strategy Session to Strengthen the Voices of Formerly Incarcerated Persons and Felons," Position Paper (Oakland: All of Us or None, 2003). See also http://www.allofusornone.org.

24. U.S. National Security Council, *The National Security Strategy of the United States of America* (2002: Section VI), available online at http://www.whitehouse.gov/nsc/nss .html.

25. Naomi Klein, "Bomb before You Buy: What Is Being Planned in Iraq Is Not Reconstruction but Robbery," *The Guardian*, April 14, 2003.

26. James Ridgeway, "Mondo Washington," *Village Voice*, April 23–29, 2003.

27. U.S. Department of State, "Bush Calls for U.S.–Middle East Free Trade Area," May 9, 2003, available online at http://usinfo.state.gov/regional/nea/summit/text2003/ 0509bushfta.htm.

HISHAAM D. AIDI

Let Us Be Moors: Islam, Race and "Connected Histories"

"*Seamos moros!*" wrote the Cuban poet and nationalist José Martí in 1893, in support of the Berber uprising against Spanish rule in northern Morocco. "Let us be Moors . . . the revolt in the Rif . . . is not an isolated incident, but an outbreak of the change and realignment that have entered the world. Let us be Moors . . . we [Cubans] who will probably die by the hand of Spain."[1] Writing at a time when the scramble for Africa and Asia was at full throttle, Martí was accentuating connections between those great power forays and Spanish depredations in Cuba, even as the rebellion of 1895 germinated on his island.

Throughout the past century, particularly during the Cold War, Latin American leaders from Cuba's Fidel Castro to Argentina's Juan Perón would express support for Arab political causes, and call for Arab-Latin solidarity in the face of imperial domination, often highlighting cultural links to the Arab world through Moorish Spain. Castro, in particular, made a philo-Arab pan-Africanism central to his regime's ideology and policy initiatives. In his famous 1959 speech on race, the *jefe máximo* underlined Cuba's African and Moorish origins. "We all have lighter or darker skin. Lighter skin implies descent from Spaniards who themselves were colonized by the Moors that came from Africa. Those who are more or less dark-skinned came directly from Africa. Moreover, nobody can consider himself as being of pure, much less superior, race."[2]

With the launching of the "war on terror," and particularly with the invasion of Iraq, political leaders and activists in Latin America have been warning of a new imperial age and again declaring solidarity with the Arab world. Some refer rather quixotically to a Moorish past. Linking the war on Iraq to Plan Colombia and to the Bush administration's alleged support for a coup against him, the erratic Venezuelan strongman Hugo Chavez has repeatedly urged his countrymen to "return to their Arab roots," and attempted to mobilize the country's mestizo and black majority against white supremacy. "They call me the monkey or black," Chavez says of his domestic and international opponents. "They can't stand that someone like me was elected."[3]

In less contentious terms, Brazil's left-leaning President Lula da Silva visited the Middle East in early December 2003 to seek "more objective" relations with the Arab world, to call for an "independent, democratic Palestinian state," and to launch a common market with the Arab world as an alternative to the North American market (particularly with many in Arab countries boycotting American products).[4] Brazil's largest trade union federation strongly denounced post–September 11 U.S. intervention in Colombia, Venezuela, and the Middle East, praising the protest movements that have appeared against U.S. and Israeli "militarism" and calling on Brazilian workers to join in the struggle "against Sharon's Nazi-Zionist aggression against the Palestinian people" and in support of the *intifada*.[5]

THE OTHER SEPTEMBER 11 EFFECT

In the age of the "war on terror," such expressions from the Western world of affinity with the Arab world are not confined to statements of political solidarity. In Latin America, Europe, and the United States, for example, there has been a sharp increase in conversion to Islam. At the first world congress of Spanish-speaking

Muslims held in Seville in April 2003, the scholar Mansur Escudero, citing "globalization," said that there were 10 to 12 million Spanish speakers among the world's 1.2 billion Muslims.[6] In the United States, researchers note that usually 25,000 people a year become Muslim, but by several accounts that number has quadrupled since September 11.[7] In Europe, an Islamic center in Holland reported a tenfold increase and the New Muslims Project in England reported a "steady stream" of new converts.[8] Several analysts have noted that in the United Kingdom, many converts are coming from middle-class and professional backgrounds, not simply through the prison system or ghetto mosques, as is commonly believed.[9] The Muslim population in Spain is also growing, due to conversion, as well as immigration and intermarriage.[10]

Different explanations have been advanced to account for this intriguing phenomenon, known as "the other September 11 effect"—the primary effects being anti-Muslim and anti-immigrant backlash and infringements upon civil liberties. Commenting on how the accused "dirty bomber" José Padilla and the shoe bomber Richard Reid converted to Islam, French scholar Olivier Roy observes, "Twenty years ago such individuals would have joined radical leftist movements, which have now disappeared or become 'bourgeois.' . . . Now only two Western movements of radical protest claim to be 'internationalist': the anti-globalization movement and radical Islamists. To convert to Islam today is a way for a European rebel to find a cause; it has little to do with theology."[11] This portrayal of Islam as an outlet for the West's political malcontents ignores the powerful allure of certain aspects of Islamic theology, and begs the question of why for at least a century, even when communism was still in vogue, minorities in the West have seen Islam as a particularly attractive alternative. Roy's formulation also neglects the critical elements of racism and racialization. At least since Malcolm X, internationalist Islam has been seen as a response to Western racism and imperialism.

Though Westerners of different social and ethnic backgrounds are gravitating toward Islam, it is mostly the ethnically marginalized of the West—historically, mostly black, but nowadays also Latino, Native American, Arab, and South Asian minorities—who, often attracted by the purported universalism and color-blindness of Islamic history and theology, are asserting membership in a transnational *umma* and thereby challenging or "exiting" the white West. Even for white converts, like John Walker Lindh, becoming Muslim involves a process of racialization—renouncing their whiteness—because while the West stands for racism and white supremacy on a global scale, Islam is seen to represent tolerance and anti-imperialism. This process of racialization is also occurring in diasporic Muslim communities in the West, which are growing increasingly race-conscious and "black" as anti-Muslim racism increases. To cope, Muslims in the diaspora are absorbing lessons from the African-American freedom movement, including from strains of African-American Islam.

Over the past two years, Islam has provided an anti-imperial idiom and imaginary community of belonging for many subordinate groups in the West, as Islamic culture and art stream into the West through minority and diaspora communities, and often in fusion with African-American art forms, Islam is slowly seeping into the cultural mainstream. Subsequently, many of the cultural and protest movements—anti-globalization, anti-imperialist, anti-racist—in the West today have Islamic and/or African-American undercurrents. At a time of military conflict and extreme ideological polarization between the West and the Muslim world, Islamic culture is permeating political and cultural currents, remaking identities and creating cultural linkages between Westerners and the Muslim world.

In sum, this chapter is about imagination and "culturalism" post-9/11. I consider why certain segments of the West are now choosing to remember their connections to the Muslim world, and how the "remembering" and "imagined solidarity" are being expressed culturally and politically. I look at the conversion trends and the craze for Arab culture that has swept parts of Latin America and the United States in the past two years, but focus on the cultural movements of "Islamic hip-hop" and the Arab European League that use the "frames" and "repertoires" of Islam and the African-American struggle as examples of the political potential of "imagined solidarities," and as instances of what anthropologist Arjun Appadurai has called "culturalism": "[the] deliberate, strategic and populist mobilization of cultural material [and] cultural differences in the service of a larger national or transnational politics."[12] I also examine how Islamic culture and motifs are becoming central to the worldwide anti-globalization and anti-war movement, and providing the cultural building blocks for an international "counter-modernity" movement.

LATINO BACK CHANNELS

Recent journalistic accounts have noted the growing rate of conversion to Islam in the southern Mexican state of Chiapas, and the often violent clashes between Christian and Spanish Muslim missionaries proselytizing among the indigenous Mayan community. The Muslim campaign in Chiapas is led by a Spaniard from Granada, Aureliano Perez, member of an international Sufi order called al-Murabitun, though he is contending with a rival missionary, Omar Weston, the Nation of Islam's local representative. Particularly interesting about the several hundred Mayan Muslims is the view of some of the converts that, though some of the missionaries are Spanish like the conquistadors, their embrace of Islam is a historic remedy for the Spanish conquest and the consequent oppression. "Five hundred years ago, they came to destroy us," said Anastasio Gomez Gomez, 21, who now goes by Ibrahim. "Five hundred years later, other Spaniards came to return a knowledge that was taken away from us."[13]

The view of 1492 as a tragic date signaling the end of a glorious era, and the related idea that conversion to Islam entails a reclaiming of that past, are common among the Latino Muslim community in the United States. That community, estimated in 2000 at 30,000 to 40,000 members, has grown in the past two years, with Latino Muslim centers and *da'wa* (proselytizing) organizations in New York, Los

Angeles, Miami, Fresno, and Houston.[14] The banner hanging at the Alianza Islamica center in the South Bronx celebrates the African and Islamic roots of Latin America: against a red, white, and blue backdrop stands a sword-wielding Moor, flanked by a Taino Indian and a black African. The Spanish conquistador is conspicuously absent. Imam (Omar Abduraheem) Ocasio of the Alianza Islamica speaks passionately about the continuity between Moorish Spain and Latin America: "Most of the people who came to Latin America and the Spanish Caribbean were from southern Spain, Andalusia—they were Moriscos, Moors forcefully converted to Christianity. The leaders, army generals, *curas* [priests] were white men from northern Spain . . . *sangre azul,* as they were called. The southerners, who did the menial jobs, . . . servants, artisans, foot soldiers, . . . were of mixed Arab and African descent. They were stripped of their religion, culture, brought to the so-called New World where they were enslaved with African slaves. . . . But the Moriscos never lost their culture . . . we are the cultural descendants of the Moors."[15] The Puerto Rican imam writes, "Islamically inspired values were conveyed ever so subtly in the Trojan horse of Spanish heritage throughout the centuries and, after 500 years, Latinos were now ready to return."[16]

In the past two years, Islam and the Arab-Muslim world seem to have entered even more poignantly into the Latin American imagination, gaining a presence in political discourse and strongly influencing Hispanic popular culture. This Arab cultural invasion of Latin America, which has reverberated in mainstream American culture, is often attributed to the Brazilian *telenovela El Clon* and Lebanese-Colombian pop icon Shakira.

El Clon, the highest-rated soap opera ever shown on Telemundo, a U.S. Spanish-language channel, reportedly reaches 2.8 million Hispanic households in the United States, as well as 85 million people in Brazil and tens of millions across Latin America. The series, which began broadcasting shortly after September 11, tells the story of Jade, a young Brazilian Muslim who returns to her mother's homeland of Morocco after her mother's death in Brazil. There she falls in love and settles down with Lucas, a Christian Brazilian, and adapts to life in an extended family setting in the old city of Fez. Filmed in Rio de Janeiro and Fez, the *telenovela* offers a profusion of Orientalist imagery—from veiled belly dancers swaying seductively behind ornate latticework to dazzling shots of Marrakesh and Fez spliced with footage of scantily clad women on Rio's beaches—and of course, incessant supplications of *"Ay, por favor, Allah!"* from Jade's neighbors in the medina. The Moroccan ambassador to Brazil, in a letter to a São Paolo newspaper, criticized the series for its egregious "cultural errors," "gross falsification," and "mediocre images" promoting stereotypes of Muslim women as submissive and men as polygamists leading lives of "luxury and indolence."

Despite the kitsch, *El Clon* has triggered what *Latin Trade* called "Mid-East fever" across Latin America. Belly dancing and "Middle Eastern–style jewelry" became "the rage in Rio and São Paolo," Brazilians began throwing "A Thousand and One Nights" parties, "Talk to a Sheikh" chat rooms cropped up online, and two new agencies opened up to offer package tours to North Africa. (In his letter, the Moroccan ambassador acknowledged that Brazilian tourism to Morocco had increased by 300 percent thanks to *El Clon.*) A journalist visiting Quito, Ecuador, found viewers of the series "wide-eyed and drop-jawed for all things Arab."[17] Even in the United States, where *El Clon*'s broadcast was almost blocked due to alleged potential controversy, it has exerted cultural influence upon the Latino community and others. In New York, observers note the *El Clon*–triggered fashion for Arab jewelry and hip scarves, the overflowing belly-dancing classes, and a recently opened beauty parlor called El Clon in Queens.[18]

Through the Latino back channel, the impact of Shakira in bringing Arab culture to the MTV audience has also been considerable. The Lebanese-Colombian singer was bombarded with questions by the media about her views "as an Arab" on the September 11 attacks, and advised to drop the belly dancing and the Arabic riffs from her music because it could hurt her album sales, but she refused. "I would have to rip out my heart or my insides in order to be able to please them," said the songstress, who expressed horror at hate crimes against "everything that's Arab, or seems Arab."[19] During the run-up to the Iraq war, Shakira's performances took on an explicitly political tone, with her dancers wearing masks of Tony Blair, George W. Bush, and Fidel Castro. Backdrop screens flashed images of Bush and Saddam Hussein as two puppets playing a sinister game of chess, with the Grim Reaper as the puppeteer. She also undertook a highly publicized tour of the Middle East (though her concerts in Casablanca, Tunis, and Beirut were postponed), during which she visited her father's ancestral village in the Bekaa Valley. Viewers across the region were delighted when Shakira appeared on Egyptian television singing the tunes of Fairuz. In Europe, the United States, South America, and even the Middle East, the belly-dancing star has fostered a reported mania for hip scarves with coins and tassels. In a random check of Cairo nightclubs, Egyptian government officials confiscated twenty-six Shakira outfits, "weighing no more than 150 grams [5 ounces]," and deemed "scandalous,"[20] but local filmmakers are currently negotiating with government officials over rights to a film project called *Shakira fi al-Munira*, about a young Egyptian girl infatuated with the Colombian chanteuse.

While the craze for Arab culture has occurred in the wake of September 11 and the ensuing war on terrorism, it is not necessarily political. Commenting on the popularity of *shawarma* and hookahs in Quito, one journalist observes that "the new fascination with Arabia comes at a time when there are new reasons for anti-American sentiment"—the recent policy of currency dollarization—but adds reassuringly that "*El Clon*'s following surely won't produce a new sect of Islamic fundamentalist terrorists in Latin America."[21] It is also not clear that conversion to Islam necessarily constitutes political or cultural resistance. Referring to the vogue for Islam and Arabic among Spanish youth, one Catalan journalist wryly observes: "It will take more than teenagers converting to an Islam lite to stop [Spanish Prime Minister José Maria] Aznar's Christian nationalism and Castilian imperialism. We need a civil dialogue about our relations with the Orient."[22] Belly dancing and learning elementary Arabic may not be acts of resistance, but such activities create important, albeit imaginary cultural linkages which can be activated for political purposes. As Miles Copeland, head of the Mondo Melodia label, who will release a film on the American belly-dancing craze in January 2004, told *PR Newswire:* "Belly dancing is about art, not politics—but in experiencing the art, you also experience the culture, and that becomes political in and of itself." Interest in Arab culture and conversions are bringing Islam into the imagination of Western youth, feeding powerful movements and cultures of protest.

FROM HARLEM TO THE CASBAH

In *No Name in the Street,* James Baldwin reflects on the "uneasy" reaction he would get when, while in France in 1948, he would "claim kinship" with the Algerians living there. "The fact that I had never seen the Algerian casbah was of no more relevance . . . than the fact that the Algerians had never seen Harlem. The Algerian and I were both, alike, victims of this history [of Europe in Africa], and I was still a part of Africa, even though I had been carried out of it nearly 400 years before."[23] Most French-born Arabs have never been to Harlem but "claim kinship" with African-Americans as they draw inspiration from the black freedom struggle. Numerous French-Arab (Beur) intellectuals and activists have noted their indebtedness to African-American liberation thought,[24] and the secular pro-integration Beur movement of the early 1980s organized campaigns and marches modeled on the U.S. civil rights struggle. But in the early 1990s, as the impoverished, ethnically segregated *banlieues* mushroomed around French cities, the discourse of *intégration* began to give way to talk of self-imposed exclusion and warnings that the children of immigrants "had gone in a separate direction." The region of Lyons, where 100,000 gathered for the famous march for *intégration* in 1983, is today cited by commentators as evidence of the failure of assimilation. Lyons, by one account, has become a "ghetto of Arabs," and fallen to Islamist influence, boasting six neighborhood boys in the U.S. military detention center at Guantanamo Bay.[25]

The generation of black and Arab Muslim youth that came of age in crime-ridden *banlieues* that periodically explode into car-burning riots, and are monitored by a heavy-handed police force, is in no mood for integration. By some estimates, 50 to 60 percent of the French prison population is Muslim.[26] French commentators are increasingly wondering if they have developed a "race problem" like that of the United States, with the attendant pathologies of ethnic ghettoes, family breakdown, drugs, violence, and, of particular concern these days, Islamism. As in the American ghetto, disintegrating family units have been replaced by new organizations—gangs, posses, and religious associations, particularly Islamic groups,[27] which provide services and patrol the *cités,* the housing projects where most immigrants live.

The confluence of Islam and urban marginality in France was displayed in a consummately post-colonial moment on October 6, 2001, when France and Algeria met in their first soccer match since the Algerian war of independence. The match was stopped prematurely when thousands of French-born Arab youth, seeing Algeria losing, raided the field chanting "Bin Laden! Bin Laden!" and hurled bottles at two female French ministers.[28] The ill-fated match, coming on the heels of September 11, led to hysterical warnings of an *intifada* simmering in the heart of France, an Islamic fifth column, the "unassimilability" of certain immigrants, and, again, an American-style "race problem." Like American pundits, the French are concerned about whether Islamic and Muslim organizations which have emerged in the *banlieues* will keep youths out of trouble or radicalize them. An American writing for the *Weekly Standard* notes, "It's the Farrakhan problem. Mosques do rescue youths from delinquency, idleness and all sorts of other ills. But in so doing, they become power brokers in areas where almost all disputes are resolved by violence and the most tribal kind of woospeh [respect, in a French accent, supposedly]. And it is that mastery of a violent environment—not the social service record—that these groups call on when they make demands on the larger society."[29]

The French media has shown a keen interest in the rising conversion to Islam in the United States and Europe—and particularly in the overlap of Islam and race, or more specifically, ethnic awareness, mobilization, and self-segregation. An exposé in an April 2003 edition of the magazine *L'Express* opened with the following statement: "Blacks, whites, Latinos, Asians . . . every year, 50,000 to 80,000 [Americans] convert to Islam. Internal enemies, members of the 'axis of evil'?" The French government's attempts to control Islamic mobilization in the *banlieues* through elections for a national Islamic council (aimed, in the words of the interior minister, at taking Islam out of "cellars and garages") backfired when the conservative Union of Islamic Organizations, inspired by Egypt's banned Muslim Brotherhood, won fourteen out of forty-one seats.

Zacarias Moussaoui, the "twentieth hijacker" awaiting trial in the United States, in many ways embodies the story of Islam and racial exclusion in France. Although he did not grow up impoverished in the *cités*, by all accounts, the French-Moroccan harbored a deep racial rage. In his youth, Moussaoui was often ridiculed because of his dark skin and frizzy hair, and repeatedly called *nègre* (nigger), but it was after the 1991 Gulf war that he became politicized. He began to consider himself "black," joining the "Kid Brothers"—a university group modeled after the Egyptian Muslim Brotherhood—and came back from a stint in London deeply hostile toward whites. "He became a racist, a black racist, and he would use the pejorative African word *toubab* to describe white people," said his brother.[30] Moussaoui raged against Western permissiveness and imperialism in Algeria, Palestine, and Chechnya.[31]

Richard Reid, the "shoe bomber," who became radicalized in the same Brixton mosque as Moussaoui, embodies the similarly distressing urban and racial situation in Britain. West Indian and South Asian youth live in benighted "mill and mosque" towns, devastated by capital flight in the late 1980s and 1990s, where the anti-immigrant British National Party is making inroads and race riots erupt frequently. Many of these youth have drifted towards radical Islamist groups. By all accounts, the petty thief and graffiti artist known as ENROL embraced Islam while in Feltham young offenders' institution to seek solace from racism. His father Robin tried to explain Reid's odyssey to Islam as a result of the difficulty of being of mixed race. "Islam accepts you for who you are," the father told CNN talk show host Larry King. "Even I was a Muslim for a little bit . . . because I was fed up with racial discrimination." In an interview with the *Guardian*, Robin continued: "About ten years ago, I met up with Richard after not seeing him for a few years. He was a little bit downhearted. I suggested to him, 'Why don't you become a Muslim? They treated me all right.'"

The mixing of Islam and racial awareness in Europe is also leading to political mobilization. The Arab European League (AEL), headed by the fiery Lebanese-born Dyab Abou Jahjah, is explicitly modeled on the American civil rights movement, borrowing slogans ("By Any Means Necessary!") and protest techniques from the Black Panthers and the Nation of Islam, and aiming to mobilize Arab and Muslim youth across Europe to lobby European governments to make Arabic one of the official languages of the European Union and to gain state funding for Islamic schools. Based in Brussels, but with chapters opening in France and Holland, the AEL has launched a cross-border Arab pride movement, and organized marches against the U.S. war in Iraq and in solidarity with the Palestinian *intifada*. Known as the "Arab Malcolm X," Abou Jahjah, who says he finds the ideas of integration "degrading," admits being inspired by the slain African-American civil rights leader, who "was also against assimilation . . . fought for civil rights and was also inspired by Islam."[32] "We're a civil rights movement, not a club of fundamentalist fanatics who want to blow things up," he told the *New York Times* on March 1, 2003. "In Europe, the immigrant organizations are Uncle Toms. We want to polarize people, to sharpen the discussion, to unmask the myth that the system is democratic for us." The AEL has also organized Black Panther–style "Arab patrols" to "police the police." Groups of unarmed Arab youths dressed in black follow the police around, carrying video cameras and flyers which read, "Bad cops: the AEL is watching you." Fusing African-American, Islamic, and Arab elements in its style and rhetoric, the AEL has become a political force to be reckoned with, even prompting the Belgian government to attempt to ban its patrols on the basis of a 1930s law that proscribes private militias.

"LE RESPECT" AND "LES PITBULLS"

> *Seul le beat aujourd-hui nous lie et nous unit.* (Today only the beat links and unites us.)
>
> —Saliha, "Danse le Beat"

Hip-hop has emerged as the idiom for the urban activism of minority youth in Europe. For Muslim youth experiencing the crackdown on immigrants, as well as state withdrawal and welfare cuts, hip-hop offers a chance to express critiques, vent rage, declare solidarity with other marginalized youth (particularly African-

Americans), and display cultural pride—to show, as New York rapper DMX says, "who we be."[33]

If American rap has been criticized for its materialism, nihilism, and political nonchalance, French hip-hop offers trenchant critiques of racism, globalization, and imperialism. Numerous groups such as Yazid and La Fonky Family deal explicitly with the challenges of being Arab and Muslim in the West, and relations between Islam and the West. In their hit single, "Je Suis Si Triste" ("I'm So Sad"), the Marseilles-based rap crew 3eme Oeil (Third Eye), made up of the Comorian-born Boss One (Mohammed), Jo Popo (Mohammed), and Saïd, offers biting social commentary over an infectious, looping bass line. Decrying hate crimes against veiled Muslim women in France, condemning police brutality and mass incarceration (with a special shout out to Mumia Abu Jamal), the rappers focus their lyrical fire on the West's "stranglehold" (*la main-mise*) on the East.

In addition to verbal release, hip-hop is used to combat racism and to promote black-white-Arab relations, as in the Urban Peace Festivals and spoken-word poetry events (*les slameurs*) organized by SOS Racisme. Hip-hop, interestingly, is also being used to counter Islamist influence in the *banlieues*. The Beurette leader Fadela Amara, who organized the march *"Ni putes ni soumises"* ("Neither whores nor submissive")—a march that has now developed into a women's rights organization affiliated with SOS Racisme—often invites Muslim female rappers to spread a feminist message. "Ni putes, ni soumises" aims to mobilize youth against ghettoes and for equality, but also to counter the Islamist organizations, such as the powerful Union of Islamic Organizations, which delivers services in the *cités* in exchange for veiling. Amara says discrimination and unemployment make many young men feel "excluded from the French project." These youths, she says, often return to Islamic traditions, opposing gender mixing and women's education, and sometimes assaulting women who do not dress according to their idea of modesty.[34] French Muslim rappers and R&B singers publicly and collectively condemned the September 11 attacks, saying the terrorists were, in the words of Ideal J, a Franco-Haitian convert to Islam, "dishonoring the faith." Al Malik of the New African Poets, a Congolese convert to Islam, noted the importance of rap and Islam to young ghetto dwellers: "Rap has opened a world to us, empowering us young men, and Islam has allowed us to flourish by teaching us respect for 'the other.' [But] the Taliban are instrumentalizing the religion."[35]

Attempts by some French Islamists to boycott American products—and market products like Mecca Cola—are failing since *banlieusards* remain loyal to American streetwear labels like Fubu and Phat Farm, often claiming that such clothing is an anti-American, but pro-black statement. More recently, local *banlieue* streetwear clothing lines have appeared with names like Bullrot (a combination of pit bull and rottweiler) and Adedi (an acronym for *Association de differences*), the latter founded by a Moroccan, a Gabonese, and a Senegalese to combat racism and extremism, and to celebrate difference.[36]

French commentators associate hip-hop with Islam, claiming that rap, like Islam, often brings rage, pathology, and dysfunction. The anti-immigrant National

Front of Jean Le Pen and its splinter, the National Republican Movement, have historically denounced hip-hop. In March 2001, both far-right parties opposed the use of public funds to finance the first Hip-Hop Dance World Cup in Villepinte, stating that "hip-hop is a movement belonging to immigrants of African origin installed in France and which constitutes a call to sedition against our institutions."[37] More recently, however, the National Front has begun to use hip-hop as a way to spread its political message, "win back" French youth, and counter Arab and American influence in French culture. The white supremacist rap crew Basic Celto, affiliated with the National Republican Movement, has as its objective to break "immigrants' monopoly" over hip-hop "which diffuses the immigrants' complaints." Basic Celto aims to promote a "national revolutionary" rap with a "Christian identity," and to draw "*français d'origine*" away from immigrant influence.[38]

But the allure of Islam, and Islam-inflected cultures like hip-hop and rai, to French youth continues to grow, prompting much editorial pondering. *Le Monde* ran a story on how Ramadan is increasingly observed in French schools, even by non-Muslims, and there have also been reports of many non-Muslim girls wearing headscarves in solidarity with Muslim schoolgirls sent home for wearing *le foulard*. Commenting on Le Pen's remark that hip-hop is a dangerous musical genre which originated in the casbahs of Algeria, rapper Boss One (Mohammed) of 3eme Oeil said: "For Le Pen, everything bad—rap, crime, AIDS—comes from Algeria or Islam. . . . The more Bush and Chirac attack Islam and say it's bad, the more young people will think it's good, and the more the oppressed will go to Islam and radical preachers. Especially here in America. Because life is hard in France, but we have a social safety net."[39]

Commentators have also blamed hip-hop for bringing social ills associated with the American ghetto to France. "[French-Arab youth] intentionally imitate belligerent Afro-American lifestyles, down to 'in-your-face' lyrics for booming rap music," moaned one observer.[40] Some have pointed to the "African-Americanization" of the speech patterns of French youth, noting that their verbal jousting is similar to that of "American rappers from black ghettoes."[41] Indeed, the culture of France's suburban ghettoes is heavily influenced by the trends of the American inner city—the urban argot, street codes of conduct, and "honor system" are strikingly similar.[42] In January 2000, a law was passed creating a police unit to monitor the behavior of pit bulls and rottweilers in housing projects where, as in the United States, such dogs had become very popular during the 1990s among urban youth.[43] The slurs used against blacks (*nègres*) and Arabs (in France, *bougnoles;* in Spain, *Moros;*[44] and in Belgium, *makkak*, which means white ape) have become commonly used terms of endearment among Muslim youth, as with the term *nigger* in the United States. But clearly, Muslim European youth have not learned misogyny and rage from hip-hop or from African-Americans. The fact that hip-hop is being used by secular urban movements to counter Islamism and racism is an illustration of the growing racial consciousness of Muslim youth in Europe, the deep resonance of the African-American experience, and how imagination can help construct a cultural world to resist state oppression and religious fanaticism.

KEEPIN' IT *HALAL*

Hip-hop's changed, ain't a black thing anymore G
Young kids in Baghdad showing 2 on 3
Holla West Coast? Nah, West Bank for life
Upside down, holla for my Moros alright
Spit rhymes in Arabic on the same level like Jada
You wouldn't know if you should head bang or belly dance playa
I'm that type of sand nigga type of Johnny Cochran yaw dig
Ya stereotype me, I knock you out like Prince Naseem.

—Outlandish, "El Moro"

The hip-hop movement has a powerful oppositional streak that makes it both attractive and troubling to political actors. Hip-hop's ability to jangle the hegemonic discourse was recently seen with Jay-Z's "Leave Iraq Alone" verse and Outkast's anti-war hit "Bombs over Baghdad," denouncing the first Gulf war, which was yanked off the air by MTV and Clear Channel when bombs began raining on Baghdad in March 2003.[45] Hip-hop artists have strongly opposed the war, without fear of the social opprobrium visited upon the Dixie Chicks and other white pop stars. As hip-hop mogul Russell Simmons put it, "Rappers don't have to worry about anything. No one likes what they have to say anyway, so they're not afraid to speak up." But when hip-hop is infused with Islamic themes and political allusions, the establishment press has found it particularly unsettling. Hence the outrage over rapper Paris' recently released—and rapidly selling—*Sonic Jihad*, the cover of which features an airplane flying toward the White House, and the alleged purging of Arabic terms and references to Hussein from Tupac Shakur's recently released *Better Dayz*, though the slain rapper was referring not to the missing Iraqi dictator, but to Hussein Fatal, a member of his Outlawz posse, which also includes Khadafi, Kastro, Komani, and Idi Amin.[46]

In the fall of 2002, accused sniper John Muhammad, formerly of the Nation of Islam, sent notes to the police that referenced lyrics from rappers who are Five Percenters—a heterodox black Muslim sect. The subsequent media frenzy triggered a soul-searching conversation within the Islamic hip-hop community that was rendered particularly urgent when Muslim hip-hoppers found themselves linked to the war on terror by Niger Innis, chairman of the conservative Congress of Racial Equality. (A similar uproar occurred more recently in the United Kingdom when a hip-hop group named Shaikh Terra and the Soul Salah crew released a video "Dirty Kuffar" ("Dirty Unbelievers"), in which they salute Hamas and Hizbullah and praise Osama bin Laden; the "hate video" drew the attention of Labor MP Andrew Dismore who described the video as "disgust[ing]" and "inexcusable" and launched a police investigation into the radical Muslim group.)[47] Shortly after the arrest of John Muhammad, Innis met with Department of Justice officials to express concern over "domestic black Muslims as a national security issue" and launched a campaign to counter Islamic recruitment efforts in the nation's prisons and colleges.[48] Muslim rappers asked themselves: should we be expected to "represent" Islam positively, and avoid the misogynist and materialistic excesses of mainstream hip-hop artists? Or should the aim be to "get paid" and gain wide success even if it means "playing with the *haram* (illicit)"? Of the U.S.-based Muslim hip-hop crews, Native Deen and Sons of Hagar have been praised for their positive political and religious messages. Native Deen, made up of three African-American rappers who won't perform in venues that allow mixed dancing or serve alcohol, have been profiled in *The New Yorker* and even received praise from the State Department, but have yet to garner airtime on mainstream radio stations. The Des Moines–based Sons of Hagar, made up of Allahz Sword (Ahmad) and Ramadan Conchus (Abdul), both Arab-Americans, and Keen Intellect (Kareem) and Musa, Irish-American and Korean-American converts to Islam, respectively, have also been praised for socially conscious lyrics. Their poignant single "Insurrection" ("It's the Arab hunting season, and I ain't leavin'/I'm pushin' the conscience button on you people/Where is the reason?"), and their track "Sisterssss" in support of polygamy,[49] are popular in the underground Muslim-Arab hip-hop scene. But Sons of Hagar have also not achieved mainstream exposure.

The Muslim rap crew that is gaining worldwide notoriety for its lyrical dexterity, stylistic appeal, and explicitly positive portrayal of Islam is the Denmark-based trio Outlandish. Made up of a Moroccan, a Pakistani, and a Honduran, Outlandish has topped the charts with hits including "Guantanamo" (the chorus: "And I got all my Moros here, Guantanamo") and "Aicha," a remake of Cheb Khaled's 1995 hit. The latter track, which saw heavy rotation on MTV Europe and climbed to fourth on the charts in Germany, has been hailed as the most positive depiction of Muslim women in a music video, with shots of pre-prayer ablution and veiled and unveiled Arab, South Asian, and African women. Rather than playing with the *haram*, Outlandish is about "keepin' it *halal* (licit)."

American hip-hop commentators note that political, cerebral rap may be popular in Europe, but if it cannot be "bling-blinged," or sexed up, it will not sell in the United States. A recent dispute between Simmons and a segment of the African-American Sunni community is illustrative. Though not a Muslim, Simmons has frequently declared his respect for Islam, and the Nation of Islam (NOI) in particular. "I grew up on Farrakhan," he said in one interview. "Where I grew up, there were dope fiends and black Muslims. If Muslims came by, you stood up straight."[50] He also tried to broker talks between the NOI and American Jewish organizations, denounced the invasion of Iraq, helped organize Musicians United to Win Without War, and is currently planning a Middle East youth peace summit. But when a recent issue of his *OneWorld* magazine ran a cover with female rapper Li'l Kim wearing a "burka-like garment over her face" and "lingerie from the neck down"—and in the same issue saying, "Fuck Afghanistan"—Najee Ali, director of the civil rights group Project Islamic Hope, demanded an apology to America's Muslims. As someone active in brokering truces in the hip-hop world, Ali cited his Islamic duty "to the people of hip-hop and humanity," and called on Simmons to apologize for the magazine cover and for the "pornographic female rapper" Foxy Brown, who in her song "Hot Spot," produced by the Simmons-founded Def Jam, says, "MCs wanna eat me but it's Ramadan."

The Li'l Kim incident instigated a discussion over other not-so-*halal* trends in Islamic hip-hop. The cover of *XXL* magazine showing rapper Nas holding a glass of cognac and wearing prayer beads around his neck outraged many Muslims. "Why he imitatin' the *kufar* (unbelievers, in Arabic) with the Hail Mary beads?!" fumed one blogger. Many Sunni Muslims have also criticized the style of some female Muslim hip-hoppers of wearing a headscarf (*hijab*) with midriff tops and the low-riding jeans popularized by Jennifer Lopez. These sartorially adventurous young Muslim women, known variously as "noochies" (Nubian hoochies), "*halal* honies," and "bodacious *bints*" (girls, in Arabic)—have provoked heated cyber-debates about freedom of expression, female modesty, and the future of Islam in America. "Our *deen* (religion, in Arabic) is not meant to be rocked!" says hip-hop journalist Adisa Banjoko, author of the forthcoming book *The Light from the East,* on Islamic influence in hip-hop. "I see these so-called Muslim sistas wearing a *hijab* and then a bustier, or a *hijab* with their belly button sticking out. You don't put on a *hijab* and try to rock it! Or these brothers wearing Allah tattoos, or big medallions with Allah's name—Allah is not to be bling-blinged!"[51]

Just as controversial are the Arabic calligraphy tattoos that women, even outside the hip-hop community, have taken to wearing. The words *halal, haram,* and *sharmuta* (whore in Arabic, but a term of endearment in certain circles these days) are tattooed on shoulders, thighs, or lower backs, and worn with bathing suit tops or hip-hugging jeans. Some of these *haram* trends in Islamic hip-hop are deliberate responses to orthodox or fundamentalist Islamic dress, like the "high-water pants" or "total *hijabs*" seen in some inner-city areas. Among young Muslim males, equally provocative are black t-shirts worn by some Shiite youth, which read in crimson, "Every Day Is Ashura, Every Day Is Karbala"—references to Shiite rituals commemorating the death of Imam Hussein in the seventh century and the Iraqi plain where he died in battle. Also troubling to some is the growing popularity of martial arts among urban Muslim youth, who say self-defense skills are necessary against gangsters and violent police. If many black Muslims in the 1960s were practicing syncretic forms of martial arts like "Kushite boxing," many of today's young male hip-hoppers are learning "Islamic wrestling." "The Prophet was a grappler," one enthusiast told *Middle East Report.* "The *hadith* (saying of the Prophet) teaches us to never hit the face of our opponent and that [Islamic] grappling allows you to win over an opponent without punching them and risking brain damage."

Russell Simmons has said that "the coolest stuff about American culture, be it language, dress, or attitude, comes from the underclass—always has and always will."[52] If so, then as Islam seeps into the American underclass and as Muslims populate the underclass in Europe, Islamic cultural elements will percolate upward into mainstream culture and society. For many American youth, Islamic hip-hop is their first encounter with Islam, and often leads them to struggle with issues of race, identity, and Western imperialism. As Bakari Kitwana has noted, "If asked about a specific political issue . . . many hip-hop generationers can easily recall the first time their awareness on that issue was raised by rap music."[53] In Europe, many North African youth are rediscovering Islam and becoming race-conscious through Five Percenter and NOI rap lyrics. For many white hip-hoppers in the United States, the sought-after "ghetto pass"—acceptance in the hip-hop community—comes only with conversion to Islam, which is seen as a rejection of being white. The white rapper Everlast, formerly Eric Schrody of House of Pain, claims that conversion to Islam and mosque attendance allow him to visit ghetto neighborhoods he could never enter as a non-Muslim white.[54] Curiously, Everlast's espousal of Islam caused static with the white rapper Eminem who accused him of becoming Muslim to deny that he is a "homosexual white rappin' Irish." One young white Latino youth explained the link between Islam and his street credibility as follows: "In the Bronx, looking like me, you don't get much respect. When I took the *shihada* (professed Islam), the brothers gave me respect, the white folk got nervous, even the police paid attention."[55]

Efforts are being made to direct the energy of Islamic hip-hop. In late July 2003, the First Annual Islamic Family Reunion and Muslims in Hip-Hop Conference and Concert was held in Orlando, Florida, with prominent imams from across the country leading three days of workshops on Muslim youth and stressing the importance of *deen*, family, schooling, and organizing. Activities included Islamic spelling bees, Islamic knowledge competitions, and performances by "positive lyricists" like Native Deen. The conference also established Hallal Entertainment, Inc. and helped launch the Islamic Crisis Emergency Response System, a Philadelphia-based organization which provides services to needy Muslim and non-Muslim families.[56] Fusing Islamic themes with the preeminent global youth culture, Islamic hip-hop has emerged as a powerful internationalist subculture for disaffected youth around the world.

"ROARING FROM THE EAST"

"The specter of a storm is haunting the Western world," wrote the black power poet Askia Muhammad Touré in 1965. "The Great Storm, the coming Black Revolution, is rolling like a tornado; roaring from the East; shaking the moorings of the earth as it passes through countries ruled by oppressive regimes. . . . Yes, all over this sullen planet, the multi-colored 'hordes' of undernourished millions are on the move like never before in human history."[57] Touré was pondering the appeal of "the East" to African-American youth in the aftermath of the 1955 Bandung conference. There, President Sukarno of Indonesia had told the representatives of twenty-nine African and Asian nations that they were united "by a common detestation of colonialism in whatever form it appears. We are united by a common detestation of racialism." Those were the days when Malcolm X met with Fidel Castro at the famed Teresa Hotel in Harlem, and when Malcolm, from his perspective of "Islamic internationalism," came to understand the civil rights movement as an instance of the struggle against imperialism, seeing the Vietnam war and the Mau Mau rebellion in Kenya as uprisings of the "darker races" and, like the African-American struggle, part of the "tidal wave" against Western imperialism.

Some commentators, pointing to the current anti-war and anti-globalization movement, have suggested that a new era of Afro-Asian-Latin solidarity may be in the offing. In the United States, the past two years has seen a political ferment and coalition-building between progressive groups—in particular between Arab and Muslim American groups and African-American groups—not seen since the 1960s when the Black Panthers and the Student Non-Violent Coordinating Committee declared solidarity with the PLO, which in turn declared solidarity with Native Americans. September 11 and the subsequent backlash have led many African-American leaders to stand with Muslim and Arab-Americans, not least because African-American Muslims are also targeted in the post–September 11 profiling and detention campaigns. Activists like Al Sharpton are mobilizing against the USA PATRIOT Act "because it is used to profile people of color" and "impacting Muslims everywhere, including Brooklyn and Harlem."[58]

Given the centrality of Islam and the Arab world to the war on terror, and the presence of *kaffiyyas* and (regrettably) bin Laden t-shirts at protests from Porto Alegre to Barcelona, it appears that the new Bandung may have a distinct Arab or Islamic cast. In the past two years, a number of Latin American leaders have called for "concrete action" to establish a Palestinian state. Castro has signed agreements of bilateral cooperation with Algeria and the United Arab Emirates, and continues to rail against "global apartheid" in general and "Israeli apartheid" in particular. Castro has also been accused of building ties with Iran and selling biotechnology in exchange for cheap oil. When he visited Iran in 2001, Castro spoke of his rapport with President Mohammad Khatami and reported that he "had the longest sleep of his life in Tehran." Most recently, he has been accused by the United States of jamming the satellite broadcasts of U.S.-based Iranian opposition groups.[59] Recent articles in right-leaning American newsmagazines claim to have discovered evidence that Venezuela is providing identity papers to suspicious numbers of people from Arab and South Asian "countries of interest" (as well as Colombians and Cubans). One article also features the claim of the former Venezuelan ambassador to Libya, Julio Cesar Pineda, to possess correspondence from Hugo Chavez stating his desire to "solidify" ties between Latin America and the Middle East—including use of the oil weapon.[60] Chavez challenged the reporters in question to produce "one single shred of evidence" for their claims.[61]

These stories of Cuban and Venezuelan ties to Middle Eastern radicals may be little more than partisan puffery, and Chavez's repeated calls for solidarity with the Arab world may be nothing more than petroleum diplomacy or an embattled leader's desperate plea for allies. Yet the Venezuelan leader's appeal to "Arab roots" is indicative of a trend in the West. Among Western subordinate groups and opposition movements that feel victimized or neglected by globalization, the Arabs are seen as bearing the brunt of the worldwide imperial assault in the era of the war on terror. As Western nationalists portray Islam as a threat to freedom and security, and launch wars to bring democracy to the Muslim world, "the multi-colored hordes" of the West are reaching for teachings and precedents (like Moorish Spain) in Islam that they hope will make the West more compassionate and free.

Islam is leaking into the West through conversion, migration, and media-driven cultural flows, and to many, the Islamic world is presenting a repertoire of alternative identities. As marginalized Westerners are finding inspiration in Islam, Muslims in the diaspora are inspired by the African-American experience. The cross-fertilization taking place among Islamic, black, and Latin cultures is creating fascinating trends and art forms. Many would argue that the fashion for Arabic tattoos, Allah chains, Orientalist soap operas, belly dancing, and hip scarves is just that—fashion. But as the Arab pride movement in Europe and Islamic hip-hop demonstrate, the vibrant cultural intermingling can have significant political implications. Cultural flows can spark forceful challenges to state policies, state-imposed identities, and the claims of Western nationalism.

For many of the minority convert communities and the diaspora Muslim communities, Islamic Spain has emerged as an anchor for their identity. Moorish Spain was a place where Islam was in and of the West, and inhabited a Golden Age before the rise of the genocidal, imperial West, a historical moment that disenchanted Westerners can share with Muslims. Neither Muslim nostalgia for nor Western Orientalist romanticism about Andalusia is new, but it is new for different subordinate groups in the West to be yearning for "return" to Moorish Spain's multiracialism. In this worldview, the year 1492 is a historical turning point. On Columbus Day in October, Chavez urged Latin Americans to boycott celebrations of the "discovery," saying that Columbus was "worse than Hitler." That the longing for pre-1492 history is shared by many minorities throughout the West is an indication of their lasting exclusion, and how the stridency of Western nationalism since September 11 has revived memories of centuries-old trauma. As one African-American activist put it recently, "The profiling and brutalizing of African-Americans didn't begin after September 11. It began in 1492."[62] In a similar spirit, after Moussaoui was arrested in the U.S. and granted the right to represent himself in court, one of his first demands was "the return of Spain to the Moors."

With African-American and Latino converts speaking of the tragedy of 1492, and with Muslim minorities in the West becoming increasingly race-conscious and inspired by black America ("*l'autre Amerique*"), the world is witnessing a new fusion between Islam and pan-Africanism. Today, however, this racialized Islamic internationalism contains elements of other cultures and diasporas as well. Islam is at the heart of an emerging global anti-hegemonic culture, which post-colonial critic Robert Young would say incarnates a "tricontinental counter-modernity" that combines diasporic and local cultural elements, and blends Arab, Islamic, black, and Hispanic factors to generate "a revolutionary black, Asian and Hispanic globalization, with its own dynamic counter-modernity . . . constructed in order to fight global imperialism."[63]

NOTES

This chapter originally appeared in *Middle East Report* (Winter 2003).

1. José Martí, "Espana en Melilla," in *Cuba: Letras*, vol. 2 (Havana: Edicion Trópico, 1938), 201.

2. Quoted in René Dépestre, "Carta de Cuba sobre el imperialismo de la mala fé," *Por la revolución, por la poesia* (Havana: Instituto del Libro, 1969), 93.

3. *El País*, April 17, 2002.

4. *Latin American Weekly Report*, October 4, 2003.

5. CUT National Plenary, Conjuntura Internacional e Nacional, Resolution 10, "Cresce a polaizaçáo politica a social em todo o mundo." Accessible online at http://cutnac web.cut.org.br/10plencut/conjtex5.htm.

6. Deutsche Presse–Agentur, April 3, 2003.

7. *New York Times*, October 22, 2001; *The Economist*, October 26, 2001. Imams and converts also made this claim in interviews carried out by Columbia University's Muslim Communities in New York Project on June 4 and June 16, 2003.

8. *Times* (London), January 7, 2002.

9. *Evening Standard*, March 15, 2002.

10. *Christian Science Monitor*, October 2, 2002. See also Yusuf Fernandez, "Spain Returning to Islam," *Islamic Horizons* (July–August 2002).

11. Olivier Roy, "Euro-Islam: The Jihad Within?" *The National Interest* (Spring 2003).

12. Arjun Appadurai, *Modernity at Large: Cultural Dimensions of Globalization* (Minneapolis: University of Minnesota Press, 1996), 15.

13. Cox News Service, August 11, 2002; see also Knight-Ridder News Service, June 28, 2003.

14. *El Diario–La Prensa*, October 6, 2001. See also *Islamic Horizons* (July–August 2002).

15. Interview with Rahim Ocasio, April 16, 1999.

16. Rahim Ocasio, "Latinos, the Invisible: Islam's Forgotten Multitude," *The Message*, August 1997.

17. Kimi Eisele, "The Multicultural Power of Soap Operas," Pacific News Service, November 25, 2002.

18. Interview with Rosa Margarita of *El Diario–La Prensa*, August 8, 2003. *El Clon*–inspired fashion can be viewed online at http://www.laoriginal.com/especiales.htm.

19. *Independent*, July 19, 2002.

20. Agence–France Presse, May 28, 2003.

21. Eisele.

22. Interview with Fernando Casado Caneque, September 8, 2003. Casado was referring to the conservative Aznar's effort to insert a reference to Europe's Christian roots in the European Union's constitution, a measure that has provoked the Spanish left and the regions of Andalusia and Catalonia who resent how the Aznar government has made Catholicism so central to the state's identity. See *El País*, July 28, 2003.

23. James Baldwin, *No Name in the Street* (New York: Dial Press, 1972), 41.

24. See, for instance, the interview with Ferida Belghoul in Alec Hargreaves, *Voices from the North African Community in France: Immigration and Identity in Beur Fiction* (Providence, R.I.: Berg Publishers, 1991), 126.

25. *Le Monde*, February 12, 2003.

26. *Jerusalem Report*, May 6, 2002.

27. See Loïc Wacquant, "Red Belt, Black Belt: Racial Division, Class Inequality and the State in the French Urban Periphery and the American Ghetto," in Enzo Mingione, ed., *Urban Poverty and the Underclass* (London: Blackwell Publishers, 1996).

28. *New York Times*, October 16, 2001.

29. *Weekly Standard*, July 15, 2002.

30. *Times* (London), September 29, 2001.

31. Abd al-Samad Moussaoui, *Zacarias, My Brother: The Making of a Terrorist* (New York: Seven Stories Press, 2003), 129.

32. *Independent*, April 3, 2003.

33. See Paul Silverstein, "Why Are We Waiting to Start the Fire? French Gangsta Rap and the Critique of State Capitalism," in Alain-Philippe Durand, ed., *Black, Blanc, Beur: Rap Music and Hip-Hop Culture in the Francophone World* (Lanham, Md.: Scarecrow Press, 2002).

34. *Le Figaro*, June 17, 2003; *Le Monde*, March 11, 2003.

35. *Le Monde*, September 27, 2001.

36. *L'Expansion*, June 11, 2003.

37. Independent Race and Refugee News Network, April 1, 2001.

38. The group's manifesto is online at http://infosuds.free.fr/082001/enquete_bc.htm. I am grateful to Paul Silverstein for this point.

39. Interview with 3eme Oeil and DJ Rebel, Bronx, New York, July 24, 2003.

40. *Jerusalem Report*, May 6, 2002.

41. *L'Express*, March 27, 2003.

42. David Lepoutre, *Coeur de banlieue: Codes, rites et langages* (Paris: O. Jacob, 1997).

43. *Le Figaro*, June 3, 2000.

44. The Spanish slur "Moro" has long been a term of endearment in Morocco and in the Moroccan diaspora—the Arabic adaptation is *moro khal al-ras* (black-headed Moor).

45. I am grateful to Zaheer Ali for this point.

46. Interview with Napoleon, March 22, 2004, New York. Tupac Shakur's former companion Napoleon, a Muslim convert who will be releasing a CD titled *Have Mercy* featuring a collaboration with the Pakistani-American crew The Aman Brothers, speaks about this allegation in an interview with the Tupac fan site HitEmUp.com, published on April 16, 2003. Accessible online at http://www.hitemup.com/interviews/napoleon-part1.html#Bush.

47. "Islamic rappers' message of terror," *The Observer* , February 8, 2004.

48. *Washington Times*, November 13, 2002.

49. When told that polygamy is illegal in the United States, Allahz Sword responded, "A lot of rappers out there talk about pimpin'—is that good? . . . I'm just talking about part of my religion." *Seattle Post-Intelligencer*, February 17, 2003.

50. Hisham Aidi, "'Building a New America': A Conversation with Russell Simmons," Africana.com, February 5, 2002.

51. Personal communication with author, August 4, 2003.

52. Quoted in John McWhorter, "How Hip-Hop Holds Blacks Back," *City Journal*, Summer 2003.

53. Bakari Kitwana, "The Hip-Hop Artist and the Racial Mountain," *Souls,* Vol. 5, No. 1 (Winter 2003): 55.

54. Interview with Adisa Banjoko, "Everlast: Taking Islam One Day at a Time," July 12, 1999. The interview is accessible online at http://thetruereligion.org/everlast.htm.

55. Interview with Columbia's Muslim Communities of New York Project, June 16, 2003 (converts focus group).

56. Sister Kalima A-Quddus, "Verily This Is a Single Ummah," *MuslimsInHipHop Newsletter,* August 7, 2003.

57. Quoted in Robin Kelley, *Freedom Dreams: The Black Radical Imagination* (Boston: Beacon Press, 2002), 60.

58. *Village Voice,* December 24, 2002.

59. *Financial Times,* July 21, 2003.

60. See Martin Arostegui, "From Venezuela, a Counterplot," *Insight on the News,* March 4, 2003, and "Terror Close to Home," *US News and World Report,* October 6, 2003.

61. Agence–France Presse, October 2, 2003.

62. Interview with Columbia's Muslim Communities of New York Project, July 21, 2003 (focus group for Muslims in NYPD and Fire Department).

63. Robert Young, *Postcolonialism: An Historical Introduction* (London: Blackwell Publishers, 2001), 2.

9. The Responsibility of the Critical Black Studies Scholar

Farah Jasmine Griffin

Eight Lessons from the Black Front: A Primer

What can the history and culture of black people in the United States teach us in these confusing and uncertain times? How can it speak to those who are angered and hurt by the tragic and inhumane loss of life that occurred on September 11? What insight does it provide for those who want to understand the impulses behind those events? Though interrogating this history cannot be a substitute for focusing on United States relations to countries in the Middle East, it can shed light on the best and worst of the nation, helping Americans to have a more multidimensional sense of their country. After all, U.S. foreign and domestic policies inform and influence each other. This is something that American citizens of all ethnic and racial backgrounds often forget. The face that this country has shown outside of its national boundaries is unfamiliar to many Americans, but certainly not to black Americans. Their history can provide undeniable evidence of our country at its worst and at its best; this country desperately needs a vision of both as we try to come to terms with the future.

What valuable lessons do black American history and culture teach us?

1. It is a history of a people who have always had to look beyond national borders for allies in their struggle to be free. This history gives us numerous examples of attempts to establish allies outside of the U.S. who would be sympathetic to and exert international pressure upon the forces that oppress us at home. Consequently, it teaches that we share a great deal in common with those beyond our borders who have suffered from inhumane policies of their own governments, especially if those governments are backed by the U.S. For this reason, many black American political

movements and organizations support the creation of a Palestinian state and were at the forefront of the fight against South African apartheid. But this did not begin in the twenty-first century. This sense of what historian Robin Kelley terms "black internationalism" is evident in the efforts of an abolitionist like Frederick Douglass, an antilynching activist like Ida B. Wells in England, Malcolm X in Ghana and Mecca, and the Black Panther Party in China or Cuba.

2. The historical experience of blacks in the United States teaches us to question who the government and the media identify as enemies. One need only recall Mike Wallace's interview with Malcolm X in the 1959 television exposé, "The Hate That Hate Produced." There is always more to the story than what we get from government press conferences or network news analysis. It is for that reason that black America has always had its own alternative press that seeks to offer the "other side" of the story.

3. Yet African-American history also teaches us to be careful of uncritically celebrating those who declare war on the U.S. The Timothy McVeighs and Adolph Hitlers of the world considered the U.S. government an enemy, but they were certainly no friends of black America. The lesson is to make distinctions between potential Hitlers and potential Che Guevaras.

4. History teaches us to look for and sympathize with the invisible victims of national tragedies, because we have so often been, and continue to be, invisible. Take, for example, the thousands of undocumented workers who were killed in the World Trade Center attacks. Our past teaches us to celebrate the heroism of the firefighters and police officers who lost their lives trying to save others, while remaining cognizant of the structural reasons for the lack of racial diversity among the heroes.

5. The history of the black freedom struggle in the United States reveals the way one group of people can enjoy economic and political privilege built on the denial of basic rights to other groups. It demonstrates the way that the privileged can maintain a willed innocence and naiveté about their complicity in the suffering of others. It also teaches us that efforts to establish independence and self-determination are often met with white resentment and state-sanctioned violence. Ida Wells's economic analysis of lynching and the destruction of black businesses, property, churches, and schools from Tulsa to Atlanta offers cogent examples of this.

6. History shows how the unchecked power of the state can pose a danger from within that is as great as terrorism from without. The Red Scare of the early twentieth century and the FBI's COINTELPRO of the 1960s and 1970s are but two instances of this. To those who are the most recent victims of American racism in the form of racial, ethnic, and religious profiling, this history would say that racism is endemic to this society. It is the place to which it automatically returns; racism is always there, ready to unleash its ugly wrath. This is a lesson for those who have wanted to distance themselves from black people as a way of being accepted, and also for black Americans who feel a sense of "I feel no sympathy for you—now you understand what we have gone through." This history says that both of these— the unchecked power of the state to survey, confine, and discipline persons thought

to be suspicious and tolerance of racial and ethnic prejudice aimed at others—are conditions we ought to be familiar with and unwilling to accept.

7. Another lesson is that black and poor Americans are always the least shocked by those things that seem to rattle the rest of the country, but are ultimately among those who will suffer the most from such events.

8. History also tells the story of a culture of resistance, struggle, and profound beauty born of the uncertainty of being black in the United States. This culture not only serves as a source of comfort when one is living in dangerous times, but also nurtures a will to be free and a vision of hope and possibility in the face of obstacles that seem insurmountable. It is a culture that does not take safety for granted, but accepts the conditions of danger and uncertainty and creates, not in spite of, but because of, them. It is a culture that privileges risk taking and a radical democratic mode of being. Listen to the lyrics of the spirituals as they recognize humanity at its most vulnerable and then democratize access to the divine. And because they have multiple levels of meaning, they insist on democracy in the here and now as well. This culture creates anew as it builds on challenges, and re-envisions the past. This is why quotation is important to jazz improvisation, sampling to hip-hop. It is a culture that documents and nurtures the movements that have challenged the U.S. to live up to its ideals and has most strongly challenged the citizens of this country to live up to a higher standard of humanity. Now, more than ever, we need to be reminded of those ideals and of that humanity, and that this country has no monopoly on either.

The history of African Americans is part and parcel of the history of the United States at large. It belongs to all of us. Its lessons are a gift born of social struggle and social change.

．

~

HAZEL V. CARBY

Aftermath

Although I have been writing and thinking about geographies of race and gender in the United Kingdom, I find it deeply disconcerting to see how rapidly many around me have adapted to a new calendar to govern their lives. They have found a way to measure time and a means by which to locate the body in relation to the world that existed before and the world that existed after September 11, 2001. By this new calendar, this way of measuring and locating the self, I do not mean to conjure the triggers for memory and positioning of the type that articulates itself as "I will never forget where I was and what I was doing when President Kennedy was shot," or, "when British troops were first sent to Northern Ireland." Rather, what I want to name, to bring into focus, is a seismic shift in public and private discourse about the relation of the self to the other, of friend to foe, of home to foreigner, that has occurred within the borders of the United States since September 11. As I write, bodies seem to be in suspended relation to each other while concepts of citizen and subject are renegotiated.

In this discursive crisis the United States, as a national body politic, is being reconfigured as "home," the exact nature of that home having yet to be determined. What has been established by the Bush Administration through its invention of the Office of Homeland Security and confirmed by the media, particularly the *New York Times* and CNN, is that the nation is a home that needs to be defended not only from an external but also from an internal threat: Within the confines of "home," its inhabitants are subject to a rapid surveillance of their legitimacy, a process overdetermined by the language and practices of racialization.

There is a vast disjunction between the everyday familiarity with the language of globalization and the utter incomprehension that the foreign policies of the United States, which cause death and destruction on a daily level abroad, have any effect at "home." Because we have just now experienced these effects, we are, as President Bush initially characterized it, on a "crusade." To protect and preserve freedom, freedom must be curtailed for some; perhaps for many it will be destroyed.

The United States is also an empire. The world's most powerful nation has enormous reach: The home has a back garden, which justifies the overthrow of democratically elected presidents of foreign countries and the invasion of Grenada; the home has international interests, which justifies the maintenance of United States troops near the oil fields in Saudi Arabia; and so it goes. When Madeleine Albright was asked on national television what she had to say about the deaths of 500,000 Iraqi children, deaths directly attributable to U.S. sanctions, she responded in the august tones of a U.S. Secretary of State that it was "a very hard choice," but "we think the price is worth it." The political calculation and weighing of bodies are absolutely central to foreign policy and the defense of the homeland. Arundhati Roy has recently called this thinking "the sophistry and fastidious algebra of infinite justice." She asks, "How many dead Iraqis will it take to make the world a better place? How many dead Afghans for every dead American? How many dead moja-hedin for each dead investment banker?"[1]

The moment of crisis—as I write, it is difficult to imagine when this histori-cal moment will end—is riven with contradiction. "Home" is full of multiple bod-ies seemingly endlessly divided, in which neighbor can be, has been, cast as potential enemy. Although these divisions appear to be absolutely transparent, exactly who should be blessed by God as opposed to subjected to his wrath (courtesy of the U.S. military), exactly who is to be unified with whom, exactly who should be embraced and comforted while others are spat upon, assaulted, even murdered, is not in fact clear. It is at this precise moment of crisis and confusion that the racialized politics of the body plays out its most deadly logic at home and abroad.

But racialization is not the only lethal weapon at work. For example, the persecution of gays and lesbians in the military has been suspended so they may go and fight for us—are "they" to be fully embraced within the confines of national domesticity permanently or merely temporarily? While the bodies of gays and lesbians are deemed suitable to be launched against the enemy, wherever it may be, their blood, which will obviously be shed in such confrontation, is not classified as suitable to be donated to the Red Cross.

We are deeply divided despite the endless sea of Stars and Stripes that hang from the porches of my neighbors, which I can see from the window of my study and out of the corner of my eye as I write in my local coffee shop. The Stars and Stripes flutter from pickup trucks, minivans, and SUVs, the favored vehicles of the small New England town in which I now live—palpable evidence, supposedly, of their drivers' love for, and preparedness to defend, this homeland, as they simultaneously belch their carbons into the atmosphere in complete disregard of the consequences. (In 2001, in Connecticut, there have already been twice as many days of "bad air" as there were in 2000.)[2] Bodies have to breathe, but, hey, we can't put limits on freedom, even if asthma is killing our children! I guess the principle at work is that we are allowed to kill our own children in order to preserve our right to pollute, as long as others don't threaten their lives. And now we march off to kill the "others" in defense of these freedoms.

Stars and Stripes, with declarations that "we will prevail" and "God Bless America," have been hastily but carefully drawn on blankets and draped over the bridges of I-95, under which I drive every morning. Stars and Stripes, cut from the pages of a local newspaper, are glued to the front of the desk of my administrative assistant as a wall of defiance should any terrorist enter our departmental office. Many of us in our department could be racially profiled at a glance as potential terrorists, with our brown skins, dark hair and eyes: We must be careful about the way we dress. My flag-waving neighbors (white) are very satisfied that they live in almost total segregation from the residents of New Haven (black), let alone New York City, a veritable Sodom and Gomorrah that very few ever visit. I do not mean that their outpouring of grief for New York is not genuine, but I do mean that One Nation under God cannot, must not, be taken for granted as an obvious historical entity. On the contrary, it is being ideologically constructed anew: It is being called into being every day; a homogeneity is being forged in front of our very eyes. It is being shaped by fear; it is being heralded by a blind jingoistic fantasy; and it is being fueled by racial thinking. Our new homeland threatens to look nothing like the international, cosmopolitan, multicultural, and multiethnic urban community that was destroyed along with the World Trade Center towers.

Meanwhile, in Britain, as gung-ho Tony Blair treads the globe rallying folks to the American cause, October is Black History Month, and the BBC Radio 4 ferrets me out of exile to talk about whether C. L. R. James should be regarded as an Uncle Tom!

NOTES

1. Arundhati Roy, "The Algebra of Infinite Justice," www.guardian.co.uk/Archive/Article/0,4273,4266289,00.html.

2. As reported on NPR, October 3, 2001, there were 13 days of bad air in 2000. There have already been 25 days of air designated as bad as of October 1, 2001.

❧

KATHLEEN NEAL CLEAVER

And the Beat Goes On: Challenges Facing Black Intellectuals

Black intellectuals these days face assaults—some subtle, others dramatic—to their sense of purpose. The tumult that turned being black into an admirable quality has subsided. The fervent sense of connection white supremacists used to impose on our community has cooled. Nearly one-third of African Americans now earn middle-class incomes, accelerating class fragmentation. An array of definitions for people simply called *black* a generation ago have popped up, and either by our own choice or by unsympathetic observers, we are now called *mainstream, afrocentric, incognegro,*[1] *oreo, biracial, conservative, radical, person of color,* or *member of the hip-hop nation.* Despite the economic and legal uplift of millions, stigmas rooted in slavery have not been eradicated, nor has racist terrorism ended. Scholars still have minimal input into the terms on which universities decide to include us; once we arrive, our presence is rarely lauded as a valuable intellectual addition.

The American glorification of personal autonomy, individual achievement, and private property gives black intellectuals a hard row to hoe. Many of our families devised strategies for coping with the segregated outside world that emphasized spirituality, artistic or athletic ability, and communal solidarity. Thus, when we engage in the interpretive work our discipline demands, some African-American intellectuals feel torn between competing value systems. Does inclusion require that we conform to alienating standards, or can adhering to ingrained community values aid the black intellectual in carrying out his or her responsibilities?

We face a pattern of difficulties—some personal, some systemic—that resembles conflicts our mentors and colleagues suffered in the past. Typically, our parents or grandparents were barred from prestigious universities, but today public policy dictates that we be accepted, if not welcomed. For example, I frequently heard the late Judge Leon Higginbotham, for whom I clerked at the federal courthouse in

Philadelphia, describe an indelibly painful incident. In the 1950s, after he'd won the Moot Court competition at Yale Law School—where he was one of the three black students—he was pained to see the disdain a white judge showed his working-class black parents, who had traveled from New Jersey to witness the ceremony honoring their son.

Today, such contempt may be less routine. Yet even while serving on the nation's highest court, Supreme Court Justice Clarence Thomas has felt its sting: A white woman getting out of a taxi in front of a hotel entrance where he happened to be standing once asked him to pick up her luggage. And Alice Walker revealed her internal conflict when she wondered about a fancy university invitation she had received: If I come, can I bring my mother?

My own mother, who met my father when they were graduate students at the University of Michigan during the 1930s, had been active in radical protest movements against segregation. She had participated in the Southern Negro Youth Congress from its inception, and my father was engaged in the NAACP's campaign to end the all-white primary election process in Texas, among other struggles. My parents created an intellectual environment at home that encouraged me to express myself and laid a foundation for my later demands that the larger community around us should respect our people's extraordinary history of accomplishment and struggle. During the late 1940s and early 1950s, my father was a sociologist who directed the Rural Life Council at Tuskegee Institute. This meant I lived within a sheltered black society molded by Booker T. Washington and George Washington Carver. Stacked on my father's shelves at home were books such as *The Marginal Man, The New Class, Das Kapital,* and *Pan-Africanism or Communism.* Guests who visited us frequently were men and women who taught in college, worked for the NAACP, practiced medicine, designed buildings, or composed music. The novelist Albert Murray lived around the corner, although I only thought of him as "Mikey's father." Years later, I met the renowned historian John Hope Franklin, at the Afro-American Cultural Center when I was a student at Yale, and he surprised me when we were introduced. He shook my hand, smiled at me in his paternal way, and told me softly, "I've known you since you were a baby. Your father and I taught at North Carolina State together."

Although such a childhood may sound atypical, it was by no means unique, particularly for that impatient generation of black college students who initiated the direct action and black consciousness movements in the Deep South. Emboldened by parents or teachers who had fought against legalized, race-based subjugation policies, we "radical" activists continued whacking out terrain where intellectuals who embodied our community's values could operate more freely. Radical artists and writers who advocated a new black consciousness during the era known as the Harlem Renaissance, the pathbreaking intellectual W. E. B. Du Bois, who laid the groundwork for our claims to self-determination, and black freedom fighters all the way back to David Walker and his fugitive slave contemporaries—all were our antecedents.

CONFRONTING INTELLECTUAL DISTORTIONS

Although we feel proud about such intellectual ancestors and stand ready to kick down walls that bar such scholarship from the paradigms recognized by our disciplines, enthusiasm alone is not sufficient. We face deeply ingrained convictions within authoritative circles that deny legitimacy—or even existence—to the work of these ancestors. Generation after generation of black intellectuals have fought to replace official interpretations that undermine our integrity as a people—renovated versions of patently bogus claims such as "Africa has no history" or "Blacks are inferior to whites because their brains are smaller"—with more coherent accounts. The fracas over Charles Murray's *The Bell Curve* demonstrates how such themes are still being recycled. Every one of us can describe some confrontation we've had with distorted scholarship or twisted intellectual conclusions that demean blacks. Several years ago, I encountered such distortion at an innovative education seminar for judges in Alabama.

Dale Segrest, a respected circuit court judge deeply concerned with enhancing pluralism within a racist structure, invited me to join him in teaching a seminar. The weekend program he'd designed was based on a law and literature model and had received official support from the Alabama Judicial Council for satisfying the state's licensing requirements. Judge Segrest, who is white, held the course at Tuskegee University, a college within his jurisdiction that he believed few white judges had ever visited. He assigned readings that introduced the works of W. E. B. Du Bois and Booker T. Washington, scholars he was certain they had not read. During one class discussion, Judge Segrest stunned me when he dismissed the prodigious intellectual work of Du Bois, asking me, "Booker T. Washington left this marvelous institution as his legacy, but what legacy did Du Bois leave?" The judge clearly recognized the material contribution that Washington had made to black advancement, but his stunted appreciation for the intellectual contributions of one of the twentieth century's greatest scholars was amazing. I thought for a moment, then replied that the legacy Du Bois left was the Civil Rights Movement, which implemented ideas he had advocated decades earlier.

Yet, when I say "Civil Rights Movement" I know that a white Alabama judge scarcely fathoms what I want to convey. The term has now become widely synonymous with the nonviolent assimilation of black people into American society. It glosses over, however, the complexity of that decades-long struggle, when radically divergent approaches and goals competed for allegiance. The words *civil rights* now have a misleading illusion of simplicity that conceals the alternative conceptions of social change that animated those who fought to end racial segregation during the 1960s.

One of the highly significant issues that gets overlooked is the debate that raged over the future direction of black institutions, such as schools. Should they be strengthened? Should the segregationists' attempts to provide so-called equal funding to maintain their separateness be encouraged? Or should we seek integration into white institutions to better serve our social and economic development?

The nature of movement leadership, particularly in local communities, is another area that is rarely considered. Instead of recognizing that powerful community upsurges were mobilized by laypeople, women, schoolteachers, union organizers, veterans, and intellectuals, conventional scholars have consecrated Martin Luther King, Jr., as the commander in chief, portraying all others as his subordinates. In reality, civil rights campaigns were frequently led by ministers, who enjoyed financial independence from local whites; in my hometown, a sociology professor named Dr. Charles Gomillion defined the struggle. He formed the Tuskegee Improvement Association, which concentrated on achieving economic and political power for black residents, deploying boycotts, lawsuits, and voter registration drives as the dominant means of attacking segregation. As a teenager, I identified with the nonviolent protests I witnessed, joined the boycotts, and walked door-to-door registering voters. But when I heard Stokely Carmichael explain that "integration was just a subterfuge for white supremacy," I was instantly converted to Black Power. What could be more clear than his explanation that black people needed the political power to determine our own destiny?

Using the term *civil rights* to represent the entire black struggle against oppression usually minimizes the anti-imperialist liberation movement that erupted in the wake of the call for Black Power. Within weeks of Carmichael's declaration during the summer of 1966, I joined the loosely woven organization he chaired called the Student Nonviolent Coordinating Committee. By then, SNCC was legendary. But, six years earlier, when James Forman, who would become the organization's first executive director, was initially considering whether to work with them, he hesitated to cast his lot with such a disorderly bunch of students. Certain qualities he saw in them, however, swayed his decision to join them. He wrote that they possessed "the energy, the talent, the brain power, the determination and the courage to change certain values in this country. One of the most important values to be changed," he said, "was that a person should work for money. These students were saying that they were more concerned with human rights than with money. They were not driven by the profit motive that dominates the society . . . and they were willing to demonstrate this with their lives. I felt that if this idea could grow among young Black people, we would usher in revolutionary change."[2] That same quality, that potential for revolution, drew me into their ranks as well.

Further, the phrase *civil rights* almost always diminishes a fundamental truth that the liberation movement recognized: Winning the war for human dignity and political equality against white supremacists would not occur without widespread violence, both defensive and aggressive. I do not believe it is an accident that this simplistic conception of the modern civil rights struggle—which in Alabama and Georgia was initiated as a clear demand for *human rights*—has become entrenched. As George Orwell observed in his novel, *1984*, when the past can be erased, the lie becomes truth.[3] America's racial oppression provides lush soil for the cultivation of lies that replace black reality and continually inspires black intellectuals to wrest control over the definition and articulation of our past and present.

BLACK DILUTED

Back when *Negro* was the conventional designation for descendants of Africans, identifying as *black* placed you in opposition to standard operating procedure within racist U.S.A. *black* then conveyed a distinct commitment to political, cultural, and economic self-determination. We who sought black liberation initiated or continued the push for academic recognition of our history and culture, brought about black studies programs through radical protest actions, promoted the Black Arts Movement, insisted upon the values of our heritage, supported African independence struggles, and challenged American racist domination in political, economic, and military spheres, including refusing to fight in the Vietnam War. Writers like LeRoi Jones, who later became Amiri Baraka, Ed Bullins, Sonia Sanchez, Eldridge Cleaver, and Alice Walker gave voice to the emerging black consciousness that led to the demise of *Negro*, fatally injured by the ideological beating delivered by Malcolm X. Those scholars, playwrights, artists, writers, and political leaders who were devoted to transforming the oppressive conditions we faced at the time began to call ourselves black scholars, black writers, and black leaders.

It is not clear that the present understanding of *black* includes a similar commitment to radical transformation. I think that any attempt to articulate the place of the black intellectual in contemporary public life requires taking changed conditions into consideration. Social dislocations left in the wake of the Vietnam War and the upheavals of the 1960s have rearranged the nature of the black/white separation and opened our communities to more sophisticated intervention by white institutions than segregation ever allowed. And although the United States is presently demographically turning into a multicultural society, ideologically it seems gripped by a reactionary return to Cold War hostility and witch hunts. Fundamentalist Christianity and neofascist mobilization resurfaced in mainstream politics, fueling high-visibility campaigns against affirmative action, immigration reform, and liberal policies of criminal justice years before the hysteria unleashed by the war on terrorism shaped public policies.

A proliferation of African-American scholars and writers has occurred during this period, and they have gained a level of visibility unthinkable merely three decades ago. But as Cornel West has noted, the "rightward intellectual drift" of American life has reconstituted a "hostile climate for the making of Black intellectuals," accompanied as it has been by the "capitulation of a significant segment of former left-liberals to new-style conservatism and old-style imperialism."[4] It seems that the concomitant success of elite racial integration, or the selective inclusion of blacks within dominant political, economic, cultural, and educational institutions, and the failure to strengthen independent black institutions that formerly nourished our scholars and writers have an ironic consequence. Despite the increase in numbers, prestige, and financial security, the new black intellectual appears to exert far less influence on public life than the old. Where are our Adam Clayton Powells, Martin Luther Kings, or Ida B. Wellses? Seeing a black intellectual like Clarence Thomas co-opted to implement state policies that enhance racist domination makes it obvious that we can no longer equate *black* with the commitment to our long-standing and still-relevant demand for self determination it used to signal. The remark I heard veteran SNCC leader Courtland Cox make sums it up: "Blackness," he said, "is necessary, but not sufficient."

Joining SNCC led me directly to the Black Panther Party for Self-Defense, where in 1967 I helped organize the urgent campaign to prevent Huey Newton's execution on charges of murdering an Oakland policeman. The revolutionaries I joined repudiated the liberal idea that our people were treated as so-called second-class citizens. Instead, Panthers asserted that the centuries of slavery and racial segregation we had endured were a form of domestic colonialism. We studied the ideological, psychological, political, and military methods of liberation young insurgents were deploying around the world and developed an analysis of how imperialism constrained our freedom. We saw clearly that our history, economic dependence, and race collided, and we did not fight to become "first-class citizens." Like Africans, Asians, and Latin Americans ejecting imperialists from their lands, we too sought liberation and self-determination. We too sought to transform racist domination into collective freedom.

Frantz Fanon's seminal work *The Wretched of the Earth*, which examined Algeria's war of independence from France, profoundly influenced us.[5] The resemblance between the colonized Africa Fanon wrote about and the conditions blacks lived under in America was striking. "The colonial world," he wrote, "is a world cut in two. . . . The zone where the natives live is not complementary to the zone inhabited by the settlers. . . . The settlers' town . . . is full of white people." But the "town belonging to the colonial people, or at least the native town, the Negro village, . . . the reservation, is a place of ill fame . . . a hungry town . . . wallowing in the mire."[6] Fanon explained that "the violence which has ruled over the ordering of the colonial world . . . that same violence will be reclaimed and taken over by the native as he surges into forbidden quarters. To wreck the colonial world is henceforth . . . a picture of action, which is . . . clear, very easy to understand. . . ."[7] We easily identified with Fanon's analysis of how violence and racism intertwined in the colonial scheme and with his psychological insight into the way revolutionary violence aided the colonized in reclaiming the dignity that white racism denied.

In America, the colonial status of blacks is so obscured by the rhetoric of democracy, it took me literally decades to understand how growing up in Alabama was akin to being colonized. After suffering defeat in the Civil War, the former headquarters of the Confederacy turned into a virtual colony of the larger industrializing United States. The political and social conditions of my segregated Alabama childhood were like those in semirural colonial regions, where independence movements erupted during the 1960s just as they did in Alabama. Now, minus its bizarre apartheid, the state is integrated into modern, corporate America, and national government policy outlaws the formal aspects of institutionalized racism there and across the United States. Does that make black people just like everybody else?

Did the abolition of segregation cancel the effects of how black people obtained citizenship? Constitutional amendments that were passed after the Civil

War conferred citizenship upon the descendants of Africans who, only a decade earlier, were deemed by the Supreme Court to have "no rights a white man was bound to respect." Do these rights, which now have to be respected, give us full-fledged membership in the democratic society—or is our situation now more complex?

I see our current status as parallel to the ceremonial end of direct colonial rule in Africa, which was quickly replaced by indirect, or neocolonial, control. Formal independence was granted, the colony gained a new name and hoisted a new flag, but the old imperial master continued to dominate the people's economic and military destiny. Similarly, the United States now tolerates black identity—the post office has even issued a Kwanzaa stamp—and allows our participation in conventional politics to expand dramatically, but little economic or military self-determination is in evidence.

A DUAL RESPONSIBILITY

The intellectual in the contemporary African-American community inherits, I think, a dual responsibility. Not only must we carry out the interpretive critical tasks for which years of training have prepared us, but we must also resist the insistent strategies that encourage black people to serve the interests of the dominant society without any reciprocal concern for their well-being. I am fully aware that this politicized component of the intellectual project is not—or is no longer—routinely acknowledged as the black intellectual's concern. The current climate of reaction encourages all scholars connected with an educational institution to cultivate ignorance of the affairs of the everyday world if they want the university's stamp of approval, a position the scholar Edward Said identifies as one of "non-interference."[8] This, he asserts, helps to conceal the interlocking hierarchies of power within government, corporations, and the academy, a fact further obscured by the rigid specialization and disciplinary separation maintained within universities. Instead of remaining silent on questions of social, economic, and foreign policy, Said calls for intellectuals to practice "interference"—to cross boundaries, confront obstacles, and break out of disciplinary ghettos.[9] Few black students being molded into scholars at major universities during the current era of retreat from democracy hear such advice. Elite institutions have modified their practices of inclusion, seeking faculty and students whom they consider non-threatening to their status quo. Unlike the early years of pell-mell incorporation of blacks, such institutions now carefully screen non-white applicants, choosing fewer American-born blacks and more foreign-born and first-generation students of African descent, favoring those students who attended private schools over the graduates of public schools. These policies contribute to the low level of activism evident on campuses and further the decline in black students' political awareness. A new crop of black intellectuals is being cultivated in places where students rarely identify with the aspirations of ordinary black folk. More often than not, students quietly acquiesce in the elite standing the institution confers upon them, no longer giving voice to any collective demands to place the enormous resources such schools command at the service of their impoverished brothers and sisters.

But to repudiate a social debt to the beleaguered community whose sacrifices and triumphs have shattered barriers to our individual advance leaves the intellectual, in my opinion, diminished and internally unbalanced. I think the frustration of sustaining that position ultimately weakens the authenticity of one's critical work. The responsibility facing those who have chosen the profession of intellectual work is not merely personal, but arises from the cultural, historical, and ethical context in which we function, whether or not we acknowledge it.

I was fortunate to receive a superb education beginning in my earliest years. The first school I attended was Children's House, an elementary school founded during the nineteenth century by Booker T. Washington the year after he established Tuskegee Institute. As a small child, I was taught by committed black women who shared my tight-knit southern black community and who steadfastly expected that their students would excel. Booker T. Washington succinctly expressed the purpose that animated that elementary school: "The object of all education, no matter what it is called, should be to fit the individual to articulate what he has learned in the schoolroom into the active everyday community in which he lives." After having studied at the best universities in the United States, I find that concept continues to animate my conduct. I think that is because Washington's idea draws upon the resilient force—the force of creativity—that enabled the descendants of African captives to transcend the beastly conditions they faced.

Our collective imagination has generated a vibrant culture interweaving old with new threads, coloring what we found in the New World with our African cultural palette. Our ancestors turned suffering into music, agony into stories, pain into dance, and setbacks into motivation. Writing about the dual status that has always plagued blacks, Eldridge Cleaver pointed out that being "both slave and Christian, . . . both free and segregated, . . . both integrated and colonized, . . . in the past has worked to our disadvantage."[10] As a revolutionary, however, Cleaver understood that the duality that used to keep us "running around in circles" would be turned "to our advantage, in the manner that we have turned Blackness from a disadvantage to a rallying point of advantage."[11] We have that brilliant legacy to encourage us.

Yet the practical conditions of existence that make black intellectuals fortunate enough to secure university positions underscore the necessity to strike a balance between loyalty to the institution and loyalty to "the race." Emphasizing the second at the expense of the first guarantees marginalization within what is an already marginalized professional life; but to displace one's identity to better serve an institution is a prescription for emotional disaster. This predicament, according to Cornel West, is scarcely of the black intellectual's own choosing, but it arises from an objective condition that isolates from both the main currents of American society and the black community the person who devotes his or her life to meticulous, critical mental tasks.[12] A truncated conception of intellectual work leaves most black folk unaware of what relevance such endeavors have for their lives, or for the world at large, and reinforces the cultural stereotype of the intellectual as insignificant. West observes that this marginalization pushes most black intellectuals into one of two camps: those he calls "successful," usually distant from and condescending toward the black community, dedicated to the prevailing bourgeois standards, or the "unsuccessful," who remain trapped within the parochial discourse of African-American life.[13] The committed few who transcend this predicament follow a different path and, in turn, they win respect from the black community. Their fundamental engagement with African-American political or cultural life, and their extraordinary talent, enable them to soar past limitations that hamper their contemporaries. To enable more to follow that path, intellectuals need to build a substantial network for each other where they can find support for their research and publication and establish means of remaining in close communication.

The reality is that African Americans have so enriched the humanities, social sciences, and arts that our culture has given the United States its international signature. Unforeseen consequences of the barbaric forced migration that dragged millions of Africans across the Atlantic now link Europe with Africa and the New World. The seeds of that diaspora flung across the continents have borne fruit and nourished a pivotal relationship of the African-American intellectual to the emerging global civilization.

CLARIFYING THE INTELLECTUAL'S ROLE

What role does the black intellectual play in public life? What *could* that role become? I suggest three areas to be examined: 1) Who constitutes the intellectual's constituency; 2) from where does he or she derive authority; and 3) what rewards can be expected for the creative or critical intellectual endeavor? The answers, of course, will not be uniform, but the range of answers will illuminate the variety of public roles black intellectuals play and focus attention on ways to enhance the significance of our work in the twenty-first century.

Let me turn first to the question of constituency. This is a troubling one for many black intellectuals who succumb to pressures to protect their institutional positions, but who divert their energies away from the concerns dearest to their hearts. My intellectual work did not start within the confines of the academy, but started when I was engaged in the fight for black liberation, so I was not compelled to recognize any claims on what I wrote until much later in life. I published articles, delivered speeches, participated in debates, spoke at demonstrations, took part in political campaigns, and sought to free political prisoners long before I returned to college, where in 1984 I earned a B.A. in history. Once I concluded that the life of professor of history would be too tame, I abandoned the idea of graduate work and entered Yale Law School, fulfilling a long-delayed goal of becoming a politically radical lawyer. Nonetheless, four years after graduating, I longed for what I assumed would be the less stressful life of a legal academic. When I began to write and speak as a legal scholar, however, it was not with the intention of abandoning the constituency with whom I grew up during my movement days. I did not stop agitating on behalf of political prisoners, speaking bluntly on political issues, or writing about the human rights struggle.

Upon arriving as a new professor at Emory Law School in 1992, I became one of the two blacks on a faculty that was torn by controversy over its long-standing lack of diversity. During my first semester, I organized a symposium titled "Diversity vs. Excellence," taking the theme from the way the entrenched faculty members framed the problem. I invited prominent scholars and law professors to stimulate the faculty's examination of this issue. After spending two years teaching law, I won a writing fellowship to the Bunting Institute in Cambridge, Massachusetts. I had quickly recognized that the conservative members of the law school's tenure committee were not the audience to whom I was directing my research and writing. When I asked for a leave of absence to accept the Harvard fellowship, one exasperated colleague of mine, a moderately conservative white legal scholar, told me I probably wasn't cut out to be an academic. The grant enabled me to resume work on a complex personal narrative to which I had already devoted years of research and writing, a narrative that revisited the massive upsurges that challenged American racism.

I struck out on the less predictable path of finding visiting positions and fellowships that allowed me the freedom to continue writing what I believed was more meaningful than patiently seeking promotion within an academic hierarchy. I've given presentations drawn from my personal narrative and my scholarship at many forums and conferences, frequently directed toward the intellectual community at universities such as Yale, Harvard, and M.I.T. I've spoken on panels at scholarly meetings such as the Organization of American Historians, the Berkshire Conference on Women's History, and the American Political Science Association; given numerous keynote speeches; and published chapters or articles in several books— none of which are likely to be assigned in law courses. So my constituency is a broad assemblage of progressive-minded folk, including scholars, activists, writers, students, lawyers, friends, and assorted intellectuals. Excluded are the institutional power brokers who might have advanced my career within the legal academy.

When I taught traditional law courses, such as professional ethics, torts, or litigation, I incorporated cases or readings that made students deal with concerns I believe are central to their legal training: sexism, illegal government wiretaps, police brutality, discrimination, and the way racial domination permeates our history and political institutions. I've created a seminar that examines cases, legal documents, historical accounts, slave narratives, and the Constitution to demonstrate how law impacts the struggle to abolish as well as to sustain human slavery. I assign the writings of scholars such as Leon Higginbotham, Herbert Aptheker, John Blassingame, and Nathan Huggins, whose work concentrates on the ramifications of the historical conflict between slavery and freedom. Students who have taken that seminar come away appreciating the intricate way the demands of a slave economy weave through the fundamental political development of America, a process rarely examined in the legal academy.

What is the source of my authority? In writing, teaching, and public speaking, I draw heavily upon our history of racial domination that I have fought for years. My personal involvement does not necessarily allow me to make critical assessments or evaluations of social policies, or to advocate directions for action. Given the admiration that prestigious universities elicit, my scholarly credentials from Yale University and Emory Law School carry significant weight. They open doors and provide connections hard to get without such credentials. Therefore, my authentic movement experience has come out of the kiln of an elite university with a fine academic glaze. Although a degree from an elegant institution can stimulate recognition, it does not in itself provide a black intellectual with the confidence to elaborate and deliver a nuanced social critique based upon a view of U.S. history that places slavery at the center. That confidence I gained from my work in the Black Panther Party. As a totally committed participant during the revolutionary phase of the liberation movement, I saw the party crushed by an awesome combination of law enforcement and intelligence agencies drawn from all over the United States. But our detractors never refuted our analyses.

What can I expect as the reward for this path I've chosen? Although I have no tenured university affiliation, I receive so many requests to give public lectures I can't do them all. I am invited to write articles for various newspapers, journals, and books, and to occasionally appear in films or on television. Witnessing the resurgent interest in the Black Panther Party gives me great satisfaction, particularly now that I am in a position to make intellectual contributions to the emerging scholarship reexamining that era. These are not the kind of intellectual or financial rewards that continuing the practice of law would have brought. But I appreciate the freedom to formulate my writing, speaking, and teaching in relation to what I learned from that movement, lessons bought with blood, exile, imprisonment, and death. If I can give voice to the core beliefs of those whose lives were extinguished in the fight for black liberation, it energizes me and enlightens my audiences, I have chosen to do what I love.

AN INTERNATIONAL SPACE

I find it disheartening to see black intellectuals increasingly distance themselves from our tradition of community solidarity and commitment to social change. Not only does that deprive the larger community of the benefit of their talent, but intellectuals attempting to navigate their internal divisions will drift in waters filled with racism's toxic refuse. Far too many of the Euro-American formulations that supposedly formed the basis of intellectual excellence still promote white supremacy. Centuries-long African-American confrontations with subjugation, exploitation, and discrimination have schooled us in problems that have no national boundaries. Although I am no fan of the globalization that spreads corporate monopoly across the world, such trends are inescapable political facts. Coupled with the innovative information technologies that reduce barriers to worldwide communication, the emerging internationalization of everything offers a stunning opportunity to expose the work of black intellectuals. We stand at the threshold of a radical transformation in the means by which knowledge is transmitted. Collectively, we possess the energy, training, and brain power to reformulate the received conceptions of history, culture, and knowledge that for the past four centuries have grounded the institutions that sustain our oppression. Can we summon the courage and vision to seize this opportunity?

A few years ago, I heard an inspiring panel discussion of black artists, including Danny Glover, Harry Belafonte, and Alfre Woodard, speak at New York University about the artist as advocate. Last, the renowned actor Ossie Davis took the podium. At eighty years old, he remains vigorous, handsome, and captivating. His commitment to our freedom struggle began before I was born and continues to this day. At the end of his remarks, he smiled at the audience and in his deep voice said, "It has taken five hundred years to win the struggle for freedom. Now take the next five hundred years to win equality." The hall fell silent as the weight of his words sunk in. Yes, freedom does not necessarily bring about equality. This sounds a clear signal to the black intellectual whose work is still committed to self-determination. We face an extraordinary opening—a realignment brought across the world by the end of the Vietnam War; the political revolution in Portugal that ensured the liberation of Angola, Mozambique, and Guinea Bissau; and the collapse of the Soviet Union. This global space is where African-American thinkers can generate radical conceptions to animate the ongoing struggle for equality. The challenge remains to choose that path.

NOTES

1. Slang term for someone who denies any affiliation with other blacks.

2. James Forman, *The Making of Black Revolutionaries*, illustrated ed. (Seattle and London: University of Washington Press, 1997), 236–237.

3. George Orwell, *1984* (New York: Harcourt, Brace, 1949), 75.

4. Cornel West, "The Dilemma of the Black Intellectual," in *Cultural Critique* (Fall 1985): 111.

5. For a detailed examination of this process, see Kathleen Neal Cleaver, "Back to Africa: The Evolution of the International Section of the Black Panther Party (1969–1972)," in Charles Jones, ed., *The Black Panther Party Reconsidered* (Baltimore: Black Classic Press, 1998).

6. Frantz Fanon, *The Wretched of the Earth*, trans. Constance Farrington (New York: Grove Press, 1968), 38–39.

7. Ibid.

8. Edward W. Said, "Opponents, Audiences, Constituencies, and Community," in W. J. T. Mitchell, ed., *The Politics of Interpretation* (Chicago and London: University of Chicago Press, 1983), 28.

9. Ibid., 30.

10. Eldridge Cleaver, quoted in *The Black Panther Movement* (Ann Arbor, Mich.: Radical Education Project, 1969), 4.

11. Ibid.,7.
12. West, "The Dilemma of the Black Intellectual," 109.
13. Ibid., 113.

∾

CLAYBORNE CARSON
A Scholar in Struggle

As my life has come full circle, my memory is often drawn to the day when I was a nineteen-year-old student attending the 1963 March on Washington for Jobs and Freedom. I suspect that the novice protester at the Lincoln Memorial would have reacted with shocked disbelief if someone had predicted that he would later teach African-American history at Stanford University or that he would edit the papers of the visionary leader of the march, who dreamed of the day that persons of all races would be judged "by the content of their character." My former self might have seen such career predictions as comparable to a possibility of walking on the moon.

I saw more black people in one day at that march than I had seen during my entire life to that point. Growing up as one of a handful of black residents in the sequestered town of Los Alamos, New Mexico, I had dutifully rehearsed for the role of First Negro (to become what many whites already were) even before gaining full awareness of life's greater possibilities. Although I had faith that doing well in school would enable me to become a famous First, my more modest pre-march ambitions centered on becoming the first member of my family to graduate from college.

Yet, even before the march, the southern freedom struggle had deeply affected my consciousness, strengthening my sense that being black (or Negro at that time) was a special identity, infused with great promise. I had come to the event from the University of Indiana, where I had attended the annual convention of the National Student Association. Howard University activist Stokely Carmichael had vividly stamped himself on my memory as he mobilized support for the Student Nonviolent Coordinating Committee (SNCC). I was impressed by his articulate militancy, even as he derided my decision to attend what he called the "picnic" in Washington rather than joining the southern struggle in Albany, Greenwood, and Cambridge, or other such movement hot spots.

Simply attending the unprecedented mass march by myself was then sufficiently adventurous to satisfy my teenage curiosity, but I was nonetheless profoundly transformed by my initial encounters with Stokely and other black activists. The evening afterward, I hitched a ride with a group of marchers returning to New York City. Arriving after midnight at Penn Station, I found my way by subway to Harlem, a place I knew only from books, but one I naively presumed would provide me a place to spend the night. Fortune smiled on me, as it would often afterward. The following day, I visited the famous landmarks of the city, enjoying myself despite the realization that my funds were sufficient only to buy a bus ticket back to Indiana, and that I would have to hitch rides from there to Albuquerque.

After tempting fate still more as a solitary black hitchhiker in middle America, I was able to return for my sophomore year at the University of New Mexico. Political activism increasingly shaped my subsequent academic career, making it difficult to imagine one without the other. I soon switched my major from mathematics to history. Nothing I learned in the classroom, however, was as instructive as my initial contacts with SNCC organizers, who demonstrated to me that Martin Luther King, Jr., was a product of a multifaceted social movement sustained by many independent organizers and grassroots leaders. A few months after the march, I encountered the most influential role model of my college years when I heard SNCC organizer Bob Moses describe the Mississippi voting rights campaign. Although I admired Stokely Carmichael's outspoken militancy, my more subdued personality was instantly drawn to Moses's soft-spoken, deferential leadership style. My subsequent activism would continue to intersect with that of Bob and Stokely; yet, despite my admiration of them and other courageous SNCC field secretaries, I continued to combine part-time activism with a full load of classes. Only gradually did my career ambitions become inextricably linked with experiences in the African-American freedom struggle.

When I transferred to UCLA in 1965, my courses became occasional distractions from a burgeoning off-campus curriculum that included involvement in the Nonviolent Action Group (NAG), which became the center of my social life in Los Angeles and led to my first civil disobedience arrest. Soon there were writing assignments for the underground *Los Angeles Free Press* (my first article was on NAG founder Woody Coleman), numerous antiwar and antidraft protests, forays to Delano to participate in the farmworkers movement, and necessary employment (an insipid advertising research job with Audience Studies on the Columbia Pictures lot in Hollywood) to pay educational expenses. Eager to contribute to SNCC's voting rights campaign, but unable to participate in the Selma-to-Montgomery march, I helped organize massive demonstrations at the Los Angeles federal building and sat in the building's lobby until I was removed by police. Later, attending the momentous May 1965 antiwar teach-in at Berkeley, I learned that Bob Moses had changed his surname to Parris in a vain attempt to free himself from the leadership role that had enveloped him. I recall that he spoke movingly about the connection between the Vietnam War and southern anti-black violence. He expressed the growing racial resentments of many black activists when he asked why white Americans had not reacted to the killing of Alabama voting rights worker Jimmy Lee Jackson as they had to the subsequent murder of a white minister, James Reeb.

In August 1965, my political activism and my undergraduate career suddenly and unexpectedly reached a turning point when a mass protest against police abuse started in the Watts section of Los Angeles. The Watts "riot" was actually an insurgency that briefly transformed large sections of south-central Los Angeles into liberated zones of the black freedom struggle. I recall standing outside NAG's Central Avenue headquarters trying to make sense of the fiery, deadly, racial rebellion that made our nonviolent, interracial militancy seem so insignificant and so inadequate. The spreading violence attracted more community support than had all of our organizing efforts. The NAG cadre, which had been held together by a shared faith in the power of interracial nonviolent direct action, subsequently disintegrated as members came to realize that black-white divisions inside and outside the group were deeper than we had imagined.

Searching for new political options, I served as cochair of the California Conference on Power and Politics held in October 1966. Those of us who organized the gathering envisioned it as the beginning of a movement for a third major political party, but instead it exposed how little we knew about power or politics. Rejecting the conventional liberalism of incumbent governor Edmund G. Brown and refusing to take seriously his conservative challenger, Ronald Reagan, we audaciously called upon voters to boycott the election, expecting that we would soon offer a serious third-party alternative. Eventually, the New Politics movement spawned the Peace and Freedom Party and inadvertently stimulated the growth of the Reagan wing of the Republican Party.

During 1965 and 1966, as New Left radicalism and black nationalism competed with one another as guiding themes of my activism and studies, I discovered posthumously the virtues of Malcolm X. I met with other UCLA students in a group called Harambee, which honored Malcolm each week by holding silent vigils beside a path leading to the UCLA Student Union. I saw myself as both a black militant and a New Left radical, but increasingly found it difficult to straddle the widening gulf between these two small segments of the student body. I began to realize that the post-Watts period represented for me a decisive break with earlier activism. I had once considered myself part of a single movement, but after 1965 it began to separate into numerous movements. Black militancy increasingly consisted of fiery oratory rather than grassroots organizing.

Parris, SNCC's best-known organizer, dropped out of sight after 1965, his whereabouts the subject of many rumors, but Stokely Carmichael's whereabouts during this period were rarely a source of mystery. He had been an effective organizer, but soon after becoming chair of SNCC he quickly transformed himself into the group's best-known ideologue. During the summer of 1966, I greeted him at a rally in Watts and responded enthusiastically to his call for Black Power. At the November 1966 Black Power Conference held in Berkeley, I was listed on the program as a "Watts organizer," rather than more accurately as a UCLA student and part-time journalist. I did my best, though, to play the role of black militant, warming the audience for Carmichael's speech and then writing a laudatory participant-observer article about the event. Fascinated by Carmichael's brash confidence that black people would unite in a revolutionary struggle, I readily allowed Black Power rhetoric to obscure the reality that SNCC and NAG had declined in their ability to organize the black people they supposedly represented. Ideological agitation increasingly obscured community organizing, as "the people" were no longer sources of innovative political ideas, but targets of consciousness raising.

College graduation in June 1967 coincided with my decision to resist the draft by leaving the United States with the intention of establishing residence elsewhere. Susan Beyer, a UCLA graduate who had shared some of my movement experiences and became my wife in August 1967, joined me in traveling through Europe and North Africa while Canadian officials considered our application for citizenship. A few of my black activist acquaintances objected to my marriage to a white woman, who was moreover Jewish, but I felt fortunate to have company in my selfimposed exile. With ample opportunity to reflect on identity issues during our travels, we found temporary refuge from the intense anti-white animus that engulfed the black struggle during that period. In the spring of 1968, after Canada rejected us and Susan discovered she had a serious case of diabetes, we were forced to return to the United States. Back in Los Angeles, distracted by the pressing need to earn a living and avoid arrest as a draft dodger, I found it difficult to reestablish myself as an activist or as a writer capable of interpreting the tumultuous events that followed Huey Newton's imprisonment on murder charges and King's assassination. Although I attended rallies in support of the Panthers and embattled UCLA professor Angela Davis, I was no longer a political journalist or a member of any political organization. I found work as a computer programmer and managed to avoid the military draft. Only a year earlier I had been a student, but I returned to a political environment at UCLA that seemed greatly transformed. My earlier movement experiences no longer seemed of much relevance to the new generation of black students who had arrived at UCLA in the aftermath of King's assassination.

By then, the effort to unite all black people under the Black Power banner had floundered because of government repression and internal conflicts within the black struggle. Black leaders competed to become the "messiah" that FBI director J. Edgar Hoover imagined "could unify and electrify the militant black nationalist movement." I was attracted to the bravery and confrontational style of the Black Panthers, initially seeing them as SNCC's urban contemporary counterparts. I ignored signs that the party's leaders had little sympathy for SNCC's consensus style of decision-making (Eldridge Cleaver later explained to me that a difference between SNCC and the Black Panthers was that the former had long meetings, and the latter had very short meetings).

In January 1969, I attended a meeting of the Black Student Union where Black Panthers and members of US ("wherever we are, US is") stood glaring at each other from opposite sides of a classroom in which intimidated students discussed how to establish a black studies program at UCLA. I had known US leader Ron (later Maulana) Karenga since 1966, when I interviewed him for the *Free Press* and was impressed by his seriousness and intelligence. Although I sided with the "revolutionary nationalist" Black Panthers in their escalating conflicts with the "cultural nationalists" of US, I was perplexed and disturbed by the Panthers' vicious verbal attacks against Karenga and his followers. I was not completely surprised two days after the meeting when the escalating tensions between Black Panthers and US members exploded into a deadly clash. Two members of US killed two Panthers, Alprentice "Bunchy" Carter and John Huggins, in a cafeteria less than one hundred yards from my office.

I would later learn that the FBI's counterintelligence program fostered these hostilities. Subsequent police raids severely damaged both groups, but for me the immediate consequence of the killings was that they reinforced my desire to maintain my distance from a Black Power movement that had become self-destructive. The Panther-US conflict also led me to become even more skeptical about the value of the prevailing rhetorical style of black militancy, which had increased competition among Black leaders while achieving scant power or racial unity.

During 1969, I considered returning to political journalism, but the emergence of the black studies movement provided a new option. While continuing to work as a computer programmer, I began auditing Professor Gary Nash's new class at UCLA on race relations in the United States. As one of a small number of black college graduates on campus, I was soon recruited by Nash to be an informal teaching assistant, leading a section of his course devoted to black political thought. Among the fifteen students in the section were the president and vice-president of the Black Student Union as well as members of the Black Panther Party, US, and the Nation of Islam. Intense class discussions provided a brutal yet instructive introduction to teaching. Political activism had once drawn me away from my undergraduate classes; now it gave me a reason to begin graduate studies. As an undergraduate, my curiosity about African-American history and political thought could only be satisfied through extracurricular study. In contrast, I thought that graduate school might transform my avocation into a vocation. I began to formulate the central question that would guide my career as a professional historian: How have oppressed people with limited resources overcome the forces that oppress them?

In the fall of 1969, I entered UCLA's graduate program in American history, part of a pioneering class of black students who were suddenly deemed more academically qualified as a result of the nationwide black rebellions following King's assassination. Although I never doubted that the black struggle had made possible my admission to graduate school, I was also convinced that the struggle strengthened my academic qualifications. I was able to draw on valuable insights from my movement experiences, even as I began to consider those experiences in a broader historical context. I soon realized that I could make an important contribution to the transformation of American historical scholarship that occurred during the early 1970s.

After two hectic years of graduate school, during which my enthusiasm compensated for the deficiencies in my academic preparation, I became an acting assistant professor at UCLA. The professors who engineered my recruitment were responding to forceful black student demands for an African-American history course taught by a black professor. My hiring followed an interview session with leaders of the Black Student Union and was made possible by an expedient decision to deny tenure to a non-black professor, Ronald Takaki, the superb historian who taught UCLA's first African-American history course. Despite my uneasiness regarding the racial politics associated with the hiring process, the suddenness of my transition from computer programmer to graduate student to professor was exhilarating (a few of my graduate school classmates had, two years later, become my students). Given my journalistic background, I worried less about pressures to publish or perish than I did about teaching courses that I had never taken, to students whose expectations were extraordinary and often contradictory—I often heard various versions of the assertion, "I don't need to read books about black history; I've lived it."

When I began graduate studies, my movement experiences initially seemed too contemporary to become the subjects of historical study, but I benefited from the willingness of a few of my professors to depart from traditional notions of historical scholarship. My maturing reflections about the modern African-American freedom struggle soon became the basis for my dissertation on SNCC, which Harvard University Press published in 1981 as *In Struggle: SNCC and the Black Awakening of the 1960s*. My research for *In Struggle* provided a welcome opportunity to reestablish contacts with many of the activists I had known during the 1960s. I was especially pleased to have the opportunity to conduct extended interviews with Bob Moses after his return from a long stay in Tanzania and with Kwame Ture (the former Stokely Carmichael) during his occasional visits to the United States from his home in Guinea, West Africa.

In 1974, I began my career as a Stanford professor, joining a small cohort of black professors who struggled to find ways to build programs, serve the needs of black students, and still produce scholarly publications. Among my colleagues was the late St. Clair Drake, a pioneering social scientist who had founded Stanford's Program in African and African American Studies and who drew upon his own political activism to inform his teaching and scholarship. Some of the younger black professors who came to Stanford (and to other universities) during this period sacrificed their opportunity to gain tenure by devoting themselves to administrative and teaching responsibilities. I experienced a degree of survivor's guilt when I gained tenure, but I found it easy to immerse myself in historical research about my chosen subject matter and felt fortunate to be paid to follow my curiosity. Although I came to see my scholarly work as my most appropriate contribution to a still-evolving freedom struggle, there were times when I longed for the activist role I had left behind. Early in the 1980s, I obtained my FBI file and was somewhat dismayed to learn that it had been closed a decade earlier with the notation, "Subject no longer warrants surveillance" (was it the station wagon that a snooping FBI agent saw in my Palo Alto driveway?).

Even after acquiring the protective shield of tenure, I learned that political struggles inside the academy were as vicious, if not as bloody, as those on the outside. So long as my classes were simply electives taken largely by black students, my presence on the faculty was accepted mainly with indifference or perhaps as one of the inevitable consequences of affirmative action. But I encountered open hostility during the mid-1980s when I became involved in the movement to alter Stanford's Western Culture requirement for all undergraduates. In 1987, responding to black student complaints, I developed an experimental course, "Western Culture: An Alternative View." It represented a modest departure from the required Great Books reading list (instituted to distinguish essential knowledge from less essential subjects, such as the African-American history courses I had taught). Along with other students and faculty members who advocated curriculum reform, I suddenly became a target for Dinesh D'Souza and other self-appointed defenders of Western culture and academic standards. The culture wars of the 1980s and 1990s served as a reminder that the freedom struggles of the 1960s had not ended, but had simply moved to new battlefields.

As the Western Culture controversy was beginning, my life's circle came closer to completion when Coretta Scott King invited me to become the editor of her late husband's papers. Because I had previously displayed little scholarly interest in King, I was surprised when she called me in January 1985. I quickly sensed, however, that the Martin Luther King, Jr., Papers Project offered a unique opportunity to study the modern African-American freedom struggle from the perspective of the leader who sometimes served as a negative reference point for SNCC activists. As I drew closer to King through studying his papers, it was no longer sufficient to debunk so-called great-man interpretations of history, as I had when I speculated at a 1986 conference on Capitol Hill, "If King had never lived, the black struggle would have followed a course of development similar to the one it did." I wanted to understand the historical significance of the person who had been the featured speaker at my first major demonstration.

Having once empathized with the young SNCC militants who challenged King, my sympathies shifted somewhat as I studied King, who was, when he died, younger than I was when I became director of the King Papers Project. During the 1960s, my own youthful impatience and impetuousness led me to agree with some of SNCC's attacks on King's moderation and his firm commitment to integration and nonviolence in the face of white racist attacks. My later acknowledgment of the limitations of the Black Power movement fostered a greater degree of humility in my assessments of King's alternative course. Although I still understood him as emerging from a freedom struggle he did not initiate, I came to appreciate him as a singularly prophetic leader who symbolized and cogently expressed many of the emergent values of the struggle. In short, he became wiser as I became older. My changing views of him have been affected not only by my personal experiences, but also by the unique opportunity I have had to study both the black movement's foremost spokesperson and its impetuous foot soldiers.

Since its beginnings in 1985, the King Papers Project and the research projects related to it have become my principal means of expressing my views about the world and how it should be changed. The project has provided an opportunity for me to work closely with idealistic and committed students as well as with other dedicated scholars in a collective research effort that has documented not only King's role in the struggle but also that of many other activists. The project's research has drawn attention to aspects of the modern African-American struggle that had been overlooked in previous writings that depicted it as a national campaign for civil rights legislation, rather than as a series of grassroots insurgencies. Realizing that some historians dismiss documentary editing as a rather mundane form of scholarship, I have appreciated the opportunity to devote my talent to the creation of publications with a value that is unrelated to transitory intellectual fashions.

Although I admire some of those who have joined the growing ranks of black "public intellectuals," as they are called, I remain a reluctant spokesperson for anyone other than myself. Only with considerable practice have I gradually become comfortable in the role of classroom lecturer and public speaker. Although I care deeply about many issues and still attend protest rallies and sign petitions, I am content to remain a teacher and writer, while more accomplished orators orate. I refrain from speaking publicly about matters that are beyond my chosen area of scholarly expertise (perhaps I still have within me some reticent qualities of that nineteen-year-old student in the crowd at the March on Washington). Nevertheless, since my area of expertise encompasses King's life and ideas as well as the struggles in which he was involved, it is hardly surprising that my intellectual life has become wide-ranging and very public, particularly during the weeks surrounding the King holiday.

Furthermore, I have enthusiastically taken on some public education responsibilities, producing popular writings and multimedia presentations about the modern African-American freedom struggle. Seeing our struggle as a valuable model for contemporary struggles, I take special pride in my works intended for popular audiences, such as *Malcolm X: The FBI File,* the docudrama *Passages of Martin Luther King,* and *The Autobiography of Martin Luther King, Jr.,* compiled from his autobiographical writings. I am grateful for the opportunity to serve as historical advisor for documentary films such as *Eyes on the Prize* and *Freedom on My Mind,* and for the museum exhibits at the King Visitors Center in Atlanta and the National Civil Rights Museum in Memphis. Even computer skills have been useful as I explore new ways to use the Internet and multimedia technology to disseminate historical information.

Thus, since that day in Washington almost four decades ago, my career has been fulfilling in many unexpected ways. Even as I complain that Stanford has not done enough to support my work, I realize that I am fortunate to have resources far beyond those available to previous generations of black scholars. I feel privileged to be able to make my own distinctive contributions—as an activist, scholar, and editor—to an ongoing, multifaceted freedom struggle. I am fortunate to have Susan as a scholarly colleague as well as a wife. Our now adult children, Malcolm and Temera, continually give us welcome assurance that our political values will survive us (our son's midnight telephone call for advice from a student-occupied Howard University building was a generation-bridging experience). In addition, I am privileged to have known and learned from a diverse collection of extraordinary and fascinating individuals—Stokely Carmichael/Kwame Ture and Bob Moses, Ella Baker and Anne Braden, St. Clair Drake and John Hope Franklin, Coretta Scott King and Jesse Jackson, Sr., students and researchers who have shared my intellectual passions, and others too numerous to name who have broadened my social, intellectual, and cultural horizons in wondrous ways.

About the Contributors

Hishaam D. Aidi is a Research Fellow at the Middle East Institute at Columbia University and works on Columbia's Muslim Communities New York Project, sponsored by the Ford Foundation.

Ana Aparicio is Assistant Professor of Anthropology at the University of Massachusetts–Boston and Research Associate with the Mauricio Gaston Institute for Latino Community Development and Public Policy. Her teaching, research, and community work are in the areas of immigration, race, youth, and activism. She is the author of *Dominican American Politics: Race, Nation, and Power in Quisqueya Heights* (UPF, 2006) and coeditor (with P. Kretsedemas) of *Immigrants, Welfare Reform, and the Poverty of Policy* (Greenwood, 2004).

Herbert Aptheker was one of the most influential historians of the black American experience in the twentieth century. The author of many books, he was best known as the editor of the writings of W. E. B. Du Bois and as the author of the classic series *Documentary History of the Negro People of the United States*.

Michael Awkward is Professor of English and Director for the Study of Black Literature and Culture at the University of Pennsylvania. He is the author of *Scenes of Instruction: A Memoir* (Duke University Press, 1999); *Negotiating Difference: Race, Gender, and the Politics of Personality* (University of Chicago Press, 1995); and *Inspiriting Influences: Tradition, Revision, and Afro-American Women's Novels* (Columbia University Press, 1989).

Lee D. Baker is Associate Professor of Cultural Anthropology and African and African American Studies at Duke University. He is the current editor of *Transforming Anthropology* and the author of many articles on the history of anthropology. He wrote *From Savage to Negro: Anthropology and the Construction of Race, 1896–1954*, edited *Life in America: Identity in Everyday Experience*, and is currently working on a book tentatively titled *Reformers, Performers, and Racists; or A History of Anthropology*.

Todd Boyd is Professor of Critical Studies in the School of Cinema-Television at the University of Southern California. A prominent media commentator, he is the author of several books, including *Young Black Rich and Famous, The New H.N.I.C.,* and *Am I Black Enough for You?* He was a writer and a producer on the Paramount Pictures film *The Wood* (1999).

Karen Brodkin teaches anthropology and women's studies at the University of California–Los Angeles. She writes on the interplay of race, gender, and class, and on social movements in the United States. Her books include *Caring by the Hour,* about African-American and white hospital workers' struggle to unionize, and *How Jews Became White Folks and What That Says about Race in America.* Her current work is about activism in Los Angeles.

Daphne A. Brooks is Assistant Professor of English and African American Studies at Princeton University, where she currently teaches courses on nineteenth-century black literature, performance studies, cultural studies, and popular music studies. She is the author of two forthcoming books, *Bodies in Dissent: Insurgent Performances in the Trans-Atlantic Imaginary* (Duke University Press, 2006) and *Jeff Buckley's Grace* (Continuum Books, 2005). Brooks is also working on a new book on black women and satire in the post–civil rights era.

Hazel V. Carby is Chair of the Department of African American Studies and Professor of American Studies at Yale University. Her books include *Reconstructing Womanhood, Race Men,* and *Cultures in Babylon.* She is researching a history of the lives of radical black women in the 1930s and 1940s and a critical analysis of the writing of Octavia Butler.

Clayborne Carson has taught at Stanford University, where he is now Professor of History and Director of the King Papers Project. He has written or coedited numerous works based on the papers, including *A Knock at Midnight: Inspiration from the Great Sermons of Reverend Martin Luther King, Jr.; The Autobiography of Martin Luther King, Jr.,* compiled from King's autobiographical writings; and *A Call to Conscience: The Landmark Speeches of Dr. Martin Luther King, Jr.*

Kathleen Neal Cleaver is Senior Lecturer and Research Fellow at the Emory University School of Law and holds an appointment as Senior Research Associate at Yale Law School. From 1967 to 1971, she was the communications secretary of the Black Panther Party, the first woman member of their central committee, and she is now the executive producer of the International Black Panther Film Festival.

Dana-Ain Davis is Assistant Professor of Anthropology at Purchase College at the State University of New York. She conducts research in both the United States and Namibia. Her research focuses on poverty policy, reproductive rights, domestic violence, and community organizing. In addition to her academic work, she works with community-based organizations on program evaluation and organizational development.

Betsy Esch is a graduate student in U.S. history and the African diaspora at New York University. She is on the editorial board of *Against the Current* magazine and is a member of the Graduate Student Organizing Committee/UAW Local 2110.

Bill Fletcher Jr. is President and Chief Executive Officer of TransAfrica Forum, a national nonprofit organization that educates and advocates for policies in favor of the peoples of Africa, the Caribbean, and Latin America. He has authored numerous articles published in a variety of newspapers and magazines.

Farah Jasmine Griffin is Director of the Institute for Research in African American Studies and Professor of English and Comparative Literature at Columbia University. Her publications include *"Who Set You Flowin'?": The African American Migration Narrative* (Oxford University Press, 1995); *If You Can't Be Free, Be a Mystery: In Search of Billie Holiday* (Free Press, 2001); and *Miles Davis and John Coltrane*, coauthored with Salim Washington (Thomas Dunne, forthcoming in 2005). She is currently working on a cultural history of New York in the 1940s as seen through the experiences and cultural productions of black women.

John Hartigan, Jr., is Associate Professor in the Americo Paredes Center for Cultural Studies, Department of Anthropology, University of Texas–Austin. He is the author of *Odd Tribes: Toward a Cultural Analysis of White People* (Duke University Press, 2005) and *Racial Situations: Class Predicaments of Whiteness in Detroit* (Princeton University Press, 1999).

Noel Ignatiev is the author of *How the Irish Became White* and coeditor of *Race Traitor: Journal of the New Abolitionism*. He teaches in the Critical Studies Department at the Massachusetts College of Art and is a Fellow at the W. E. B. Du Bois Center at Harvard University.

John L. Jackson Jr. received his bachelor's degree in communications from Howard University in 1993 and his doctoral degree in anthropology from Columbia University in 2000. After three years as a Junior Fellow at Harvard's Society of Fellows, Jackson is currently Assistant Professor of Cultural Anthropology and African and African American Studies at Duke University. He is author of *Harlemworld: Doing Race and Class in Contemporary Black America* (University of Chicago Press, 2001) and *Real Black: Adventures in Racial Sincerity* (University of Chicago Press, 2005).

Audrey Jacobs is a consultant who has more than a decade of experience working with nonprofit organizations. Her areas of emphasis include income security/

poverty, early childhood education, and HIV/AIDS. She works with nonprofit organizations in the areas of strategic planning, program planning and evaluation, and fund and board development. She is a graduate of Barnard College, Columbia University, and the New York University School of Law and has conducted research on race and the law.

Robin D. G. Kelley is Professor of Anthropology, African American Studies, and Jazz Studies at Columbia University. He is the author of several books, including *Hammer and Hoe: Alabama Communists during the Great Depression* (1990), *Race Rebels: Culture Politics and the Black Working Class* (1994), and most recently, *Freedom Dreams: The Black Radical Imagination* (2002). He is currently completing a biography of pianist/composer Thelonious Monk, tentatively titled *Thelonious: A Life.*

Jeffrey R. Kerr-Ritchie is a teacher and scholar of slavery, abolition, and emancipation in the modern world. He did his undergraduate work in the United Kingdom and obtained his graduate degrees from the University of Pennsylvania. He has taught at Wesleyan, the State University of New York–Binghamton, and Columbia University. He seeks to bring politics into scholarship and scholarship into politics.

Eric Klinenberg is Associate Professor of Sociology at New York University. He is the author of *Heat Wave: A Social Autopsy of Disaster in Chicago* (University of Chicago Press) and coeditor of *The Making and Unmaking of Whiteness* (Duke University Press). He is currently completing *Fighting for Air: Big Media and the Asphyxiation of Local News* (Henry Holt) and doing research on urban isolation.

Akemi Kochiyama is a graduate student in the Department of Anthropology at the Graduate Center of the City University of New York.

Leith Mullings is Presidential Professor of Anthropology at the Graduate Center of the City University of New York and is the author of several books on the study of race, class, and gender in African-American communities, including *Cities of the United States: Studies in Urban Anthropology* (1987); *On Our Own Terms: Class, Race, and Gender in the Lives of African American Women* (1997); and, with coauthor Alaka Wali, *Stress and Resilience: The Social Context of Reproduction in Central Harlem* (2001). With Manning Marable, Mullings coedited *Let Nobody Turn Us Around: Voices of Resistance, Reform and Renewal—An African American Anthology* (2002) and *Freedom: A Photographic History of the African American Struggle* (2002).

George Derek Musgrove is Visiting Lecturer in the Department of History at Trinity College in Hartford, Connecticut. He is currently working on his dissertation, titled "The Second Redemption: Race, Party Realignment, and State Power in the Post–Civil Rights United States."

Gary Y. Okihiro is Professor of International and Public Affairs and Director of the Center for the Study of Ethnicity and Race at Columbia University. He is the author of eight books on U.S. and African history, including *Common Ground: Reimagining American History.*

Andrea Queeley is a Bay Area native and graduate student in anthropology at the City University of New York. She is currently conducting research for her dissertation on race and ethnicity in eastern Cuba.

David Roediger is Babcock Professor of African American Studies at the University of Illinois. His recent publications include *Working toward Whiteness* (Basic-Books) and *History against Misery* (Charles Kerr Company). He is the editor of the Modern Library edition of W. E. B. Du Bois's *John Brown* (Random House).

Assata Shakur, a former Black Panther framed for the shooting of a police officer in the United States in 1973 and sentenced to life plus thirty years by an all-white jury, escaped from jail in 1979 and eventually made her way to Cuba, where she has lived in exile since 1984. She has spoken and written frankly about Cuba over the years.

Nikhil Singh is Associate Professor of History at the University of Washington. He is the author of *Black Is a Country: Race and the Unfinished Struggle for Democracy,* winner of the Liberty Legacy Foundation Award from the Organization of American Historians. His articles have appeared in *American Quarterly, Social Text, Radical History Review, South Atlantic Quarterly,* and *American Literary History.* He is currently at work on a book on U.S. imperialism.

Barbara Smith's articles, essays, literary criticism, and short stories have appeared in a variety of publications, including the *Black Scholar, Gay Community News,* the *Guardian, Ms.* magazine, the *Nation,* the *New York Times Book Review,* and the *Village Voice.* Among her other books, she is the general editor of *The Reader's Companion to U.S. Women's History* (with Wilma Mankiller, Gwendolyn Mink, Marysa Navarro, and Gloria Steinem; Houghton Mifflin, 1998) and the author of *That Never Hurts: Writings on Race, Gender, and Freedom* (Rutgers University Press, 1998).

Julia Sudbury is Canada Research Chair in Social Justice, Equity, and Diversity at the University of Toronto and Associate Professor of African Diaspora Studies in the Department of Ethnic Studies at Mills College. She is author of *Other Kinds of Dreams: Black Women's Organisations and the Politics of Transformation* (Routledge, 1998) and editor of *Global Lockdown: Race, Gender, and the Prison-Industrial Complex* (Routledge, 2005). Julia is a founding member of Critical Resistance and the Prisoner Justice Action Committee (Toronto).

Beverly Thompson is a Ph.D. candidate in political sociology at the New School University. She is currently writing her dissertation on the anticorporate movement, direct action, and radical law collectives.

Howard Winant is Professor of Sociology at the University of California–Santa Barbara, where he is also Founding Director of the New Racial Studies Project. He is the author of *The World Is a Ghetto: Race and Democracy since World War II* (2001); *The New Politics of Race: Globalism, Difference, Justice* (2004); *Racial Conditions: Politics, Theory, Comparisons* (1994); and *Racial Formation in the United States: From the 1960s to the 1990s* (1994), coauthored with Michael Omi.

Tim Wise is among the nation's most prominent white antiracist essayists and educators and the author of two books: *White Like Me: Reflections on Race from a Privileged Son* (Brooklyn: Soft Skull, 2005), and *Affirmative Action: Racial Preference in Black and White* (New York: Routledge, 2005). He has contributed to dozens of edited volumes and trained educators, government officials, and community groups on methods for dismantling racism in their institutions.

Index